M.D.

M.D.

One Doctor's Adventures
Among the Famous
and Infamous from
the Jungles of Panama
to a Park Avenue Practice

B. H. Kean, M.D.

WITH TRACY DAHLBY

BALLANTINE BOOKS
NEW YORK

Library of Congress Cataloging-in-Publication Data
Kean, B. H. (Benjamin Harrison), 1912–
M.D. : one doctor's adventures among the famous and infamous from the jungles of Panama to a Park Avenue practice / B. H. Kean with Tracy Dahlby.—1st ed.
p.   cm.
  ISBN 0-345-35821-X
  1. Kean, B. H. (Benjamin Harrison), 1912–   .   2. Physicians—United States—Biography.   I. Dahlby, Tracy.   II. Title.
R154.K24A3   1990
610'.92—dc20   88-92876
[B]   CIP

Manufactured in the United States of America
First Edition: February 1990
10 9 8 7 6 5 4 3

For
COLLETTE

Contents

A Doctor's Warning

Truth, we are told, is stranger than fiction. From what I've seen in fifty years of practicing medicine, the evidence does strongly point in that direction. Take, for example, the incident irreverent reporters referred to at the time as the "Curious Case of the Kissing Nuns."

The year was 1965 and the place, the normally quiescent, upper middle-class suburb of Lakewood, New Jersey, was in an uproar. Thirty-seven sisters at the local Roman Catholic convent had come down with a serious, highly contagious infection. Community concern focused less on the specter of epidemic disease, however, than on a single, acutely embarrassing complication: the illness in question, common on college campuses but rare in nunneries, was thought to be transmitted mainly through a process indelicately known as "wet kissing." When word of this provocative mode of transmission hit the newsstands, scandalized parishioners began yanking their children out of the convent school where the morally suspect sisters taught with such abandon that the institution seemed permanently doomed.

In the rush to public judgment, however, the people of Lakewood overlooked one important medical clue. The diagnosis had been made solely on the results of blood tests done as part of an annual health checkup. But when I was called down from New York to confirm the finding, a funny thing happened. I examined all thirty-seven sisters and not one of them displayed the slightest clinical symptoms of the disease. Indeed, all seemed to be in perfect health! How could this be?

I followed my nose to the local pathology lab, a shabby, cinderblock facility in the town's commercial center, where I found what I suspected: an absent-minded technician who, while inspecting the convent corpuscles, had squirted acid into the test tubes when he should have squirted alkaline. The result was thirty-seven false positives for infectious mononucleosis and the ensuing consternation in the community.

My deductions were hardly Holmesian; unfortunately, mistakes of this kind are all too common in the normal course of medical practice and the alert physician will always look with suspicion on lab results that refuse to jibe with the clinical evidence. Still, the nuns, now restored to innocence, didn't know this and so I shamefully basked in a chorus of grateful hosannas. As an added reward, the mother superior arranged for me to visit the Vatican to accept the thanks of the head man himself, Pope Paul VI, which I modestly declined.

Modesty did not prevent me from recounting my exploits to my second-year class at Cornell University Medical College, however. But the larval doctors were not impressed. Over the years, it seems, I had acquired the reputation of a "raconteur"—in other words, somebody who seldom lets the facts stand in the way of a good story. That I smoked Cuban cigars, brought Carnoustie, my West Highland terrier, to listen to my lectures, and awarded my students bottles of Dom Perignon for high test scores was interpreted as further evidence of a cavalier attitude toward scientific truth. (As far as I know, there has never been any law against medical students having fun while they learn to be doctors, though the practice is still generally frowned upon.) The result was that subsequent efforts to buttress my nun story with hard scientific fact were greeted by my pupils with the usual groans of suspicion.

This reaction might have upset me, but it didn't. Quite the contrary. I was thrilled, and let me explain the reason why. Good teaching is good theater. No matter how arcane the subject matter, wrapped in an intriguing tale it is understood and remembered. Supplying such stories is rarely a problem. Any doctor's practice provides an unending stream of everything from low comedy to high drama. In my case, I have spent most of my career dividing my time between the teaching of tropical medicine at Cornell (when I wasn't traipsing off on a research project to some flyblown savannah or pestilential swamp halfway across the globe) and treating patients in private practice a few blocks away on Manhattan's Park Avenue. That has made scripting my lectures a fairly simple matter of flipping open my casebook and letting the colorful characters contained therein, both patients and the attendant cast of pathogenic villains, elbow their way into the limelight.

My goal in all of this has been a simple one: I wanted to do to my students what my teachers had long ago done to me; I wanted to infect them with a fascination for the kaleidoscopic puzzle of medicine that presents itself in different guise each time a patient walks through the consulting room door. If my students were skeptical, hallelujah! Skeptics make wonderful doctors.

Over the years some five thousand students have been subjected to my brainwashing techniques. Not a few have encouraged me to put down my medical yarns in book form—perhaps on the theory that, in the process, even I might get tired of retelling them. I had always intended to write such a book anyway, of course, but my students deserve the credit—or the blame, as the case may be—for that initial push. In any event, this joint parentage has resulted in a curious offspring; the book before you now is the collection of stories about the memorable cases and scientific investigations my students wanted, although I have chosen to tell them within the context of one man's life in medicine in the perhaps farfetched hope of giving an otherwise checkered career some semblance of order.

Giving birth wasn't easy. For years, I wrestled with the ethical dilemma any doctor faces when he undertakes to write about his patients: how to be as faithful to the facts as memory and documentation allow and yet not breach the right of every patient to confide in his doctor without fear of disclosure.

Thus the reader deserves a word of warning: while all recol-
lections in the pages that follow are based on incidents that really
happened, and have been rendered in a truthful spirit, names and
physical details have, in a few cases, been altered where and to
the extent necessary to protect doctor-patient confidences. I
therefore feel especially grateful to the many brave souls, patients
and friends who, knowing all too well my idiosyncracies as doctor and man, went ahead and gave permission for use of their
real identities anyway!

Others deserve thanks, as well. Tracy and I are indebted to
David Halberstam, who first introduced us to one another and
then offered his wise counsel and friendship throughout the most
satisfying of collaborations during which Ben Kean became a
better writer and Tracy Dahlby became a passable "physician"
and amateur parasitologist. We are grateful to Charles Scribner,
Jr., for making the other critical connection, introducing us to
Betsy Rapoport at Ballantine Books, whose surgical skills as editor are exceeded only by the most gracious manner in dealing
with the clinical miseries of authorship. Special thanks go to
Adair Russell, my longtime medical editor, without whose dedication and attention to detail the book would never have taken
shape. Space is limited and the list of those patients, friends, and
colleagues who made the journey through medicine both exciting
and enriching is a long one. Suffice it to say that they are remembered with gratitude and affection, and they will find their
footprints scattered throughout the following pages.

A special category of gratitude is hereby established for
Toshiko Dahlby, who lovingly endured two years during which
"Dr. Dahlby" found the time to sort through medical anecdotes,
personal artifacts, and hundreds of hours of conversations and
then actually sit down and write the ensuing narrative, all the
while holding down a demanding job at *Newsweek* magazine.

Reconstructing the past would not have been possible without
the help of Elizabeth Bradburn, who read the book for factual
accuracy. We have endeavored to acknowledge specific sources
with the appropriate credits and regret any omissions that might
have occurred. For their help in corroborating the complicated

events surrounding the Shah's medical odyssey, we would especially like to thank Joseph V. Reed, Robert Armao, Michael DeBakey, and Hibbard Williams. Moreover, the work of authors Pierre Salinger, William Shawcross, Hamilton Jordan, and Dennis Breo, among others, prevented memory from becoming totally self-serving. We are also grateful to experts in various fields who have read individual chapters for scientific accuracy. The authors take sole responsibility for the scientific oversimplifications which are inevitable in a book intended for the general reader.

A final word of caution. Reading this book will *not* be harmful to your health. We hope, in fact, it will shed some light, however faintly, on the joys and challenges one doctor had the incredible luck to encounter during his first fifty years in medicine. Let the reader be alerted, however, that the telling of such a tale would be all but impossible without describing the occasional graphic biological fact of life. Such detail may fascinate some, while others will find it indelicate or just plain grim. To those who find themselves in the latter category, I can only apologize in advance and say that, in dealing with a man who has been parasitologist, pathologist, and physician all his adult life, the fleas, as it were, necessarily go with the dog. Enjoy and be well.

B. H. KEAN, M.D.
New York, 1990

Last Flight from Lackland

December 14, 1979 was a dismal day at Lackland Air Force Base on the outskirts of San Antonio, Texas. Gray and cold outside, sickness indoors. Still, as I sat there watching my patient, I couldn't help marvel. Anybody else in his condition would be flat on his back in bed. Yet this man moved like a caged jungle cat, pacing quickly up and down his narrow room as if he were trying to outmaneuver death itself.

But death was gaining on him fast. The man's disease was roaring back to life after a pitifully short remission and was visibly taking its toll. He looked hollow-eyed and haggard. His large head, with its mane of iron-gray hair, seemed to wobble as he moved. His faded red bathrobe whipped about a pair of wasted, matchstick legs. It took no medical genius to see that he was losing weight rapidly—dying, quite literally, by the pound.

Complications had prevented us from operating, but now we could afford to wait no longer. "Your time is running out," I told him adamantly. "You've got to let us operate."

The man in the bathrobe said nothing but slowly shook his head, as if deep in thought, and kept on pacing. Amazing, I thought. Even the most hardboiled of patients would have acquiesced long ago. Yet this man, so proud, erect, and regal, even in his illness, had made up his mind that he would not be operated

3

on, and no amount of medical bullying was about to make him change it.

But then, this was no ordinary patient. This was Mohammed Reza Pahlavi, the self-proclaimed Shahanshah, Light of the Aryans, Vice Regent of God, and I, God help me, was his doctor.

The Shah's improbable journey had started on January 16, 1979, when week after week of violent antigovernment rioting had brought his administration to its knees, and the man who had ruled thirty-eight million Iranians from the majesty of the Peacock Throne was forced into exile in disgrace. For months the world watched as the Shah fled, unwanted and unwelcomed by his former friends and allies, from Egypt and Morocco to the Bahamas and Mexico, while the Ayatollah Khomeini's Islamic revolutionaries howled for his blood and vowed to send assassins to murder him in midflight.

With typical wit and irony, the Shah referred to his odyssey as his hegira, an Arabic word meaning flight from danger and toward safety and succor. Throughout it all, though, the ailing monarch, more than any of the retainers, diplomats, friends, and foes who swirled around him as he traveled, seemed to understand the paradoxical nature of his journey and stoically accept the presentiment that, from his intricate tangle of life-threatening problems, both political and medical, there could ultimately be no escape.

I had joined the hegira in Mexico in September of 1979. By that time, the Shah was suffering from at least five serious illnesses, any one of which was perfectly capable of killing him. Medically speaking, the choice was simple: the patient had to receive the comprehensive care only a first-rate public hospital could provide, or he would be dead within a matter of weeks. Faced with the grim facts, President Jimmy Carter had reluctantly agreed to let him enter the United States where he would be treated at New York Hospital in Manhattan under my supervision. That was in late October. Now, a mere eight weeks later, Carter wanted him out of the country—just as fast as was medically possible.

Carter had his reasons. On November 4, a little more than a week after the Shah arrived in New York, militant students had overrun the U.S. embassy in Teheran where, as Christmas approached, they continued to hold fifty-three Americans hostage, threatening to kill them if the Shah wasn't returned to stand trial for "crimes against the people." No president in his right mind could consider a deposed monarch an acceptable trade-off for American lives. Carter had decided the Shah would have to go. The president's political expedient and the medical interests of my patient were about to collide, and I was caught squarely in the middle.

On the face of it, I was an improbable character to be involved in such high political drama. For nearly forty years I had been a professor of tropical medicine. Quite by accident, I had also become a general practitioner with an office on Manhattan's Park Avenue. Over the years I had treated my share of idiosyncratic patients from the world of business, finance, the arts, and entertainment. I had even treated a few heads of state. I was familiar with the ironies of caring for the rich and the famous, chief among them being the sorry medical care they often received because of their insistence on having their egos massaged by high-priced doctors in hothouse clinics, while ordinary people, unencumbered by exalted status, were treated at large public hospitals, simply, democratically, and properly.

But I had never experienced a case as uniquely frustrating as the Shah's. Other famous people could, if they wanted, mask their identities, enter a good hospital under a false name, and thus elude publicity for a time. Not the Shah. The media blitz accompanying his escape from Teheran, his search for a country of permanent exile with its bizarre political complications, and now his forced flight from Lackland for an uncertain future, all combined to guarantee that a hiding place was one luxury he couldn't buy at any price. Thorough, routine care was another. Before it was all over, rival teams of doctors from France, Mexico, Panama, Egypt, and America would fight over the privilege of treating him. In the confusion, they would not only fail to cure him, but contribute to his early death.

But all that lay in the future as I sat in that bleak room at Lackland and kept vigil with the restless Shah. In a few minutes I would be forced to confront the president's men who had gathered nearby and try to cut a deal to help save my patient's life. What a mess, I thought, as the full force of my predicament suddenly hit me. How had I, a tropical medicine man and Manhattan internist, gotten swept up in this strange star-crossed odyssey? Someday, I knew, I would have to answer that question for myself and it would require going back to the start of my own medical odyssey, a story that begins with a frightened young man who never wanted to become a doctor at all.

PART I

BECOMING A MEDICAL MAN

CHAPTER 1

A Red-Hot Poker

Sixty years ago, when the idea of going to medical school first entered my brain, the prospect of actually becoming a doctor horrified me. As far as I could tell, doctors were little more than glorified plumbers who spent most of their time banging on chests, checking the pressure in the pipes, and encouraging urine samples to flow. Worse yet, they exchanged what mundane knowledge they had for *money*. Most undignified. Secretly, of course, the thought of taking responsibility for the life of a fellow human paralyzed me with dread.

No, I had decided on a much more promising line of work: I would become one of the great medical scientists of the twentieth century. True, I hadn't given much thought as to what field I would inflict myself on. Nor had I ever so much as cracked a medical book. That I happened to be a college freshman who couldn't have distinguished a pathogen from a spare tire if my life depended on it didn't seem to bother me, either. Fortunately, as it turned out, I would have very little to say about the directions in which life was about to propel me.

When I was born in Valparaiso, Indiana, in 1912, my parents were students at the University of Valparaiso, a school known in those days as the "Poor Man's Harvard" because of its high academic standards and low tuition. The small college town had one other advantage as far as my parents were concerned: it was only 160 miles north of New Harmony, the spot on the Wabash River, where, in 1825, British social visionary Robert Owen had established his version of Utopia. Like hundreds of other communes then sprinkled across the country, Owen's colony was based on free housing, free education, and brotherly, if not necessarily free, love.

My parents had planned to join the Owenites as soon as they finished school. For reasons obscure to me, they moved instead to East Orange, New Jersey, when I was five years old, and a few years later to Manhattan's Greenwich Village. These changes of venue, however, did little to dilute my parents' Owenite fervor. Determined to pass on their down-to-earth idealism to me, they required me to perform a variety of daily chores, including the critically important task of washing the dog each and every day of the year, a ritual that continued long after most of the poor beast's hair had fallen out from overbathing.

Enforced reading was also a part of the Owenite regimen. So at the age of eight, I was confined to my father's cramped study, where I proceeded to stumble doggedly through the verbal mine field of Gibbon's *Decline and Fall of the Roman Empire*. Somewhere along the line I managed to embrace the music of Beethoven and Scott Joplin and to become mesmerized by bridge, baseball, tennis, and the Civic Repertory Theatre on Fourteenth Street and Sixth Avenue, where the elegant Eva Le Gallienne starred in the plays of Ibsen, Turgenev, and Shakespeare and infected me with a lifelong passion for the theater.

Growing up in Lower Manhattan in the twenties, I exhibited the unmistakable symptoms of chronic wanderlust, a disease that has plagued me to this day. At fifteen, I would stand at the southbound exit of the newly completed Holland Tunnel and thumb rides from the passing stream of cars. When an accommodating driver would ask where I was headed, I'd tell him, "Anyplace you're going as long as it's south." The north, with its wintry landscapes and low gray skies, held little fascination for me. Ah, but the south! That was the direction of sunshine, adventure, and the promise of exotic new discoveries. Though neither I nor anybody I knew had ever set foot there, the tropics already seemed to be in my blood. I've always found it a little eerie, this slow, inexorable process of being pulled toward the light and the warmth, something I would later learn a biologist refers to as tropism—the tendency of plants and animals to be moved by external stimuli, as a flower turns toward the sun.

Sixty years ago, hitchhiking wasn't the death-defying enterprise it has now become. The epidemics of drug and alcohol abuse, kidnapping, and rape had yet to wash over our society. Still, my unannounced disappearances appalled my mother. To her credit, though, she did nothing to stop me. She assumed, quite inaccurately as it turned out, that I would one day outgrow my juvenile restlessness.

In spite of my wanderings, I did remain a more or less dutiful son. I was an avid student and a ravenous reader, and I confined my hitchhiking escapades to weekends and holidays, so as not to miss any school. But I could never quite shake my desire to strike out for new horizons. When I went to medical school years later, and the study of tropical medicine grabbed my lapels and started tugging hard, my restlessness simply shifted gears, moving smoothly from the tangible world of asphalt to the more abstract terrain of books and learning, where the lure of the open road was every bit as potent.

When I was eighteen, I enrolled at the University of California at Berkeley, a decision based on the unassailable logic that it was as far away from New York—and home—as I could get and still be in the United States. And so, in August of 1930, I left New York harbor aboard the liner the USS *President Wilson*, bound for San Francisco via Havana and the Panama Canal. As befits a first foreign adventure, it was a low-budget affair (the one-way ticket to California cost eighty-four dollars) and the prospect of the thirteen-day voyage through southern waters struck me as wildly romantic.

But I was hardly a romantic figure. Slight, blond, and given to quick, nervous movements, I was already a little stooped at the shoulder and weighed no more than 120 pounds soaking wet. I spoke rapidly and emphatically in a kind of pseudo-academic patois—a pathetic effort to appear smart and convincing. I was neither, especially outfitted as I was in a cheap blue seersucker suit I'd specially selected to meet both my budgetary requirements and the sunny California climate.

Thus attired, I soon found myself standing in the bleak steerage compartment of the *President Wilson* being critically appraised by the chief purser, a profane, blustering, bearded old sea dog. He seemed to regard my existence as a personal affront, and fussed and fumed over my steerage-class ticket in the salty language of the sea. His fury, as it turned out, had less to do with me than with my fellow passengers in steerage—forty-five Filipinos, illegal immigrants who had been caught working at menial jobs in the fruitless attempt to better their lot in life and for their efforts were being shipped back to their impoverished homeland courtesy of Uncle Sam. Since I was officially classified as "white" and the deportees were "nonwhite," shipping company policy dictated, in those days of unabashed racial discrimination, that the accommodations be divided into separate areas.

Grumbling loudly, old Neptune proceeded to divide steerage into two parts, assigning me an enormous amount of space encompassing several cabins and a large sea galley, while the hapless Filipinos were forced to huddle in the dingy, narrow part of the hold. When I protested this arrangement as unfair to my fellow travelers, the purser proved as deaf as he was vocal. In 1930, *desegregation* had yet to make its debut as a meaningful part of the American vocabulary. The Filipinos stayed in the hold.

It was a lonely voyage. Isolated in my officially bestowed "whiteness," I had no one to talk to. Moreover, hitchhiking hadn't prepared me for the physically confining spaces of sea travel. I became homesick and seasick at roughly the same time.

Eventually, though, a few of the first-class passengers, peering down from the upper deck, spotted a solitary figure stretched pathetically over the rail in the depths of steerage, and came down to visit.

By the third day, when I had mastered the trick of keeping down solid food, one of my benefactors invited me up to the posh main dining room for lunch. I felt guilty about being elevated to the good life of steak and potatoes while my Filipino friends were eking along on meatless stew but, as far as the ship's officers were concerned, I was free to come and go as I pleased. It would have been much smarter, of course, to simply upgrade me to third- or even second-class, thus making all of steerage available to the miserably cramped deportees. When I pointed this out to the purser, however, he was horrified. "Do you realize what you're asking?" he said incredulously. "That would violate the provisions of the eighty-four dollar ticket!" In 1930, people in authority, not just at sea but everywhere, tended to run very tight ships, indeed.

Three days out of New York we steamed into Havana harbor. All of the passengers clambered into the old colonial city for sightseeing, with the exception of the Filipinos, of course, who languished in their shipboard prison. Timid and frightened, I hung back with the deportees. When I finally emerged from steerage, however, I was in for a pleasant surprise. The sun, high and fierce, was producing an incredible heat. This was my first experience of the temperature of the tropics, and I found it exhilarating. My body quickly adapted to the sauna-box conditions and, as the sweat gushed out of me and I toured the hot, sweet-smelling waterfront, with its stately colonial buildings and lively cantinas, I knew that my southern tropism had been a reliable guide.

Three days later, we sailed into Colón at the Atlantic entrance to the Panama Canal. After the glories of Havana, the grubby port city, with its crumbling wooden shanties, begging children, and dirty bars, seemed to have little going for it. That night the ship anchored in Gatun Lake, close enough to the island of Barro Colorado for me to hear the primal sounds of the Panamanian jungle. Having now almost completely insinuated myself into first-class life, I stood on the upper deck under a crescent moon, smoking one of my first Cuban cigars, and tried to peer into the heavily enfoliated landscape.

I could see nothing except the vague, brooding outline of Panama's low hills. I don't know what I expected exactly, maybe some kind of tacit sign of welcome from my now beloved tropics. But if there was any telepathic signal out there in the shrieking night that I would return to Panama in exactly seven years to earn my spurs as a doctor, and then stay on for seven more, I couldn't detect it. All I got from behind the impenetrable curtain of jungle darkness was the occasional sound of some invisible animal crashing noisily through the underbrush. Unable to decipher anything of interest, I went below to steerage and bed.

I arrived at Berkeley on schedule and fell into line with other freshmen to sign up for classes. I couldn't help but notice that, while I, the "sophisticated" Easterner, still wore my blue seersucker, now severely puckered with dirt and overuse, the rest of the world seemed to be dressed in either blue jeans or grimy yellow cords. Feeling out of place, I determined then and there to flatten my fellow students with my academic brilliance. So I did the only logical thing for a budding scientific genius—I enrolled myself as an English major. After all, I reasoned, a great scientist had to write well. How else would anybody know what he was talking about? In truth, of course, I was far more interested in Shakespeare, the theater, and jazz than in scientific theory.

Then, in the fall of 1932, something happened to change all that. I'd just started my junior year when the celebrated British historian of medical science, Sir Charles Singer, arrived on cam-

pus as a visiting professor. Sir Charles was a bulky, aging specimen, almost totally bald, with a mercilessly adenoidal British
accent. To me, however, he was a godlike figure. His lectures
were marvels of literacy, organization, and enthusiasm, all driven
by a quiet, powerful intellect. I was enthralled. At the advanced
age of twenty, I had at last found my calling: I would not become
just another great scientist per se, but a great historian of science,
just like Sir Charles.

So I was crushed with disappointment when my term paper
on the history of malaria was returned to me marked "Unread."
Leafed inside, a little oddly, I thought, was an invitation to tea
from Sir Charles himself. A few days later, when I found myself
uncomfortably balanced on the edge of the great man's sofa, I
worked up the courage to ask him why he had rejected my manu-
script.

Sir Charles looked at me and blinked huge owlish eyes through
bottle-thick eyeglasses. "Perusal of your references made it
clear," he said, making it sound perfectly obvious, "that you had
not read the original sources, and I have no time to review hand-
me-downs."

"But Sir Charles," I protested, "it would be impossible for
me to read Greek, Latin, French, Italian, and German," the lan-
guages in which the pioneering studies on malaria had been done.
Sir Charles shrugged his heavy, tweedy shoulders. "Why then,"
he said dryly, "did you not pick another subject, such as the
'Contributions to Malaria By Those Who Wrote in English'?"

Chastened, I quickly retreated to the safety of my English
major and put my scientific plans on hold until medical school.
If I couldn't be a great historian of medicine, I reasoned, at least
I could be a literate doctor.*

---

*Forty-four years later I answered Sir Charles properly. *Tropical Medicine and
Parasitology: Classic Investigations*, a collection of approximately two hundred
original papers on parasitology, translated (by others) from nine foreign lan-
guages, was published by Cornell University Press. As senior editor, I gave
ten years to the project.

In the fall of 1933, I entered Columbia University's College of Physicians and Surgeons in New York City and my now rekindled ambition for a role in major-league research enrolled with me.

That was just as well, I suppose, because back then, medical science needed all the help it could get. In this country, pneumonia and tuberculosis were still the major killers; cancer remained an inexorable death sentence. Worldwide, malaria infected several hundred million people and killed ten million every year with brutal regularity. (In its long, malignant history, that one tropical scourge alone had up to that point slaughtered more of humankind than all other diseases combined.) Dysentery continued to devastate the tropics at a ferocious rate.

To treat these plagues, we had at our disposal only four basic drugs—morphine for pain, digitalis for heart failure, quinine for malaria, and aspirin for everything else. Doctors struggled heroically just to keep from killing patients out of sheer helplessness. Oftentimes, we'd simply make hollow, reassuring noises at the patient, give him a stock remedy—and pray. We might just as well have consulted palm readers or astrologists. It was, by today's technologically sophisticated standards, like practicing medicine by Ouija board.

So there was much work to do—and plenty of room for a young overachiever like myself. Still, I lived in fear of somehow being seduced into becoming a regular physician, taking care of people with mundane aches and pains. My vision was to crack the code of illness and piece together cures that would astound my colleagues with their unconventional brilliance. It would be the life of a medical pioneer, lonely, austere, and exhilarating. It all seemed pretty straightforward. Unencumbered by common sense or a shred of practical experience, I continued to dream on.

When I entered the second year of medical school, the time came for me to decide on a specialty, the arena in which I would make my mark. It was then, while I was whipsawed with indecision, that I first heard "the call." Looking back, I guess it was a little odd that the message should be rendered in an Irish accent. At the time, though, that only stood to reason, because the voice was that of an irascible Irishman named Francis W. O'Connor.

O'Connor, professor of tropical medicine at Columbia P & S, entered my life one spring morning in 1934 when he strode into the lecture hall of the pathology department. It was a breathtaking entrance. As was his custom, O'Connor wore morning clothes to class—gray pinstriped trousers and a cutaway coat. He carried a bowler hat and an ebony cane. A hundred second-year medical students swiveled from their microscopes and gaped in wonder. O'Connor, elegant, imperious, civilized, stared back, as if he were peering through his microscope at a wholly predictable, if mildly amusing species of protozoa.

We weren't only stunned, but confused. The "experts" in our class, the intrepid few who had flipped through the textbook for a quick preview of the course, pronounced tropical medicine to be a complete waste of time. We knew—or thought we knew—all we needed to know about the animal parasites of man—the tapeworm, the roundworm, the flatworm, worms of all conceivable shapes and sizes. We knew them to be writhing, grubby, disgusting creatures for the most part, connected in our minds with foul smells and fetid matter. And what could they possibly have to do with us? Parasites bedeviled distant lands. They were hardly likely to afflict anybody we would ever treat. (I would remember this years later when, lecturing to each new crop of second-year students, I would always take pains to point out how, at that very moment, each and every person within earshot harbored one or more common parasites, some potentially dangerous.)

But now here stood before us the humbling presence of Francis W. O'Connor, and suddenly I sensed my education was about to begin.

O'Connor quickly proved himself a shameless Gaelic spellbinder. Speaking in a mellifluous, rolling baritone, he eschewed the medical jargon that routinely scrambled our brains and muddled our attempts at recall. When he talked of parasites as creatures of great beauty, there was a touch of poetry in his words. He wasn't so much a medical lecturer as a storyteller, a spinner of parasitological tales that had the effect of etching the little monsters on your mind in a way that made them hard to forget.

The microscopic blobs responsible for amebic dysentery, for instance, took on dramatically contrasting personalities. *Entamoeba histolytica*, O'Connor explained, was the "evil genius," the dangerous one, an active, intelligent, fastidious, nimble parasite, far too crafty to stick around the microscopic field long enough to have its photograph snapped. *Entamoeba coli*, the pretender, on the other hand, was nothing but a common hooligan, a filthy little particle with indiscriminate eating habits and questionable self-esteem, a disgusting lowlife too lazy to swim out of the microscope's hot ring of light where it simply withers and fries in its own juices. After two years of medical school—two years of lectures so tedious as to be almost life-threatening—O'Connor's class was as exciting as sex, another subject about which most of us knew very little at the time. I was hooked.

Over the next two years, as my classmates drifted toward the more "respectable" specialties of gynecology, obstetrics, and surgery, I attached myself to O'Connor like a New Guinea tapeworm. I became a regular fixture in his laboratory, washing bottles, doing simple slide preparations, scanning stool samples for the more obvious parasitic intruders, and generally sucking in every morsel of knowledge that came my way.

Feisty, opinionated, a man with no known personal friends, O'Connor at first barely tolerated my presence. Gradually, though, he must have seen through the layers of obsequiousness, ambition, and insecurity that made up my youthful persona to the kind of burning curiosity that appealed to him. Because, slowly at first and then with growing enthusiasm, he began to teach.

And how he could teach! O'Connor drew crayon sketches for me in his quick, deft hand of all the important parasites and their complicated life cycles—"mug shots," he called them. Starting with malaria, he explained how all parasitic diseases have three things in common: they all feature a scene of the crime, the human body or the host, where the evil business is done; each involves a third-party accomplice called a vector that helps transmit the infection (in malaria, the mosquito); and all involve a cunning culprit, the parasite itself (usually with a fancy name, like *Plasmodium falciparum*, the cause of malignant malaria).

Nipping at a flask of Irish whiskey he kept stashed among his beakers and test tubes, O'Connor would spend hours regaling me with stories about the "grand old days" of tropical medicine. The hero in many of these tales was Sir Patrick Manson, the widely acknowledged father of tropical medicine. It was "Mosquito" Manson, a trailblazer in the study of insect-borne infection, who founded the London School of Hygiene and Tropical Medicine in 1899 and who authored the classic textbook on tropical diseases, our bible. It was Manson who, while working in Amoy, China, discovered that the mosquito was the transmitter of filaria, the parasite causing elephantiasis in man. He later suggested to Ronald Ross that the mosquito might also be responsible for the spread of malaria, a hunch Ross ultimately confirmed and for which he won the Nobel Prize in 1902.

Of Manson's many parasitic triumphs, perhaps the most fortuitous was his encounter with "Tso-Tong," a Chinese mandarin. While sitting in Manson's office on April 24, 1880, Tso-Tong raised a wad of phlegm in his throat and, missing the spitoon, spat the blood-stained sputum on the floor. Instead of being "angry and disgusted," Manson wrote later, he put some of the material on a slide and examined it under the microscope. Patience had its reward; the Englishman became the first human to lay eyes on the eggs of the Oriental lung fluke, *Paragonimus*. "I was not looking for a parasite when I found those eggs," he noted, "for a man may search for a shilling and find a sovereign. The important thing is to search."

O'Connor took pride in having been a disciple of the great man himself, although his feelings about Manson were understandably mixed. As a young instructor at the London School, O'Connor had expected to eventually inherit not only Mosquito Manson's academic mantle, but the old man's daughter as well, for the lonely, socially timid O'Connor had fallen madly in love with the beautiful, if somewhat fickle, Edith Margaret Manson.

Unhappily, Miss Edith had not fallen for O'Connor. Her heart belonged to yet another promising young parasitologist, a man of German extraction named Philip Bahr, who, to further complicate things, had also apprenticed himself to her father. O'Connor and Bahr exchanged escalating unpleasantries. The situation took a critical turn when O'Connor, shortly after the First World War, chose a solemn academic occasion, a conference on parasites, to rise from his chair and call Manson-Bahr (who had by now married Edith and added the famous parasitologist's name to his own) a "hyphenated Hun." There was talk of a duel. Then, suddenly, O'Connor withdrew. Being Irish in an English world, he shrewdly surmised that, having caused a public scandal and lost the hand of the fair Miss Edith into the bargain, his chances of going much farther with his career in London were, as he put it, "so slim as to be nonexistent."

So he did what seemed the only sensible thing: he exiled himself to Western Samoa. There, in the remote South Pacific, O'Connor engaged in what may seem strange solace for a heartbroken lover, though perfectly understandable for an Irish parasitologist with a poetic flair; he spent the next two years studying the effects on the native population of elephantiasis, one of whose most astounding attributes is its ability to cause the scrotum to swell to the size of a burlap potato sack.

O'Connor routinely used adversity to sharpen his scientific edge. During the First World War he had allied himself with C. M. Wenyon, the great English protozoologist. The two men moved into a tent at British army headquarters outside Alexandria, where they studied the impressive array of Egyptian protozoa then waging offensives in the intestinal tracts of thousands of British tommies stationed there awaiting repatriation. O'Connor issued each homesick soldier an empty wooden latrine bucket. Along with the receptacle each man received an ulti-matum approved by the military high command: fill the bucket and return home to England, refuse and stay in Egypt. "You can be sure," O'Connor said when he told me the story years later, "that the soldiers were literally overflowing with enthusiasm."

It was this aspect of O'Connor, his role as a great medical de-tective, that really captured my imagination. By the time I be-came his student in the mid-thirties, his sleuthing exploits had become the stuff of legend. During the summer of 1933, for example, O'Connor had been called in to help solve the riddle of what the newspapers had dubbed the "mystery plague" of the Chicago World's Fair. Hundreds of fairgoers, having returned to homes all over the country, had suddenly taken to their beds with rattling fevers and violent bouts of diarrhea. Sixty people died. Attendance at the fair plummeted, and there was talk of shutting down entirely.

The disease continued to baffle fair officials and local doctors, but it didn't fool the wily O'Connor for very long. No sooner had he gotten a good look at a sampling of victims' stools than he identified the villain as *Entamoeba histolytica*, the cause of ame-bic dysentery, one of the very diseases he and Wenyon had stud-ied so meticulously in Egypt. But the big question still loomed: Why had this ameba, a parasite commonly associated with filth and squalor, and spread by contact with infected feces, struck a modern, comparatively sanitary city like Chicago?

It was the epidemiologist's classic conundrum and a torture to the maniacally curious O'Connor. When he could stand it no longer, he decided to pay his own way to Chicago and spent the next several weeks interviewing victims in the Chicago area. He tracked down others across the country and grilled them by tele-phone. The questions—repeated hundreds of times—were al-ways the same: What did you eat before you got sick? What restaurants did you frequent? What hotel did you stay in?

His food-related questioning got him nowhere; not enough

people had eaten the same things or even in the same restaurants to create a meaningful pattern of infection. Not so with the matter of lodging, however. Practically everyone he talked to had had one thing in common: they had all been the guests of the stately old Congress Hotel, one of the Windy City's finer hostelries, which faced Lake Michigan in the middle of what is now the Loop.

The answer came to O'Connor in a flash. He rushed to the Congress, descended into the dank basement, and there found exactly what he had been looking for: two rusty pipes. One pipe carried tap water to the guest rooms; the other channeled raw sewage out of the building. Somehow, the pipes had accidentally fused ("a marriage of inconvenience," O'Connor called it), and the hotel's supply of drinking water had become a lusty breeding ground of the deadly amebas. O'Connor had saved the day.

Not according to the newspapers, however. The press exuberantly declared Dr. Herman Bundesen to be Chicago's medical savior. Bundesen, then president of the Chicago Board of Health and a big name in public health, had lent his name to the blue-ribbon commission appointed to study the disease and was therefore mistakenly credited with having solved one of the great epidemiological mysteries of the twentieth century. The lack of publicity didn't seem to bother the taciturn O'Connor; he hated to write and was content to let others appear in the medical literature. "The uncloaking of amebas," he reminded me, "is reward enough for any man."

In any event, the medical historians eventually got the facts straight. Reading about the "mystery plague" and then falling under O'Connor's spell only two years after his cracking of the case had a powerful effect on me. I still had no intention of becoming a practicing doctor. I'd long since given up on becoming a medical historian. No, I had finally decided what I wanted to do with my life. At the ripe, old age of twenty-four, I knew that I, too, more than anything, wanted to become a medical detective—especially if I could do it in a place where the sun was always shining and the weather was warm.

A RED-HOT POKER

Francis W. O'Connor seemed positively clairvoyant in his capacity to confidently anticipate every step I should take to implement my new plan and when I should take it. He proceeded to map out my career like some kind of elaborate military campaign.

It was an ambitious plan. After medical school I would go to Panama, where I'd spend two years as an intern at Gorgas Hospital in the American Canal Zone, then widely regarded, at least clinically speaking, as the "mecca of tropical medicine." Next would come a two-year stint at O'Connor's alma mater, the London School of Hygiene and Tropical Medicine, the pinnacle of parasitological research. If all went smoothly, I'd then labor two years in each of the hot, gritty vineyards of tropical disease— Africa, China, and India—and learn firsthand the modi operandi of the pathogenic villains peculiar to each continent.

If I somehow managed to avoid succumbing to a fatal dose of exotic parasites myself, I would emerge, at the advanced age of thirty-five, as qualified, in O'Connor's eyes, to eventually take over from him the chair in tropical medicine at Columbia P & S. What O'Connor didn't count on was his own untimely death in 1938 at the age of fifty-four. That, and the outbreak of the Second World War, would change my plans—and my life—in ways that even the canny O'Connor couldn't have foreseen.

For the time being, though, I was simply eager to please my mentor. I enthusiastically went along with everything O'Connor said, including his desire to see me start my medical trek in the tropical surroundings of the American Canal Zone.

Gorgas Hospital had many attractions. Along with the excellent training I would receive there, it was south and the climate was lushly tropical. Gorgas also paid its interns eighty-five dollars a month, an unbelievably lavish salary for those hard Depression times. (Most hospitals paid interns nothing at all and even then fired them if they got married or cohabited in an obvious fashion. When the interns at Mount Sinai Hospital in Manhattan went on strike for a thirty-dollar-a-month laundry allowance in 1936, they were promptly declared "communists" and let go on the spot.)

With so many things going for Gorgas, the field was crowded with contenders; eight hundred medical school graduates applied for a mere eight openings. I knew in my bones that I didn't have a prayer. Then a letter arrived from the chief health officer of the Canal Zone, Colonel H. C. Pillsbury, informing me that I had been selected for the Gorgas internship along with seven other candidates from cities all across the United States. I was stunned at first, but the more I thought about it, the more I had to hand it to the members of the selection committee. Imagine, they had waded through that enormous pool of applicants and, somehow, at least in my case, managed to pick out the truly talented and deserving. Their wisdom astounded me.

Later on, when I got the chance to peek at my Gorgas records, I would discover the secret of their acuity. O'Connor, it seems, had written a letter to Colonel Joseph Franklin Siler, head of the Army Medical School in Washington, D.C. The colonel, having developed the first practical vaccine for the prevention of typhoid fever, carried a lot of clout in the Army Medical Corps, which also happened to operate Gorgas Hospital. Siler had written a compelling letter of his own.

"Dear Governor," he wrote to Colonel Clarence S. Ridley, the American plenipotentiary for the Canal Zone whom he must have outranked. "Enclosed is a letter from my friend, Dr. Francis W. O'Connor, in behalf of one Kean, who desires an internship at Gorgas Hospital. I do not wish to offend Dr. O'Connor and you don't dare offend me. See that Kean gets the job."

Thus did merit cement the cornerstone of my career.

I began my real journey into medicine when I went to say goodbye to Francis W. O'Connor. I was leaving for Panama the very next day and was hungry for a few final words of wisdom.

Until then, O'Connor had been the single biggest influence in my life. What if I failed to live up to his expectations? Worse yet, what if cures for all major human diseases were discovered before I could finish my marathon training course and make my contribution? I was desperate for O'Connor to issue one last set of instructions that would magically erase all doubt about traveling the road that now stretched ahead of me into the unknown.

O'Connor did not appear sympathetic. He looked at me with his cool blue eyes—it was as if he could see life rushing by me while I stood frozen in my tracks. "Stay on your toes, Kean," he shouted at last. Stay on your toes?! What the hell kind of advice is that, I thought. Frankly, I had expected a little more from the great doctor, so I pressed him to elaborate.

O'Connor sighed heavily and reached for his favorite metaphor—the old-fashioned fireplace poker. According to the Irishman's formulation, you either had a "poker up your arse" about something, or, God help you, you didn't. "*Your* poker," he said, thickening his Celtic brogue for dramatic effect, "is of the red-hot variety, and, if your colleagues don't beat you to death out of sheer spite for your ambition, you might make a decent scientist one day."

With that, O'Connor ordered me out of his laboratory. He despised sentimentality in any form—he said so anyhow. Besides, he had work to do. Not knowing whether to burst into tears or explode with joy, I went home and packed my bags. It was June 1937, and I was sure of one thing and one thing only— my poker *was* red hot and, at that particular moment, it was pointing straight toward Panama.

CHAPTER 2

Coming of Age in Panama

My career as a practicing physician began in earnest one steamy Saturday night in Panama, and it was not an auspicious start.

At the time, though, I was convinced internship was going to be a real snap. After all, I'd been at Gorgas Hospital less than a week and already I'd been put in charge of supervising the weekend shift in the emergency room. Obviously the senior doctors had great confidence in my talents as a healer or they wouldn't have assigned me this important honor. It never occurred to me that ER duty was a standard part of the ritual initiation for raw interns, the medical equivalent of Marine boot camp. I chose to interpret it as a sign of big things to come. The thrill lasted all of twenty minutes.

It took me that long to size up my new surroundings. What served as the emergency room at Gorgas by night was, by day, the main operating theater, a spacious, brightly lighted oval lined with surgical cabinets and almost luminous in its whiteness. The nurses were all white, too—mostly fresh, young, and sassy women who invariably hailed from places in the Deep South, especially Alabama, Mississippi, and Louisiana. The male orderlies, on the other hand, were all black, all Jamaican or Barbadian emigrés, and all seasoned veterans of the Gorgas service.

Standing by the open windows mopping my forehead with a handkerchief and watching the blades of the huge ceiling fan knife slowly through the hot, dead air, I savored the feeling of power accompanying my first medical command. Despite the enervating humidity, the nurses glided through the ER going about their chores with great decorum and efficiency. Only one thing puzzled me: they seemed to be laying out enough gauze and antiseptic to bind the wounds of an army. When I asked one of them to explain, she looked at me as if nothing could be plainer. "Why, Doctor, honey," she laughed. "It's Saturday night in Panama City." I didn't know what she meant, but I was about to find out.

It was then that I heard the noise. Faint and far off at first, it sounded like the muffled bellowing of some large farm animal. As it grew closer, however, I realized that what I'd mistaken for the call of a prize bull in heat was not some barnyard serenade at all, but the sound of a human voice, singing loudly, with great feeling, and badly off key.

The nurses heard it, too, and looked up from their work. As the source of the caterwauling headed in our direction, the lyrics, though slurred, became audible: "Mine eyes haf seen-ah glory uffa cummin uffa Lo-o-o-rd . . ." Oh Lord is right, I thought, for I knew that whatever was slouching toward the ER making that infernal racket spelled nothing but trouble.

Trouble arrived when the emergency room doors swung back to reveal three American sailors, grinning and wildly disheveled. They swayed in the doorway for an instant while their eyes adjusted to the incandescent brightness of the operating theater. The singer—a blond, sunburned, fuzz-cheeked youth of about twenty—stood, or rather hung, between two larger, semi-erect swabbies, while he continued to declaim, ". . . G-a-l-o-o-r-e-e g-a-l-o-o-r-e-e hal-lay-looo-yah." As they lurched forward, I quickly diagnosed his problem. Even I could see that the singing sailor's head had been laid open from ear to ear. His scalp was a geyser of blood.

All at once, my dilemma hit me with full force. I had gone to a good medical school for four long years. I had studied hard. But now I realized how utterly useless all that book learning had been for the situation I now faced.

In those days, Columbia P & S, like other top medical schools around the country, prided itself on producing scientists, scholars, and professors. It did not consider itself an incubator for the general practitioner. The practical aspects of medical training were passed over for the teaching of the so-called "fundamental principles of medicine." Many of my wiser classmates, fearful of graduating without any practical experience whatsoever, signed up for volunteer work in local clinics where they could familiarize themselves with flesh-and-blood patient care.

I couldn't be bothered by such mundane concerns, of course. Since I'd never wanted to treat patients anyway, I spent all my free time at the microscope with O'Connor. I was a doctor only in the most theoretical stretch of the imagination. I had never drawn blood from a single vein or sewn one measly suture. And now, here in faraway Panama, I had collided with the most terrible truth of all: I was utterly paralyzed by the sight of blood.

This was not the way I'd pictured the first encounter between doctor and patient. I had always imagined a moment of triumph, a young doctor skillfully attending to his patient as the nurses and orderlies nodded in admiration and approval. Instead, I stood there bewildered, staring blankly at the young sailor as he lapsed closer and closer to bleeding to death. The nurses, who had called me "doctor" with such deference only minutes before, were now staring at me, expecting the results the title assigned.

I picked up a piece of gauze and daubed timidly at the man's spurting wound, but my half-hearted efforts did nothing to stanch the prolific flow of blood. It didn't take the head nurse long to recognize I knew absolutely nothing about treating a patient. She observed my technique for a moment, and then, with a disapproving cluck of her tongue, ripped the gauze from my hand, grabbed the sailor in an authoritative headlock, and applied maximum pressure to the top of his skull.

Having been exposed as a complete medical fraud, I contemplated the end of my career. Just then, however, I felt someone poke me gently in the ribs. "Dok-tor," said a soft, thickly accented voice, "you will be needin' these." I turned to see Edgar, the senior orderly, calmly holding a pair of surgical gloves in his outstretched hands. Numbly, without stopping for the washing ritual, I inserted first one shaky paw, then the other, as I searched Edgar's rheumy eyes for confirmation of impending catastrophe.

Edgar only smiled. A mountainous black man with great ebony promontories for cheeks and a fringe of close-cropped, salt-and-pepper hair, Edgar was a figure of great respect at Gorgas, a Jamaican emigré who had worked as a surgical assistant at the hospital for more than thirty years. During that time, he had guided many a fumbling young intern through the terrifying rites of the emergency room; now he would do the same for me.

Edgar prepared the patient for surgery by shaving his head in what struck me as a most ruthless fashion. Shielding the patient's eyes with an enormous hand, he poured a mixture of iodine and peroxide into the wound. The sailor didn't scream as I had feared. He wasn't sober enough for that. Instead, he only winced dumbly and continued mumbling his battle hymn, but at reduced volume. Edgar handed me the suture and forceps, took my hands in his, and began guiding me in tying stitches through the thick, ragged pieces of scalp.

I was horrified. "Edgar," I protested, "We haven't given this man any anesthetic!" Edgar chuckled at my innocence. He explained how there were very few nerves in the scalp to begin with, adding, "Be-zides, theez mahn he got so much all-coh-hole een heem now heez gone to feel noh way worze."

Amazingly, the wound seemed to close. The bleeding stopped. The stitches even appeared to assume a modestly organized pattern. Edgar quickly applied a compress bandage, wrapped the incoherent sailor in a white headdress, and discharged him with a stern, fatherly injunction against the wages of sin and alcohol. Turning to me, he smiled approvingly and said in a voice loud enough for everyone in the emergency room to hear, "Niize whork, Dok-tor." I have never felt more gratitude toward any human being than I felt for this honorable wise man that night.

I prayed that no more cases would come our way that shift. But that was a very tall order indeed. On a Saturday night, Panama City, crossroad of two continents, bustling ocean port, was one of the bawdiest, toughest fleshpots north of the Equator. Countless bars, clip joints, and brothels routinely spewed onto the pavements battalions of hapless GIs reeling from booze and sporting a breathtaking variety of contusions, abrasions, and lacerations acquired in the usual ways—brained by a bartender over a disputed tab, straight-razored by some jealous woman of the night, or simply beaten senseless by a fellow comrade-in-arms.

All night long, wounds, concussions, black eyes, and broken limbs flowed through the ER in a steady stream, while Edgar directed operations with skill and patience. Anything remotely serious he took charge of himself. Around five o'clock Sunday morning, having observed Edgar in action for many hours now, I worked up the courage to remove a microscopic shard of beer bottle from the breast of one of the American girls who danced at Mamie Kelly's, a local nightspot. Edgar pronounced the operation a brilliant success, the girl gave me a moist smile of gratitude, and I stumbled back to the intern quarters at dawn, wondering through a haze of exhaustion just exactly what kind of life medicine held in store for a doctor scared stiff by the sight of blood.

I had come into the Canal Zone on June 28, 1937, when the *Ancon*, the new flagship of the Panama Canal Line, docked at Colón on the Atlantic side. (The "old" *Ancon*, then recently retired from service, had been the first ship to navigate the canal when it was opened on August 15, 1914.) I was now twenty-five.

The first thing I noticed was how everything in Panama seemed to have a double identity. Cristobal, the Canal Zone port, had its Panamanian twin, Colón. Opposite Cristobal–Colón on the Pacific side was Balboa–Panama City. The two sets of cities were connected by a railway owned and operated by the Panama Canal Line, where a steam locomotive steadily made its way along a single line of track, through mountain and jungle, toward the Pacific.

Although I had passed through the canal for the first time en route to Berkeley seven years earlier, I had never really seen Panama. From the deck of a ship, elevated and distant, you couldn't see much beyond the first layer of jungle. Now, however, seated at the open window of a train, I got a real glimpse into the hot, moist, noisy heart of Panama. Ships steamed through the canal as the huge lock gates clanged shut behind them. In the bright sunlight, stretches of thick, impenetrable jungle were interspersed with stops at the Canal Zone depots of Fort Davis, Gamboa, and Pedro Miguel. In village after village that lined the Panama side of the track, ragged children played, dogs barked, women spoke in a mixture of staccato Spanish and the local Indian dialect. Strange, unidentifiable odors rose through the jungle as the train chugged through the steamy landscape. What romance!

The heady rush of strange new sights, sounds, and smells, made our arrival in Balboa all the more disappointing. What immediately struck me about this place that was to be my new home was how clean and orderly everything looked. Instead of the exotic squalor I'd anticipated, the scene was straight out of Palm Beach, Florida. Neat white houses sat amid immense, rolling lawns, lavishly irrigated and manicured. The streets were spotless. And there, on top of a large hill, dominating the entire scene, was the huge white Administration Building, the symbol of the United States' presence in Panama.

While I struggled to find my steamer trunk on the station platform, I was approached by a man in a chauffeur's uniform. "You must be Dr. Kean from New York," he said, breaking into a friendly grin. "I'm Sam. Dr. James is waiting for you at the Union Club." Sam's assistant grabbed my baggage checks and ran off down the platform. When I protested, Sam held up an admonishing palm. "Don't worry," he said. "We'll take your bags to the hospital. But you really can't keep Dr. James waiting."

Who the hell was Dr. James? Then I remembered. O'Connor had spoken of the great William James many times. According to legend, he was an extraordinarily capable internist, best known for his research on amebic dysentery, O'Connor's pet disease, and blackwater fever, a particularly malevolent complication of malaria. Until that moment, I simply hadn't connected James with Panama. In any event, I wondered what this medical giant could possibly want with me.

Sam shoved me into a long, glistening Buick, and we headed into Panama. The length of a football field was all that separated the aseptic Canal Zone from the teeming streets of Panama City, and, as we drove across Fourth of July Avenue, we were suddenly back in that other world I had glimpsed from the train, the poor, rotting, enticing world of Panama's Spanish-speaking slums. I was amazed. I'd never before realized how only a few hundred yards could make such a big difference in the way people lived.

The Union Club, the gathering place for the Panamanian elite and a few rich American expatriates, sat on a low, palm-studded bluff overlooking the dazzling blue waters of Panama Bay. The club was well equipped for its primary function—the drinking of alcohol—boasting, as it did, three large, self-contained bars on the ground floor and two more upstairs. The hallways were cavernous, dark, and cool, and after a few minutes of aimless wandering I found Bill James.

The dark, polished bartop mirrored a pair of shotglasses, a bottle of Old Parr Scotch, and the huge, round face of the great doctor. James was an enormous man—broad, fat, and tall—with an astonishing capacity to consume liquor. A Southerner, he was also a famous talker, and he had a little of the Baptist preacher about him in the dramatic way he hammered home a point.

James greeted me with a baleful stare. "We need you down here, Kean," he said, pausing to peer through the bottom of his empty glass in microscope-fashion at a liver spot on the back of his hand. "When you've finished at Gorgas, of course, you'll join us at Herrick," he said with finality. James headed the Herrick Clinic in Panama City, a small, exclusive hospital that specialized in caring for the wealthy upper crust of Panamanian society. "There are too many of us old folks down here trying to care for too many sick people. Young Dr. Kean, look no farther. Here is where you belong, and here is where you shall stay."

Dr. James then launched into a lengthy overview of the local tropical diseases; malaria and amebiasis were his favorites. Warming to his topics, he lectured me on them individually and in great detail. All the while, he managed to keep my glass filled to the top with Old Parr whiskey.

How exciting it was to be in the company of the great! Obviously Dr. James found me fascinating, too. Why else would a famous man like him devote so much of his precious time to an unknown like me? I hadn't yet recognized one of life's fundamental principles—that the teacher is frequently far more desperate for a student to enlighten than the pupil is to receive said enlightenment. So my instruction continued as afternoon faded into a cool tropical evening and the bar began to fill up with other club members. Dr. James would interrupt his lecturing just long enough to greet various local dignitaries who approached to pay their respects.

There was only one problem. Although I now considered myself a seasoned man of the world, I still was not a very experienced drinker. As the hours rolled by, and the Old Parr river flowed on, I began to notice an odd clinical phenomenon involving my own body. This consisted of the deliriously euphoric sensation that I was about to float away from the bar like a helium-filled balloon. So I hooked my feet firmly under the brass bar rail and continued to nod in agreement with everything Dr. James said. It did not occur to me that I might be drunk.

But drunk is what I was. I was also beginning to develop a distinct queasiness in the pit of my stomach. No lunch had been served on the train, and Dr. James was far too busy discussing the sexual habits of the anopheline mosquito to think about dinner. I struggled valiantly to keep up with James's line of argument, as well as his alcohol consumption. Alas, I was no match for the great doctor in either department. The evening flew by in a haze.

Around eleven o'clock, I realized I was in serious trouble. I didn't want to offend my host. On the other hand, I was quickly losing out to a more powerful urge to fade into oblivion, amebas or no amebas, or whatever point Dr. James happened to be embellishing at the moment. I was also troubled by my sudden loss of memory. Deep down in the rubble of my mind, I had the distinct feeling that I had come to Panama for some specific purpose, that I had a mission to fulfill. Try as I might, though, I couldn't quite put my finger on it. At midnight, trusty old Sam appeared at my elbow, and he and Dr. James carried me out to the Buick.

The next morning I awoke in a strange room. Hovering over me, crooning softly, was a pretty young woman with golden limbs and a beatific smile. Her English was limited, and my head was about to explode with pain, so it took me a while to grasp what she was doing there. At length, I managed to put things together: the woman was Dr. James's maid and she was there to persuade me to join the great man for breakfast. Having solved the mystery, I groaned three times, rolled over, and tried to go back to sleep.

But Dr. James had trained his staff well. Like Sam the Persistent, the maid wouldn't take no for an answer. She sat me up, shoved a cup of coffee into my trembling hands, and then provided a razor and soap, which I used to inflict several large cuts on my face before starting down to the dining room. Halfway there, I suddenly remembered why I had come to Panama—the minor matter of my internship at Gorgas Hospital! I would have to tell Dr. James at once; he would surely order Sam to drive me there immediately.

Downstairs, Dr. James was in an ebullient mood. If it had been hard to sneak a word into our conversation the night before, it was downright impossible now. The doctor had a plan. Since it was far too nice a day to practice medicine, he said, he would cancel his office hours and take me on a complete tour of Panama City. I protested weakly that I thought I really ought to be getting to Gorgas to start my medical career. "Nonsense, young man," bellowed Dr. James. "What you need is to see Panama through the eyes of an old-timer. You'll see all you want of your blasted hospital soon enough."

Outside, Sam revved up the Buick and we embarked on what struck me as a remarkably well-orchestrated tour: a trip out to the old city to see the ruins left by Sir Henry Morgan, the pirate; a jaunt over to the Miraflores locks on the canal to see them in operation as a big tanker steamed through; a visit to a local Indian village, Rio Abajo, to observe preparations for an important cockfight that evening. As one high point led to the next, I discreetly fished for clues about the general location of Gorgas Hospital. But whenever the question arose, Dr. James always spotted some crucial landmark that cried out for explanation.

When the noon whistle blew we just happened to find ourselves passing in front of the Union Club. "What a happy coincidence!" Dr. James declared. Inside, he held up two fingers and the barman produced a pair of gigantic rum drinks. Three rums later, when I was beginning to feel myself again, we resumed our tour. By 4:30, however, we were back at Dr. James's famous corner in the Union Club. Again, the Old Parr flowed. Again, the evening grew faint, then disappeared altogether. And again Sam and Dr. James carried me out to the trusty Buick.

The next morning I woke up in a cold sweat. Panicked, I realized that this was my third day in Panama and I still had absolutely no idea where to find Gorgas Hospital. That noon, battered and unkempt, the cuts on my face now infected with some unfamiliar tropical bacteria, I decided to make a run for it. While Dr. James was occupied jawboning a local politician from his usual perch at the Club, I made an excuse and headed for the toilet. There I scrawled a note thanking him for his "extraordinary hospitality" and promised to get back in touch as soon as I'd settled in at the hospital.

As I was about to slip out the back door, I ran into Sam, who tried to block my path. I brushed past him, ran out into the street, and hailed a carrometa, one of the colorful, horse-drawn taxis that plied Panama City in those days. I climbed in and told the driver to take me to Gorgas Hospital on the double. He turned and looked at me like I was crazy—didn't I know the hospital was only a few blocks away?!

We crossed Fourth of July Avenue, drove past the old Tivoli Hotel and the Episcopal church, and headed up the palm-lined streets of Ancon Hill.

And then I saw Gorgas Hospital. Long, white, and imposing, it sat on the brow of "the Hill" and seemed to sprawl endlessly in all directions. A long, circular driveway, lined with more palm trees, wound up the slope to the main entrance, a double porte cochere. As I bounced up and down in my seat from the gentle rattle of the wooden wheels, the driver's religious gewgaws and charms dangling wildly and the horse's hoofs heralding approval as they hit the hard pavement, I couldn't help thinking, despite my still delicate physical condition, how exciting this all was. My first hospital! The tropics! Here I was at last.

The assistant superintendent of the hospital was less enthusiastic about my arrival. He greeted me with a sneer: "Where in the hell have you been?" Then, after taking a closer look at my bedraggled condition, he added sarcastically, "In the whorehouses of Panama City, I suppose."

"No such luck," I replied. "I was met at the train by Dr. James and . . ."

The man's whole manner suddenly changed. "Oh, my God! Another friend of Dr. James." He laughed explosively. "We're going to have to start sending somebody over to Cristobal to meet the boat and save some of you young fellows from falling into his hands." Obviously I hadn't been the first intern to be so lavishly entertained by the great Dr. James. Somehow I felt a little disappointed.

The deputy administrator showed me to the intern quarters. Gorgas was laid out in the pavilion style then typical of hospitals in the tropics, with five one-story wings, each a separate patient ward, communicating with one another through a central hub, which itself housed a main operating room, clinic space, and administrative offices. As we walked the long, airy corridors, my sense of excitement grew. Old sepia-tinted photographs on the walls showed women dressed in long, flowing robes ministering to the sick. From the looks of their flamboyant "flying nun" hats, I knew they could only have been the Sisters of Charity, the French Roman Catholic nursing order.

It was then that I remembered the stories O'Connor had told me about the old French hospital, L'Hôpital Central du Panama. Informally known as Ancon Hospital, it had consisted of some fifty buildings that once occupied the very same grassy knoll overlooking the Pacific where Gorgas's modern concrete shell, built in the early twenties, then stood. Opened in 1882 and operated by the French Canal Company, with space for five hundred beds, it was the medical arm of the French effort to dig a canal in Panama—an effort doomed almost from the start by tropical disease.

Triumphant in building the Suez Canal, the great French engineer Ferdinand de Lesseps came to Panama, then part of Colombia, in 1881 to start construction of a sea-level canal across the forty-mile-wide isthmus. The magnitude of the new undertaking dwarfed Suez. The anticipated cost of $130 million was half again as great (to say nothing of the $290 million the French actually spent before they were forced to abandon their undertaking). "Apart from wars," wrote historian David McCullough, "it represented the largest, most costly single effort ever before mounted on earth."*

---

*David McCullough, *The Path Between the Seas* (New York: Simon and Schuster, 1977), 11.

But it wasn't the engineering challenge that defeated the French; it was disease. Suez was hot, dry, and dusty; even insects couldn't thrive there. Panama, on the other hand, was a wet, humid jungle, the perfect breeding place for a staggering variety of mosquitoes, including those transmitting yellow fever and malaria. Unfortunately, it wasn't until 1900 that U.S. Army Major Walter Reed, following the lead of Dr. Carlos Finlay, demonstrated in Cuba that the mosquito was the carrier of yellow fever. (Three years earlier, Ronald Ross, working under the influence of Sir Patrick Manson, had exposed the insect's role in transmitting malaria.) In the meantime, the French, who wrongly attributed their constant struggle against disease to mysterious vapors thought to rise from rotting jungle vegetation, died in appalling numbers.

The French stuck it out for ten years before funds ran out and they had to give up on de Lesseps's ambitious plan. But disease had long since sapped even the French élan. Medical historian John Gibson described the scope of the problem:

> A single ship arrived at the isthmus [in 1883] bringing seventeen French engineers, only one of whom lived to return to his native land. Twenty out of twenty-five Sisters of Charity who began their duties at Ancon Hospital at the same time succumbed to the ever-present agent of death. In September 1884, twenty sailors died of yellow fever in Colón harbor. Only a single member of the crew of a British brig was alive when the epidemic subsided. During the same epidemic 160 yellow fever cases occurred among the white men of the coast city, two out of every three resulted fatally. Is it surprising that to the Frenchmen this part of the world became known as "the white man's graveyard?"*

---

*John M. Gibson, *Physician to the World—The Life of General William C. Gorgas* (Durham, N.C.: Duke University Press, 1950), 99.

est, Darling took one last look at his slides to confirm his failure—and immediately broke into a smile! True, the microbes
he'd isolated were dead ringers for *L. donovani*—in every respect,
that is, but one. The telltale parabasal rod (that eventually develops into flagella) inside the single-celled creature was missing.
These were not the beasts responsible for kala-azar after all. Darling's honor was saved!

Better yet, he had stumbled across a brand new disease, for
on closer inspection, Darling's parasite turned out not to be a
parasite at all, but a fungus. The discovery—the most important
of his career—became known as the histoplasmosis of Darling.
Ever since, millions upon millions of pigeons throughout the
world have obligingly guaranteed Sam Darling's immortality, as
subsequent studies have shown that the disease bearing his name
is found virtually everywhere the ubiquitous birds deposit their
feces, the prime vehicle for the growth and transmission of the
fungus. To this day, histoplasmosis remains stubbornly prevalent
in the Midwest, especially in Ohio and Wisconsin, infecting millions of Americans but sparing no part of the world. Usually
asymptomatic, it may cause a prolonged, low-grade fever. Occasionally, in X rays of the chest, it is confused with tuberculosis.

The job of ridding Panama of epidemic disease was plenty big
enough to test the reputations of Gorgas and his intrepid band
of scientists. In Havana, the colonel had been able to eliminate
yellow fever in eight months; in Panama, it took twice as long.
The mosquito slayers cleared large areas of vegetation, drained
ditches, pools, and creeks, and laid a blanket of oil diluted with
kerosene across large bodies of water. Darling improved on this
mixture by concocting something he called PCL (Panama Canal
Larvicide), consisting of crude carbolic acid, rosin, and caustic
soda which, at a cost of seventeen cents a gallon, emulsified in
water and spread rapidly along the grassy margins of ditches and
stream, killing mosquito larvae as it went.

The screening of all Canal Zone dwellings took more time and money, but Gorgas used his consummate political skills to obtain the necessary funds. When Colonel George Washington Goethals, the man in charge of building the canal, complained that each mosquito Gorgas killed cost the American taxpayer ten dollars, Gorgas replied, "But just think, one of those ten-dollar mosquitoes might bite you, and what a loss that would be to the country."*

Gorgas created a water supply for the Canal Zone and its twin cities that was one of the best in the world. In 1910 (or even today), only a fool would drink tapwater in Paris, Leningrad, or Mexico City. Thanks to Gorgas, the water supply in Colón and Panama City became as safe as in New York or London, infant mortality dropped quickly, and the diarrheal diseases, themselves the causes of many deaths, very nearly disappeared. During their tragic decade in the territory, the French had lost a total of 22,000 men to yellow fever; in the ten years it took the Americans to finish digging the canal, only seventeen succumbed to the disease. Malaria was not wholly eliminated, but significantly reduced—all thanks to Gorgas and his team.

Unfortunately, not all Canal Zone traditions were as commendable as its scientific legacy. When Teddy Roosevelt declared the canal "a shining path of progress between the seas," most Americans took it for granted that the waterway should bisect Panama with a zone of U.S. occupation. The canal was flanked on either side by an American sector ten miles wide, a line that historically helped divide Panamanian loyalties and accounts for the powerful love–hate relationship its people feel for the United States to this day.

The canal was primarily built not by the Americans, the French, or, for that matter, the Panamanians, but by labor imported from the West Indies, principally Barbados. When it was completed on the eve of the First World War, the white Amer-

---

*McCullough, 573.

icans kept the empire, the Barbadians and Jamaicans stayed on to work on the canal and in the hospital, and the Panamanians nursed their wounded national pride.*

Working in the Zone as a doctor was generally the same as working in the States. Living there was almost identical to living somewhere in the Deep South. That is where the vast majority of the four thousand whites who operated the canal and administered the Canal Zone were recruited from, and they brought their cultural prejudices along with them. Mint juleps and bourbon were the popular barroom drinks. Racial segregation, except in the workplace, was pervasive and rigidly observed. During the building of the canal, whites were paid in gold and blacks in silver, and the coinage worked its way deep into the social fabric of the Zone by providing the euphemistic means by which all public facilities—housing, toilets, water fountains, movies, and buses—were separated.

---

*That a drug-contaminated dictator like Manuel Antonio Noriega would come to power in Panama in the 1980s was only the logical outcome of the trauma inflicted by the circumstances of history that neither the United States nor Panama has understood sufficiently.

The villainy of Noriega and the quixotic personality of his predecessor, Omar Torrijos Herrera, have been widely reported elsewhere. It should be pointed out, however, that their behavior represents only a variation of a time-honored pattern of corruption in the Panamanian leadership. In the late thirties, for instance, it was public knowledge that for many years the red-light establishments in Panama City regularly contributed one-tenth of their daily revenue directly to the office of the president. During my period at Gorgas, one of the grand old men of Panamanian politics died while visiting a high-class "house" in Rio Abajo and was rushed into the Canal Zone for emergency treatment at Gorgas Hospital where he was declared dead—quietly and for the first time. The patriarch's still-warm body was then rushed back across the line and into his official residence where he was declared dead for a second time—this time officially—so that he could die with honor in his own country.

Detailing the political corruption of Panamanian leaders should not be interpreted as an attempt to trivialize the bitterness of Panamanians toward the gringo. They properly resented the role of inferiority assigned to them by the Americans who ran the canal and routinely referred to locals from all walks of life as "spics."

The microcosm of Gorgas Hospital mirrored these same social divisions. The "gold service" was composed of the doctors and nurses, all American citizens and all white, while those on the "silver service," the orderlies, cleaning ladies, laundry women, and cooks, were categorized as "colored," whether they were local mestizos, San Blas Indians, or the indispensable black emigrés from Barbados and Jamaica. White nurses made ten times the salary of black orderlies for much the same work. Edgar may have been the animating spirit of the emergency room and my savior, but he and I could not drink from the same water fountain.

Patient wards were strictly segregated—"gold" for the Caucasian canal workers and their families, as well as American military personnel, "silver" for local Panamanians and the blacks. This meant that each specialty ward—pediatrics, obstetrics, internal medicine, and surgery—had its gold and silver divisions, and it was the custom for interns to spend six weeks in each learning the ropes.

The big diseases were pretty run-of-the-mill stuff. Gold patients routinely suffered all of the maladies of Mississippi and Alabama: hypertension, heart disease, pneumonia, alcoholism, syphilis, and gonorrhea. Their silver counterparts had the same diseases—only more of them, and more often badly neglected. Among the female patients on the silver service, diabetic gangrene forced frequent amputations; fibroid uteruses when removed could weigh twenty pounds; and cancers of the breast might be huge and ulcerated.

Some 10 percent of both gold and silver cases, however, were anything but routine. These involved the diseases of the tropics, including malaria, leprosy, leishmaniasis (which causes disfiguring ulcers of the face), Chagas' disease (the New World variety of African sleeping sickness), amebiasis, and practically every form of diarrhea, both deadly and benign, known to humankind.

There could be little doubt that William Crawford Gorgas had done an excellent job cleaning up the Canal Zone. Nonetheless, Panama proper, the land beyond the antiseptic American pale of concrete buildings and immaculate streets, remained a pesthole with few rivals in the Western Hemisphere. There the parasites—those of malaria, chief among them—vied with nonparasitic villains to inflict their miseries. Take, for example, the spectacularly explosive vomiting death brought on by the eating of the poisonous fruit of the Akee tree, first brought to the Caribbean in 1778 by the notorious Captain Bligh. Then there was the bizarre, though relatively benign affliction called ainhum, which mysteriously seals off the circulation in the feet, causing the toes to fall off one by one. The list was endless, fascinating, and depressing. By the time I left Panama, I had written some thirty-five papers on such diseases and had successfully established myself as a major expert on some of the world's most minor afflictions.

After a few weeks on the job, I was beginning to feel more confident about my ability to cope with the unending flow of the unexpected and the usual. Having released myself from near-total paralysis at the sight of blood, I now encountered pressure of a different sort, though, for I suddenly realized that I'd now been at Gorgas for almost two months and I still hadn't made a single major scientific discovery. But how did one go about unraveling such a mystery? Then it hit me! I remembered the story of the lovelorn Francis O'Connor and how his star-crossed affair with Edith Manson had propelled him to the South Seas, where he'd made his mark studying elephantiasis, the most destructive clinical manifestation of a disease called filariasis. So what if filariasis had never been recorded in Central America? That was obviously the result of some gross scientific oversight, which I was now prepared to remedy.

Captain James Cook was the first European to give an account of elephantiasis when, in 1774, he described the grotesque swelling of limbs he saw while visiting Tonga, where native lore attributed the disease to the eating of unripe yams. But it was none other than Mosquito Manson, O'Connor's mentor and hoped-for father-in-law, who demonstrated how the filaria, the white threadlike parasite causing the disease, worms its way into its victims. After the tiny creatures are injected into the skin by the mosquito, they burrow into the body and ride the circulatory system to the lymph glands of the groin. Having achieved this existential feat, they then die—and that's when the real trouble starts. Decomposing, their bodies give off chemicals that trigger an intense inflammatory reaction that blocks the normal return of lymphatic fluid from the arms, legs, and testicles. The result: an elephantine swelling of these extremities.

Before 1948, there was no cure for filariasis. Victims simply endured the disease as it ran its slow, steady course, frequently over the space of many years. Surgery could provide some relief if, of course, a surgeon was handy, which wasn't often the case in the South Seas. Visiting Samoa in 1934, the distinguished tropical disease expert Victor Heiser noted in his memoir, *An American Doctor's Odyssey*, the local demand for scalpel-wielders: "Any surgeon who could cut out one hundred and twenty-five pounds of excess tissue [in a single afflicted patient] naturally found favor in the eyes of the Islanders."

What fired my enthusiasm for finding filariasis in Panama was the fact that the tricky filaria often lies dormant in the blood of its victims for years before causing the obvious manifestations of disease. So I set up my own small laboratory—a microscope and a few bottles of stain—in an abandoned broom closet at Gorgas, determined to document the frequency of infection in the Canal Zone and about to demonstrate in the process how dangerous a little knowledge can be.

The worm's nocturnal habits presented the first challenge. Although a simple blood smear can easily reveal the presence of the parasite, only the prick of a patient's finger between the hours of 10 P.M. and 2 A.M. can provide the right sample, for that is when the worm leaves the snug safety of the internal organs to circulate freely in the peripheral blood. (This timing is also what makes possible the midnight rendezvous between the worms and the mosquitoes that transmit them, since the mosquitoes are also nocturnal creatures.) So I prowled the wards by night, collecting blood for slides that could be scanned for filariae at a more reasonable hour.

Naturally, my ambition made me an object of suspicion among my fellow interns. They considered me an irritating over-achiever, and they told me so. Hoots and laughter accompanied me as I embarked on my nightly rounds only to invariably bump into my colleagues as they set off to prowl the beer gardens of Panama City's bawdy bar district. Secretly, of course, I longed to join them, but I could not weaken now. O'Connor was counting on me. We'll see who laughs last, I thought, when Kean hits parasitic pay dirt.

After five weeks of work I had assembled more than five hundred slides, stained and ready for examination. Hour after hour, I hunched over the microscope, scanning for the fiendish filaria, but without success. I found not a single parasite. Filariasis was not fated to be a pathogenic feature of the Canal Zone. It never had existed there and probably never would.

My failure did not seem to shock O'Connor, when I wrote him with the bad news. "I did not think you would find anything," he wrote back, adding, a little condescendingly, I thought, "But, then, looking is the thing, is it not?" He was right, of course. But I resented it at the time.

Failure did have a hidden advantage, however, in that it seemed to make me more acceptable to my fellow interns. Now that I was perceived as having had some of the starch knocked out of me, I was deemed suitable for friendship. Rodney Rau Beard— a rotund, affable Stanford man—made the first approach. Rodney, who eventually became a professor of public health at his alma mater, loved ecclesiastical music and went to the Episcopal church at the foot of Ancon Hill every Sunday to feast his ears. When he was married there a year later, I was his best man, even though it meant sacrificing my weekly golf date.

Bob Kaiser was a big, boisterous kid from Columbus and followed every game of the Ohio State football team by long distance as if it were a search for the Holy Grail. He routinely loaned me enough money on the twentieth of each month to last until payday, a favor I was reminded of thirty-five years later when his son passed my course at Cornell with flying colors. Then there was the intern referred to simply as "the brilliant one," the most intelligent and capable of all eight of us, who drank too much and persisted, when in his cups, in the embarrassing and eventually self-isolating habit of pinching the nipples of any and all females in his vicinity.

For all our differences, however, we all had one characteristic in common: the hard medical lessons of the intern's life.

There are painful lessons in every doctor's life, although their relative inexperience makes interns particularly susceptible to feelings of guilt, which revolve around the self-indictment, "If only I had known more, I might have saved that patient's life." In my case, the date of July 21, 1937, remains forever emblazoned on my memory, for that is the day I killed my first patient.

I'd just been assigned to my first six-week rotation in "Pediatrics—Silver," when I was handed the chart of a nine-year-old Panamanian boy with a confirmed diagnosis of malaria. Too sick to swallow, the patient was unable to take the quinine capsules then normally given for the disease. Since this was my very first malaria patient and the complications bothered me, I rushed to Colonel Frank Clampton for advice. "No problem," said the easygoing chief of pediatrics, "just administer half the standard dose intravenously."

Three weeks into my internship, needles, sutures, and the other paraphernalia of the medical profession no longer frightened me. So I prepared the quinine mixture, sucked it up into a syringe, and placed a tourniquet on the little boy's arm. When the vein had enlarged sufficiently, I inserted the needle, removed the tourniquet with a flick of my free hand, and then slowly, gently injected the medication—just as we had been taught.

I had barely started the inoculation when the boy's eyelids began to flutter. His eyes then rolled back in his head, which began lolling eerily from side to side. In the next split second, the youngster started to shake violently. A chill of panic shot from the base of my spine to explode in my brain—"This kid is dying!" I quickly removed the needle, and the syringe clattered to the floor. But it was too late. As I stood helplessly by, a volley of convulsions of ever-greater force racked the child's body until, suddenly, he lay completely still. The whole process took no more than a few seconds. Time enough, however, to see myself metamorphose from healer to killer.

To this day I have no idea if the child died of malaria or if my injection did in fact kill him. Other, more experienced doctors had patients die under similar circumstances. New orders were posted. We were required to dilute the quinine in greater amounts of water and administer it by drip feed instead of syringe. But those few panicked seconds in Panama were all it took to teach me a lifetime of respect not only for malaria, but for the hidden dangers even the simplest, most frequently recommended forms of drug therapy can entail.

Lessons were lurking around every corner at Gorgas. A few weeks after the malaria tragedy, the normal rotation brought me to "Pediatrics—Gold." The unspoken, racist implication was that you'd be allowed to get any really serious mistakes out of your system while caring for the Panamanians and blacks on the silver ward before dealing with the army "brats" and children of the Caucasian canal workers on the gold. Whoever had devised this theory, however, had failed to make allowances for an intern like me.

Like many young doctors, I was too busy trying to impress those around me with the extent of my knowledge to learn the first thing about practicing medicine—the art of how to listen to the patient. Listening is a basic tool of the physician because it is the only way of discovering the particulars of a patient's complaint, the complicated physiological and emotional factors that distinguish the real-life patient from the textbook model. If the doctor doesn't know how to listen, he doesn't get the clues he needs to make a reasoned diagnosis and the patient is in big trouble.

In contrast to me, Colonel Clampton was one of the best listeners I have ever seen. He was gentle, patient, and very "unmilitary." He was also very old—or at least he seemed so to us interns, who considered his diagnostic technique hopelessly outdated. The colonel hardly ever used a stethoscope or examined a child with his hands. He simply sat at the patient's bedside, watching and listening. Flared nostrils and raspy breathing? Pneumonia. A tendency to bend the right leg, touch the lower right quadrant of the abdomen, and whine? Appendicitis. Odd neck movements and high fever? Meningitis.

The colonel's diagnoses were remarkably accurate. That cut little ice with my colleagues and me, however. All that watching and listening drove us to distraction. If not addlepated to begin with, the old boy, we were convinced, was galloping toward senility at an accelerating clip.

During this period when I was busy feeling superior to Clampton, a boy of five or six was carried, arms and legs flailing, into one of the examination rooms, where he proceeded to throw his little head back and emit a series of earsplitting screams. No one seemed to know what was wrong with him or why he had been admitted to the hospital. The boy himself was no stranger to any of us, however. He belonged to a doting, middle-aged colonel, whose sole hobby was to spoil his son rotten. This he accomplished in part by ordering the wives of various enlisted men to act as the child's unpaid nanny. The unending stream of strangers, who weren't always successful in hiding their lack of enthusiasm for the assignment, had the effect of both flattering and frustrating the little tyke beyond belief. At the advanced age of six, he had become a confirmed hypochondriac, and we were all weary of his many time-consuming, unnecessary trips to the hospital.

While three nurses pinned him down, and the patient continued to wail, I turned him over on his stomach and slipped a thermometer up his rear end. He had a very minor fever. I then pried open his mouth with a tongue depressor and discovered the faintest signs of a sore throat. Since it was already 5:30, I told one of the nurses, "Give him an aspirin, and I'll be back after dinner to see what happens."

At the mention of the word "aspirin," the kid stopped howling long enough to shout, his face an explosive shade of red, "I don't want aspirin! I can't take it! You can't make me!" We'll see about that, I thought. Turning to the head nurse, I said, a little callously perhaps, "Shove it down his throat, and I'll be back."

The staff dining room was a quarter of a mile away, down one of Gorgas's long, pavilion-style wards. As I walked along, I could hear the kid still shrieking in protest at the aspirin. I arrived at the dining room and sat with my colleagues to await dinner, which was always promptly served at six o'clock. No sooner had the kitchen doors swung open with the soup course, however, than I was called to the telephone. A distraught nurse was on the line: "The colonel's son is dead!"

My seven colleagues and I raced down the corridor to the child's bedside. Fortunately, the nurse had spoken prematurely. The kid wasn't dead yet, but he was fading fast. He had lapsed into a coma and his breathing had stopped. Shattered, I watched as my calmer, more experienced colleagues started artificial respiration followed by oxygen and injections of adrenalin. After what seemed like an eternity, the little boy batted his eyes several times and drew a long, labored breath. I leaned over in gratitude, close enough to hear him say, "I told you not to give me aspirin. I'm allergic to it." The patient survived my stupidity to make a full and speedy recovery.

Years later, as I sat in my green leather chair on Park Avenue listening to a patient tell his story, I would always remember that child. My last question before proceeding to the examining room has always been, "What do you think is the matter with you?" Not infrequently, the patient is right.

Dr. Howard Tuttle was famous for his unconventional teaching techniques. Dour and balding, Tuttle was chief of surgery at Gorgas and, although a veteran of twenty-five years in the canal service, he still spoke with a clipped Massachusetts accent. He was the quintessential surgeon, brusque, efficient, and overwhelmingly self-confident, and he took an exceedingly dim view of even the slightest surgical error committed by one of his interns. We all dreaded rotation under Dr. Tuttle's steely gaze.

I had more reason for worry than the others. I simply wasn't cut out to be a surgeon, and I knew it. To say that I hadn't been blessed with great manual dexterity would be putting it mildly. I was downright clumsy. I was sure that I had no business anywhere near an operating table. Each time I entered the OR, Hippocrates's famous injunction to medical people—"First, do no harm"—rang in my ears. I was, at least in my own mind, a surgical accident waiting to happen. And so I lived in mortal terror that Dr. Tuttle would assign me to a major operation for which I was not qualified.

Naturally, that is exactly what happened. Near the end of my rotation, he ordered me to assist him on a particularly intricate gallstone operation. My hands shook violently as I scrubbed down alongside the cool, silent Dr. Tuttle, while the patient, a 250-pound Jamaican woman, was wheeled into the operating room. A resident administered a spinal anesthesia and I took my assigned position across the table from Tuttle.

The old surgeon made a huge incision in the patient's abdomen, then looked up at me and said, "Kean, you've been working very hard lately; I think you should do this operation." Tuttle's words hit me like an ice-water transfusion, and with the predictable effect—I froze. I opened my mouth to protest but no sound came out. Dr. Tuttle, meanwhile, calmly laid down his scalpel on the draped belly of the patient and walked out. I rushed to the surgeon's side of the table, motioned to the second assistant to take my place, and started mopping up the blood, wondering how on earth I was going to survive this experience, to say nothing of the patient's chances.

It was then that I noticed something peculiar about the woman in front of me. Her blood was blue. Her breathing had stopped. So had her pulse. Panicked and horrified, I dropped my instruments and rushed through the swinging doors and into the corridor, shouting, "Dr. Tuttle, Dr. Tuttle, come back! She's dead!"

Dr. Tuttle turned and smiled thinly. "Of course she's dead, Kean. You don't think I'd let you operate on a live patient, do you?" The spinal anesthesia had killed her, as it did one patient in every three thousand or so.

In his wisdom, Dr. Tuttle had already divined that, for the next few years anyway, I would show considerably more aptitude dealing not with the live patients on the operating table, but with the dead ones on the autopsy slab. After a brief intermission, I was destined for the Gorgas morgue.

CHAPTER 3

European Interlude

Francis W. O'Connor died during my first year in Panama, and the sudden loss of my mentor devastated me. I was now completely on my own. There would be no authority figure around to make all the big decisions for me. Would I stay on in Panama where things were leafy and comfortable? Or would I continue to follow O'Connor's blueprint for me, spending the next ten years traveling the globe, rootless and poor, trying to qualify as a tropical medicine man?

The prospect of leaving the Canal Zone horrified me; I loved the place, I loved the work. But, deep down, the old wanderlust stirred. I decided to press on to the next stop on the itinerary: the London School of Hygiene and Tropical Medicine.

After two years of internship and residency in Panama, I'd been able to pay off school debts of a thousand dollars, save nearly four hundred more, and borrow an equal amount. Eight hundred dollars would get me as far as England, cover tuition at the London School and, if I managed my money sensibly, allow me to squeak through the year without starving to death.

Sensibility in the money department had never been my strong suit, however. I immediately set about planning a whirlwind tour of Europe, based on the not wholly unreasonable theory that I owed it to myself, an embryonic man of the world (a world so far composed largely of Valparaiso, Greenwich Village, Berkeley, and Panama), to get a feeling for the Continental life before buckling down for more studies. The first stop, obviously, would have to be Paris.

Once again, I arranged to make my voyage in steerage, this time on a French liner, the *Lafayette*. The passage from New York to Le Havre cost eighty-four dollars, exactly the same price I'd paid for my first trip through the Panama Canal via Havana on the *President Wilson* ten years earlier. And again, as the day of departure drew nearer, I found myself tormented by the prospect of an expedition into the unknown.

I wasn't worried about the London School; I knew I had probably learned enough about parasites in Panama to stand me in pretty good stead there. But what would I do afterward? How would I fund the rest of the O'Connor program? I had no money for further studies and now, with O'Connor himself out of the picture, my one living link to the medical establishment back in the United States was severed. I felt lost and alone. Then, en route to Paris late in that summer of 1939, adventure beckoned once again, and this time it spoke not in the Irish tones of O'Connor or the exotic accent of Paris, but in the tongue of Flatbush Avenue, Brooklyn.

The *Lafayette* left New York harbor on August 10. Steerage on the French liner was a vast improvement on the *President Wilson*. The food was terrible, but the wine was cheap and plentiful and the atmosphere festive. In contrast to the unfortunate Filipino deportees on the *Wilson*, the bowels of the *Lafayette* were filled with a wide variety of lively, interesting people of many ages and nationalities. Before leaving Panama, I had purchased a secondhand tuxedo and, by dressing the part of a young swell, I was able to ascend to the first-class deck, where, to my surprise, people seemed genuinely interested in talking to a fidgety doctor from the tropics. As I drifted between the earthy camaraderie of the lower decks and the refinement of the upper spheres, the eight-day voyage took on new promise.

If style and sophistication inhabited the upper decks, romance was booked in steerage. As I was leaning over the lower-deck railing one day early in the voyage, the high, musical voice of a young girl spoke to me in a language that was pure New York. "Yuuwa an American, ain'tcha?" How sweet, I thought—Kean, you've acquired a little admirer. I pictured a schoolgirl on her way to Europe with her parents and turned to give her an avuncular word or two.

Suddenly, I found myself staring into the lush bosom of a remarkably tall young woman with a head of flaming red hair and the clean, sharp facial features of a film goddess. "Hi, I'm Colleen O'Neill," she said, revealing a set of stunning white teeth. I was dumbfounded.

As she hooked herself over the railing beside me, revealing an extra yard or two of seductive curves, Colleen got to the point quickly. She explained that she was something called a pigeon dancer, that she was on her way back to Paris, where she practiced this intriguing profession—and she was lonely. Would I mind keeping her company? "Tell me more about the pigeons," I stammered.

The Folies Bergère, Colleen said, had an act in which a half-dozen girls danced on stage, each performer clad only in three pigeons—one to cover each strategic point of the female anatomy. Just before the curtain was about to fall, there would be a loud blast of music from the orchestra, the frightened pigeons would fly off into the wings, and the bevy of international beauties would be left fully, if fleetingly, exposed. Colleen was very proud of the fact that she was one of the first Americans ever to have been hired for this artistic extravaganza.

Colleen had a checkered past. She had been a showgirl on Broadway under the "protection" of a notorious New York mob boss, one of whose boys, it seems, had become understandably smitten with the curvaceous Catholic kid from Flatbush and had decided to elevate her status to that of gangland moll. Colleen was terrified. She worked up the nerve to go straight to the mobster himself and ask for help. Although from all accounts the man was a pathological killer, he must have harbored a shred of chivalry somewhere in that twisted soul of his, because he called off his amorous goon and gave Colleen the money for her passage to Europe.

Of Colleen's many charms the one that was manifestly welcome to an eager, if inexperienced, twenty-eight-year-old male was her near-total preoccupation with sex. Don't get me wrong—Colleen knew where to draw the line. Under absolutely no circumstances would she consent to what she referred to as "shootin' the moon." Her compromise was a simple one; she would happily engage in any and all forms of sexual gratification up to but short of the consummate act itself. Aside from Colleen's insistence on maintaining her technical virginity, this meant we were only limited by our somewhat innocent 1930s imaginations.

Together we spent night after night in my tiny cabin, my roommate having discreetly disappeared, cavorting at all sexual levels except the ultimate. Toward the end of the voyage, however, Colleen experienced a change of heart. She now insisted on "shootin' the moon," adding in the same breath, and with conviction, "I'll make yoos a wonderful wife."

To prove it, Colleen said she'd even consider the supreme sacrifice—giving up the pigeon act. Determined to become a famous scientist, I had never for a second entertained thoughts of marriage. Until now. Somehow the prospect of life with the beautiful Colleen didn't seem all that bad. I was weakening rapidly when, on the last night of the voyage, as I lay entangled in our narrow seabunk, O'Connor's ghost appeared to me in a dream. The old man, his eyes like blowtorches, brandished his red-hot poker and was ready to brain me for having the temerity to give up on his plan in such a predictable fashion. I woke up drenched in sweat.

The next morning I was obliged to exercise an uncharacteristic degree of self-control. Over breakfast, I told Colleen, in the most tongue-tied way possible, that I couldn't marry her. Full of the confidence of youth, Colleen didn't seem in the slightest way put out. "You'll change yer tune," she said, with a saucy waggle of her hips. "Jes think watcher gonna be missin'." I thought. Suddenly, and for the first time since I'd fallen under the spell of Francis O'Connor five years earlier, the prospect of spending my life in the lonely pursuit of parasites seemed to lose a little of its glamour.

The excitement of visiting Paris for the first time was enough to take Colleen off my mind for a few days. Docking in boisterous Le Havre, taking the boat-train to the Gare du Nord, ordering a taxi to drive me around the Champs-Elysées, the Arc de Triomphe, and the Place de la Concorde—this was the stuff of dreams! (Years later, a close friend would diagnose this state of intense enthusiasm that overcame me in the presence of anything new and different as "Fishforkitis"—based on the assumption that I hailed from the mythical hamlet of Fishfork, Idaho—Pop. 30, and so found even a traffic stoplight a source of rapt fascination.)

I stayed at a small hotel of dubious sanitation near the Madeleine called the Hotel Newton, where the landlady seemed to be clairvoyant. Bulky in soiled sweaters, with crumpled hankies protruding from the sleeves, she spoke no English, but made it plain enough that absolutely no guests, especially *les femmes*, would be permitted to visit my room. Somehow she'd seen through my polite exterior to a mind boiling with fantasies of romantic conquest in the City of Lights.

That was just as well, I suppose, because my room—narrow, overheated, and crammed with ancient furniture at three dollars a night—was on the fifth floor overlooking the air shaft and not at all suitable for amorous adventure. For all her mind-reading talents, the landlady was a miserable cook and something of a cheapskate. Breakfast, served in a dusty little room off the kitchen on the first floor, consisted of a thimbleful of orange juice, a miniature croissant, and some bad French coffee. But who cared? Paris awaited.

Day after day, I walked around the city, thrilling to the sights. I hiked to the Louvre and then sauntered over to Notre Dame. I tramped up and down the Champs-Élysées, ending up at the Hôtel des Invalides. I spent hours patrolling the Left Bank, browsing through the tiny book and art stalls there, determined to soak up the mood and history of this most civilized of cities. I purchased a beret. My execrable French improved, but not enough to get me into any serious trouble. Somehow, in all that walking, though, I managed to totally ignore the rumblings of the war that was now only weeks away.

Yes, the days were glorious. The nights, on the other hand, grew increasingly lonely. They were filled with half-hearted attempts to divert myself with more walking. I strolled through Montmartre, with its hundreds of lively bistros and small, cozy nightclubs. For two dollars I bought a bamboo pole from a boy and fished the Seine. I stayed in my cramped room and tried to decipher some old French books I'd bought on the history of tropical medicine. Finally, I could stand it no longer. I went to see the pigeons.

The act at the Folies Bergère was everything Colleen had described and more. Though difficult to believe at first, the other dancers were every bit as statuesque as the gorgeous Colleen. All the same, I couldn't help notice how the pigeons, startled by the all-important trumpet blast that signaled the moment of full disclosure, had the nasty habit of defecating on stage as they flew off toward the wings. The parasitologist in me was appalled. Just the way to spread at least three terrible diseases, I said to myself. Obviously, as the only parasitologist in the house, it was my professional duty to sit through the last show of the evening to confirm this menace to public health. Secretly, of course, I longed for the tender caresses of my beautiful pigeon dancer.

Backstage, to my relief, Colleen was happy to see me. She threw her arms around me and introduced me to the other members of her troupe, two dark Italians, two bouncy, flaxen-haired Brits, and a voluptuous golden Pole with piercing blue eyes. All the girls lined up and, stepping forward in turn and bending coquettishly from the waist, planted sisterly pecks on both cheeks.

The girls had little to do in the daytime and more or less adopted me. In the afternoons I fell easily into the habit of walking up the Rue Royale, past Maxim's and the sidewalk cafes, arm in arm with two or three of these lovely creatures. Not infrequently, the men would crane their necks at us, seeming to wonder how on earth a modest physical specimen such as I had managed to stage such a *coup d'amour.*

My duties as mascot also demanded that I drop into the Folies each night just in time to watch the pigeons explode toward the wings in a hail of feathers and feces. After the midnight show, I would walk the girls home, stopping on the way for a light supper at a sidewalk cafe. Instead of making the lonely trek back to the Hotel Newton, I was usually rewarded, after the pulling of various long faces, with an invitation to stay the night at the girls' apartment. Waking up in the mornings, with two or three lovely nude bodies draped over the limited bed space, I began to harbor dark thoughts. Did I really want to spend the best years of my life poking around the pestholes of Africa, India, and China?

I might have done something drastic had my sex life not been as frustrated as ever, despite all the outward appearances of amorous success. The European girls remained faithful to their lovers, and Colleen had laid down the law: No engagement ring, "no shootin' nothin'."

However much the idea of becoming an international playboy appealed to me, my timing was bad. Ominous things were beginning to happen in Paris. Sitting in my favorite outdoor cafe on the Rue Royale one evening, I noticed that the streetlights were flickering oddly. From then on the city seemed to grow darker and darker with each passing night. It was now the end of August 1939, and even I could no longer ignore the fact that the lights of Paris were being absorbed into the shadow of the approaching Nazi storm.

A few nights later I was awakened long after midnight as first one girl, then another, plopped down on my bed, and we huddled there listening to the cadenced stamping of boots as hundreds, then thousands, of French soldiers marched toward the central railway station. We sat there for a long time, taking turns voicing our anxieties about the coming war, wondering how it would change our lives and debating whether we should make plans to abandon Paris. I reported how many of my Italian and Spanish acquaintances from the *Lafayette* were already returning home. The girls were silent for a moment, then they began making up imaginative, if wholly unrealistic schemes for escaping Hitler's stormtroopers.

Over the next three days, everybody who had anywhere to go packed up and went. The girls and I reacted to the sad prospect of so many splintered friendships by throwing a big party at their apartment, the windows papered over for the blackout. Hard liquor, then in extremely short supply, materialized in large quantities as departing friends expressed their generosity of spirit by showing up with numerous bottles of Scotch, gin, and wine under their coats. Still, the conversation was hushed, conspiratorial, and devoted mainly to talk of exit routes. A handsome young Italian couple was going back to Palermo, a winning Frenchman was signing up for the army the following morning, the two British pigeon ladies were returning home to England on an early tide.

When asked about my plans, I shrugged my shoulders and said that, if things got really rough, I'd just go back to the States. All other murmuring in the room ceased and a voice said, "But how will you get in?"—a question that had never before occurred to me. Before I could speak up, one of the girls replied, "Oh, he has an American passport, the lucky stiff."

I was lucky. Other than Colleen, I was the only American citizen in the room and, for the first time, I appreciated the value of having American travel papers. Instinctively, I clutched my breastpocket and confirmed that, yes, my passport was still there.

The time had come to leave Paris. The City of Lights was now completely blacked out. The lovely Colleen was going back to Brooklyn and begged me to go with her. But I had no interest in returning home to New York, where unemployment, and, quite possibly, a vengeful, lovelorn mobster awaited. Everyone else I knew was either fleeing France or going underground. I decided to declare an end to my Continental expedition and to go on to England where I would enroll at the London School, just as Francis O'Connor would have wanted.

The two British pigeon girls proved helpful, and, with the assistance of their Italian stevedore boyfriends, who worked for a big shipping company, the three of us managed seats on what we understood to be the last boat-train for London.

Early the next morning I found myself wandering around the unfamiliar city. For the first time in weeks I was without the benefit of female companionship and felt very lonely. I'd taken the addresses and telephone numbers of the pigeon girls—and then never saw them again. They were relieved to be back in England but distressed by the loss of their dancing jobs and worried about their Italian beaus returning to the questionable mercies of Benito Mussolini.

The London sky was filled with dozens of fat antiaircraft balloons—protection that, even to a military ignoramus like me, seemed wholly inadequate against the might of the German Luftwaffe. The city was silent, frightened. A rumor ran through the streets that the fiendish Jerries were poised to launch a poison gas attack. I bumped into an American businessman who told me that gas masks were being distributed free of charge at the American embassy and I didn't want to be caught maskless in an emergency.

While searching the thoroughfares for the embassy building, I straggled past 10 Downing Street, where a small, quiet crowd was kept back from the door by bobbies with unsheathed night-sticks. Everyone was waiting for the prime minister to emerge and make an important announcement. The thought that photographs would immortalize that dreary London morning scene for posterity would have seemed ridiculous to me then. Still, it was obvious something big was about to happen, so I stuck around.

A few minutes later, the door of No. 10 opened and out stepped Neville Chamberlain, tall and grim. He made a brief announcement in his high, tremulous voice—Britain had officially declared war on Germany! It was Sunday, September 3, 1939.

I stumbled from that dramatic moment in the history of Western Civilization toward the American Embassy. Arriving at the palatial building at 9 Prince's Gate, I presented my passport to the duty officer, signed the register, and was directed to an office on the ground floor where the gas masks were being handed out.

The masks themselves were pretty amateurish affairs, a pair of thin glass goggles fitted to a filter the size of a can of chewing tobacco. But they were useful, if only as a psychological defense against the feeling of utter helplessness that comes from being an expatriate in a foreign world newly at war. There were already a dozen or so Americans in the room clumsily trying to assemble the ill-fitting masks, which they then awkwardly placed on their heads, mangling protruding ears, noses, and eyeglasses in the process.

While I was similarly engaged, Joseph Kennedy, the American ambassador, walked in. He was of medium height, with thinning gray-black hair and horn-rimmed spectacles perched halfway down his nose. He seemed to be trying to reassure his distraught countrymen that all would be well, but his words were having the opposite of the effect intended. I could see a state of subdued panic overtake several of my fellow mask-assemblers as I overheard him saying, "You should leave England as soon as possible. Don't linger. Difficulties are coming—very, very soon."

When he got to me and asked what I was doing in England, I told him about my plans to study at the London School. He looked at me as if I had taken leave of my senses before puffily warning me, "You should return to the U.S. as soon as possible, young man. You can bet the London School won't be holding any classes this term."

In that case, I told the ambassador, I would join the British army medical corps. Kennedy's eyes widened in disbelief. He seemed genuinely flabbergasted. I was a little stunned myself, since this was the very first instant the idea had popped into my brain.

"What, and join the losing side?" Kennedy blustered. He then proceeded to inveigh against British weakness, predicting loudly that the war would last only a few days before Germany would "clobber the Brits." When he saw that his message wasn't getting through, he resorted to strong-arm tactics. "If you join the British service," he said, his face turning from red to purple, "it is up to you. But I will personally see to it that your American passport is taken from you and that you will never again return to your country."

"Mr. Ambassador," I said, getting a little emotional myself, "your personal views on the Nazis are your own business, but you have no right to deprive me of my passport. I'm not a traitor. Britain happens to be our ally."

Kennedy was apoplectic. He continued to rant on about my "treachery." Everybody in the room dropped his mask and seemed to share my wonder that such a respectable figure as the American ambassador could allow himself to get so worked up in public. An aide soon appeared and led him away, Kennedy still shaking his head in disgust.

Twenty years later I mentioned this incident to his son, Robert Kennedy, when I ran into him in the lobby of the Carlyle Hotel in New York, where both of us had apartments at the time. John Kennedy was president then, and Bobby was his attorney general. When I described his father's behavior, he didn't seem shocked. "Mr. Kennedy," he said with an ironic smile, "was a very angry man in those days. Most of us did not share his political views, but, even today, I'm reminded how strongly he felt about matters."

The conversation did nothing to relieve me of my image of Kennedy Sr. as a cantankerous old coot, ready to deprive me of my citizenship for sticking up for a loyal ally.

The next few days in London were dreadful. It was now early fall and, even for England, the weather was unremittingly cold and damp. Every few hours the ghostly wail of the air-raid sirens drove everyone into underground shelters. At night, there was a total blackout. People girded themselves for the German onslaught from the air—and then nothing happened. The atmosphere of fearful anticipation was totally exhausting.

The biggest letdown of all, however, was waiting for me at the gates of the London School of Hygiene and Tropical Medicine. By the time I got to the famous old building at the corner of Keppel and Gower Streets, the doors were locked tight and sandbagged. Old Joe Kennedy had been right—at least about this one thing. A sign proclaimed that classes had been canceled until "further notice." When would that be? No one seemed to know. None of the professors were around. The skeleton staff busily closing down the school didn't have the "foggiest."

I telephoned an old academic ally of O'Connor, Professor Clayton Lane, whose number I'd brought with me from Panama. Invited for tea that afternoon, I soon found myself in the presence of a gracious, elderly gentleman, who, though preoccupied with the new war, took great delight in confirming the stories of O'Connor's bellicose exploits in the old days at the London School where they both had been budding parasitologists. Lane also gave me the distressing news that, although he was confident the school would reopen, it wouldn't do so in London but in a safer spot somewhere out in the countryside. When that would happen he had no way of telling.

So that decided it. I would now make good on my threat to Joe Kennedy and join the British army. The next day I visited two British recruiting centers, but they were completely disorganized and no one seemed to know what to do with me. It was becoming clear that I had no choice but to return to the United States and try to resume my career, as makeshift and boring as that was likely to be. It was a depressing moment. The great plan—Panama, England, Africa, China, India, and back to New York to claim O'Connor's mantle at Columbia P & S—had blown away with the winds of war.

But how to get safely back home? Ships from England to the United States were still available, although wolfpacks of German submarines were greedily patrolling the North Atlantic and U-boat scares were numerous. I decided to test my luck by first crossing the Irish Sea, spending a few days in Dublin for one last holiday fling, and then making the run for it across the Atlantic.

The ferry ride to Ireland was long, nearly eight hours, and the ship was in total darkness, or as close to it as was humanly possible. Those who tried to light cigarettes were sharply rebuked. The British liner *Athenia* had been torpedoed in these very same waters a few nights before with three hundred Americans on board, and nerves were on edge. Gradually, though, the mood improved. There were plentiful supplies of stout on board, which helped cushion the shock of being at war and in the dark. In the happy confusion, I met an attractive young lady, the niece of the American ambassador to Ireland; visits to the Abbey Theatre and long walks in Dublin kept me busy until it was time to leave for home.

I sailed from Cobh on the *President Harding*, the sister ship of the *President Wilson* that had taken me to California ten years before. Despite the excitement and experiences of the intervening decade, however, I didn't feel either older or wiser—only worried about what awaited me back in New York. The ship was packed to the railings with returning American expatriates and tourists. People slept on cots set up in the emptied swimming pool. I was lucky enough to get a small cabin, where I bunked with three Irish-American priests, who spent most of their time tippling in a suite belonging to a trio of merry, heavily made-up widows from Miami.

Discipline was obviously breaking down under the strain of war. Despite my second-class ticket, I was assigned to take my meals at a first-class table, where I found myself among five interesting companions. There was Congressman Hamilton Fish, who had been in Germany meeting with Hitler and making friends with Hermann Goering, chief of the Luftwaffe. Anti-British in the extreme, Fish shared Joe Kennedy's feelings that the war would be over quickly and that a Europe controlled by Hitler would be better than a Europe controlled by Stalin. Today such views are considered embarrassing; people tend to forget how many so-called respectable citizens held them then.

Then there was a middle-aged lady, elegantly coiffed and beautifully gowned, who was, quite literally, dripping with expensive jewels. The estranged wife of a Dutch diamond magnate, she cheerily announced that she wore her diamonds to bed as she felt this was the safest place for them. These declarations, I got the distinct impression, were accompanied by the unspoken hope that one of the male members of the group might be inspired to visit her cabin late some night and personally confirm her security arrangements.

Fred Spiegel, the mail-order king from Chicago, was also at the table, heading back to America to start building his great fortune in the postwar boom that would boost the buying power of the middle class to stratospheric new levels. There was also Dr. Tom Spies, a brilliant medical researcher who did much of the pioneering work on vitamin deficiencies, and who would remain my close friend until his death at New York Hospital a decade later.

The fifth member of this disparate group was a short, pudgy

German banker who said little except a noncommittal "v-e-e-ry in-ter-resting" whenever he was called upon to comment on some controversial statement. (When I met him two decades later in his lavish Fifth Avenue apartment, he had become one of the richest of the new breed of Wall Street entrepreneurs. After all those years, he finally told me his story. "At the bottom of my large suitcase were these seven oil paintings which I had had removed from their frames," he said, pointing to the walls. I immediately recognized three of them—a Picasso, a Cezanne, and a Modigliani. The $100,000 he borrowed using his master-pieces as collateral had got him started in America. V-e-e-ry in-ter-resting, indeed!)

Everyone dressed formally for dinner, with the exception of Tom Spies, a confirmed populist who held his cotton workman's pants aloft with a belt fashioned from a length of rope. Wine flowed freely and so did the talk, which veered dangerously close to a showdown between the right-wing Fish and the left-wing Spies a few times, before all agreed to steer clear of sensitive political subjects. The result was a lively, entertaining group, more suitable to a happy sea cruise than a nerve-racking retreat from war.

Tom Spies and I devoted the time between meals to our military studies. Each morning we repaired to the ship's bulletin board to peruse the latest news dispatches from the front. Tom had a map on which he carefully recorded the progress of the German army through Poland, while noting that the enemy was making thirty miles a day without any difficulty whatsoever. When the Germans did pause, he pointed out, it had nothing to do with the strength of the resistance, but was merely a regrouping necessitated by the startling speed of their advance. As it turned out, Spies calculated almost to the day when the Germans would reach the Russian lines.

I kept insisting, in my romantic ignorance, that the Polish cavalry and the heroic Polish people would hold the marauding Germans point by point. There was a lot of inflated talk about heroism in those days, especially from people far away from the front line. Tom looked at me forlornly, knowing full well that, for the time being at least, there would be no stopping Hitler's war machine. The Germans planned first to mop up on the eastern front, and then turn to the more important business of subjugating France and invading England. Tom predicted, again accurately, that the Maginot Line would be of little consequence in this war and that the English Channel would become the key demarcation.

Against all realistic assessments, I clung to my optimism about the capacity of the French to hold off the Germans. I'd apparently already forgotten the dilapidated state of the French army recruits I had watched tramp toward the train station on those dark Paris nights, with their badly fitting uniforms, poor discipline, and low morale.

At last—after eight nervous days at sea, with everyone fearing sudden attack from a German sub and daily bulletins suggesting that things were going very badly at the front—we arrived in New York.

So what now? O'Connor was gone. I had no other contacts in the medical community. And for all my youthful bravado, I still had little confidence in my skills as a healer. Still lacking any semblance of manual dexterity, I was as ill-suited as ever to life as a surgeon. I was still afraid of flesh-and-blood patients, which seemed to rule out most areas of clinical medicine. Dr. Tuttle had been right, I thought glumly: I was much better off dealing with dead people than treating live patients.

It was then, while I was staying with my parents in Greenwich Village and feeling sorry for myself, that a letter arrived from none other than the old New Englander himself. How would I like to return to Panama? A new regime was in place at Gorgas Hospital. He, Dr. Tuttle, had spoken personally to the new chief health officer, one General Morrison Clay Stayer, and to Dr. Lewis Beals Bates, head of the Board of Health Laboratory; together they had come up with a job tailor-made for my talents.

It was the position of assistant pathologist, whose chief task was to assist in conducting autopsies on all Canal Zone fatalities.

What luck! For one thing, pathology meant a return to work at the microscope. Moreover, it was considered sound basic training for any specialty in medicine. So, once again, my poker was pointed toward Panama, and this time it would take me straight to the Gorgas morgue.

CHAPTER 4

The Fatal Martini

B odies rot quickly in the tropics, and the thermometer inside the autopsy room at Gorgas Hospital in the early afternoon of Monday, June 21, 1943, had long since snapped the hundred-degree mark in defiance of the slowly revolving ceiling fans. So I was prepared to work swiftly when Alleyne, my Jamaican assistant, wheeled Gorgas Autopsy No. 14092 through the swinging doors and handed me the case history.

The deceased was identified as Robert E. Sherwood, a captain in the U.S. Army Quartermaster Corps, who I proceeded to describe for the stenographer as "a fairly well-developed adult white male weighing a hundred and fifty pounds, measuring seventy-three inches in length, and appearing about the stated age of thirty."

At first glance the body looked normal enough, but outward appearances, as they not infrequently did, belied the true nature of death. Only an hour earlier, the handsome young captain had, in a burst of superhuman strength, snapped the canvas shackles pinioning him to his bed, leaped to his feet, and punched the duty nurse hard in the face before crumpling to the floor where, screaming, drooling, arms and legs jerking uncontrollably, he died a few minutes later.

Captain Sherwood, circumstantial evidence strongly suggested, had succumbed to rabies. If that was indeed the case, I knew, the Canal Zone could be staring down the barrel of a particularly gruesome epidemic: small but utterly deadly. As I prepared to wield my scalpel, I took one last moment to reconsider the medical record.

Robert Sherwood had been admitted to the Gold Pavilion at Gorgas on the afternoon of Thursday, June 17, complaining of shortness of breath and painful muscle spasms in his upper left leg. His other symptoms—headache, nausea, fever, and difficulty in swallowing—while not unusual in themselves, had persisted and worsened over the course of the next twenty-four hours.

Other features of the captain's behavior were a little harder to fathom. The approach of sunset, for instance, terrified him and unleashed wild, hallucinatory fears about the coming of the night. The sight of a glass of water made him pull the bedcovers over his head. Routine blood tests turned up nothing remarkable. For lack of more conclusive evidence, Sherwood was diagnosed as having a mild case of strep throat for which he was given a sulfa drug.

When the patient grew more and more aggravated and irrational the following day, a neurologist was summoned. The brain man found no serious irregularities, but came up with a diagnosis anyhow: "psychoneurosis with anxiety hysteria on the basis of an acute situational reaction with respect to an episode with his commanding officer." Translation: Sherwood had had a row with his CO and it had driven him temporarily insane.

This diagnosis was short-lived, however, for an hour later the patient was found wandering around the parking lot outside the hospital, muttering incoherently. The neurologist was forced to concede that even a real SOB of a CO would have a hard time inducing this advanced degree of blithering in one of his officers. By now Sherwood's speech was thick and slurred. His eyes moved back and forth rapidly like pinballs in a chute. His temperature shot up to 106 degrees. And still his symptoms baffled the doctors.

But not the head nurse. A laconic chain-smoker from Alabama, she had kept her eyeballs trained on the patient for nearly two days now. Sherwood's fear of water, as far as she was concerned, could mean only one thing—the man was dying of hydrophobia, the old-fashioned but graphically descriptive name for rabies. When Old Eagle Eyes could stand the dithering of the doctors no longer, she advised them to "wake up and smell the coffee," which they did.

The diagnosis of rabies caused an uproar—and for good reason. Humans usually acquire the disease from the bite of a dog, a cat, or—especially in the tropics—a vampire bat, whose brain has been invaded by the rabies virus. That meant the killer, trotting or flying, could still be on the loose, busily spreading the infection. Thanks to Louis Pasteur, a vaccine for rabies did exist and, although it would do Robert Sherwood no good (the treatment had to be started within a few days of exposure), it might save the lives of whoever else was now at risk. First, however, we had to try to find out where Sherwood had been bitten, by what, and when.

I had been busily attending to my chores in the Gorgas morgue, which occupied a large white building with a red-tile roof about a quarter of a mile from the patient wards, when word filtered down to me of the rabies scare. Gloved, masked, and gowned for protection, I dropped everything and dashed up the hill and entered Sherwood's room as quietly as possible. Rabies victims are often highly volatile, drifting uneasily between stupor and hysteria, and you don't want to take them by surprise. At the moment, however, Sherwood, strapped tightly to his bed, was alert and cooperative. "Hello, Doctor," he croaked hoarsely.

When I asked him how he thought he'd gotten sick, he'd just shaken his head. No idea. "Okay," I said, "let's try it this way. How many unfriendly animals have you met lately?"

"Now that you mention it," Sherwood said, "there was this crazy little dog at the airport in Managua." Sherwood explained how, on a flight down from the States several weeks back, his plane had made a brief stopover in Nicaragua for refueling. Leaving the aircraft to stretch his legs, he was approached by a small, scruffy mongrel. The dog had wagged its tail in a friendly way, but when Sherwood reached out to pet the animal, it had bitten him twice on the fingers of the right hand. "They were just scratches," Sherwood said, so he had simply applied some iodine and forgotten about them.

Managua, Nicaragua. Mongrel. Scratches. Well, as clues went, they weren't much, I thought, as I stood there in the autopsy room days later staring down at Sherwood's body. But at least they gave us a starting point in our search for other possible victims. Before that, though, a meticulous postmortem would show us exactly what we were dealing with.

Thanks to TV and the movies, the word *autopsy* often conjures up a series of ghoulish images straight out of the city morgue— a corpse on a granite slab with a tag on its toe, the victim of some horrible crime; the dour pathologist in his rubber apron delving into the body for forensic clues; the hardboiled detective hovering in the background waiting for leads to whodunit.

Although the autopsy does frequently help solve crimes, the postmortem is of enormous value to our society in other ways. Broadly speaking, it sheds important light on the still confounding mysteries of how people get sick and die. That may explain why, to the committed pathologist, each autopsy is not some macabre enterprise entered into only out of a grim sense of professional duty or legal obligation, but a fresh adventure, a new medical riddle waiting to be solved.

One of the most ruggedly persistent misconceptions Americans harbor about their doctors is that the family physician or, at the very least, the specialist in charge of a particular case, knows why a patient dies. In truth, even the best doctors have pretty dismal track records in that department. Fifty years ago, physicians accurately pegged the cause of death in only a quarter of all patients who died while in their care. Today, despite our breathtaking advances in medical technology, the ratio is still not much better. That's where the pathologist comes in.

From the days of the pharaohs, through the beginning of the modern medical revolution in the nineteenth century, and right up to the present, a good part—probably most—of what we know about the human anatomy and the nature of disease and its treatment stems from the examination of the dead. The autopsy has shown us how cigarette smoking causes lung cancer and how impaired insulin production is related to diabetes; it has helped mitigate our ignorance about such villains as multiple sclerosis, Alzheimer's disease, and AIDS. You name the disease, and the record will show that morbid anatomy (as pathology was once called) has defined it.

So the question arises, why then is the postmortem today facing virtual extinction? (Only 10 percent to 15 percent of all patients who die in American hospitals nowadays are autopsied, compared to four times that number four decades ago.) Fear is one great inhibitor. Recent studies have shown that, despite major improvements in diagnostic techniques, as many as a quarter of all patients died following a significant error in diagnosis. While that's nothing particularly new,* many doctors, who find themselves practicing in an age of escalating malpractice suits, have adopted the unfortunate attitude that what the deceased's loved ones don't know can't hurt them—*the doctors.*

The rapid spread of high-tech ignorance tells the rest of the story. Necropsy has long since been dropped by many medical

---

*In 1912, the year I was born, Dr. Richard C. Cabot, reporting on the results of 3,000 autopsies done at Massachusetts General Hospital, disclosed that antemortem diagnoses missed up to 84 percent of the more common diseases afflicting patients. More important, Cabot showed that the outcome of illness, i.e., death, might have been different in about 35 percent of the cases had the correct diagnosis been known.

schools as a cornerstone of a doctor's education because too few bodies are available for postmortem study. No wonder many younger physicians seem to think that autopsies have lost their relevance in an age of CAT scans and other supersophisticated methods of diagnosis. They are dead wrong. They are also missing out on one of medicine's great adventures.

The quest begins when the pathologist inspects the outside of the body for any wounds, scars, or other irregularities that might have a bearing on the death puzzle. Next he makes a sweeping, T-shaped incision running from one armpit to the other and then down the full length of the chest and abdomen to the pubic mound. Having opened the chest, the pathologist then examines the heart and lungs in situ before removing them. He excavates the abdomen, taking out and weighing the liver, the kidneys, the spleen, the pancreas—each of the ten major organs there. He takes samples of all bodily juices—the blood, the urine, the spinal fluid—for later testing. Meanwhile, an assistant opens the skull so the pathologist can examine the brain and the pituitary gland.

A skilled pathologist can gather important clues by simply studying the way various organs look and feel. The chest cavity of the TB victim may be shot through with a waxy, cheese-like substance. The alcoholic's liver, faded, knobby, and dessicated, is an organic record of abuse. An enlarged heart with areas of scarring signals hypertension and coronary disease. Sometimes the stomach is replaced by a hard mass of cancer, or pus may fill the abdomen from a ruptured appendix. The brain may disclose hemorrhage, infection, tumor, or trauma from a physical blow. The examples are endless.

Sometimes, this gross examination, which takes about two hours, is enough to establish a definitive cause of death. Not infrequently, though, the answer lurks in tissue samples sliced from all the important organs, which the pathologist examines under the microscope. His findings may reveal anything from a garden-variety illness to an exciting rarity. Like snowflakes or fingerprints, no two autopsies are ever alike, each having its own unique denouement encoded somewhere inside the decedent's biological mechanism.

In the Sherwood case, I proceeded quickly through the examination of the thoracic and abdominal cavities, all the while shouting my findings at Anita Larson, a veteran Gorgas stenographer, who had been banished to a remote corner of the room for her safety. Only the victim's abdominal muscles, ruptured by repeated, violent convulsions, showed any signs of abnormality. While I removed the major organs, Alleyne stripped back the scalp and sawed his way through the calvarium to remove the brain, a hard job that he did with speed and skill, his muscular forearms bulging, his tongue curled over his upper lip in concentration.

Starting with the brain, I examined the entire central nervous system with great care. Too impatient to wait the twenty-four hours normally needed to prepare the sections for microscopic study, I simply smeared an ultra-thin layer of brain tissue on a glass slide, dipped it in alcohol, and then added a home brew of two dyes, methylene blue and fuchsin, that would make the masses of rabies virus, called Negri bodies, stand out against the microscopic field.

Heart pounding, I peered through the microscope and . . . Eureka! There, in some of the large nerve cells, were the pink, densely packed, oval clusters that shouted "rabies!" Here was incontrovertible proof that the late Captain Robert Sherwood had indeed been a victim of the dread disease.

Now that I had identified the killer virus, the next step was for Army investigators to start hunting for the last key piece in the epidemiological puzzle—the agent of transmission. But, although dead men tell no lies, particularly on the autopsy table, Captain Sherwood, while still alive, had unwittingly thrown the epidemiologists a few curve balls.

According to Sherwood, the dog had attacked him on the tarmac in Managua on the afternoon of May 1. When investigators checked the flight manifest, however, there was no record of any refueling stop on or around that date. They were tempted to simply attribute the late captain's story to the ravings of a dying man. Then suddenly Sherwood's name popped up on a passenger list. The aircraft in question had indeed made a stopover, not on the first of May, but two weeks earlier, on the nineteenth of April. And in the wrong country! While the plane had stopped briefly in Nicaragua the day before, the refueling had been done at the Ilopango airport in neighboring El Salvador.

Investigators soon zeroed in on the Pan American Airlines building at Ilopango, where they questioned the airport manager, a Mr. J. M. Kappaccicci. He vividly recalled Robert Sherwood and said how surprised he'd been when his friendly little pooch—a cute, white mongrel of undetermined but panoramic parentage—had attacked him. That was the first time the animal had shown the slightest trace of antisocial behavior. From then on, however, the dog had turned plain nasty, snapping furiously at (though fortunately not biting) a number of airport employees. The Army report concluded:

> The dog refused to eat and, because of its unfriendliness, Mr. Kappaccicci gave it to a young girl named Miss Baby Pacomo on April 22, who took the dog to her home. While in her possession it bit her niece and a local doctor was called. Since the dog appeared unwell, he decided to administer the Pasteur rabies treatment, not only to the niece, but to a nephew and the grandmother of Miss Pacomo, since they had all been in close contact with the dog and might have suffered slight abrasions . . .
>
> The doctor [while very probably saving three lives in the Pacomo family through exercise of his good judgment] failed to mention that the dog should be kept under surveillance. Because the animal was considered unfit to be about children, it was passed on to a friend of Miss Pacomo,

one José Boza on April 23. On April 24 the dog died in a state of violent convulsions. Mr. Boza did not consider it necessary to have the dog examined. He merely threw it in the garbage can which was collected by the Sanidad.

Poor Captain Sherwood. He had been the victim of unhappy circumstance. Fortunately, though, the disease, as far as we were able to determine, caused no more deaths. Thus ended my first—and last—case of rabies in Panama, a case fairly typical of my lot as a pathologist in a place where the exotic came to life on the autopsy table.

I was lucky to have that privileged position at all. The Gorgas morgue enjoyed a big reputation in the international medical community, and the few positions there were strenuously contended for. Although my return to Panama had been engineered by the powerful trio of Tuttle, Bates, and Stayer, on arrival I was horrified to find that there never had been a real job for me in pathology—only the promise of one. So there I was, in the winter of 1940, lured back to Panama—and then told to be patient, my number would come up.

Patience had never been my strong suit, but I needed the work. So I accepted a job as regular physician in the Canal Zone, with a yearly salary of $3,600. I gloomily entertained visions of metamorphosing into a typical clock-punching "Zoner," my dreams of becoming a great parasitologist evaporating into the "good life," Panama style—membership in the local golf club and a permanent place alongside Dr. Bill James at the Union Club bar until my liver gave out.

As usual, events proved me wrong. During my escapades in Europe, which had lasted barely three months, a conservative revolution had occurred in Canal Zone medicine. Patient care was tightened up, professional rounds were made more professional, and a new dedication to scientific excellence was in the air. There was a big, new broom sweeping clean at Gorgas Hospital, and it belonged to General Morrison Clay Stayer, who, as the new medical chief, was not only my ultimate boss, but the man who would now take over from Francis O'Connor the role of guiding me through the next phase of my education.

Stayer was a Pennsylvania Dutchman who displayed all of the stereotypical attributes of his breed—he was a stern, stubborn, no-nonsense administrator, highly skilled in the art of telling people what they needed to know but didn't particularly want to hear. The old man would have long since retired a major general, an unusually high rank for a medical officer, if not for the war and the pleadings of his old friend, General George C. Marshall, then military chief of staff at the Pentagon, for him to stay on and help bolster the sagging morale of the Army Medical Corps.

During my first year back in Panama, Stayer quickly sensed how unsettled I was, so he decided to inflict on me the medical equivalent of boot camp training before bestowing the honor of working with the Gorgas cadavers. This involved spending three months as the sole physician at the Palo Seco leper colony, where I rubbed rotting limbs with chaulmoogra oil when I wasn't injecting it into somebody's backside. (The treatment was later determined to be worthless.) I was next dispatched to the San Blas Islands off the coast of Colombia to study the phenomenally low blood pressure of the Cuna Indians. I ran a diabetic ward for black women (the rate of diabetes is high in Jamaicans) at Gorgas Hospital and was sent into the bush armed with quinine and a new drug, Atabrine, to combat the spread of malaria in the villages up the Chagres River.

Waiting for me at the end of my labors was, as promised, the coveted Gorgas morgue. I was named to the post of assistant pathologist on April 20, 1940, and was thrilled to be finally getting the chance to become a bona fide medical sleuth. Each specialty of clinical medicine has always had its own unique appeal, but since the days of Sir William Osler—the Johns Hopkins professor who pioneered the proper training of medical students in pathologic anatomy—pathology has been one of the most respected among physicians themselves.

Nothing pleased me more than the idea of returning to the microscope, for pathology combined the gross examination of the organs with more detailed microscopic study of tissues. Going back to the microscope was like going home; since my training at Columbia P & S under O'Connor, it was there that I'd always felt most comfortable.

As head of the lab, Dr. Bates—tall, bald, and flabby, with a slightly eunuchoid appearance amplified by a high tenor voice— was both a master of the autopsy and an excellent teacher. When I was finally liberated from the Palo Seco leper colony, it was Bates who enthusiastically showed me to my new office, where I would spend the next six years being Dutch uncled by this shy, gentle, highly professional man. The room was the size of a large coat closet, with a small wooden bench and a microscope of great age. But it was my first private office and I was thrilled. I had finally found a home.

Next door to my office was the autopsy room, the domain of Alleyne, the venerable Jamaican autopsy assistant. Alleyne was the very first "silver" employee hired by the Board of Health Laboratory, where he'd been stepping lightly among the autopsy tables and specimen jars since before I was born and would continue doing long after I'd left the Zone.

So there I was at Gorgas, standing on the shoulders of the great pathologist Samuel T. Darling, having inherited his laboratory, his assistant, Alleyne, his desk, and all his instruments except his microscope. No self-respecting pathologist ever leaves his microscope behind.

The Canal Zone was a pathologist's paradise. To begin with, it was a genuine melting pot, made up of white American Zoners, the Caribbean blacks employed on the "silver" service, GIs from all across the United States, and the local Panamanians—whites, mestizos, and San Blas Indians. Adding to the variety was the fact that the usual forms of human demise—heart disease, cancer, traffic accidents—were augmented by the more offbeat tropical diseases. All of this guaranteed a rich, steady, and varied reservoir of what we somewhat impersonally referred to as "autopsy material."

There was one further aspect of mortality peculiar to the Canal Zone. No matter what their race, creed, or citizenship, everyone who died there was subject to the immutable fact of death referred to as "Bates's Law." As head of the Board of Health Laboratory, Lewis Beals Bates exercised total temporal control over the Zone dead and his orders were simple: No postmortem, no burial.

This grim dictate provoked surprisingly few objections. The civilian Zoners, eager to ship their loved ones back home for burial in American soil as quickly as possible, complied without a whimper. (The corrosive humidity required the speedy assistance of an undertaker, and the only one in the entire Canal Zone happened to report directly to Dr. Bates.) U.S. military personnel raised no fuss; to them, Bates's Law was simply further proof, if proof be needed, that the Army's long, authoritarian arm reached not just into every facet of daily life but beyond the grave, as well. The locals, for their part, were happy with the Bates protocol, for it meant that the U.S. government, in its generosity, would shell out the lavish sum of twenty-five dollars for a handsome wooden casket in which to house the departed.

So the morgue was a busy place. Stateside, a hospital autopsy rate of 50 percent was considered quite good in those days. In the Canal Zone, thanks to Bates's Law, it was very nearly 100 percent.

In 1942, General Stayer saw to it that I was duly inducted into the U.S. Army Medical Corps with the rank of first lieutenant. Despite my new military status, however, life changed very little. I wasn't required to wear a uniform, and for many months I didn't even own one. In 1945, the old man bucked me up both the medical and military ranks, making me senior pathologist and captain. I performed my last postmortem—No. 15732—on

THE FATAL MARTINI

September 9, 1945, on a man who had died of diesel burns following an oil explosion on the canal. During my six years at the morgue, we carried out a total of 3,460 autopsies, and I had personally either performed or supervised easily half that number.

As the war unfolded, Panama became not only a jumping-off point for troops headed for the South Pacific, but a training ground for combat doctors, as well. The war was being fought in some of the world's most spectacular pestholes—places like New Guinea, Malaya, and southern China—and to see hundreds of these physicians shuttle through on their way to do battle with humankind's most villainous parasitic foes was almost more than I could stand. I repeatedly asked General Stayer to let me go where I could do some good, but Stayer repeatedly said no—he needed me right where I was, to help in the training effort.

I did my best to subdue my warlike impulses and threw myself into my work at the autopsy table. It was there I learned how right old man Stayer had been about the need to educate stateside doctors in the mysteries of tropical medicine. And it was there that Stayer himself turned up one stifling afternoon to peer over my shoulder at the body of a soldier who had died suddenly of cerebral malaria.

"Eight malaria deaths in the past two weeks," he said, shaking his head. "That's a hell of a lot."

"More than I've seen in that short a time since I've been here," I agreed.

No shrinking violet when it came to making decisions, Stayer boomed, "Okay, Kean, consider yourself on detached duty. I want to know what the hell is going on here. Get to the bottom of this malaria business and have a report on my desk—in a week."

I got very little sleep for the next few nights as I plowed through decades of documents recording the ebb and flow of mosquito populations in Panama, changes in temperature and rainfall, the incidence of malaria infections among troops on maneuver—virtually every factor that might have a bearing on sudden, unexpected malaria deaths. I quizzed anyone in the Canal Zone and in Panama City who might yield a clue, from sanitary engineers, malariologists, and hydrologists to a few old-timers whose memories stretched back to the days of the French.

On the morning of the seventh day, I ascended Ancon Hill to see the general.

"Well?" said Stayer, looking up from his desk.

"I've found the cause," I said, trying to suppress a smile.

"What is it?"

"More important than *what* it is is *where* it is," I said, somewhat cryptically.

The general, who had no patience for riddles, exploded. "Goddamnit, Kean," he said, "have it your way. *Where* the hell is it?"

"Rochester, Minnesota."

The general looked as if he could murder me on the spot. "Do you mean to stand there and tell me that an outbreak of malaria in Panama comes from Rochester, Minnesota? Are you out of your mind?"

"Yes, sir—I mean, no, sir. I mean I am not out of my mind. The Mayo Clinic of Rochester, Minnesota is responsible."

Defeated, the general slumped back in his chair as I explained. Stayer knew as well as I did that many a medical neophyte has "murdered" a malaria patient by not recognizing the diversity of the initial symptoms, by making a wrong diagnosis, by treating for the wrong disease—and, finally, by not appreciating the speed with which malaria claims its victims.

So where did the Mayo Clinic fit in? Simple. On its way to the Pacific theater, a field hospital unit mustered from the Mayo Clinic had recently arrived in Panama for training in tropical medicine. For the physicians from the far north, it was their first brush with jungles or tropical parasites. Very soon, they were confronted with soldiers presenting a dizzying array of symptoms, including intense abdominal pain, headache, slurred speech, and loss of motor reflexes.

Experienced diagnosticians, the doctors from Rochester confidently confirmed cases of everything from appendicitis to alcoholism, strep throat to psychoneurosis. Unfortunately, these were diagnoses of the higher latitudes, not of the tropics—and every single one of them was wrong. All eight men had had malaria, all had been misdiagnosed (each by a different doctor), and all had died. The reason: The men from Minnesota, all competent doctors on their own turf, did not know the first thing about the disease they had encountered on Panamanian soil.

General Stayer no longer seemed angry. Quite the contrary. "Good work, Kean," he said. "Go back to your lab. I'll put a stop to this epidemic but quick."

The next morning Stayer issued orders requiring that before any soldier was ever examined—for whatever reason—his temperature was to be read. If the mercury topped ninety-nine degrees Fahrenheit, a blood smear for malaria had to be taken and examined under a microscope within two hours, either in the field or at the nearest station hospital. The general then added a personal note of the kind for which he was famous by suggesting an unappetizing fate for any officer who lost another soldier to malaria. His exact words were: "I will send him back to Rochester demoted and without his balls."

The Mayo Clinic unit, manhood intact, went on to distinguish itself in the South Pacific, and I went back to the autopsy table, swallowed my pride, and nursed a deep envy of those lucky medics at the front. Before long, however, I, too, was called into action, although of a decidedly different sort.

In October of 1943 a cable arrived from the War Department in Washington ordering me to report immediately to the commander in chief, Franklin Delano Roosevelt. FDR?! Me?! Like many Americans then, I regarded Roosevelt with an awe that was certifiably religious. Now I would get the chance to meet the great man face to face. What incredible luck! Still, it struck me as a little odd that the agent responsible for the introduction should be none other than *Carcharodon carcharias*, a species of man-eating shark.

With the coming of war, the debate over the attitude of the shark family toward the human race had entered a period of renewed frenzy. The question loomed: Did sharks eat men? The disappearance of large numbers of American flyers who had been forced to bail out over the Pacific suggested, at least circumstantially, that the answer was a resounding yes. Still, in those pre-"Jaws" years, there were those in scientific circles who argued strenuously that the shark was being framed, blamed for injuries inflicted by proven aquatic menaces like the barracuda. These pro-shark hard-liners were right about one thing. Scientifically speaking, the case against their noble fish had yet to be made. Anecdotes were numerous; solid proof was lacking.

That situation resolved itself on the afternoon of September 23, 1943, when a U.S. Navy PT boat chuffed into a shallow cove off Rey Island in the Gulf of Panama and dropped anchor. Having experienced engine trouble, the skipper thought something might be fouling the propeller. Twenty-year-old Radioman 3d Class Raymond Nault volunteered to dive down and take a look.

From then on everything happened very fast. In the same instant that Nault popped to the surface and waved the all-clear signal, his crewmates on deck caught sight of a large dorsal fin knifing through the turquoise waters. Horrified, they watched as the fin materialized at closer range into the body of a seven-foot shark. The fish lunged. Nault screamed. His head disappeared beneath the waves. By the time he resurfaced a few seconds later, rifles were already trained on his assailant. But Nault's agonized fellow sailors couldn't open fire. In the tangle of fish and man that thrashed off the stern, there was no way to shoot the fish without shooting Nault, as well.

When the shark finally lost interest and swam away, the badly damaged swimmer was hoisted aboard. Blood spurted from a series of nasty wounds on his lower limbs and tourniquets were quickly applied, one to each leg. Deep in shock, Nault was rushed to the U.S. Navy hospital in Balboa, where he died three hours after the attack. By nightfall, the sailor's muscular body rested on the autopsy slab at Gorgas.

As I inspected the corpse, I could only shake my head in anger. If anybody still doubted the shark's enthusiasm for human flesh, I thought, they should take a good, hard look at this. The victim's left leg, or what was left of it, was a road map of aggression. Starting at the foot, a half-dozen sets of wounds, indicating a wide, arching jaw, telescoped up the leg just beyond the knee. The pattern suggested multiple rows of very large teeth. The great snapping jaws had completely pulverized the left knee joint. Large gashes lacerated the front of the right thigh.

This tragic situation had one positive feature, however. For anybody requiring further evidence of shark attack, the fish had obligingly deposited the tips of three of its teeth in the body of its victim.

As I was about to start the autopsy, Dr. Tuttle walked in and examined the corpse. So I would not be operating under any illusion, the chief of surgery, in typically abrupt fashion, observed, "Not the first case of shark bite in these waters, of course."

Tuttle then recounted the story of how a ten-year-old Panamanian boy had gone for a swim one Sunday afternoon off Taboga Island, about thirty-five miles from the spot where Raymond Nault was later attacked. Picnicking on the beach, the swimmer's family looked on in horror as a shark rose from the depths, ripped off one of the youngster's legs, and swam away. On its second pass, the fish clamped the remainder of the child in enormous jaws and headed for open ocean. The boy's father and uncles pursued the beast in open boats and, somehow, managed to catch up with and kill it. When they slit its belly open, out came the boy's torso, still wearing his red swimming trunks.

"The evidence," said Dr. Tuttle disapprovingly, "was not considered conclusive at the time. Some people said it begged the question of whether another fish might not have swallowed the swimmer and his bathing trunks, and then, in turn, been swallowed by the shark." This line of reasoning, he observed, was an admirable attempt to show the marine food chain at work, but made little practical sense. So Tuttle encouraged me to rush my autopsy report to the War Department. "Maybe this will wake them up," he said.

I had serious doubts. Knowing something of the murky ocean of officialdom, I fully expected my shark report would quietly settle to the bottom of some bureaucratic trench and stay there forever, unread and unappreciated. But I was wrong.

Two weeks later, the governor of the Canal Zone received an urgent cable from Washington ordering me to report to the White House. The president, it said, wanted to see for himself the evidence in the Nault case. Nervously, I stuffed my autopsy records, slides, and blocks of tissue into a big suitcase, even though I knew these were of only secondary importance. The real clinchers I would carry in my breastpocket—the three shards of shark tooth I had picked out of Raymond Nault's wounds.

My trip north was delayed in order for me to get a uniform in which to meet the commander in chief. I had so far spent most of my military life in hospital clothes, and there had been little call for proper Army attire. My one outfit of tropical khakis looked more like a large, limp, baggy pajama suit than the uniform of a captain in the United States Army Medical Corps. Ultimately, the quartermaster at Fort Amador came to the rescue, producing a crisp, new wool uniform which very nearly fit and was, in any case, more suitable for conducting official military business in the cold north.

My first stop was not Washington, but New York. There I hoped to obtain expert testimony that would help confirm the diagnosis I had rather hastily recorded in my autopsy report—"death due to shark attack"—without all the necessary scientific specifications. I wanted to confirm the identity of the aggressor by showing my three teeth to a recognized authority on sharks.

THE FATAL MARTINI

That was John T. Nichols, Curator of Recent Fishes at the American Museum of Natural History at Seventy-Ninth Street and Central Park West. Nichols—tall, thin, and cadaverous—received me in an office so small and crammed with books, reprints, and the odd jawbone of shark, that one false move threatened to send the whole business crashing down on our heads. Hospitable but nervous, Nichols crossed and uncrossed his legs over and over again, exposing a hole the size of a quarter on the bottom of his right shoe through which poked a patch of pink flesh.

After a fumbling attempt at small talk, Nichols said, "Let me see the tooth." I fished around in my breastpocket for the largest of the fragments and placed it on his desk. "Shark, species *Carcharodon carcharias*, approximately seven feet long," said the Curator of Recent Fishes, without even bothering to pick up the evidence.

"Are you sure?" I said, a little troubled by the casual speed of the diagnosis.

"Of course, I'm sure," he said testily. "But I can see you want a second opinion." Lunging from behind his desk, Nichols flung back the door and shouted down the corridor, "Breder, come in here! I need your advice." Breder—Dr. C. M. Breder, Jr., Curator of the New York Aquarium—emerged from his office and, looking perplexed, stood in the middle of the hallway about ten feet away and blinked his eyes like some large species of codfish dressed in a moth-eaten tweed jacket. Nichols placed the tooth chip between thumb and middle finger and held it aloft. "Breder," he demanded, "what is this?"

"*Carcharodon carcharias*, seven and a half feet," said Breder, turning back to his office, visibly irritated at having had his ruminations interrupted to answer such an obvious question.

I thanked Nichols and headed for the elevator. I was overjoyed; I had now established the conclusive evidentiary link between shark and man. Still, I couldn't help feeling a little sorry for Nichols and Breder. To think that men so accomplished in their fields had to endure such shabby circumstances! Obviously, they were very poorly paid.

The elevator was an antique car with an elevator man of similar vintage. "How long have you worked here?" I asked.

"Almost thirty years, sir," he said proudly. "Almost as long as Mr. Nichols himself."

"Mr. Nichols seems like a wonderful man," I said.

"Oh, yes sir, the best. Only a wonderful man would give millions of his own personal fortune to rehabilitate this old museum."

Up to that point I hadn't had much experience with the very wealthy and I still had a few things to learn. Little did I suspect that there would be many men and women in my future, who, like the wonderful Mr. Nichols, would think nothing of donating small mountains of gold to charity and then recoil in horror from the price of a pair of socks, a ten-dollar taxi fare, or a twenty-five-dollar medical bill.

The next afternoon I arrived an hour early for my audience with the president and waited nervously in the White House vestibule. Right on time, Roosevelt, dressed in a double-breasted gray suit and puffing away at his trademark cigarette holder, greeted me in a small room on the second floor where he sat behind a large desk. Also present in the room were three men wearing the highly decorated uniforms of the War Department staff—one Army, one Navy, one Marine Corps. Sweating profusely in my new wool uniform, all I could think of was that here I stood in the presence of the leader of the Free World with three shark's teeth in my pocket.

"I understand," said Roosevelt in his jolly patrician voice, "that you did an autopsy on a sailor who died following bites by a fish. Tell me," he said, pausing dramatically, "how can you be certain the fish was a shark?"

I numbly repeated the evidence as reported by the crew members on board the PT boat and described how I had autopsied the sailor and removed the three teeth. Reaching into my pocket, I produced the offending fragments, while I recalled my encounter with Nichols and Breder in New York. Roosevelt listened intently. When I had finished, he turned to his aides and said, "That settles it. It was a shark."

The president thanked me for coming. Although the meeting had lasted less than ten minutes, the encounter with FDR left me dazed. As I stumbled out to Pennsylvania Avenue, I wondered why on earth I'd been summoned all the way from Panama for that. Only later did I discover that Roosevelt, who had served as assistant secretary of the Navy during the First World War, not only took a great interest in naval affairs in general, but was particularly pained by the thought of downed flyers being eaten by sharks. He had personally ordered dozens of sharks captured in Florida, where experiments were underway in an effort to develop the first reliable shark repellent.

Alas, not one of the tests was successful. The sharks continued to feast on flyers until the collapse of Imperial Japan in 1945 eliminated their supply. Still, I like to think I served the president in some small way. At least he could continue ordering the incarceration of sharks in Florida with a clear conscience, for we now knew—scientifically—that man was most definitely on the shark's menu.*

Writers, I have always thought, are an especially gutsy breed. Like doctors, they spend an inordinate amount of time dealing with the grim realities of life and death, but they do so without the emotional buffer of the scientific perspective.

Take Sherwood Anderson, for example. In his memoir, *A Story Teller's Story*, Anderson described how, sitting before the magnificent cathedral of Chartres, he experienced an epiphany:

---

*I originally published an account of my adventure in "Death Following Attack by Shark Carcharodon Carcharias" in the *Journal of the American Medical Association*, vol. 125, 845–846, 22 July 1944.

"I thought that if I were suddenly to be confronted with death in the form of the old man with a sickle in his hand, I would be compelled to say, 'Well, it's your turn now, old fellow. I've had my chance. If I had done little enough, it's my fault, not yours.'"

Anderson was being modest. A prolific writer, the author of *Winesburg, Ohio* accomplished a great deal in his career, including the nurturing of young writers like Hemingway, Faulkner, Wolfe, and Steinbeck. He did seriously miscalculate the nature of his demise, however, for when Old Man Death eventually did come for him, he was armed, not with a sickle, but with a toothpick.

I know because Anderson, age sixty-four, died at five o'clock on the afternoon of March 8, 1941, at Colón Hospital on the Atlantic side of the Canal Zone. In keeping with Bates's Law, the author's body was rushed by overnight train to the Gorgas morgue for autopsy. So it was that when I reported for work the next morning at 8:30, I was surprised to find Anderson there waiting for me.

This was not our first meeting. A denizen of Greenwich Village, Anderson had been a friend of Maxwell Bodenheim, the author of *Naked on Roller Skates*. In the mid-thirties Bodenheim, not yet completely destroyed by booze, was in the habit of holding court in a seedy apartment on Eighth Street. One summer, while toying with the idea of becoming a writer myself—a sportswriter—I had dropped in on a few of these sessions and had met Sherwood Anderson, whom I regarded with the awe of a downtrodden undergraduate for anyone remotely famous, creative, or intelligent.*

---

*In *A Moveable Feast*, published in 1964, shortly after his own death, Hemingway described his early days in Paris with Gertrude Stein: "When I first met her she did not speak of Sherwood Anderson as a writer but spoke glowingly of him as a man and of his great, beautiful, warm Italian eyes and of his kindness and his charm. I did not care about his great beautiful warm Italian eyes but I liked some of his short stories very much. They were simply written and sometimes beautifully written and he knew the people he was writing about and cared deeply for them. Miss Stein did not want to talk about his stories

So now, here at Gorgas, I felt a little emotional as I surveyed his body lying there on the granite slab. Very soon, though, I was totally engrossed in reviewing the author's medical history, for it became apparent that no one, not the doctor on board his ship, nor the physicians at the hospital in Colón, had the faintest idea of what had killed him.

The patient had sailed from New York on February 28, aboard the SS *Santa Lucia*. The hospital report noted "a history of indiscretion in eating and drinking at farewell parties" for several days prior to departure. Then, aboard ship on March 1:

> The patient did not eat lunch because he felt "stuffy." He experienced cramps across his lower abdomen but noted neither true pain nor tenderness. On March 2 he was given magnesium sulphate and . . . felt much improved but continued to have cramping pains. On the morning of March 5 the patient felt better, ate eggs and drank tea. This was followed by abdominal pains which continued to increase in severity throughout the day, necessitating the administration of morphine. On the evening of March 5 the patient was transferred from the ship to Colón Hospital.

It was then that Anderson's condition took a sharp turn for the worse. On March 8 his pulse began to race, accelerating until he lapsed into a state of delirium, delirium became coma, and he died. Although his doctors had diagnosed his problem as an acute intestinal obstruction "cause and location undetermined," it didn't take me long to pinpoint the exact cause of death.

No sooner had I started the autopsy than I saw signs of great turbulence in the abdominal cavity. At first, I thought it might be his appendix. Everybody knows that a ruptured appendix is serious business. Bursting, the organ spews the foul contents of the bowel into the peritoneal cavity, causing an intense inflam-

---

but always about him as a person." There is no mention of the color of his eyes in my autopsy report.

matory reaction and a buildup of pus that poisons and, untreated, eventually kills the patient. But Anderson's case, although strikingly similar to an exploded appendix, had one highly unusual feature.

As I noted in my autopsy report, "A large amount of purulent exudate surrounds the sigmoidal portion of the colon, and fills much of the pelvis." And then the startling find: "A toothpick is found projecting through a diverticulum of the colon at a point 28.0 cm proximal to the anus. The toothpick is wooden, well preserved, and measures 6.0 cm in length. The broad end extends for 2.5 cm into the peritoneal cavity, whereas the pointed portion, 3.5 cm in length, is present within the diverticulum and sigmoid."

Sherwood Anderson had been killed by a toothpick! A diverticulum is an out-pouching of the large intestine, something not unlike an appendix. Many people, especially those over the age of fifty, have them, although they do little damage unless one ruptures. (That's one reason why we eat bran nowadays—to keep food moving quickly enough through the gut to avoid becoming trapped in these outpouchings and causing infection.) In Anderson's case, the fatal toothpick had passed through the stomach and small bowel, gotten caught in a diverticulum, and perforated it, so that the liquid stool poured into the closed chamber of the belly, producing large pockets of pus around the bladder.

As a pathologist at Gorgas, I had performed hundreds of postmortems. I had come across some rather surprising findings: a .45 caliber bullet that had pierced the brain of its victim and somehow wound up in his liver; the blockage of the intestines of a four-year-old boy by a bolus of two hundred roundworms the size of nightcrawlers; an extra baby found in the abdomen of a mother who had given normal birth a week earlier. For all that, though, I had never encountered an agent of death quite so bizarre as a toothpick. But you can't fight the physical evidence, and there it was—a shapely, substantial, three-inch-long toothpick of the kind used in the finer bars and restaurants. The obvious question arose: How in the hell did a toothpick get there in the first place?

Dr. Howard Tuttle was something of a prude. He was the product of a severe New England upbringing, and his long years in the tropics had done nothing to soften his starchy, moralistic view of the world. He took a particularly dim view of "liberal" writers like Sherwood Anderson and said so. Nonetheless, it became obvious that he had read every page of *Winesburg, Ohio* with great care.

When Tuttle dropped by the laboratory that afternoon, as was his habit, he peered down his gold-rimmed spectacles at me and announced in his nasal Massachusetts tones, "Kean, I hope you never become a martini drinker."

"Why not?"

"Well, you saw what happened to that author fellow, didn't you?"

"How do you know he drank martinis?"

Tuttle was shocked. Was I incapable of following a perfectly logical train of thought? "How on earth do you think that toothpick got into him?" he said sourly. "By magic?"

"Okay, how then?"

"The chronology of his trip makes the hour of his swallowing the toothpick clear as day," he said, pacing up and down the big, airy room, as Alleyne darted out of his way. "The night he left New York there was a party aboard ship. He got drunk. When he went after the olive in his fourth or fifth martini, he was no longer able to distinguish olive from toothpick. He swallowed both. That was February 28. Three days later, on March 1, he experienced upper intestinal symptoms—just the right time for the toothpick to have passed through the small intestine. By March 2 the toothpick had wedged itself in the diverticulum, producing the ultimately fatal perforation."

I was impressed by Dr. Tuttle's theory and decided to put it to the test. Later that afternoon I called on Anderson's widow,

Eleanor Copenhaver, who was staying at the Tivoli Hotel at the base of Ancon Hill. She was a gracious, gray-haired woman and greeted me warmly when I introduced myself as an old acquaintance of her husband's from Greenwich Village who wanted to pay his respects.

I also told her that I was the one who had performed the autopsy on her husband. I reported that all arrangements for shipping the body back to the States had been made. Then, as diplomatically as possible, I asked her if there had been a farewell party the day the ship left New York.

"Indeed there was," she said.

"Did your husband consume any alcohol that night?"

"Oh my, yes," said Mrs. Anderson, a little apologetically. "I tried to restrain him, but you know how it is. He must have had five or six drinks."

"Did your husband drink martinis by any chance?"

"Nothing but," she said, pausing a moment before adding, "He liked them very dry—and with an olive."

Sherwood Anderson was probably not the first victim of the venturesome toothpick; he was certainly not the last. The *New England Journal of Medicine* carried the following letter on October 16, 1986, under the heading, "Martini Toothpick Warning":*

To the Editor:

We are writing to call attention to a new and potentially serious hazard associated with the hasty ingestion of martinis (or indeed Gibsons, as in the present case). One of us was partaking of a Gibson (gin, ice, essence of vermouth, and several cocktail onions speared on a flat wooden toothpick). As the beverage and onions were quickly consumed,

_____

*This letter is reprinted with permission from an article by Daniel Malamud, Ph.D. and Mary Harlan Murphy, M.D. in *The New England Journal of Medicine*, vol. 315, 1031, 1986.

the toothpick floated from the glass into the oral cavity and lodged, uncomfortably, in the posterior pharynx. An attempt to dislodge it by regurgitation resulted in transferring it up into the posterior nares [deep in the nose], pointed end first. A trip to the emergency room brought the first author of this letter into contact with the second. Actually, this meeting occurred one hour later, after several encounters with other hospital personnel, who took the history by asking such questions as: "You have a toothpick caught where?" "Are you the man with a toothpick up his nose?" "This couldn't happen—why didn't the olive stop it?" Fortunately, the adroit second author was able to extract the offending obstruction deftly with an alligator forceps. The first author was sent home with the suggestion that he have a drink, sans toothpick. We caution imbibers to consider this potential danger at the end of a difficult day.

I read this letter with a certain twinge of jealous pride. After all, my unheralded discovery of the dangers of the toothpick predated theirs by more than forty years. But I felt a little guilty, too. Had I been more public-spirited in those days I might have prevented untold toothpick swallowings over the years. One study places the number of toothpick injuries in the United States alone for the years 1979 to 1982 at 8,176. Of the three deaths recorded, one—that of a sixty-three-year-old man—was caused by "perforation of the bowel by a toothpick."

Would the publicizing of the strange circumstances of a celebrated author's death have helped reduce the toothpick toll? Who can say? As it was, a highly respected national magazine based in New York mistakenly reported at the time that Sherwood Anderson had died of a brain tumor!

CHAPTER 5

In A German
Salt Mine

Throughout the war I lobbied hard for reassignment to a combat theater. I longed to be in the Philippines or one of the islands in the South Pacific, where battles were raging and malaria was dropping GIs in terrible numbers. That, I felt strongly, was the perfect place for the malaria man I had become. I pestered General Stayer, and, after he was transferred to North Africa, I petitioned the War Department in Washington—all without success. Then, three months after the war ended in Europe, the Army, in its bureaucratic wisdom, ordered me to Berlin, without specifying how my skills as a tropical medicine man would be utilized in Northern Europe.

Through a chain reaction of snafus, unbelievable even for the military, it took me exactly fifty days to make the trip from Panama to Berlin. The last leg of the journey was the worst. It was mid-December and we had been snowbound in Newfoundland for a week when our battered B-16 finally took off for Scotland and flew straight into a storm over the North Atlantic. Ten officers and thirty enlisted men, fresh from liberty and badly hung over, strapped themselves into the aircraft's bucket seats and immediately turned deep shades of green. The fuselage pitched and rolled wildly. For some, the strain of remaining upright was too great. Releasing their harnesses, they spent the rest of the flight bouncing in the muck, bloodying their faces on the steel deck, and spitting out the occasional tooth.

Somewhere over the Atlantic I managed to learn that the invisible hand behind my transfer belonged to none other than General Stayer, who had himself recently been reassigned to occupied Germany and the job of chief health officer for the American zone. So when I arrived in Berlin, shaken, unshaven, and grubby, I went straight to Stayer's office to thank him for finally springing me from Panama. When I entered his den, however, the old lion looked at me blankly for a few seconds, as if he didn't remember having sent for me, and growled, "Kean, what the hell are you doing here?"

I showed him the telegram appointing me chief of the U.S. Army medical laboratory in Berlin. "Oh, that," he chortled. "That post has been filled for weeks now. Guess we'll have to find something else for you."

I stood there in my wrinkled "FDR" uniform feeling slightly ridiculous as the general pondered my fate. "Okay, Kean, I've got just the thing," he said. Reaching into a drawer, he produced a large ring of keys which he thrust into my hand. "Penicillin," he declared. "Kean, you're now in charge of administering our entire penicillin supply in Germany."

He had to be kidding—I had never "administered" anything before in my life. But he was not. "There's precious little of the stuff as it is and what there is is disappearing like crazy," Stayer explained. "I want you to set up a proper system. Do whatever you have to, but if I hear of any nonsense, I will personally break every bone in your body."

In 1945, penicillin was serious business in Germany. Bomb-cratered and bleak, Berlin looked like the surface of the moon. Germans throughout the country were sick, starving, dying. Gonorrhea, pneumonia, meningitis, the grim handmaidens of war, raged almost out of control. Penicillin, discovered in England in 1928 by Sir Alexander Fleming, was the new magic bullet against these plagues, but the ammunition was in woefully short supply. The Russians had none. The British and French fretted over minuscule stocks. The United States had a near-total monopoly on the drug in Europe, but there wasn't nearly enough to go around.

So the Army, its wisdom functioning enigmatically as ever, decreed that penicillin in Germany would be reserved solely for the treatment of two privileged groups: American soldiers—and German prostitutes!

The GI part of the equation was easy to understand. Wartime logic dictated that keeping our troops in fighting trim took precedence over the needs of a vanquished enemy. Prostitutes were a different matter. Though not an officially sanctioned part of the GI fitness program, even the U.S. Army realized the sheer impossibility of keeping sexually frustrated GIs and seductive fräuleins apart for very long. To ignore the hookers was to guarantee an astonishingly high rate of venereal disease infection among our soldiers.

Clever though it was, this policy had one serious flaw. In order for the "working girls" to be treated, the penicillin was doled out to a select number of German hospitals, a maneuver which vastly underestimated the ingenuity of the American fighting man. Our resourceful GIs identified all strategic clinics with stunning speed and accuracy. Within a few days, soldiers had formed long lines outside hospital gates for the sole purpose of picking up the "clean" prostitutes as they were discharged. Epidemiologically speaking, the logic was sound. Each girl, the soldiers reasoned, would be good for a few gonorrhea-free exchanges before becoming reinfected. More adventurous troops, using ladders and crowbars, broke into the wards at night to search out "safe" girls where they lay in their beds and had to be hauled off to jail by the MPs.

The "penicillin for prostitutes" program, as it was unofficially known, caused an uproar. The Allies, with the interesting exception of the more permissive French, criticized the move as uncharitable and morally suspect. General Stayer was unmoved.

He was a medical realist. During his long career, he had cleaned up bordellos in China, the Philippines, and Panama, all for the safety of the American serviceman. He now insisted that the same preventive measures be applied in Germany.

Others were nervous. General Lucius Clay, military governor of the American zone and Stayer's immediate boss, worried not so much about his reputation among the Allies as about the reaction of the nonstop delegations of U.S. Congressmen, American correspondents, and VIPs of all stripes, who were now swarming the country, observing the novel phenomenon of American military dictatorship in action. "How's this going to 'read' from the pulpit in Poughkeepsie?" Clay wanted to know.

Stayer, never one to pull punches with his superiors, replied, "To hell with Poughkeepsie, General. Tell those goddamn snoops we plan to send our boys home clean!" Clay let the matter drop.

The penicillin shortage caused problems of a more serious nature for the Germans. As the demand for the life-saving drug mounted, pharmaceutical forgeries began to flood the black market. The ersatz penicillin consisted of granulated clay of the same orange coloring and consistency as true penicillin powder. The stuff was then bottled in "official" GI-issue ampules scavenged from hospital garbage dumps.

The side effects were brutal. Every ounce of German clay, like soil anywhere, contained millions of tetanus germs. Diluted and injected into the human body, it produced a wide variety of agonizing results—horrible local abscesses if the users were lucky, death in violent convulsions if they were not. Scores died in this gruesome, criminal fashion. Orders to all U.S. military facilities to destroy the penicillin bottles before they were thrown away did little good, since thousands of the smoked-glass containers had already hit the black market.

That winter, just when the penicillin shortage was at its peak, epidemics of pneumonia and meningitis swept the country. Children were dying in great numbers. Each morning I walked a gauntlet of angry German mothers who would line up outside

Allied headquarters in Berlin to greet me chanting *"Fur Hüren ja, fur mein sterbendes Kind nein!"*—"For whores, yes, for my dying baby, no!" I was cursed for withholding the drug. I was spat on. I took to keeping a supply of fresh uniforms at the office so I could doff my spittle-flecked clothes after each foray outside. It was a heartbreaking situation. But my hands were tied. There simply wasn't enough penicillin for everyone who needed it, and not even the righteous fury of motherhood could change that.

To relieve my depression, I fell into the habit of walking the bomb-shattered Berlin streets at twilight, trying to imagine how the unfortunate city had looked in better days. While strolling through the old Reichstag area one evening, I suddenly got the chilling sensation that someone was following me. Stepping into a doorway, I looked back and saw two Russian soldiers, rough and unsavory in their fur hats and great coats, standing in the middle of the street. They looked befuddled, as though trying to figure out how I had managed to elude them. Obviously they had wanted to rob me, I thought, and was glad to have given them the slip.

The next evening they were back on my tail again. And again I thought I'd lost them when, turning a corner, my heart nearly flew into my mouth. Standing not more than six feet in front of me, blocking my path, was the taller of the big Russians. When I got a good look at him, though, he didn't look very menacing at all. Grinning a big, mischievous, toothless grin, he patted a battered suitcase he clutched to his chest and cooed softly, "Pen-nah-see-lin, pen-nah-see-lin." He had to repeat the curious phrase several times before I caught his gist. Penicillin?! Of all people, he wants to sell *me* fake penicillin, I thought. Boy, what a joke!

But the Russian was no longer smiling. In fact, he looked like he was about to burst into tears. Frustrated at his inability to make himself understood, he repeated, more fervently now, "Pen-nah-see-lin, pen-nah-see-lin," and then opened his suitcase a crack. My jaw dropped. The container was stuffed, not with fake drugs at all, but with what appeared to be American dollars. Then the Russian revealed another phrase in his limited repertoire of pidgin English: "Ten-tou-zand, ten-tou-zand." Still puzzled by the charade, I walked off, leaving the Russian pounding his forehead with a gloved fist.

The next night at dinner I reported the strange incident to General Stayer. "You idiot," the old man shouted. "The Russians were trying to bribe you!" He explained that $10,000 was the going rate for a vial of penicillin.

"Quite frankly, General," I said, "I find that a little hard to believe. Where could the Russians lay their hands on that kind of cash? And why on earth would they pay so much for so little penicillin?"

Stayer explained that the Russians were swimming in greenbacks "liberated" from German bank vaults and blackmarketeers. And they were willing to spend them liberally, if it meant escaping the one thing every Russian soldier dreaded more than a Stalinist purge—the Russian army treatment for gonorrhea.

The standard treatment, Stayer said, called for an injection of turpentine directly into the victim's urethra so that the infected lining would slough off and be washed out in the urine flow. One can only imagine the pain. "Tell me, Kean," the old man asked, "if you had the clap and could lay your hands on $10,000, what would you do?"

By late 1946, the penicillin shortage had abated. The turpentine-shy Russians got more, and so did the other Allies, as large stocks from the United States became available. Most of the penicillin in the world at that time was still being manufactured in an old Brooklyn factory. Its manager, John L. Smith, had transformed his vinegar vats into fungus farms, where the golden, hairlike fibers were grown and harvested. The "pickle" factory expanded into a business that grew almost as fast as the penicillin it produced, and the company, Pfizer, became one of the world's larg-est pharmaceutical concerns.

Expanding American production, however, didn't solve the problems of the German public, which needed a source of supply closer to home. So I came up with a plan. Producing penicillin is theoretically very easy. All that's needed is a large vat, a small inoculum of fungus, and a way of siphoning the mold as it grows. Even in their dilapidated state, I reasoned, the German drug com-panies could manage that. Why not allow the Germans to pro-duce enough penicillin themselves to meet the needs of their civilian population?

General Stayer hated the idea. To him, the Germans were still the reviled enemy. He was particularly concerned that some of the old-line drug companies belonging to the I. G. Farben cartel that had added economic muscle to Hitler's cause might benefit financially. After weeks of needling, however, the old man fi-nally softened up and agreed to let me authorize production in a tiny factory I'd discovered on the road between Frankfurt and Wiesbaden, a company with no apparent links to the Nazi past.

The U.S. military contract I presented to the eager board of directors provided $15,000 to grow, bottle, and test-market pen-icillin. The experiment got off to a shaky start when the inoculum they first used, which came from Britain, not Brooklyn, failed to produce "clean" penicillin. Looking back, though, I suppose the company's efforts might now be judged something of a triumph, considering that today the struggling shanty enterprise of long ago has metamorphosed into Hoechst, a chemical and pharmaceutical empire with worldwide annual sales of $23 bil-lion.

I had been in Germany three months when I got a new job. General Stayer appointed me chief health officer for the state of Hesse, a post for which I was eminently unqualified, having never supervised anything bigger than the pathology laboratory in Panama. Now I would be responsible for the health and welfare of four million Hessian citizens, who had suddenly become wards of our military government. Stayer brushed aside my protests with the curt order "Get cracking, Kean," so I shrugged my shoulders and went to take command of my military fiefdom.

Division was the nature of everything in Germany then. Berlin had been divided into four zones, each occupied by one of the Allied victors. The entire country had been similarly parceled up, with Russia getting the major portion east of the Elbe. The remainder was split unequally among the United States, Britain, and France. The American zone, the largest of the three, was further partitioned into three administrative sectors: Baden-Württemberg had its headquarters in Stuttgart; Bavaria had its GHQ in Munich; and Hesse, the most populous and, in terms of industrial potential, the most important, housed American military rule in its baroque Palace of Justice in Wiesbaden.

As CHO, it was my primary duty to prevent epidemic diseases from killing off the civilian population and thus complicating the task of administering the Occupation. In the process, I was to see to it that hospitals, medical schools, and clinics, all of which had been heavily bombed, went back into business as soon as humanly possible. In the incongruous way of the Army, responsibility for the sector's prisons, abundant whorehouses, and impressive, though badly damaged museums had been thrown in for good measure.

As a doctor in Panama, the biggest health crisis I had ever faced was the day 150 Chiriqui Indians, dazed by fever and suffering from alastrim, a cross between smallpox and chicken pox, had drifted out of the hills and into the emergency room at Gorgas Hospital. By comparison, the problems in Hesse were enough to induce cardiac arrest. Thousands upon thousands of people were holed up in cellars or living in bombed-out houses that had been sealed off with boards. Conditions were filthy and degrading, further complicated by the steady stream of refugees pouring across the border from the even bleaker Russian zone. Tuberculosis, malnutrition, and venereal infections mocked our feeble efforts to combat disease.

Other medical supplies were only marginally more plentiful than penicillin. The biggest obstacle, however, was finding enough qualified medical personnel to handle the crisis. My American staff consisted of less than a hundred physician-officers, and they were stationed only in the largest cities. Other than displaying remarkable enthusiasm for monitoring health conditions in Hesse's houses of ill repute, few of them had any real interest in caring for a former enemy. They were generally eager to "divorce" their live-in fräuleins and return home to their wives and medical practices in the States.

That left me with the Germans themselves, and a major dilemma. Obviously, the sensible way to establish a decent health care system was to put to work the large pool of indigenous professionals already on hand—four thousand doctors, three times as many nurses, and several thousand pharmacists, veterinarians, and sanitary engineers. Unfortunately, though, the vast majority of these people were *verboten*—unavailable to us because they had been Nazis or Nazi sympathizers. So our de-Nazification experts said, anyway.

That was stretching things a bit too far. After all, Hitler had been in power for over a decade. During that time, every important, and many of the unimportant, positions in the German establishment were occupied by Nazis or individuals who were obliged to swear allegiance to the Nazi creed. At the beginning, our Nazi hunters made their definition of a Nazi so all-encompassing as to prevent nearly every professionally qualified German from holding down a public sector job on political grounds. Very soon, it became impossible to run anything.

Few fields of human endeavor had been so thoroughly Nazified under the prevailing definition as the medical profession. Many of the capable doctors left behind after the Nazis shipped the Jews off to concentration camps were fellow Nazis. That meant that every time we located good candidates for public health officer, nurse, or dog catcher, the Counter Intelligence Corps, which was responsible for keeping tabs on Hitler's former minions, would leap forward to expose them. Ultimately, we were reduced to determining not whether someone was professionally qualified to practice medicine, but to establishing the degree to which he or she had been a Nazi.

I found out just how seriously the CIC took its job one afternoon shortly after my arrival in Wiesbaden when the telephone rang and I was called to an office in the basement of the Palace of Justice. The caller said there'd been a "medical emergency." But when the door was unlocked, and then locked again behind me, I found two CIC officers calmly smoking cigarettes and looking at the body of a man lying motionless on the floor.

Turning the body over, I could see right away that he had been stabbed. There was a large wound where the knife had penetrated the upper portion of the victim's abdomen, just below the sternum. From the enormous pool of blood that had collected on the floor, I suspected the death weapon had nicked the aorta, the main vessel pumping blood from the heart. The man, whoever he was, had bled to death—and very, very rapidly.

"What happened?" I asked one of the officers, a short, stocky man with a Midwestern accent.

"Well," he said, "we're just interviewin' this fella here, and, wouldn't you know it, he turns out to be one a them Nazis, and a very obnoxious Nazi at that. We get to slicin' his third button off when he goes and grabs my knife and stabs himself. Kills himself deader 'n a doornail."

Now it all made sense. The officers had been playing the "button game." This consisted of having the suspect stand at attention while being questioned. In those days German men invariably wore three buttons on their narrow-lapeled jackets. If the answers proved unsatisfactory, it was not unusual for the interrogator to take out a knife and hack off the top button. Sometimes, the removal of a second button was necessary to achieve a confession. By the time the CIC men reached the third button, they would normally conclude they were dealing with a hard-boiled Nazi of the first order and promptly declare him unsuited for public sector employment. On this occasion, the ritual had moved in quick succession from menace to murder.

I say murder because it strains the imagination to think a middle-aged German could, in that time of malnutrition and malaise, summon the speed and power required to wrest a knife from a muscular, young American, and then to commit a Teutonic form of *seppuku* while his questioners looked on. Much more likely, the interrogators themselves, angered by the man's responses—or lack of them—had buried the knife in their charge's belly. If that was the case, though, the CIC men showed not the slightest trace of remorse.

I'll blow the whistle on these bastards, sure as hell, I thought angrily. To do that, though, I knew I'd need the corroboration of a coroner, so I demanded that an honest German colleague I knew be brought in. When Johann arrived, however, he took one look at the stony faces of the CIC men and promptly pronounced the case a suicide. At that point I realized how foolish it would be to try to contest the testimony of two hardened CIC men who were more in step with the unforgiving mood of the times than a well-meaning doctor already suspected of being soft on his "Nazi" colleagues.

Although it has now been more than forty years since that episode, my dreams are still occasionally haunted by the specter of that prostrate German and the surprised expression on his face when I flopped him over on his back. I can clearly make out the three missing buttons on his jacket as I agonize about what to do, wondering, in my sleep, if this makes me an accessory to a murder.

My first few weeks in Wiesbaden were haunted by a specter of a different sort—the looming certainty of failure. How did one go about setting up a health care system for millions of people without the benefit of medical supplies or doctors? I was ready to call it quits, acknowledge my inability to cope with the situation, and throw myself on the mercy of General Stayer when salvation suddenly arrived.

It appeared in the unlikely form of an elderly German, tall, gaunt, and grim, with a shiny bald dome—an exact clone of Konrad Adenauer—named Wolfgang Spemann. Herr Doktor Spemann, whose official title was Chief Public Health Officer, was my civilian counterpart, and he offered several unique qualifications for the job. In the first place, Spemann was not, and never had been, a Nazi. After a long, honorable career as a public health official, Spemann had retired well before Hitler rose to power. He'd spent his life battling tuberculosis, diphtheria, scarlet fever, and other contagious diseases which were now making a furious comeback in the aftermath of war. Moreover, he was a figure of great respect among Germans from all walks of life.

Spemann was quick to size up the scope of our problems. Before long, the walls of his tiny office were plastered with charts showing statistical evidence of a rising tide of tuberculosis and malnutrition, a merciful ebbing of typhus (DDT was successfully wiping out typhus-bearing lice by the trillions), the stubborn persistence of typhoid and the childhood infections, and a continuing groundswell in the number of refugees flooding in, bringing fresh supplies of pathogens with them along with their fevered hopes for survival.

The search for qualified German physicians took on new urgency when I received orders from GHQ requiring the reduction of American medical officers in U.S.-occupied Germany from 450 to 45 within nine months. I would be left with a total of fifteen American doctors to monitor health care in all of Hesse.

Dr. Spemann, who hated the Nazis more than anyone, was undaunted. He simply got his hands on an old register for the German Communist Party and used it to recruit scores of doctors who had been forced underground by Hitler's anticommunist fanaticism. When I protested, Spemann calmly pointed out, "Innocent people are dying. We have no choice." The ubiquitous CIC agents, who despised communists almost as much as they did the Nazis, managed to disqualify a few of these Marxist medicos, but they were never entirely successful in keeping up with the resourceful Dr. Spemann.

Eventually, the doctor crisis, like the penicillin shortage, began to ease up. With Germany still in ruins and the Russians busily stitching together the Iron Curtain, the CIC became more interested in protecting Germany from the communist hordes and dialed back on its de-Nazification regulations. Still, the severe shortages of practically all medical supplies persisted. I traveled to Berlin time after time to try and pry more bandages, drugs, and surgical equipment out of General Stayer, but always received the same reply: "You think you're the only one with problems," he would say. "Quit bellyaching and make the best of a bad situation."

Returning from one such ill-fated trip, I walked into my office in Wiesbaden to find my adjutant, Captain Bill Hamilton, talking to Colonel Henry Twilight. Twilight was a career officer in his mid-fifties, a wiry little fellow with a crinkled, ugly face that gave you the impression he was smiling cynically even when he was not.

"Welcome back, Major," said Twilight. "I hear you've been raising hell with the brass in Berlin."

"Not quite," I said, "but trying to get the general to cough up more supplies isn't easy."

Twilight smiled—or not—it was hard to tell. Taking a long pull on his "liberated" meerschaum, an heirloom doubtlessly acquired from some desperate German family in exchange for a bar of soap or a pair of rayon stockings, he said, "I've just been talking to Hamilton here about that salt mine up at Salzgitter." He added diffidently, "That's your baby, you know?"

I smelled a rat. What the hell was Twilight up to now? Like everybody else, I'd heard sketchy reports about Salzgitter, a small town about eighty miles northeast of Wiesbaden famous for a cavernous, centuries-old salt mine. But under my jurisdiction? That was news to me. I looked to Hamilton for guidance.

"Sir, it's apparently an enemy military dump loaded with medical supplies," he said.

"Good god!" I shouted. "Can we get at them?"

"Oh, you didn't know?" Twilight said innocently. "A patrol stumbled across the old mine up there about a year ago. Turns out it's a huge place, with hundreds of chambers and a small railroad system of its own. Surprised you didn't know about it, Kean," he said, giving Hamilton a wink.

"Also turns out," Twilight continued, making an obscene sucking sound on his meerschaum, "that the Jerries used the place to salt away most of their reserve medical supplies. Trouble is— trouble at least as far as you're concerned—is that they also used it to store their old ammo. Black powder. Rusty shell casings. Tons and tons of the nasty stuff. Why, there's enough explosives there," Twilight said merrily, "to blow up what's left of Germany and probably take Luxembourg with it."

"That's not important," I said impatiently. "The important thing is that we get those medical supplies to the people who need them."

"Well, we *can* make a deal," Twilight said, looking at me with sly, hooded eyes. "I just happen to have received permission to transfer all captured enemy materiel now under my control, except the ammo, to those departments of the military government that may desire them for distribution to the German citizenry. That's where you come in, Kean." Whipping a piece of paper out of his breast pocket, he said, "Sign this, and the supplies are yours."

"Not so fast, Colonel," I said, in my I-wasn't-born-yesterday tone. "What about the ammo?"

"Yes, that is a problem, isn't it," Twilight chortled. "If you sign for the mine, you don't only get the medical supplies. You're responsible for the explosives, too."

I started to pace the room. "Look, Twilight, we need those supplies desperately, but, damn it, the health department can't be responsible for live ammunition. Be reasonable! I don't know a .45 caliber bullet from a howitzer. What if the place blows while we're evacuating the medicine?"

"Precisely," said Twilight. "And that's why I can't be held responsible. If you want the supplies, you'll have to go down there and get them. Of course, if the mine doesn't blow, you'll agree to hand the ammo back to me so I can take credit for salvaging it."

Now everything tumbled into place. Twilight was going to use me the way coal miners used a caged canary to make sure the air in the mineshaft was safe to breathe—if death waited down there under the Hessian soil, my men, not his, would be the first to expire. But he had me. We needed those medical supplies!

"Okay, Twilight," I said, "you've got a deal."

The next day I drove up to Salzgitter, not too far past Fulda and hard by the Russian zone, which would soon become East Germany. The weather was pleasant. The snow had now completely melted, and the countryside was fresh, green, and vibrant. The car climbed into the hills, and the air grew colder. After a few unanticipated detours, I succeeded in finding a dilapidated sign, "Salzbergwerk," announcing my arrival at the mine. The GI sentry was startled to see me, a VIP out for an afternoon spin, and waved me through the gate with a hesitant salute. He knew trouble when he saw it coming.

I drove up to a large shack with smoke pouring from a tumbledown chimney. Braking a little too hard, I sent up a spray of gravel across the siding that must have sounded to whomever was inside like a machine-gun strafing the front porch, because suddenly a pair of plump, short-skirted German girls ran shrieking from the house and disappeared around a corner. I stomped in, making even more noise, and found Master Sergeant Oswald Franke in his tangled boudoir.

"Hi, Major," he grinned sheepishly, kicking a pair of red rayon panties under the bed. "Nobody told me you were coming."

Franke—large, stooped, and heavy—quickly pulled a rumpled

pair of fatigue trousers over his gray, woolly long johns. "Glad to see you, sir," he said ingratiatingly. "Sort of wish we'd known you were coming, though. You're the boss from Wiesbaden, aren't you? How about a drink?" He took a large skeleton key from his pocket and opened a hall closet, disclosing an astonishing array of liquor—the finest Scotch, bourbon, brandy, and liqueurs I'd seen since arriving in Germany.

"You realize you could be court martialed for this," I said gruffly. "In the meantime, though, a Scotch wouldn't do me any harm." He seemed to sense that his secrets were safe with me.

"What's going on here, Sergeant?" I asked, finding a seat in Franke's cluttered office and lighting up a cigar. "And start from the beginning, because frankly I don't have a clue."

"This is a gigantic mine, Major," Franke said, with a disarming smile. "The whole mountain is riddled with tunnels. I've been down there many times, but even I haven't seen it all. I stopped counting when I got to forty-five, but there must be a couple hundred more. At one time, they say, the Third Reich stashed a lot of its major artworks down there, but all of that stuff was carted away by the Allies before I got here."

"Exactly what's down there now?"

"Don't really know."

"No inventory?"

"There's a half-dozen inventories, but we don't know which one to trust. The Jerries moved stuff in and out like crazy."

"Why haven't you done an inventory yourself?"

"Meaning no disrespect, sir, but I've only got five enlisted men. It would take us forever to go through all that stuff. Meanwhile, we can't keep it from being stolen, but there's so much of it that it will take years to make a dent. The Nazis left a caretaker here; maybe he can give you a better idea. I'll introduce you to him."

We headed to the main entrance of the mine and descended the depths in a narrow, creaky elevator. Only four people could squeeze into the wire-mesh cage at one time. After one or two lurching stops on the way down, we finally reached bottom.

Given the complete lack of activity on the surface, the goings-on in the bowels of the mine were startling. Narrow rail cars, resembling toy electric trains, clanged noisily and moved in all directions, manned by a crew of German workers, who, under the questionable direction of Sergeant Franke, kept the salt operation humming.

We boarded one of the tiny cars and were driven through the darkness, around an endless series of curves, to another part of the mine, where we got out and started walking. Corridor after corridor, tunnel after tunnel, room after room was packed with crates of hospital clothing, medicine, bandages, surgical gloves, scalpels, mosquito netting, iron-frame beds, and autoclaves. In addition, hundreds of suspicious-looking wooden ammunition boxes glowered from their caves, just waiting for a single spark to blow us all to kingdom come.

I had a few of the medical crates opened for inspection. Most of the material was in good shape; the mine was very dry and the temperature uniform, so decomposition wasn't a big problem. The atmosphere reminded me of a cellar I had visited in Dublin before the war which contained, for the benefit of tourists, three mummies, whose chief attribute consisted of having resisted rotting for several hundred years. I shook hands with one of the specimens for the good luck the guide assured me would follow.

So I was shocked when what appeared to be another subterranean cadaver walked out of the shadows of the German mine. This one was small, bald, and pockmarked, and wore shiny gold-rimmed spectacles and a sharply pressed blue suit. Like the Dublin mummies, his skin gave off an eerie, greenish luminescence. Franke introduced the apparition as Herr Kluge, the pharmacist–caretaker left behind by the Nazis, the man who supposedly carried the full inventory of medical items in his head.

That was apparently no longer the case, however. "As you see, Major," the pharmacist said in heavily accented English, "things are in a very disorganized state. At one time," he explained with a mirthless grin, "I knew *pre*cisely what was here.

Alas, the supplies have been looted so many times that all is *kaput*."

"Who did the looting?" I asked.

"Ah, those terrible Russians," the pharmacist cackled. He explained how Soviet troops, who had sneaked across from their zone, had broken most of the bottles containing surgical sutures to get at the alcohol in them. "Pity," he said, with ghoulish delight, "they could not distinguish alcohol from formaldehyde. We found eight bodies in Russian uniforms here when we returned.

"Then, of course," he went on, "you Americans came, first one regiment, then another and another. Your countrymen have a good eye for value. Most of them were looking for microscopes they could sell on the black market."

"How much of this stuff do you suppose was stolen by the Germans?" I asked coolly.

The pharmacist grimaced. "Very little, my dear Major. You must remember that, despite our current difficulties, we are a very disciplined people."

The cadaverous German was beginning to irritate me, so I suggested we head for the elevator, the surface, and a drink. Once again seated in Franke's office, I asked the sergeant how long it would take to bring up all the medical supplies.

"Jesus, Major, one hell of a long time. There's only this one small shaft and another farther down the hill. The elevators work only a couple of hours a day because there's so little coal for electricity."

"I suspect there are a few hidden entrances," I said. "That might explain . . ."

"Nothing can be brought up," the pharmacist interrupted, "until a new inventory is completed. And that will take two or three years."

I looked at the German, then at Franke. "Sergeant," I said, "we're going to clean out that mine beginning tomorrow. We're bringing up everything, everything, that is, except the ammunition."

"But Major," Franke protested, "we haven't got the manpower. We haven't got the coal. And where will we stow all that stuff once it's topside?"

"Leave that to me, Sergeant. Meanwhile," I said, pointing a finger at the smirking pharmacist, "fire this man immediately. If he's seen on the grounds again I'll have him put in jail. I'll be back in a week."

On the way back to Wiesbaden I calculated I'd need at least a hundred workers, tons and tons of coal, and more warehouse space than probably then existed in the whole of Germany. It was an impossible job. No, not impossible, I thought. It's just a job for Herr Doktor Spemann.

Five days later Captain Hamilton telephoned me from the mine. "Major, you won't believe this," he said. "Old man Spemann shows up a couple days ago with a handful of Germans, and I think, nice try, but this will never work. Yesterday morning sixty—yes, sixty!—more report for duty, saying Herr Spemann's sent them. A few hours later a train arrives and starts dumping coal on the siding. Starting today we're going on a twenty-four-hour shift using both elevators."

"That's wonderful," I said, congratulating myself on having put Spemann in charge.

"You've never seen anything like it," Hamilton gushed. "These guys are so organized. As soon as the stuff is brought to the surface, it's inventoried, loaded on trucks, and driven away."

Driven away?! I had expressly told Spemann that I wanted the supplies to stay at the mine site until we could arrange for securely guarded warehouse facilities. "Where did he find the warehouses, I wonder," I said, trying to sound nonchalant.

"Oh, they aren't using warehouses."

"What the hell do you mean, they're not using warehouses?!"

"Well, in order to facilitate distribution, Spemann said the stuff was being shipped straight to the four big German drug companies. That's where the trucks and the men came from—from the drug companies. Didn't you know that?"

Suddenly, everything clicked. I'd been so wrapped up in trying to free the materiel as quickly as possible that I'd overlooked one important consideration. Medical supplies were in such high demand that whoever put them on the market stood to reap enormous profits. No wonder the mine was being cleaned out at such a furious pace. The drug companies must have thought they'd lucked into an incredible windfall. "Get Spemann in here on the double!" I bellowed through the wall at my secretary.

A few minutes later, Spemann walked in, wreathed in smiles and seeming to anticipate a vote of thanks. Somehow I contained my anger long enough to ask him, "How are things going at the mine?"

"Magnificent," he said, clicking his heels and trying to contain his enthusiasm. "It is beyond all my fondest dreams!"

"What about the warehouse situation?"

Spemann hesitated for a moment, as though smelling trouble, then plowed ahead. "The disposal of goods presented too big a problem for health department channels, so we decided to utilize a natural system."

"What do you mean, 'natural system'?"

"Throughout Germany, the usual channel for distributing medical supplies to the hospitals is through the wholesaler and local pharmacists. So, we have turned the materiel over to a few highly reliable drug companies, and they are very helpfully arranging things. They will handle distribution in the fastest, most efficient way possible, I can assure you."

"And did I hear you say without profit?"

Spemann flushed a deep shade of scarlet. "Well, naturally they will be allowed a small profit. To cover costs, you understand."

I could contain myself no longer. "There are no medical supplies left in Germany. I am turning over to you millions of dollars' worth of materiel, and you have the gall to restock the shelves of these companies for general sale. Do you think they can resist raking in big profits when goods are unavailable elsewhere? Spemann, I'm disappointed in you."

Spemann looked crushed. "These are reliable, honest companies," he moaned.

"Don't hedge, Spemann. Are these companies Nazi outfits or what?"

"They were, of course. But management has now been replaced by politically acceptable individuals. I tell you there are no other companies big enough to help us."

He had a point there. "Fine," I said. "But there can be no profits made by any Germans in this deal." I then announced my plan: The goods would be sold at a cost 20 percent below prewar list prices to the German government, which would, in turn, sell them to the hospitals and dispensaries at a markup of 2 percent for handling. The drug companies could act as agents for the government and claim the two percent.

"But Major, these companies are in business to make money. Would you consider 15 percent?"

"It's two percent or nothing," I said. "Now get the top men from those companies here tomorrow at nine o'clock. No excuses."

The next morning a half-dozen men filed into the conference room at the Palace of Justice. Gray, middle-aged, and distinguished, they looked as if they might belong in any corporate boardroom in the United States.

"Gentlemen," I began, "I called this meeting to discuss the evacuation of the Salzgitter mine. I would like to hear your plans for distributing the medical supplies."

One of the executives, a large, overfed man with thinning blond hair, cleared his throat. "After the mine is completely evacuated, Major, we will review the inventory and publish a list of all supplies available in the newspapers. Whatever anyone needs can be applied for. Naturally, the hospitals will be our first priority. We trust," he concluded silkily, "these arrangements are satisfactory?"

"Oh, entirely," I said. "And allow me to commend you on your cooperation in an effort as big as this one—particularly when no profit will be permitted."

The executives gasped in unison. They looked at Dr. Spemann, wondering whether they'd heard me correctly. "Oh yes," said Spemann, a little sheepishly, "I failed to mention that one detail." He then repeated my plan in German to make sure everybody understood.

A second executive protested vehemently—a small, round man, smoking a big cigar that made him look like a George Grosz cartoon capitalist. "Major," he said, "no one desires to benefit from the unhappy situation our country finds itself in, let me assure you. However, work on the mine requires the use of virtually all our facilities, and for this some recompense is due."

"This is strictly a humanitarian deal," I said. "You cannot—will not—make a profit on it."

"In that case, Major," said a third executive, his jaw set defiantly, "it would be to the advantage of my company not to accept your generous offer of participation. Even in such times as these, we have obligations to our stockholders."

Spemann had told me to anticipate this reaction, and I was ready. "I understand perfectly," I said. "Of course, the military government could always arrange to simply expropriate your businesses and order you to comply, but I see no reason why we should force the German people to help themselves. If you decide not to proceed, I will release an announcement to the effect that the materiel in the mine is available, but, because the German drug companies would not remove it without making a profit, the military government has decided to offer it for sale elsewhere in Europe."

The executives looked shell-shocked. They needed no reminding of how angry the German people already were with big business in general and its role in fueling the Nazi cause. After a long pause the first executive spoke up: "All right, Major, for patriotic reasons we will dispose of the goods at the price you set."

"Excellent," I said, preparing to throw my final bomb. "And since you will be simply acting as agents for the German government, you will, of course, agree to your companies remaining anonymous."

"But why?" cried the squat executive, his cigar now dangling from his lower lip.

"Because," I replied, "I don't want either you gentlemen, or any of your companies, to gain one ounce of prestige or positive publicity out of this deal. Is that clear?"

"It is clear, Major, that the military government wants to ruin us," stammered the first executive angrily. "This is nothing but socialism."

"Call it what you will," I said. "The truth is, we are simply going to use you, and you are not going to use us. And now, gentlemen, good day."

The executives rose together, fired off a series of snappy bows, and departed. The cunning old Spemann was delighted, and, for a moment, forgot his dour Teutonic demeanor. "Wonderful, wonderful!" he said, clapping his hands and prancing around the office like a Bavarian slap-dancer. "There is nothing like an order to make a German understand."

Spemann was right—we had won the battle of the Salzgitter mine and victory was sweet.

It was also short-lived. A week later I received a severe reprimand from GHQ in Berlin. General Stayer was furious. What was the big idea of undermining the profit motive? How did I expect Germany ever to get back on its feet, if I went around trampling on free enterprise? I was baffled. What had happened to the policy that the Germans were our enemies and were to be treated as such? What about the goal of busting the Nazi machine into such tiny pieces that it could never be reassembled?

"Times have changed, you numbskull," bellowed Stayer over the telephone. "Germany is our ally and she must be allowed to rebuild. It's the Soviets we're worried about now, not the blasted

Krauts." Without my having noticed it, the Occupation had suddenly entered a new phase.

Our efforts at combating disease in Hesse left little time for me
to fulfill my other official role as American *oberführer* for Hesse's
cultural treasures. Taking a break from routine chores one day,
however, I decided to make an inspection tour of the Museum
of Fine Arts across the street from our offices in the Palace of
Justice.

No sooner had I set foot in the long, low granite building,
though, than I was surrounded by a half-dozen guards, who,
with a zeal that seemed a little excessive, demanded to see my
credentials. With some difficulty, I managed to persuade them
that they in fact worked for me and went inside. But when I
entered the first exhibition area I was shocked. What did these
crazy guards think they were protecting? The museum was
empty!

Walking from room to room—each one barer and darker than
the last—I came upon a large wooden door that was barred and
nailed shut in a very conspicuous fashion. I asked the guards,
who had been nipping at my heels, what was in the room. Nobody knew. I asked for the key. No key, I was told. Having
worked myself into a state of intense curiosity now, I summoned
the commander of the guard unit, a man with a scarred face and
an eye patch. Like the others, he pleaded ignorance. All he knew
was that six months earlier he'd been ordered to assemble a team
to protect whatever was inside "at all costs." Surveillance was
to be around the clock. He would be held personally responsible,
he said, drawing an ominous finger across his throat.

To the commander's dismay, I called for hammers and a crow-
bar and directed his men to break down the door. Inside, there
in the center of yet another large, empty room, was a single crate
measuring about five feet square. I knew better than to attack
the box with hammers, so the museum curator, who had by

now appeared on the scene, arranged for a team of curatorial experts to show up the following day.

The next morning I rose early and returned to the museum with Captain Hamilton, determined to get to the bottom of the mystery. The work of decrating was already underway. One of the experts, an attractive young brunette, had the annoying habit of shouting, *"Achtung! Achtung!"* as each nail and board was removed. When the last bit of excelsior had been cleared away, the museum curator, the young woman, and I all gaped in amazement. Sitting in the middle of the gray granite floor was one of the wonders of the ancient world—the exquisite, sculpted head of the Egyptian Queen Nefertiti!

According to legend, Nefertiti, the wife of the Pharaoh Akhenaton, who ruled from 1377 to 1360 B.C., was the most beautiful woman who had ever lived. In Egypt, German archaeologists had excavated her famous head—about twenty inches high and made of limestone—on the eve of the First World War and then spirited it back to Berlin where it was eventually put on display at the Kaiser Wilhelm Institute. For years, angry Egyptians demanded the return of the peerless national treasure. Adolf Hitler himself neatly summed up the German attitude toward these entreaties: "The German nation does not give up what it has!"

When the tide of war began to turn against the Germans, they decided to move Nefertiti to Wiesbaden. This was based on the shrewd assumption that the Allies would resist bombing the daylights out of a city they might eventually want to use as a hub of occupation. (German farsightedness wasn't 20–20, though, since British pilots managed to blast large sections of Wiesbaden, having somehow mistaken it for Frankfurt.) The Nazis were also eager to keep Nefertiti's beautiful head from falling into greedy Russian fingers. Then, during the last, chaotic days of the Third Reich, the head had vanished.

It took the curator only a few seconds to declare that the uncrated specimen was indeed the lost head, the original. So here I was, the Doctor from Fishfork, in total command of an Egyptian queen!

I immediately ordered a special pedestal built so that I might personally place my goddess upon it. An electrician was instructed to rig up lighting that would bathe her in a royal glow night and day, showing off her best angles in the process. The lock on the door was changed and only two people were given keys. Not the curator; he was an ex-Nazi and I did not trust him. No, one key was given to a Colonel Watson, the adjutant, who placed it in a sealed envelope that was stored in his safe at the Palace of Justice. The other one stayed in my pocket until I left Germany for home.*

Twice each day, I made the short pilgrimage across the street to pay homage to the Queen of the Egyptians. Whenever important visitors came to see us at the Palace of Justice, I took them to meet my "girlfriend." Few real women have ever exerted that kind of hold on me.

One day in the fall of 1947, General Stayer strode into my apartment in Wiesbaden unannounced and demanded a drink. I dutifully poured him two jiggersful of Scotch and followed him out to the veranda. Sitting there in silence, I noticed for the first time how old and tired he looked. His hair, what was left of it anyway, was stone gray. His hands were mottled with liver spots and trembled as he raised a cigarette to his lips. He was old, I wasn't getting any younger, and our adventures in Panama suddenly seemed light-years in the past.

"Kean," he said at last, "I'm going home . . ."

"But General . . ." I protested.

" 'But General' nothing. Shut up and listen. I haven't come down here to talk about old times. I'm going home and I want you to take my place. I've spoken to General Clay and he agrees."

I was flabbergasted. "General, I'm flattered. But you couldn't make a worse choice. Suppose I don't agree with the policy?"

---

*The bust of Nefertiti is now on display in the Egyptian Museum in West Berlin.

"That doesn't matter. All you have to do is act as though you do. You'll get your orders. But above all, you're a doctor, and, deep down, you don't want war. Who could better represent our country?"

This was not the kind of offer that came a reluctant major's way everyday and I knew it. Top policy, top decisions, a general's star on my uniform—these were the glimmerings of greatness Stayer now held out to me.

The old man looked at me through watery eyes. "Kean," he said, "you're closer to me than my own son, and nothing has ever made me happier than to be able to give you this chance. Don't make up your mind right now. Think it over, think it over. Now pour me another shot."

Since Panama, Stayer had been a constant source of inspiration and opportunity for me. He had taken up the role of teacher and guide in the wake of Francis O'Connor's death. This, his final favor to me, was tempting indeed. As I turned it over in my mind, though, I realized that the whole reason for having teachers in life is for them to guide you to a point where you can make your own decisions. Now, at the age of thirty-five, I knew that I had finally reached just such a point. I turned to the general and said no. I wanted to be a scientist, a parasitologist, not a military man. And to do that, I knew, there was only one place for me now—New York, New York, my long-abandoned hometown.

PART II

PARK AVENUE
PHYSICIAN

Hard Times in Manhattan

You can never go home again, or so people say. But in the fall of 1947 I had no choice. I sailed from Bremerhaven on a troopship that was crowded and smelled of diesel fuel, wet wool blankets, and urine. It was a rough voyage, with high seas, soupy fogs, and unseaworthy infantrymen vomiting in narrow bunks. Somehow I managed to rescue myself from the pervasive misery by meeting a lovely redhead who worked for an American ambassador in Scandinavia. Being of the same sympathetic makeup as Colleen O'Neill, the woman who had guided me on my maiden voyage to Europe a decade earlier, she soothed me all the way home. That was the last I would see of both redheads and fun for a while.

I was back in New York after ten years and the city had changed. Everything now seemed so expensive, the nickel cup of coffee having followed the nickel cigar into prewar oblivion. Before leaving Germany, I had stuffed into my duffle bag a powerful Zeiss microscope with elegant brass fittings, which I purchased on the black market for three cartons of Lucky Strikes. That and a meager bank account represented my entire net worth. A smoking, secondhand Buick and the deposit on an apartment, a side street walk-up on the corner of 77th Street and Third Avenue, ate up most of my savings. Gone was my chauffeur-driven

Mercedes-Benz limousine, along with the uniform of a lieutenant colonel (the promotion had been General Stayer's parting gift to me), and all the bowing and scraping a general's aide commanded.

It was a depressing time and I needed a job. So I went north to 168th Street and Broadway to see Robert Loeb, chief of medicine at Columbia P & S. This was a big moment for me. Here I was, after ten years of foreign medical adventuring, returning to my alma mater, armed with a sheaf of scientific papers I had authored while in Panama. I was now ready to assume my rightful role of succeeding Francis O'Connor as professor of tropical medicine, the post O'Connor had promised me when I left for Central America that long-ago day in 1937.

Loeb was friendly but not terribly sympathetic. After we'd trudged through some desultory small talk about Panama, it dawned on me that he had no intention of offering me a job. I was shocked. I reminded him of O'Connor's promise, adding—shrewdly, I thought—that I didn't expect the top job right away. I'd be happy to take a junior post for a year or two—"so as not to ruffle any feathers, you understand." I was suffering from the general delusion among veterans at the time that they would be allowed to return to their old jobs, or to ones they might have obtained had they not been called to military duty.

Loeb, a powerful, brilliant, arrogant medical man, was not impressed. O'Connor's promise meant little to him. Times had changed, he said. In my absence, another man, an industrious, capable physician, had stepped in to fill the late O'Connor's shoes. An intestinal disability had kept the man out of the military and, during the war, he had proven himself an invaluable member of the department. The unspoken message came through loud and clear: While I was off chasing parasitic rainbows in Panama and playing the big shot in Germany, academia had carried on quite well without me, thank you. There was no job for me.

I was heartbroken—but I was also hungry for work and status. So the next morning I ventured to a crumbling brick building on the Lower East Side across from Bellevue Hospital to track down William Von Glahn, a former teacher from Columbia P & S, who now headed the pathology department at New York University. Von Glahn hadn't changed. He was still the sleek, debonair, charming man I remembered from my student days. A championship ballroom dancer and something of a dandy with his snappy bow ties and his Douglas Fairbanks, Sr. good looks, Von Glahn glided smoothly around his small, musty office as though it were the Taj Mahal.

Spreading my reprints out on his desk, he looked at them like a riverboat gambler sizing up a hand of stud. Then came the snap decision. "Kean," said Von Glahn, "you're hired. Assistant professor of pathology. Report for duty tomorrow morning."

I was ecstatic. The job paid $4,000 a year. I would teach every day of the week, except Sundays. There would be no more Mercedes or castles on the Rhine in my future, and very little champagne and caviar, but if I managed my budget frugally, I would survive.

I had no difficulty arranging my courses to meet the needs of my students. Most of them were demobilized MDs like myself, who were using the GI Bill to enroll in refresher courses before returning to full-time practice. I had new opportunities for learning, as well. Sigmund Wilens, who had been chief resident at Columbia P & S in my day, was now chief pathologist at Bellevue Hospital. He and Von Glahn met every day at lunchtime to review all new surgical and autopsy slides. As I did my teaching in the mornings, I sat in on these sessions and watched the two masters of the microscope at work.

For all my hours at the autopsy table in Panama, I was still pretty much self-taught as a pathologist. So I now drank greedily at the well of academic knowledge, as my mentors dipped effortlessly into deep reservoirs of experience to appraise the slides that were passed around a table strewn with milk cartons and tunafish sandwiches. I was pleased at how much I had learned on my own at Gorgas, but fearful that a few bonehead errors that had crept into my scientific papers would now be exposed to the ridicule of these seasoned pros.

Very occasionally, I would find myself in the heady position of knowing more than either Von Glahn or Wilens about a particular parasitic disease, accidental death, or even some rare manifestation of tuberculosis—the major killer in Panama. The roles would then temporarily reverse themselves, and the sages would listen to me. I was eventually permitted to lecture second-year medical students on tropical diseases. I was in heaven!

On the same floor, halfway between where Von Glahn presided over his roundtable and the lecture hall where I did my teaching, was the pathology laboratory of New York City's Chief Medical Examiner, Milton Helpern. Milton, a big, cheerful man, with chubby cheeks and a constant smile, was an exceptionally gifted medical detective. That stood to reason, since he had been trained by Thomas A. Gonzalez and Morgan Vance, the fathers of forensic medicine in America, the men who helped introduce the concept of the medical examiner's office to police departments all across the country. As a part-time coroner's physician in the Canal Zone, I had studied their book, *Legal Medicine and Toxicology*, more than once. The chapter on how to distinguish suicide from murder had come in particularly handy in unpredictable Panama.

Milton and I became good friends, and he fell into the habit of stopping me on my way out of the lecture hall to "show me a slide." That was his way of asking for help, for while he was a fine gross pathologist, he became hopelessly disoriented whenever he peered through the microscope and entered the unfamiliar territory of the cell. So while Milton was busy studying the course a fatal bullet had taken through the skull of some hapless cadaver, I would try to round out the anatomy of violent death by scanning the histological evidence for signs of alcoholism, drug abuse, or other relevant conditions.

Later on, when my medical practice was big—and death not infrequent—Milton repaid the favor many times over. This he accomplished by accepting without question my clinical opinion on the cause of a patient's death, thereby helping to speed the glum process of getting the body of the deceased from home to undertaker without the depressing, time-consuming detour of a trip to the medical examiner's autopsy table.

Milton was nothing if not a humanitarian, and, once or twice, he permitted me to bend the medical record on those grounds. When Mr. T, a distinguished financier with a reputation around Manhattan as something of a playboy, committed suicide after his business collapsed, I found a note near the body accusing his wife and father-in-law of withholding financial help that would have saved him from humiliation. I telephoned Milton and read it to him. He paused a moment, then asked, "Is the evidence of suicide clear?"

"Good god, Milton," I said, "there are empty bottles of sleeping pills all over the place."

"Any children?"

"Yes. Young ones."

Helpern's voice took on the formal tone of the medical examiner. "Tell me, Dr. Kean," he asked, "did the decedent leave any kind of suicide note?"

I got his message. "No," I said.

When Mrs. P, socialite and heiress, died suddenly at her suite in the Plaza one night, her husband and two daughters were away traveling in Canada, unaware that the poor, confused woman had just been jilted by the latest in a long line of greedy, manipulative lovers. Once again I found myself called in by a family friend and stood there looking at the body sprawled on the huge silk bedcover while I telephoned Helpern.

"She's had a bad heart for years, Milton," I lied, pocketing the empty Seconal bottle. Playing God is dangerous business, so I tried not to push my luck. But I knew that the wise Milton would let me know if I was overstepping the unwritten rules that allowed the medical examiner to take both the law and humanity into account and, when the situation warranted, to err on the side of humanity.

After two years in New York, I had learned a great deal about becoming a better pathologist and an acceptable teacher. But the learning curve was now beginning to flatten out with a vengeance, and I started to get the sinking feeling that I was going nowhere fast. I was also piling up debt at a worrying pace. So I went to Bill Von Glahn and demanded a raise. My salary was increased to $4,400 a year. This had the immediate effect of increasing my income to exactly half the level of my expenditures.

The Continental tastes I'd acquired in Germany had gotten the best of me. Most of the good restaurants of that time—Baroque, Soule's Pavillon, Le Chambord—are gone now and so are the funds I so assiduously funneled into them in long-forgotten efforts to woo a woman, impress a friend, or simply feel a part of the Manhattan social swirl. Good seats to the theater, which forty years later would cost an outrageous $45 apiece, were then, in proportion, every bit as outrageously priced. These were not, suffice it to say, the habits appropriate to an assistant professor of pathology.

But Von Glahn would give me no more money. Instead, he came up with the unwelcome suggestion that I augment my income by going into private practice on the side. He offered to free me from my teaching duties two half days a week to help get me started.

The thought appalled me. I was still as uninterested in caring for patients as I'd been in medical school or as an intern in Panama. The laboratory was my métier. Who the hell wanted to deal with patients? Patients were boring, demanding, and frightening. Pathogens, on the other hand, were fascinating, their behavior more predictable—and they didn't talk back. But harsh economic realities were already quietly reshaping my attitudes. Private practice it would have to be. But private practice of what?

Von Glahn observed me from behind his desk, his poker player's eyes glittering mischievously. "Why, coprology, of course," he said. Coprology? Yes, he acknowledged, it was not one of medicine's glamour specialties. On the other hand, there was always work for someone who could scan human stools for pernicious microbes. But where would one do such a thing, I asked. "Al Barach's got a big office," said Von Glahn. "Go see him." I wrote down the address—929 Park Avenue.

Dr. Alvin Barach was a distinguished professor of medicine at Columbia P & S and a specialist in pulmonary disease. He also ran a flourishing private practice on Park Avenue and, with its brass lamps, walnut endtables, and leather armchairs, it was an impressive office, all right. To my astonishment, Barach agreed to induct me into this medical pleasure palace for the modest sum of $150 a month. Three other junior colleagues also paid $150 each. This, I later calculated, netted Barach an amount exactly double what he paid for leasing the entire office. But I didn't begrudge Barach his spirit of free enterprise. Having successfully installed myself on Park Avenue, I intended to stay.

My new professional quarters were somewhat less impressive than those of my colleagues, however. This had largely to do with the fact that the "office" I had rented wasn't really an office at all, but a toilet. Fortunately, though, 929 Park was a big, old building, and the toilets were very large. I hired a workman to remove the unnecessary porcelain and, with the help of prefabricated partitions, divided the area into three separate rooms. One room I made into a small laboratory, where I deposited my black market microscope from Germany; a second cubicle, with its miniature desk and one chair, I designated my "consultation room"; the third room remained a toilet. I was now ready to practice medicine. So I sat back and waited.

It was a long wait. Four weeks later my first patient arrived. Tall, willowy, and high-strung, she was the debutante daughter of a leading New York family, and she had an embarrassing problem. She suffered from severe diarrhea that invariably seemed to strike at some all-important high society function. I gave her a jar and told her to return with a stool sample the next day, which she did. I then spent the following night with her specimen, sitting up till four in the morning conducting an exhaustive exploration for parasites.

But she did not have parasites. Nothing was wrong with her except a chronic case of nerves. I confess to having been a little disappointed with the discovery, since I would not now have the opportunity of rescuing this lovely creature from some rare tropical disease, as I had fantasized. Science, I had noticed, was frequently uncooperative that way.

In any event, the following morning at eight o'clock, bleary-eyed and unshaven, I slipped a five-page, typewritten report documenting the debutante's illness under the door of her regular physician, Dr. Harold Hyman, a prominent man on Park Avenue. That noon the telephone rang. It was Hyman, calling to congratulate me—he said he had never before seen a single stool produce such a volume of scientific analysis. He promised to send me more patients.

So I was now in business, if just barely. Word spread on Park Avenue that there was somebody in the neighborhood who did stool examinations, but building up a practice was a slow process. ("Quick! Is there a coprologist in the house?" wasn't something one was likely to hear very often.) In hindsight, though, I suppose my timing was exactly right. International travel, which had been prohibitively expensive, was just then becoming as relatively cheap as it was fashionable. I soon found myself inundated with stool samples from members of New York's burgeoning jetset, travelers who began to bring home from their foreign escapades a textbook variety of parasitic infections. What a relief! Every right-minded parasitologist knows his proper place is in the tropics. But I no longer needed to feel guilty about living in Manhattan, thousands of miles from the nearest pestilential swamp. The tropics would now come to me.

Coprology also offered unique competitive advantages. Other doctors didn't routinely do proctoscopic examinations: too messy and too hard. They didn't study the stool: they hadn't been trained for it. In short, I was the right man for a job nobody else wanted.

In 1949, Al Barach began to instruct me in the public relations of private practice. "Kean," he advised, "you've got to develop a new gimmick every two years." Publish a scientific paper. Write a newspaper opinion piece on some new form of therapy. It didn't really matter in Barach's book—just as long as the word went out. "People will start coming to you," he said, "not for what you have done, but simply because they've read your name somewhere."

Following his own theory, Al had come up with his first major gimmick during the war by pioneering the use of the oxygen tent in pulmonary therapy. That was all well and good for Al Barach, I thought, but something about his advice bothered me. Was it really ethical to lure in patients with what amounted to cleverly disguised advertising? "Don't get them in, can't help them," was Barach's brusque response.

I decided it made sense. Try as I might, however, I could not come up with a gimmick of my own. Then one morning I woke up to discover that the left side of my face was paralyzed. I stumbled to the bathroom and gave myself a neurological examination in the mirror. My diagnosis was reassuring. I was not having a brain hemorrhage; I had Bell's palsy.

To this day the cause of Bell's palsy remains a mystery. Recent studies suggest that it may be caused by a viral ambush of the facial nerve as it winds through a convoluted bony canal at the base of the skull or as it exits through the stylomastoid foramen, a tiny hole in the front part of the skull, to join the soft tissues of the face. Whatever the origin, there is swelling, tearing, and a ghoulish distortion of the facial features.

I needed a doctor. So I went to see Harold Hyman, the man who had sent the diarrhetic debutante my way. He confirmed my diagnosis of Bell's palsy and sent me away, weeping involuntarily and unable to control my saliva. There was as yet no treatment.

That night, about ten o'clock, Hyman telephoned me. "Ben," he said, sounding distraught, "come down to my office right away." When I arrived, it was like looking into a mirror. Dr. Hyman's face was twisted into the same Hunchback-of-Notre-Dame configuration as mine. The left side of his face twitched uncontrollably. It was my turn to confirm his self-diagnosis: Bell's palsy.

We were faced, quite literally, with a medical rarity—a two-man epidemic. We sat down and tried to figure out what had happened. Bell's palsy had never been known to be contagious. It normally struck no more than one individual in any given household. Had we both been exposed to the same patient with a virus? Had Dr. Hyman acquired the virus from me earlier in the day and then developed the disease in an amazingly accelerated fashion? We were stumped.

The infection passed quickly but left me imprinted for life with an asymmetrical smile that has often been misinterpreted as the sign of a cynical nature. My left eye still tears involuntarily, leading people who don't know me very well to draw other equally erroneous conclusions about my emotional state. According to Barach's rules of publicity, I should have written a paper on this strange incident. I did not.

But word got around all the same. Before I knew what had hit me, I'd become an "expert" on Bell's palsy. People began calling me from various parts of the world seeking consultation. One woman flew all the way from Australia to meet the great authority on the disease. I explained to this patient, as diplomatically as I could, that I knew no more about Bell's palsy than an aborigine witch doctor. I had no secret therapy, no magic potion. She did not believe me. She berated me for my lack of sympathy. When I mentioned this incident to Al Barach, he nodded sagely—now I knew exactly what he meant by the power of a good gimmick.

About this time a terrible thing happened to me: I found myself beginning to actually enjoy being a doctor.

This was an alarming revelation. Since medical school, I had remained committed to my goal of someday becoming a great scientist. Doctoring was something one did to get through medical school and internship. But curiosity had always been the bane of my existence, and now, while I was busily trying to avoid bankruptcy, my patients did a nasty thing to me—they became interesting.

They were an idiosyncratic bunch, to be sure. One bouncy, blond socialite, who reminded me of the cartoon character Betty Boop, would show up at my office for her regular checkup and remove a full-length sable coat, then a second—revealing only a lush, blemish-free anatomy underneath!

Before I knew it I was no longer a lonely coprologist but a fully fledged internist with a growing roster of colorful patients. Take Ian McGrath, for example, the ferocious necktie baron, whose third-generation family company dominated the American market for many years. Tall, irascible, hard-of-hearing, he carried, even as a young man at Princeton, a big walking stick, which he wielded ruthlessly, pounding on desks and doors, and threatening virtually anybody who did not obey. His wife, Lady Evelyn Barlow, a British aristocrat, was a serene, gracious woman who somehow found happiness with this difficult man. Whenever I'd had my desktop thumped by her husband's cane, she would console me: "Well, that's Ian, but he's really very lovable when you get to know him."

Ian chose not to display this sweeter side in his dealings with me. Me—whom he considered a smart-alecky young physician—he did not trust. He was constantly haranguing me about my "exorbitant charges," which normally amounted to $20 for an agonizing office visit. Then at two o'clock one morning I found myself in his residential suite at the Ritz Tower, ducking his cane and trying to put him on an ambulance stretcher.

McGrath's phlebitis had suddenly flared up, and without emergency surgery (called the Ben Hogan operation, after the great golfer) he would be dead by sunrise.

The operation went smoothly and, after several weeks of major care, I sent him a bill for a thousand dollars. From then on I lived in dread of the moment when he would arrive on his crutches and hammer down my door. But nothing ever happened. Instead, McGrath sent me two checks, one for $1,000 and the other a bonus of $10,000. The next month, when he came into the office for a routine physical, I sent him a bill for $25. Two days later he was on the telephone, howling at me for my modest rate increase, "You shyster, you! You used to charge only twenty. Why is it now twenty-five?"

Within about two years, my toilet practice was literally bursting at the seams. I was now caring for several hundred patients. I was no longer broke. And I was beginning to get some exciting work that would help me combine the hard-to-reconcile allures of parasitology and the practice of general internal medicine.

In 1951, I became medical consultant and pathologist to the Arabian-American Oil Company, and twice each week I'd receive via their courier plane tissue samples of employees who had been stricken with rare diseases while stationed in the Middle East. In 1956, I was hired by the newly created Ford Foundation to help set up a health care system for their branch-office representatives around the world. Amebic dysentery had become my primary "gimmick," although I would soon take my fascination with the illness to a new stage by embarking on a long-term research project in Mexico to help solve the mystery of every tourist's enemy, Montezuma's Revenge.

For all that, though, the old restlessness was still with me. I left Al Barach's office and moved my practice a few blocks south to a new building at 710 Park Avenue. The rooms were roomier there, and I could now afford to serve my colleagues in the neighborhood better by expanding my laboratory capabilities. In addition to coprology, my staff and I could now also do blood chemistries, Pap smears—the whole gamut of clinical pathology. And, of course, I continued to see my growing gallery of eccentric patients on a private basis.

Every wanderer needs a home. In the spring of 1952, I decided it was time to put down stronger roots in my academic career, as well. I applied for a tenured post in tropical medicine at Cornell University Medical College on the Upper East Side.

I was particularly interested in this job because it was so much like the one denied me by Robert Loeb at Columbia P & S five years earlier. There was only one hurdle to clear first, and it was a high one—an interview with the redoubtable David Prestwick Barr, the chief of medicine at the New York Hospital–Cornell Medical Center. Barr, then in his late fifties, was a big name in medicine, having been responsible for an encyclopedic, multiauthored, three-volume work, *Modern Medical Therapy in General Practice*, that had strained the eyes and stretched the imaginations of several generations of medical students.

Portly, silver-haired, and soft-spoken, Barr had the courtly manner of a man trained in the old European tradition. (On retirement, he became the personal physician of Chiang Kai-shek in Taiwan.) Behind this fatherly exterior, however, ticked one of the shrewdest medical minds in the country. So when I was summoned to his office I was in a state of quiet panic. Failure was in the air. There was certainly little reason to expect that I'd be spending the next thirty-five years walking the corridors of Cornell.

Barr was famous for having perfected a bedside manner that extracted the maximum amount of information in the minimum amount of time without the patient being aware that he had been questioned at all, an experience a colleague once likened to having your appendix removed through your pants pocket while you were watching a baseball game. He had little trouble excising the pertinent details of my life—Columbia P & S, O'Connor, Panama, Germany, NYU. At the end of the interview, almost as an afterthought, he said, "Oh, that reminds me. You've been interested in malaria, haven't you?"

"Yes, sir," I said proudly. "I wrote several papers on malaria during my time in Panama."

"Well now, that is interesting," said Barr, sitting back in his big chair and forming a steeple with his fingertips. "You know, we have in the hospital at the present time a young child with malaria. I wonder . . ." he said, blushing with embarrassment, "I wonder if you might help all of us here understand exactly what we're dealing with."

Dr. Barr knew all about malaria, of that I was quite sure. This was the trick question, cloaked in disarming innocence, I had been told to expect. My future at Cornell, I was willing to bet, rested on my ability to give the professor a satisfactory response. So I proceeded with caution, asking him to outline the case for me. He explained that the child was ten years old and suffered from thalassemia major, a blood disease of children in which the red cells, normally elliptical in shape, become rounded. The defective cells are easily destroyed by the body, and the result is high fever, enlargement of the spleen, and, all too often, early death.

Barr continued: "The child developed a high fever and, because it persisted for several days, we finally decided it would be wise to look for malaria. As it turns out, that is precisely what he had. But how did a child contract malaria in Manhattan?"

I had one question: "Has the child ever been out of the United States?"

"Never."

With the audacity that comes from an intimate knowledge of the subject, I announced peremptorily—and perhaps a little too loudly: "The child is of Italian extraction. A transfusion was given with the father's blood. He is in all probability a shoemaker who left Sicily twenty years ago. The type of malaria the boy has is quartan. He can be easily cured."

Dr. Barr seemed impressed. "You have heard about this case then?" I said no, and went on to explain the reasoning behind my diagnostic conclusions. Because of its wholesale destruction of the blood, thalassemia major requires its victims to undergo frequent transfusions. Forty years ago, most transfusions were still given by a direct donor—almost invariably the father.

To a malariologist, the rest was simple. It was obvious the father had unwittingly infected his son with the malaria parasite. He hadn't suffered the symptoms of the disease for years, otherwise he would not have offered to transfuse his son. Quartan is the only type of malaria that survives in the human host so quietly for so long. After twenty years or so, the parasite would be hard to detect in the routine screening of the donor's blood prior to the transfusion.

How did I know the father was Italian? That was easy. Thalassemia major is a hereditary disease, particularly common among the children of first-generation Italian immigrants. Quartan malaria is also endemic to the Mediterranean. The part about the Sicilian shoemaker I threw in for dramatic effect.

My snap diagnosis worked like magic on Dr. Barr. Instead of offering me one job, he offered me three—head of clinical tropical medicine at New York Hospital, head of the parasitology laboratory at the same institution, and assistant professor of public health at Cornell. It was a package deal, he said—"all three or nothing." Not knowing whether to laugh or cry, I accepted, and then immediately regretted the decision. How on earth was I going to find the time to keep my private practice going on Park Avenue and hold down three separate jobs at Cornell? Altogether, they paid $5,000 a year—only slightly more than I was making at my one NYU job.

Practice on staid Park Avenue, meanwhile, was becoming more and more offbeat. I hadn't been in my new office at 710 Park Avenue long, for instance, when Salvador Dali walked through the door. The great surrealist suffered from amebic dysentery, and another physician had referred him to me.

The waiting room was small, narrow, and dull, with a sparsely upholstered banquette and two equally uncomfortable chairs. Even so, Dali entered it as though walking onto a floodlit stage. Elongated, aristocratic, and haughty, he wore a black silk cape and a high black felt fedora, and carried a walking stick with a gold ornament on top. The other patients lowered their magazines to get a good look at this strange vision.

Cora Burke, my receptionist, said, "Take a seat, Mr. Dali. The doctor will be with you shortly." Dali gazed down his long aquiline nose at Cora and snorted. With a flourish of his famous high-twirled mustachios, he spun on his heel, his cape whipping around, and strode into the L-shaped waiting area. I happened to be passing Cora's desk in time to see him come to an abrupt stop in the middle of the floor. He hoisted a monocle to his brow and inspected the wall with obvious fascination.

On the walls were three paintings. There was a Manet—a cheap reproduction costing only a few dollars—depicting a misty country scene. There was a faded, yellowing lithograph of Van Gogh's "Sun Flowers" of similar value. The third piece was an original of which I was proud, a watercolor of a hobo who bore an uncanny resemblance to my old friend from Greenwich Village, the writer Maxwell Bodenheim. I'd purchased it on a sidewalk in the Village from the artist himself, and it had set me back nearly sixty dollars.

As Dali continued to survey my collection of ersatz art, his nostrils began to quiver as if he'd caught a whiff of something exceedingly foul. He raised his walking stick over his head and, for a moment, I thought he would strike either the paintings, one of my other patients, Cora Burke, or myself. Instead, he simply twirled about once again, summoned a large wad of phlegm from his throat, spat into the center of the waiting room carpet, and walked out.

That was not the last I'd see of Dali, however. The artist's dysentery was chronic, and he was forced to return often. He was invariably accompanied by his ferocious wife, Gala, who also suffered from the illness. This was hardly surprising considering their lifestyle. In New York, they lived at the St. Regis on the corner of Fifth Avenue and Fifty-fifth Street. In Spain, where they spent most of their time, however, they returned to the earth—which meant eating the local vegetables and drinking the water. They were constantly reinfecting themselves, though eventually I had some luck in treating them.

Gala was a formidable woman—almost as tall and spindly as Dali, with the hooked features of one of Macbeth's witches and an accent more Russian than Spanish. She was maniacally jealous of Dali and made sure that no one spoke to him for more than a few minutes without interrupting—and terminating—the conversation. But to Dali she was the Madonna, his angel, his Platonic ideal of Woman. His depiction of her as a voluptuous creature dominating the foreground or hovering in the background of so many of his paintings came as a shock to anyone who had ever met her in the flesh.

For all her faults, though, Gala's devotion to Dali was admirable beyond question, even if it did tend to run to extremes. It was her habit, for instance, to inspect Dali's every bowel movement personally. She would then plan the artist's diet for the following day based upon her interpretation of the great man's stool.

I wasn't totally ignorant of Dali's reputation. I knew, for instance, that his surrealism and his status as an artist meant that he did not, as a rule, paint people's portraits. On a dare, however, I was persuaded by a friend, a woman of great persuasive beauty, to ask Dali if he would consent to do her portrait. To my surprise, Dali knew the woman and agreed.

This brought up the embarrassing question of price. How much did someone of Dali's caliber charge for a personal portrait? Dali didn't appear the least bit embarrassed. "If you wish me to do the head—only the head," he said in his accented, highly nasal English, "it will be five thousand dollars."

Five thousand dollars was a lot of money, but, considering

Dali's stature, and that his paintings were then fetching many times that amount, it sounded like a reasonable deal.

"Of course," he continued, "if you wish to include the torso, too, that will be ten thousand. If you wish a full-length portrait, that will be fourteen thousand."

I was curious about how the artist might render his subject. "Oh, that is no problem," he said. "The painting will be that of a fish."

"A fish? Do you mean the subject will be recognizable as a person within the fish, or that she will become a fish herself?"

"That," he said, flinging his hands in the air, "is not something that can be decided now. That must wait until the first sitting."

I was confused. "But if it's a head, for instance, will it be a fish?"

"Yes."

"What if it's a torso?"

"A fish."

"A full-length portrait will be a fish, too?"

"Of course," said Dali, with a heavy sigh.

I thought I was catching on. "You mean it will be the same fish, regardless of whether you do the head, the torso, or the full-length portrait?"

"Exactly!"

"Same size?"

"Same size."

"Same fish?"

"Same fish."

"Then what's the difference?"

"There is no difference to me, only to you. If you want the head, you will get the head. If you want the torso, I'll give you the torso, and so on."

I was confused again. "All three will be the same fish but each with a different price?"

"Why, of course!"

I decided against commissioning the painting. Obviously, I still had far too much to learn about the world of art.

Ignorance of that magnitude can be dangerous, as I soon discovered.

A few blocks south of my office at 710 Park was a large, turn-of-the-century mansion owned by Henry Esterhase, financier, banker, philanthropist. By the time I met him in 1950 he was dying of old age. His regular physician would ask me to visit the big house from time to time and draw a blood sample or do a urinalysis. Toward the end, my trips became more frequent as his medical care intensified. Then one day, shortly after one such visit, I read in the newspaper that he had died.

Three months later, I received a telephone call from Esterhase's attorney and executor. It was an embarrassing exchange. "Dr. Kean," he said, "we would appreciate it if you would allow yourself to be interviewed by a private investigator, who has been retained by the estate and by the Metropolitan Museum of Art."

"Why?"

"We want to obtain information about a very valuable piece of porcelain that is missing from the Esterhase collection. It was willed to the Metropolitan, and now it has disappeared."

What did that have to do with me, I asked, a little indignantly. "Think nothing of it," he said airily. "We simply want to talk to anybody who was in the mansion during the last couple of weeks before Mr. Esterhase's death." Then, ominously: "You may have your lawyer present, if you wish." My pulse quickened and my mouth went dry. Obviously, I was being considered a prime suspect in this terrible crime.

That afternoon the detective appeared in my office, a man who had obviously never read Dashiell Hammett, for he was small, sleek, well-mannered, and nattily dressed. He was also informed, persistent, and irritating. He explained that an extremely valuable Lalique vase—blue, eight inches tall, irreplaceable—had disappeared from the Esterhase household. A subsequent search had failed to find it. It had been stolen.

"Why are you asking me about it?" I blurted out. The detective stared at me, his eyes narrowing with suspicion.

"Well, Dr. Kean," he said, "you *did* visit Mr. Esterhase the day before he died. And the vase *was* in the room." He went on to explain that others had confirmed that the piece was in the room, on the far mantle, up to the time of my visit. After that, its whereabouts had become murky. Did I remember seeing it?

I did not. I denied knowing anything about the jar. I huffily assured the investigator that I didn't take it, all the while fighting to keep my anger in check. "Let me remind you," I said, "I went to that house to care for a sick man."

He seemed to accept the implausibility of a doctor copping a piece of art from a dying man's room. He closed his notebook, rose from his chair, and walked into the outer office. Suddenly, I heard a commotion. The detective was shouting, "There it is! There it is!"

When I emerged from my office, I saw him pointing to something on the desk belonging to Cora Burke. Perched on one corner was a small, exquisitely decorated blue vase filled with pencils. I vaguely remembered having noticed it before, but then it wasn't my habit to stop and examine pencil holders, however attractive.

The man, whose whole demeanor had given way to intense excitement, continued to shout, "That's the vase! That's the Lalique!" He picked it up, dumped the pencils on Cora's desk, and, hands trembling, examined it for chips and scratches. He then looked up at me, an expression of grim satisfaction on his face. "Never heard of it before, huh?" he said sarcastically.

Inwardly, I heard the prison doors clang shut. "Cora," I asked, "where did you get this jar?"

Cora promptly burst into tears. "Oh, I knew I shouldn't have done it, Dr. Kean," she wailed. "But it's so beautiful."

"But Cora, how did you get the jar?"

"It came from Mr. Eh-eh-esterhase," she blubbered. "The day before he died, the butler brought over this brown paper bag with a urine specimen inside. The specimen was in the jar." My jaw dropped in unison with the detective's. Cora continued: "I took it back to the lab and told Alice Moeller to do the urinalysis. I told her to wash the jar very carefully, and I would use it on my desk. It's so-o-o pretty."

The mystery had solved itself. Told to provide a urine specimen, Esterhase, confused and dying, had availed himself of the most convenient receptacle, which just happened to be his priceless Lalique vase. The detective departed without another word. Presumably the elegant urinal eventually found its way to the Metropolitan Museum of Art. I never had the courage to check.

CHAPTER 7

A Tapeworm from the Tundra

H arry Benjamin was one of the great heroes of Park Avenue medicine. Small, bald, pink-cheeked, Harry was a devout Swiss Lutheran who eventually gained national recognition as the father of the sex-change operation in America. Beginning in the late forties, he pioneered the standard method for liberating those men who, desperately trapped inside male bodies, felt Nature had always intended for them the role of women. Over the years, Harry helped ease the psychological hardships of hundreds of such patients, including those of the famous Christine Jorgensen, the subject of the first widely publicized gender modification involving an American citizen.

But in 1955, Harry was ready for a change himself, and so was I. He wanted to retire and I needed a bigger office. So I quickly assembled the extravagant sum of a thousand dollars that Harry wanted as down payment on his luxurious office at 728 Park Avenue, moved in before he could change his mind, and set up the private clinic that would serve as my base of operations for the next three decades. Most of my patients, rich or not-so-rich, accomplished or anonymous, were quiet, unassuming, solid citizens. Still, the ranks of certifiable eccentrics continued to grow. None perhaps was more unusual, or challenging, however, than Charles Putnam Tetchner, the Canadian uranium king, who turned up unannounced on October 27, 1955, to report an odd fluttering in his upper intestine.

Tetchner was then well up into his seventies and counted his fortune in the billions. Until the tender age of fifty-seven, he had eked out a living as a hermit prospector on the lower cusp of the Arctic Circle. Then one day, while digging a new outhouse for himself, he had accidentally shoveled his way into the mother lode. Ever since, "Tetch," as his few friends called him (or "Tetched," as he was known to his many enemies in tribute to his maniacal temper), divided his time between a remote miner's cabin on the Yukon River and an ornate penthouse atop the Queen Elizabeth Hotel in Montreal. Gnarled and taciturn, Tetchner was short—barely five feet tall—with catlike green eyes buried in a wizened walnut of a face. It was a face that advertised dark ferocities and people instinctively gave him a very wide berth.

Still, this tough little character from the creeks wasn't prepared for the news when I told him his X rays showed that, deep within his washboard-hard belly, he harbored a beef tapeworm the length of the average garden hose.

The old man reacted belligerently, demanding to know why I was wasting time "jawing" when "that sonofabitch is suckin' out my life's blood." I hurriedly made arrangements with the patient for a follow-up visit the next day and managed to see him to the waiting room door without violent incident. Heaving a sigh of relief, I paused to ponder just what to expect from Mr. Tetchner and his parasitic intruder: the worm, I concluded, would be the least of my problems. One thing intrigued me, though. The tapeworm normally ran in pretty predictable company, afflicting the world's poor in astonishing numbers. But it was a rare disease for a billionaire. One of the titans of mining with a tapeworm? How the hell had he become infected?

The beef tapeworm, *Taenia saginata*, is one of a group of gutless, segmented flatworms that flourishes in the upper reaches of the human small intestine, just beyond the stomach. Pale yellow in color, it bears an uncanny, if unappetizing, resemblance to a single, very long strand of pasta—a sort of indented fettucini. Although the worm is as timid and generally benign as it is ugly, it suffers from a terrible image problem, which has to do with its two most horrifying attributes—its enormous length (often twenty feet or more), and a preference for some remarkably flamboyant toilet habits.

As parasites go, *T. saginata*, like its close cousins the pork tapeworm, *Taenia solium*, and the fish tapeworm, *Diphyllobothrium latum*, is a relatively well-behaved guest, causing little physical discomfort in its human host. Otherwise healthy individuals are apt to be oblivious to the presence of their helminthic intruder, although this state of blissful ignorance only intensifies the trauma when the inevitable day of reckoning arrives.

That day is usually accompanied by a highly predictable series of events. The worm, having grown longer and longer, is now obliged to jettison its posterior segments, or proglottids, to make way for new growth. Deposited in the bowel, a chain of these proglottids, usually measuring from two to three feet in length, is then expelled with the feces. Imagine the consternation of the unsuspecting victim when, casually turning to inspect his stool, he discovers several feet of worm writhing and wriggling in the toilet bowl! (Occasionally, a string of particularly muscular proglottids forces its way from the anus and crawls down the thigh on its own power, causing, in the words of one medical textbook, "a slight tickling sensation." Tickling sensation? Utter showstopping panic may be more like it!)

Of all the species of tapeworm, *T. saginata* is the ultimate cosmopolite, infecting an estimated fifty million people in a broad geographical band that covers sub-Saharan Africa, the Middle East, parts of the Soviet Union, South Asia, the Philippines, and Latin America. Humans everywhere acquire the parasite the same way—by eating raw or undercooked beef or lamb that has itself been infected. Less than a hundred cases are now reported in the United States each year, but like other diseases hard to justify to the folks at home, foreign travelers do occasionally bring tapeworms back as unintended souvenirs.

Even though few North Americans ever experience a tapeworm visitation, you can be quite sure that the sight of a chorus line of proglottids doing their macabre dance in the toilet bowl is enough to propel the unlucky few in the direction of the nearest parasitologist with considerable velocity.

It is hardly surprising then that C. P. Tetchner was a man in a hurry. He arrived thirty minutes early for his appointment the next morning and demanded immediate attention, despite a waiting room full of patients. He was accompanied by an "actress" of ambiguous credits named "Baby," a voluptuous blonde easily half his age and nearly twice his height.

The old prospector had been giving his "monster" some thought, he said, and had decided he'd acquired it during a trip to the Orinoco mines in the Amazon jungles of Venezuela earlier that same year. The trip, to inspect his considerable Latin American holdings, had been one of the "damn fool" mistakes of his life. It was the first time he had left North America and, he gave me to understand, it would be his last. He had been quick to appreciate the folly of foreign travel and, less than twenty-four hours after arriving at the Orinoco site, he was winging his way back to Canada. But he had not acted quite fast enough, because, somehow, he had acquired a tapeworm.

It was a pretty good diagnosis for a uranium king. In any event, his doctors up north—"damn quacks" he called them—had failed, after repeated attempts, to accurately diagnose his complaint. Eventually, one of the much-abused Canadian physicians threw himself on the mercy of Dr. Barr, begging him to get the redoubtable Tetch to New York and off his back. Dr. Barr, naturally, unloaded him on me.

"I hear tell you know worms better than any man alive," Tetchner said. "It's an unusual calling, I'll admit. But it's about time one of you blasted sawbones helped out a man with a god-damn monster gnawing away at his innards."

Tetchner was right. Hunting for tapeworms was an unusual way of making a living, but I felt his own vast peculiarities hardly qualified him to criticize my professional idiosyncrasy. Besides, I didn't like him. He made me nervous. Sitting on the edge of my examining table, taut and distrustful, he looked like a timber wolf sizing up its lunch. Next he demanded to know how I planned to "deliver the goods."

"The standard treatment," I explained uneasily, "is to have the patient swallow ten 100-milligram tablets of a powerful drug called Atabrine. The idea is to paralyze the worm's nervous system, causing it to release its suckers." I was then obliged to tell him that, unfortunately, it didn't always work that way. It took hours for the tablets to dissolve in the stomach, and, by that time, the medicine reaching the head of the parasite was usually so heavily diluted with gastric juices it did little good. If the suckers didn't release, you didn't get the head. No head, no cure.

Tetchner's green eyes narrowed menacingly, whereupon I hastened to assure him that his case would be different. For him, I said, I would roll out the heavy artillery. For him, I would create a "bullet" of chemicals so potent that no worm could possibly survive.

"First," I explained, "we pass a narrow tube through the nose, down the gullet, into the stomach, and out the pyloric sphincter into the duodenum. Once the tube is positioned near the parasite, we then shoot a full gram of medicine directly onto the worm's head. That provides a blast a thousand times more powerful than simply taking the drug orally. Three hours later you take a strong dose of salts, your bowels move, and the worm, now knocked out cold, is flushed from your life forever."

Tetchner's whole manner changed. Though a man of little formal education, he was quick to grasp the concept of treatment. He liked the idea of—as he put it—"clonking" the parasite on the head. Baby was full of maternal concern, however. Did the medicine have any dangerous side effects? Would the nasal tube hurt? What if the treatment didn't kill the worm, but only succeeded in getting it angry? Might it not go on a rampage "inside Tetchie's tummy"?

I assured Baby that the many tapeworms I had known were all pretty docile creatures, and I'd never observed the slightest hint of a vengeful spirit. As far as the operation itself went, I told her that it was virtually risk-free. The procedure was so simple, in fact, that—though I didn't tell Baby this—it could have been performed with excellent results in an igloo.

Tetch was raring to go. He wanted to check into the hospital the very next day. He had one stipulation, however. He wanted a small room, the smallest—and the cheapest—the institution could provide. Medical treatment was so outrageously expensive, and besides, he said, people were always trying to "take advantage" of a man of his means. Anyhow, he observed shrewdly, "nothin' ain't ever done in a big room that can't be done in a little one." I might have known C. P. Tetchner, like many of the superrich, was a cheapskate.

I picked up the telephone and called the hospital. The woman in admissions told me that all rooms, both large and small, were fully booked. The only thing available was a luxury suite on the seventeenth floor, a room normally reserved for foreign dignitaries, oil sheiks, or the just plain filthy rich. The going rate was a hundred and fifty dollars a day—or roughly a thousand dollars at today's prices.

A hundred and fifty dollars? Tetchner turned pale and looked as if he might go into cardiac arrest. Recovering momentarily, he said he'd changed his mind. He no longer wanted a room; he now wanted an entire floor. The woman on the telephone gasped. The hospital had never had such a request, she said, in a voice which made the whole idea seem somehow obscene.

Warily, Tetchner agreed to settle for the big VIP suite, a spacious corner empyrean in the Baker Pavilion which commanded a sweeping view of the East River and the stubbly outcroppings of Queens beyond, the room now destined to become the scene of the great Canadian worm hunt.

I was now totally absorbed with Tetchner's worm. Believe me, I wanted that parasite very badly. I had no intention of winding up on the old geezer's list of "goddamn quacks."

When the last patient left that evening and the office was quiet, I retired to my laboratory to prepare for the showdown. Unlocking my glass-paneled medicine cabinet, I reached for a large brown bottle marked "Atabrine" and poured ten tablets out on the table, huge yellow horse pills compacted like small chunks of concrete and covered with a thick protective glaze. Wrapping them in a single ply of waxed paper, I used a small sledgehammer to crush them into a fine powder. Pulverization was the key— even the tiniest granule could block the nose tube or syringe, and that meant certain failure. So I gave the powder a few extra whacks for good measure and then mixed it into thirty cubic centimeters of water. I prepared three batches, just in case. I was taking no chances.

At three o'clock the next afternoon, Charles Putnam Tetchner entered New York Hospital with all the fanfare of a midget general riding into battle. He was accompanied by the bounteous Baby, MacGregor Flood, his "financial advisor" and sidekick, and his bodyguard, an ex-Mountie of mountainous proportions with a lantern jaw and the implausible though not inappropriate name of Eddy Nelson. Dr. Barr, gracious and smiling, was on hand to welcome him to the VIP suite. Curious interns and residents, trying to appear nonchalant, crowded around for a look at the uranium baron.

To everyone's surprise, Tetchner proved himself to be a model patient. Normally an eater of huge volume, he tamely accepted a liquid diet for the evening. Offered a mild sedative at bedtime, he politely refused, saying that getting to sleep had never been a big problem for him. To be sure, the sound of deep, prodigious snoring was soon thundering through the corridors and gently rattling the windows in the "Tetchner Suite."

At precisely 6:30 the following morning, I walked into Tetchner's room. Flood, the Mountie, and Baby were already gathered around the bed, fluffing the old man's pillows and speaking words of encouragement. Sitting glumly in the middle of his nest, blinking his eyes nervously, Tetchner looked like a scrawny baby bird with ruffled feathers. "Today's the day, Tetchie," said Baby, patting the old man's hand. Tetch, his steely gaze fixed on the bedposts, appeared not to be listening.

I went to work quickly. Sitting Tetchner on the edge of the bed, I carefully cooled a four-foot length of clear rubber tubing in a tray of crushed ice. Then, raising his chin slightly, I inserted one end into the right nostril. No go. Despite the fact that Tetchner sported an enormous, hawklike proboscis for a man his size, the passageway was too tight.

Next I tried the left side. This time, the tube threaded easily, so I pushed it into the nasal cavity as far as it would go, dangled it for a moment at the top of the gullet, and then eased it down Tetchner's throat. The patient swallowed hard, and I continued to slowly feed more line until the tube entered the stomach. I then moved Tetchner onto his right side and into a semifetal position. From experience, I knew the natural undulations of the stomach muscles would do the rest. Within the hour they would jiggle and coax the tip of the tube through the pyloric sphincter and into place in the duodenum.

So far the procedure had produced only a few muffled grunts on Tetchner's part and none of the cussing and caterwauling I had feared. With all going smoothly, I slipped out to make quick rounds of other patients in the hospital.

At 7:30, when I returned to administer the knockout dose, the eyes of the Great White North were upon me. Baby, Flood, and Eddy Nelson, looking pale and frightened, stood frozen to their spots around the bed.

I filled a syringe with the predetermined amount of Atabrine solution. Then, with a dramatic gesture involving the wrist, I raised the nozzle of the nasogastric tube, tested the syringe in my other hand by giving it a tiny pre-ejaculatory squirt in the air, inserted the needle in the tube, and sent the yellow fluid coursing through the pipeline. I watched sixty seconds tick away on my wristwatch before flushing the medication down with another ten cubic centimeters of water. I then withdrew the tube gently and swiftly from Tetchner's beak.

"All done!" I said. "Now, Mr. Tetchner, you've got to wait patiently for the next three hours while the drug goes to work. Don't get up. Don't eat or drink anything. Above all, do not vomit. If you do, you won't retain enough medication to destroy the worm and all our efforts will have been wasted. So lie back, close your eyes, and try to relax."

Tetchner said nothing, but eyed me with hostility and nestled his head against his oversized pillows. Before Baby and I could tiptoe out into the hall, the sound of Tetch's guttering snores once again echoed throughout the wing.

"In about three hours," I whispered to Baby, "we'll give him a laxative to drink. Once that goes to work, the worm will be ours."

Just before nine o'clock I arrived at my Park Avenue office to start seeing my regular patients. Ten minutes later Cora Burke was on the intercom. Eddy Nelson was calling from Tetchner headquarters at New York Hospital.

"Dr. Kean? He's just turned over on his left side," said Nelson. "Is that significant?"

I assured him there was no problem and hung up. A few minutes later there was another call. This time, it was Flood on the line, speaking in a thick Gaelic brogue.

"Tetch 'as jest burped, laddie. What does that mean?"

The drill was repeated all morning long. No sooner had one

hung up than Miss Burke would buzz me again: "It's the other one."

At eleven, Flood telephoned with the astounding news that the nurse had just entered the room and looked like she was going to try to make Tetchner drink the laxative.

"Aren't you comin' over to administer it?" asked Flood, rolling his r's plaintively.

"No, that won't be necessary. All he has to do is drink it." And so it went.

Then came the big news. Around three o'clock Baby telephoned, her normally high-pitched voice now almost inaudibly squeaky with excitement. The worm was coming out, a full hour ahead of schedule. Good, I thought, that megadose of Atabrine has accelerated the climax.

To keep Tetchner company, Flood and Eddy Nelson had squeezed into the toilet with him. Hovering nearby at the end of a telephone extension cord, Baby treated me to a graphic, play-by-play of the action. There were sounds like those associated with heavy lifting and then the scuffling of feet, as if large pieces of furniture were being moved around the room. Occasionally, a deep male voice would shout out what could have been a rodeo cheer. Several minutes went by during which the whooping and hollering in the background died away to a confused, barely audible muffle of voices. Then came a long silence. Suddenly, Baby let out a bloodcurdling shriek.

"It's out! It's out!" she cried.

The nurse came on the line to confirm that the basin was indeed filled with an enormous tapeworm. I asked her to telephone Patricia Daniels in the hospital's tropical medicine unit and have her keep an eye on things until I could get over there. If we had been lucky enough to get the head of the worm, Pat, a master lab technician, would be able to identify it immediately.

Before I could duck out of my office, the telephone rang again. This time, it was Pat Daniels, and she sounded panicky.

"Dr. Kean," she said, "you've got to get over here fast."

"What's the trouble?"

"There's a man with a gun over here."

"What?"

"Yes, Tetchner's people have removed the worm from the bedpan. They've got it draped back and forth on that big couch at the end of the room. It must be at least thirty or forty feet long. They've got what looks like the head end lying on a cushion. Mr. Tetchner's got a hand lens and I guess he's trying to find the head himself. But he doesn't have a stitch of clothes on. The man with the gun, a heavy-set little fellow, who calls everybody 'laddie'—"

"That would be Mr. Flood—"

"Yes, he's standing behind the couch waving a pistol, saying, 'Nobody's gonna look at that thing except for Mr. Tetchner or Dr. Kean.' "

"Is that all?"

"Well, the lady they call Baby seems to be hysterical. She's running back and forth wringing her hands and laughing and crying all at once. Then there's a tall man without a gun who's just standing in the corner looking like he's going to be sick."

I put down the receiver, ran out into my waiting room, and, seeing it filled with patients, shouted, "Emergency" at the top of my lungs and rushed out the door.

When I arrived at the hospital, the scene was just as Pat had described. Flood was brandishing a revolver all right, and clearly had the drop on the worm, which, at the moment, appeared to be reclining peaceably on the couch. I told Flood I thought I could take it from here and moved in to pick up the parasite. Starting with the posterior segments, I wound the seemingly endless body around a glass cylinder. I finally reached the proximal tip where the head was normally found and, pressing it between two glass slides, borrowed Pat's low-power microscope to have a good look.

"Mr. Tetchner, victory is ours! Meet *Taenia saginata*, the beef tapeworm!"

Tetch was still keyed up. "Are you sure?" he said, peering through the lens at the tiny suckers protruding from a head no bigger than that of a pin. He turned from the microscope to compare what he'd seen there with diagrams in medical textbooks he'd strewn around the suite. Gradually, though, I could see that he was allowing himself to accept the fact that our mission had been a success.

"Okay, we got it," he said at last. "Now take that big bastard out of here."

Pat took the worm, as instructed, and fled. Meanwhile, Tetchner's condition was already visibly much improved. Still clad only in his birthday suit, the uranium king, grinning wildly, strode up and down the room, pounding his chest with his stubby fists.

"I cannot believe this!" he crowed. "The worm is dead! The sonofabitch is a goner!" With an exuberant gesture, he then motioned everyone to clear out of the room with the exception of Flood and myself. "Flood," he said, "get the suitcase."

The chubby moneyman went into the closet, rummaged around for a few seconds, then emerged with a ragged leather grip, which he opened on the bed. My eyes popped. It was filled to the brim with hundred-dollar bills. Tetchner grabbed a fistful of money, started to count it out loud, then changed his mind, and proceeded to shove fistfuls of bills into my coat pockets.

The sight of so much cash rendered me momentarily speechless. When I finally found my tongue, I stammered something ridiculous about it having been a great honor knowing him and, backing toward the door, I promised to telephone him later that evening to see how he was getting along.

Tetchner simply looked away and grunted. "Come on, Flood," he said, "let's get the hell out of here."

The wheels of the taxi barely seemed to touch the ground as I skimmed home with the cash bulging in my pockets. My mind spun with daydreams about how I would spend it all. I could see myself standing on the beach at Cap d'Antibes on the Riviera, deeply suntanned and looking out to sea. I tooled along the boulevards of the mind in a low, sleek Jaguar of midnight blue. Surely Tetchner's energetic stuffing of greenbacks would, at 1950s prices, put such treasures within my grasp.

When I reached my apartment, I bolted through the door and headed for the bedroom, picking myself up a double shot of bourbon on the way. I emptied my pockets on the bed and started counting. One, two, three, four, five. . . . Before I had tallied up a thousand dollars, the telephone rang. It was Charles Putnam Tetchner calling from his suite at the Waldorf.

"Kean, you still got that money I give you?"

"Of course, I do. It's been less than an hour since you gave it to me."

"Good," said the uranium king. "I've been thinking. How'd you like to go into business with me?"

I could scarcely believe my ears. "Mr. Tetchner," I croaked, "I would be delighted."

"Okay," Tetchner said. "Bring that money down here pronto and we'll get the deal rolling."

I rushed to the kitchen and found a brown paper bag to carry the money in. Before long, I was standing, sack in hand, in the chandelier-lit radiance of the penthouse on the thirty-fourth floor of the Waldorf. (On his trips to New York, Tetchner either stayed there or across Lexington Avenue at the Beverly Hotel, where a double room then cost eight dollars a night.)

Tetchner had added to his attire since our last meeting. He was now wearing a suit of red long johns, a pair of scuffed black oxfords, and argyle socks. At the moment, he happened to be dancing a kind of Indian rain dance, tempo allegro, in the middle of the thickly carpeted parlor, punctuating spry steps with ear-splitting war whoops. He interrupted his movements when he saw me come in.

"Kean," he said, "that goddamn worm was sucking out my life's blood. But he's gone now, the little pissant. Look here, I can even dance again."

While Tetch demonstrated a few more steps in slow motion, Baby joyously clapped her hands, making little birdlike hops on the balls of her feet. Flood and Eddy Nelson stood close by, beaming and silent. The boss was whole again, and the world was spinning in its grooves.

When Tetchner stopped dancing, he motioned for Flood and me to join him in the master bedroom. "Flood," he ordered, nodding in the direction of my paper sack. "Count that money."

"Eight thousand three hundred dollars, Tetch."

"Okay, Flood, here's what you do. Take Kean's money and match it. That'll give you about sixteen thousand. Then go buy some mining leases for the Doctor here. We'll make a rich feller outta him yet."

Again, I found myself struggling for words. "Mr. Tetchner," I said, "I don't know how to thank you. Just let me say it's a great honor to be going into business with you."

Tetchner smiled benevolently, like a not wholly trustworthy Rumpelstiltskin. "Don't mention it, Kean. Just one thing, though. Don't tell nobody about our little deal till Flood here gets back to you with the details. Around Christmastime, I'd reckon."

The next morning I hurried to Dr. Barr's office at Cornell.

"Dr. Barr, we're rich," I declared, reporting in detail the transactions of the previous evening. Great wealth was a new experience for me, and I was suddenly flush with feelings of magnanimity and good will toward my fellow man. I told Dr. Barr I was cutting him in on the deal. It was only fair that we split the proceeds down the middle, since he had introduced me to Tetchner in the first place.

Dr. Barr, always the soul of honor, said that his position at the hospital prevented him from accepting the money as a personal fee. He would be quite happy to take it on behalf of medical research, however. How appropriate, I thought. Charles Putnam Tetchner would serve not only the interests of Ben Kean, but through Kean the noble cause of scientific advancement. And all because of the humble tapeworm! I told the good doctor I'd let him know as soon as word came from Montreal.

The weeks passed slowly. Just before Christmas, a letter arrived from Montreal by certified mail. The envelope announced, in authoritatively raised letters, that it was from the offices of C. P. Tetchner. With its heavy, textured paper, it had the very heft of great fortune.

I had to marvel at the way these business tycoons operated. Say what you would about the cut and thrust of major league business, these fellows knew how to keep to a bargain. Jumpy with excitement, I raced to Dr. Barr's office with the unopened letter burning a hole in my vest pocket.

I found Dr. Barr, normally a genial but subdued man, in rollicking spirits. It was the funniest thing, he said, but he, too, had received a letter from Tetchner that very minute. Without further delay, we each tore open our respective envelopes.

The letters were identical. They each began, "Dear Friend," a tone that struck me, quite frankly, as just a little impersonal for an exchange between fellow mining magnates. I read on.

In the sprightly manner of the form letter, it said that, for the Yuletide holidays, we were each being sent five pounds of Canadian smoked baby bull jerky. Mr. Tetchner, the letter said, hoped that we would enjoy this traditional frontier delicacy as much as he did himself.

I looked at Dr. Barr. His face was flushed with embarrassment. I must have looked stunned, too, because I distinctly remember feeling my mouth hanging open. After a long pause he looked at me with an odd expression, something between a smile and a grimace, and quietly said, as if to himself, "Bull, indeed."

Suffice it to say, Charles Putnam Tetchner and I did not become fellow uranium barons. Tetchner never again mentioned the leases, and I was too embarrassed to raise the issue myself.

Our relationship didn't end there, however. For better or

worse, Tetchner remained my patient for nearly twenty years, and, for most of that period, religiously flew to New York every six months for his regular checkup. On one such visit, when he was well past ninety, he checked into New York Hospital for a battery of tests designed to determine if he had a serious ailment of his head or chest or gut, each of which had their own agenda of chronic complaints.

Just before he left the hospital I worked up the courage to ask him about the issue that had nagged at our doctor–patient relationship all those years.

"Mr. Tetchner," I said, "do you recall years ago when I cured you of your tapeworm right here in this hospital?" Did he recall how he had crammed my pockets with eighty-three hundred-dollar bills and how, an hour later at the Waldorf, he had relieved me of the money on the promise of mining leases that never materialized? Flood, I told him, had never got back in touch.

Tetchner did not appear astonished by the news. Quite the contrary. The old man cackled maniacally.

"Yes," he said, "I remember just as plain as day. I guess ole Flood sort of put one over on you."

"Put one over on me?"

"Yes, I don't recall that he ever did buy those leases for you," the old man said, his green eyes twinkling with malicious delight. "You ought to be more careful who you do business with."

CHAPTER 8

Curtain Calls

T he trouble with you, Ben," an exasperated Edna Ferber once said, as the author of the bestselling novels *Saratoga Trunk* and *Giant* perched herself on the edge of my examining table, "is that I want to talk about my blood pressure and all you want to talk about are my plot lines!"

This kind of allegation used to make me angry. But I don't deny it anymore. How could I? A search of my files would be just as likely to disgorge a newspaper clipping about a patient's latest financial coup on Wall Street (or his arrest in an insider trading scam) as his medical history, or turn up a review of another's controversial new screenplay along with her chest X rays and blood tests.

Yes, I must confess that ever since I stopped being afraid of them my patients have never ceased to fascinate me. So many of them have led such exciting lives! Lawyers who defended famous gangsters. Financiers who dealt in billions. Writers who won their Pulitzers. Long before a successful play would be produced, an important movie released, a great book written, the early plans, the dreams, and the agonizing work would be reviewed as I was about to listen to a heart or pass a proctoscope. It still surprises me that I actually got paid for caring for these unusual, stimulating people.

CURTAIN CALLS

Patients make marvelous captives. Once you've got them in an examining gown with a tongue depressor down their throat they are usually ready to surrender stories that give new meaning to the phrase "the human condition." Willie had spent ten days in Alaska on a fishing trip—or so his wife thought. In truth, he had been holed up in the Waldorf all that time with her sister. Mrs. T, married to an international playboy for thirty years and before that the girlfriend of many men-about-town, finally let me do a Pap test. She was a virgin! Mr. P had three sons. Mrs. P stated that each had a different father—none her husband.

But of all the patients who have come through my door on Park Avenue over the years, I must confess a fatal attraction to one special breed—the doers in the theater. I can't fully account for this affliction, but it had a reasonably precise date of onset—1925.

That was the year my family moved from East Orange to Bank Street in Greenwich Village. Not too far way—a short, exhilarating hop on roller skates—was the Civic Repertory Theatre, where Eva Le Gallienne, who was probably the best known actress for two or three generations of theatergoers, was the headliner. Chekhov, Turgenev, Ibsen, and Shakespeare were the playwrights. I guess I must have nursed a boyhood crush on the beautiful, elegant Le Gallienne, but I know I fell in love for keeps with the plays. At twenty-five cents, matinees were relatively cheap, and I was soon hopelessly addicted. Small wonder theater people became my favorite patients.

Going over some old medical records, I was amused to find a bill dated July 1, 1958—"Oscar Hammerstein, For Professional Services Rendered, $100.00"—with the further notation, "This includes complete medical survey and physical examination, X-ray studies, electrocardiogram, basal metabolic test, multiple laboratory examinations, and chemical studies." Today, the same review would run upwards of $500. Could rates have been so much lower back then?

Oscar Hammerstein II was born on the Upper West Side on July 12, 1895, and named for his grandfather, O. H. I, one of New York's great impresarios of opera and the musical stage. His father, William, was a director of the Victoria Theatre, a vaudeville house in Times Square. In 1942, he teamed up with Richard Rodgers and their collaboration eventually produced such Broadway hit musicals as *Oklahoma!, The King and I, Carousel, South Pacific,* and *The Sound of Music.*

Hammerstein was a big, lovable bear of a man, with a round, pitted face, a bulky body, and a lumbering gait. Not exactly what you would call handsome, but his personality radiated a gentle, thoughtful, caring intelligence that was hard to resist. I became his physician in the early fifties when I "inherited" him from Harold Hyman, although it was really his wife Dorothy's hostility toward me that was responsible for bringing us together in the first place.

Following my return to New York in 1947, it became my custom to dine at the "21" Club at least once a month. In the City's rigid social pecking order, "21," originally a Roaring Twenties speakeasy, prided itself on being not so much a restaurant as a private club, where the service one received varied sharply according to one's status. If you were known to the management, it was a four-star restaurant. If you weren't, it was a no-star restaurant.

Seating determined everything. Unspoken rules designated the dining room on the second floor for the care and feeding of the "tourists"—those who would occasionally turn up to gawk at the celebrity clientele, none of whom, unfortunately, were ever on the second floor. I did my gawking on the ground floor, the epicenter of the serious hobnobbing. But even there the pecking order was rugged business. The first room on the left, smaller than either the one in the center, or the secluded area just beyond the standup bar, was *the* fast lane. Above the tinkling of martini and champagne glasses could always be heard a litany of big names—Bing Crosby, John O'Hara, Harold Ross, the Drexels, the Woodwards, the generals, the financiers, the politicians.

From where I usually sat, on the outer perimeter just a table away from being bumped upstairs into coach class, it took a good pair of ears to stay tuned into the social swirl.

Then one evening there was a fortuitous mix-up. When we entered the lobby, my date and I were inexplicably shown to a highly strategic table within the charmed circle. Instead of reveling in my good luck, however, I began to feel uncomfortable, sure that at any moment the maitre d' would discover his error and banish us in humiliation to a lesser location. While I was stewing, Oscar Hammerstein and his wife, Dorothy, walked in. We exchanged greetings (Harold Hyman, who was still Hammerstein's doctor in those days, had previously introduced us) and they were seated—but not at a "good" table.

The next morning at ten o'clock, I received a telephone call from an apoplectic Dr. Hyman. "What the hell do you think you're doing, Kean," he fumed. What on earth did he mean? Dorothy Hammerstein had just called him, he said, to complain about my "behavior."

"I don't remember doing anything wrong," I protested weakly.

"Oh no?" said Hyman. "For starters, you had a much better table than Oc and Dorothy, and she finds that completely unacceptable." He then explained that, on general principles, Dorothy felt that a "young doctor" (I was then a mere slip of a lad at thirty-seven) had no business being seen in a place like "21," since it was obvious that I could not possibly afford it. "Wise up," concluded Hyman, in his usual diplomatic fashion, and hung up.

Chagrined, I didn't return to "21" for several months. When I did manage to work up my courage and go back, the senior owner, Mac Kriendler, whisked me to a choice table and reported that dinner that evening would be with the compliments of Mr. Oscar Hammerstein, who hoped I would accept his apologies, dinner, and a bottle of the best champagne. I found out later that Oc had learned of Dorothy's diatribe on his next visit to Dr.

Hyman and wanted to make amends. I was never again consigned to social Siberia. Oc Hammerstein and I became friends.

One afternoon in the early winter of 1951, while I was busy seeing patients at 728 Park Avenue, Hammerstein telephoned me from New Haven, Connecticut, where he was rehearsing *The King and I* for its debut on Broadway. He was calling about his leading lady, Gertrude Lawrence, and he sounded desperate.

"Ben," he said, "Get up here right away. Gertie's lost her voice."

How long had she been sick? "Almost a week, Ben," said Oc, adding with obvious pain, "This is the most expensive production we've ever done. We've got an extraordinary cast. But everything depends on Gertie. It's just a week till opening night here, and she can't sing a note. She can't even talk. We're sunk."

I told him not to panic, I would be right up. I then called Sam Rosen, the best nose and throat man I knew, and within the hour we were racing up the Merritt Parkway toward New Haven in my little black Ford.

When we arrived at the Taft Hotel, Oc Hammerstein and Dick Rodgers were waiting to usher us into Lawrence's room. Gertie, wearing a silk robe, no makeup, and the languid expression of a patient at the end of her rope, was propped up in bed on multiple pillows. Standing guard, with arms crossed in a belligerent pose, was Fanny Holtzmann, a well-known Manhattan attorney who represented Gertie.

The impresarios departed and left us with our patient, but Holtzmann refused to budge. Under no circumstances, she said, would she permit us to examine her client if she were not present.

Sam shrugged his shoulders and went to work. He took an otolaryngologic history from the patient, who responded "yes" or "no" by nodding or shaking her head. Finally, it came time for the standard physical examination. But when Lawrence rose and started to disrobe, Holtzmann nearly blew a gasket. "No," she said, "there will be none of that." She would permit us to examine nothing but the throat itself. Rolling his eyes heavenward, Sam pulled out his instruments and proceeded to conduct a thorough reconnaissance of the throat, pharynx, and larynx.

Sam and I then retired to our room. As soon as I closed the door, I asked Sam what he'd seen. "Nothing," he replied. "I didn't see a damn thing. This is the strangest case of laryngitis I've ever come across." We decided to go ahead and treat the patient with a special spray Rosen had developed and simply hope that her condition would improve.

For the next three days, Sam and I lived next door to Gertrude Lawrence. Every four hours, Sam slipped into her bedroom to spritz her nose and throat with a concoction of glycerin, adrenaline, and sugar. After more than a dozen treatments, the star of the show was still unable to utter a single vowel. Sam and I were stumped. We called a conference with Oc and Dick, and Rosen told them how, medically speaking, there was no reason Lawrence shouldn't be able to warble like a songbird. Her vocal cords weren't paralyzed, they moved under proper stimulation, but no sounds came out. "I am useless to you," Sam declared and left for New York that evening.

Rodgers and Hammerstein were now in a complete state. They pleaded with me to stay on, suggesting I try all known traditional methods of treatment, including having the patient breathe vapors from a steam kettle. That night I attended the rehearsal next door at the Schubert Theater. It was now less than three days until opening night. Yul Brynner, the "King," was bothered by all the delays, but the show simply could not go on without Gertie.

At three o'clock the next morning I suddenly sat up in bed. I had the solution! Somehow, my subconscious had been working on a cure all along, and now I had it. I called a groggy Hammerstein and said, "Oc, I know what's the matter with Gertie. Sam Rosen can't help her. I can't help her. But you and Dick can." Fifteen minutes later Oc, Dick, and I met in Hammerstein's room. The impresarios were sleepy-eyed but listened intently.

"Gentlemen," I said, "there's absolutely nothing the matter

with her voice, and nothing we do medically will bring it back. She can't sing for one very good reason—she wants to dance."

Dick Rodgers looked at me as if I had lost my mind. "What do you mean, she wants to dance?" he said irritably. "She *is* a dancer. She started out as a dancer. She's danced all her life." I was perfectly aware of the fact that Gertie Lawrence had come to America from England as a chorus girl in the 1924 production of *Charlot's Revue*; Dorothy Hammerstein had been a member of the same cast.

"That's just it," I said. "She thinks of herself as a dancer, not a singer. Two things are driving her crazy. One, she has no dance number in the show. Two, she is being overshadowed by Yul Brynner and needs another song or two—especially a song that she can sing." Everyone knew Gertie's singing was not as accomplished as her dancing.

Rodgers looked stunned. If Oc was big and ursine, Dick was the small, quick, sharp-witted fox. He could be suave, gracious, cool, and brilliant. At the moment, however, he was wound exceedingly tight. Turning to Hammerstein, he said, "I always thought you were making up these stories about 'Kean's miracle cures,' but now I realize this man is either completely crazy or he's on to something. Anyhow, it's worth a try. If she wants to dance, we'll let her dance. We'll go to work on a couple of extra songs."

They worked fast. At eleven o'clock that morning, Oc, Dick, and I went to Lawrence's room. Rodgers did the talking. "Gertie," he said, "voice or no voice, you're still the star of our show. So we've decided that, even if you can't sing, we'll take advantage of your talent and your beauty anyway. We're going to add a new dance number for you, and, somehow, we'll proceed that way until you get your voice back."

Rodgers described one of the numbers the boys had been working on that morning. It was a dance in which the English governess, the Lawrence role, circled the King's bed while it slowly dawns on the monarch that she happens to be a very fetching woman. It would be accompanied by an expanded version of the song, "Shall We Dance," which could, if necessary, be whispered. Gertie nodded her head in approval. There was another song, a brand new one, said Dick. It was called "Getting to Know You." He hummed a few bars. Gertie tilted her head and smiled.

That night Gertrude Lawrence, as Anna Leonowens, appeared on stage for the first time in a week and proceeded to dance lightly around the King's bed. The next day she was able to render the words of "Getting to Know You" in a kind of soft croaking voice. Two days later her laryngitis was completely cured. Opening night in New Haven, February 26, 1951, was a triumph. I returned to New York in high spirits, humming the melody of "Getting to Know You" under my breath all the way home. Along with a check for services rendered, the boys sent me two tickets for the Broadway opening on March 29. Afterwards, I went back stage and on to a party at Sardi's. To this day I don't know if Gertie ever knew how she got her immortal song.

Medicine is like waiting on tables, hairdressing, or auto repair in at least one important respect: one satisfied customer leads to four. Oc Hammerstein introduced me to a couple of his friends and, before I knew it, I had a large roster of patients from Broadway and Hollywood. None of them was more memorable, however, than the irrepressible Sigmund Romberg.

Romberg—cheery, rotund, more Viennese than schnitzel (no, he was more Hungarian than goulash)—was America's answer to Gilbert and Sullivan, a one-man operetta factory with a long list of early hit shows to his credit, including *Maytime, The Student Prince, The New Moon,* and *The Desert Song.*

For all that, though, Rommy had few pretenses about his talents as a composer, director, or musician. "I'll always be able to write good music," he liked to say, "just as long as I'm able to steal from Mozart." He liked to joke that the only difference between Dick Rodgers and himself was, "I steal and don't conceal it, whereas Dick steals, but spends a lot of his time trying to cover his tracks. Everyone steals from Mozart."

One day in 1950 I received a telephone call from Romberg's wife, Lillian. "Come quick!" she cried. "Rommy's just cut off his thumb!" For a man who was then making much of his income traveling around the country playing pop music in concert because he had grown tired of the rigors of composing, the loss of a thumb was a major catastrophe. I rushed over to the Ritz Tower at Park Avenue and Fifty-seventh Street, where the Rombergs had an apartment, and hammered on the door.

When Lillian let me in, I found Rommy, Oc Hammerstein, Ben Hecht, and Gene Fowler sitting calmly at a card table playing a round of bridge. They looked up, smiled, said, "Hello, Ben," and went back to their game. I couldn't help but notice that around Rommy's right thumb was wrapped a white silk handkerchief soaked with blood. Over the loud protests of the other players, I managed to persuade the wounded Romberg to step into the bathroom so that I could determine the extent of his injury.

He had damaged himself, all right. A pseudo-marble bathroom gadget had shattered while Rommy was trying to loosen a knob and had inflicted a deep cut on the undersurface of the thumb. Since the victim wasn't able to bend the distal thumb joint, I knew the tendon must have been severed. I returned the patient to the sitting room and announced that the game would have to be postponed while Rommy and I went to the hospital to get his thumb sewn up.

Rommy howled in protest. "I'm not going to go," he insisted, sticking out his little cherub's chin. "This is the first time Gene has been East for months, and this bridge game is much too important to be interrupted by surgery. I'll go to the hospital tomorrow."

"If you wait till then," I warned, "the ends of the tendon will separate, and it will be impossible for the surgeon to bring them together. We've got to go right now."

Rommy grew contemplative. "What happens if I don't have the operation?"

"The skin will heal, but the tendon won't—you'll never be able to bend that thumb again."

"All right," he announced peremptorily, "that's the way we'll leave it. I won't be able to bend my thumb. Thank you very much." He ordered me to bandage him up so that the card game could continue.

Lillian was outraged. "Rommy," she screeched, "you can't do this! You've got to use that thumb or you won't be able to play the piano properly."

Rommy pondered the offending digit. "Ben," he said, "show me how my thumb will perform if I don't have the operation." I kept my thumb in a rigid, upright position and indicated how it would move if the distal joint couldn't be bent. He studied the movement closely, then reclaimed his seat at the bridge table. "There's no need for the operation," he announced with finality. "The way I play the piano, nobody will know the difference."

Ever since I forced an aspirin down the throat of that unhappy child during my intern days at Gorgas Hospital, and very nearly killed him in the process, I've tried my damnedest to listen to what my patients are trying to tell me. But it was Oc Hammerstein who proved the importance of listening in a way I would have given anything to avoid.

On the morning of August 16, 1959, Oc came to see me at 728 Park Avenue for his annual checkup. As in past years, he had no significant complaints. To all appearances, he was in excellent shape for a man of sixty-four. The usual tests were done, all of which turned out to be within acceptable limits. So, as we sat in my consulting room, and I leaned back in my green leather chair and lighted a cigar, I was pleased to give him the good news. "According to my records," I said, "this is the sixth examination we've done and we've never found anything yet. Come back next year for a repeat performance."

"I'm glad things look so good," he said, before adding a little hesitantly, "There's just one thing I forgot to tell you that's different from last year."

"Oh, what's that?"

"I've always been a pretty sound sleeper, you know, but a couple of times this past month I've woken up in the middle of the night and couldn't get back to sleep."

The interruption of normal sleeping patterns has any number of causes, none of which are normally very serious. It can be a simple case of stress. Or, if frequent trips to the toilet are involved, one has to consider the possibility of an enlarged prostate, a common problem which often begins in the sixties.

"What happens next?" I asked him.

"That's the funny part," said Oc, chuckling to himself. "I feel hungry, so I go to the kitchen and get a glass of milk and a few crackers. That takes care of it, and I go back to sleep."

"Well," I replied, "that doesn't sound like much to worry about. Go on home." Still, I felt uncomfortable for some reason.

A few minutes later, something clicked. I ran out to the street, found Oc standing on the corner waiting for the light, and asked him to come back to the office.

"Oc," I said apologetically, "I'm pretty sure it's nothing, but there's no point in taking chances. I want to arrange for you to have a stomach X ray and a couple of other tests." He agreed, and within twenty-four hours, our studies were completed. Bad news. The tests revealed carcinoma of the stomach, far advanced.

That same week, Dr. Frank Glenn operated on Oc at New York Hospital, removing that part of the stomach containing the tumor. He spent the next eleven months with his family at his beloved country home near Doylestown, Pennsylvania, where he died on August 23, 1960, at the age of sixty-five. The world had lost a marvelous talent. I had lost a good friend and been reminded—the hard way—about the importance of an old medical lesson: Listen to the patient!

_____

Over the years, my patients taught me many wonderful things of a nonmedical nature. (Jack McFadden, the Memphis cotton king, who owned a massive art collection, was able, after much effort, to get me to distinguish a Modigliani from a Monet; the Monet was the one with all the lilies.) But mostly they reinforced the notion that the rich and famous are indeed an eccentric bunch.

Billy Rose was a case in point. He was never a favorite of anyone, but then he was never boring either. The great Broadway showman was small, smooth-skinned, pink, and bouncing, with a whining, falsetto voice. He was also belligerent by nature, deceitful by habit, and absolutely brilliant. Billy started his career in the unlikely role of secretary to Bernard Baruch, the professional advisor to presidents. He got his start in show business by staging the Aquacade with his then wife-to-be, Eleanor Holm, after she had been kicked off the Olympic swim team by Avery Brundage for drinking a celebratory glass of champagne.

The years brought Billy escalating success and the ownership of the Ziegfeld Theater, a townhouse on Beekman Place, a country estate in Mt. Kisco, New York, where he kept a large collection of Soutines, and the "Old Rocking Chair" estate in Montego Bay, Jamaica. He was proud to be the sponsor of his bevy of chorines, "Billy Rose's Long-Stemmed American Beauties," and the largest stockholder of AT&T. Money (of any denomination), sex (of indeterminate configuration), publicity (of any and all kinds) drove his hyperactive ego. After Eleanor came Joyce Matthews, and then Florence Vidor. Somewhere along the line came André Gide.

"Ben, you read books," he said one day when he called me from his office at the Ziegfeld. "I need to talk to you right away." I went over to Sixth Avenue and Fifty-fourth Street to see him. He sat behind a high enameled desk on an elevated revolving chair.

"I've been thinking about producing a play based on Gide's *The Immoralist*," he said abruptly. "Will it be a hit?" Frankly, I was a little surprised at the choice. Here was a producer of musical extravaganzas typically featuring partially nude dancing girls, prancing elephants, and all manner of fans, feathers, and frills. Now he was talking about producing a play set in Algeria, which featured a Frenchman who becomes hopelessly enamored of a beautiful young Arab serving boy. Not exactly his cup of tea, I thought.

"Billy, you can't produce that play," I said, a little undiplomatically, I'm afraid.

"Why not?!" he demanded truculently.

"It will bomb. You'll lose your ass."

"That's all right," he said, seeming to relax a little. "Screw the investors. All I want is the prestige."

I had suspected that his interest in Gide had less to do with Gide than with his desire to shed his image as a man of elephants and dancing girls. Billy Rose wanted to become known as a sensitive litterateur! I would fix him.

"Gide is prestigious all right," I said, pausing thoughtfully, "but Proust would be so much better, of course."

"Okay," said Billy enthusiastically, "you got it. What plays did Proust write?" He was furious when he later discovered that Proust had written no plays. He went ahead and produced *The Immoralist*, and it was hailed as the great artistic success of the 1954 season. The investors got clobbered, but Billy got what he was after. He was stepping up the social ladder in high style.

In the early sixties I became Frank Loesser's physician when Frank moved from Hollywood to settle in New York. Referred to me by Abe Burrows, who had co-written the book for *Guys and Dolls* with him, Frank was a real-life replica of the memorable mobster character, Nathan Detroit, and spoke and acted like a cross between Humphrey Bogart and George Raft. Under the tough-guy facade, however, lurked an educated, cultivated human being. But for me, it was his wife, Lynn, who was the unforgettable member of the family, for it was Lynn Loesser who first showed me how to "click."

One day when Lynn, a tall, lanky ex-showgirl with frizzy

blond hair and an engaging smile, was in my office discussing Frank's misbehavior, I asked her what she did when he was "busy"—our euphemism for a husband not being at home when he should have been. "Well," she said, "I spend most of my time clicking." I had never heard of clicking, I said, whereupon Lynn replied, "Close your eyes and turn around facing the wall, and I'll show you how to click."

I wondered whether this was going to be the kind of exhibition a doctor had better observe in the protective presence of his nurse, but did as instructed. The next sound I heard was that of a loud, sharp "click," a little like the single snap of a castanet. "What was that?" I asked. I was told to turn around and see for myself.

Lynn was standing in the middle of my office, bending forward from the waist. She then tossed back her head with considerable force and, as she did so, she threw the heel of her right foot in the opposite direction. The "click" resulted when her foot tapped the back of her skull. "I can do it with my left heel, too," she said proudly. "Watch!"

The fact that she wore a billowy cotton dress did not seem to concern her in the slightest. She clicked again. "That's simply remarkable," I said, really meaning it.

"It's very healthy," Lynn announced. "I used to be a tap dancer in the circus, and that's where I learned how to click the back of my head. Whenever I get a headache, I go 'click, click,' and it doesn't take long to knock the pain right out of there."

Lynn clicked every morning upon rising from bed and each night before retiring. I'd often wondered why our conversations never seemed to make much sense to me. Now I knew—it was all that clicking. When I mentioned this to Frank he confirmed the diagnosis. "Yes," he said, "her brains are completely scrambled."

Sometimes, patients taught me more subtle skills. I learned, for instance, to keep my antennae up for gossip about myself in the interests of avoiding professionally embarrassing situations. In practicing medicine, the chances for being misunderstood present themselves daily. In spite of my precautionary tactics, however, embarrassment was sometimes unavoidable. This proved to be the case in the early winter of 1966 when, working away in my lab at Cornell, minding my own business, I received a telephone call from my colleague Connie Guion asking me to see one of her patients, an accomplished actress and Hollywood sex symbol we'll call Miss L. Then at the peak of her career as a leading lady, the lovely, childlike Miss L had a gravelly, Tallulah Bankhead voice, in surprising contrast to her quick, nervous movements. She also had the reputation of being a bit, shall we say, high-strung.

Dr. Guion alluded to this when she called me into consultation. "Please be very careful with her," she said, "because she's, well, a little flighty, and her husband [a well-known publisher] thinks she's made of bric-a-brac and will shatter if a harsh word is spoken tó her."

I didn't take this warning personally, although I was aware that I myself had something of a reputation for plain speaking that was occasionally misinterpreted as harshness. On the other hand, I knew myself to be unfailingly gentle toward all beautiful movie actresses, so I wasn't worried.

"What ails her?" I asked.

"A worm," said Connie.

"What kind of worm?"

"We think it's ascaris."

Ah, my old foe, the roundworm, I thought with pleasure. That was one character I knew how to make very short work of indeed. "Okay," I said, "I'll have a look."

I flipped through our laboratory records and found that there had been several stool examinations done on the stunning Miss L, but all had failed to turn up the slightest evidence of the roundworm or its eggs. Under the circumstances, I failed to understand how a diagnosis of ascariasis, or roundworm infection, could have been made.

I took the elevator up to the Tower (as the twelfth through seventeenth floors of New York Hospital's Baker Pavilion are called), found the patient's room, introduced myself, and asked her what seemed to be the trouble.

"I have no symptoms now," she said, her large blue eyes widening coquettishly, "but they say that I have within me a worm."

"Where are you supposed to have acquired this worm?" I asked.

"On location in Mexico," she replied.

I was still puzzled. "If you do have a worm," I said, "there should be some evidence in your stool, but the tests done in our laboratory were negative. What seems to have convinced you and Dr. Guion that you have a worm?"

"Let me show it to you," she said. Hopping pertly from the bed, she opened a drawer and produced a large folder of X rays of her intestinal tract. "I had a tummy ache," said the actress, "and the doctors thought it would be a good idea if I had a barium X ray. This is what they found."

I examined the X ray and, indeed, in the small intestine, halfway down, was radiographic evidence of an eight-inch roundworm, *Ascaris lumbricoides*, a creature closely resembling an overgrown earthworm.

"Well, you do have a worm," I told Miss L, "and I think the thing to do is to treat you for it."

Treatment in those days wasn't nearly as simple or as safe as it is now, but we did have drugs that would eliminate the worm with fair reliability. In this case, I told the patient that she would begin medication, whereupon we would check the content of her stool for a few days to see whether the monster had been flushed from its lair.

"Medicine, did you say? You want me to take medicine?" The smile disappeared from the star's dreamy face for the first time in our twenty-minute relationship and was replaced by a frown of dramatic intensity. "I don't take drugs," she said, looking as if she were about to burst into tears.

"Miss L," I said, trying to be gentle, "there is no possible way to remove this parasite *without* taking medicine."

"What will happen if I just leave it alone?"

"Nothing will happen," I said. "It will probably live on there for a few years, grow old, loosen its grip on the intestinal walls, and be passed through your bowel without too much harm. However, if you get a fever, whatever the cause, the worm may migrate to another part of your body and cause more serious symptoms. I suggest you get rid of it right away, and to do that I need to give you some medicine."

"Let me think about it," she said, her brows knitted in thought. "Please come back tomorrow."

That night I spoke to Dr. Guion, confirming her diagnosis and suggesting a course of therapy. Connie was the epitome of all that was good about the New York Hospital–Cornell Medical Center in those days. Gray-haired, bespectacled, and a little over-weight—everybody's benevolent aunt—she was regarded as one of the finest doctors in New York City and had been Vincent Astor's personal physician for many years. Invariably polite, pleasant, and prim, she said, "Thank you very much, Dr. Kean. Please see if you can persuade her to take the medicine." She then added a warning: "But be careful. She's a very sensitive, allergic type of person—and a Jehovah's Witness most of the time."

The next morning I returned to Miss L's room, prescription in hand, prepared to use all my powers of persuasion, limited though they were, to get her to accept drug therapy. The patient was lying in bed, covered with a sheet, and studying her X ray. After the usual greetings, I tried to impress on her the importance of taking the medication.

"No," she said, with a big, cinematic smile. "I have been thinking about this the whole night through, and I have come up with a better plan to eliminate the worm. Was it not you who told me that the worm remains in the intestines by stretching itself across the walls of the bowel, more or less as a man in a small closet might push both walls with his extended arms?"

"That's right," I said. "The medicine paralyzes the musculature of the worm, so it loses its power to suspend itself across the intestinal chasm. When its grip is broken, it flows out with the rest of the intestinal contents."

A look of grim determination now overtook the actress. "Okay," she said, "here's my plan. I am going to make that evil old worm release its hold by making it so dizzy that it will fall into the intestinal tract on its own."

This was a form of therapy new to my experience. "That's an interesting concept," I said. "How do you propose to make the worm dizzy?"

She said, "Let me show you." Suddenly, the gorgeous Miss L, star of stage and screen, a woman thought to be one of the most magnificent creatures in the world, flung back the sheet, sprang to her feet, and stood on the bed—wearing absolutely nothing. "Watch!" she said. I did as I was told.

The actress proceeded to hurl her abdominal muscles into a series of circular convolutions of an intensity previously unknown to medical science. After a minute or so of clockwise rotation, Miss L reversed gears and everything, driven by her undulating hips, went in the opposite direction—around and around and around. She was extraordinarily adept in the use of her abdomen, but how she could have produced motion of such verve and duration was then—and remains to me now—a complete mystery.

So there I stood, glued to my spot at the feet of the film goddess by a mixture of fear and fascination, as her wildly pelvic bump and grind continued. While I was trying to decide whether professional ethics would permit me to shift my gaze from her abdominal muscles to the rest of her body, Dr. Connie Guion, the conscience of Cornell University Medical College, walked in. She looked at the nude performer standing on top of the bed, then at the stunned physician at the foot of the bed, and asked, "What in heaven's name is going on here?"

"The patient will explain everything," I stammered, and ran from the room.

That brought down the curtain on my treatment of Miss L. It was the last I ever saw of the film star, not to mention the last time Dr. Guion ever trusted me with one of her patients.

Wheel of Fortune

S omething was up. Dr. Barr, my mentor at New York Hospital, was not in the habit of making private calls on junior colleagues, but there he was in my laboratory at Cornell, absentmindedly fiddling with one of my Bunsen burners and bursting to tell me something.

"I've got another one for you," he said cryptically. Like many distinguished men, Barr hid a prankish sense of humor behind an exterior of grave respectability. He told me he was entrusting me with a "special patient." Man by the name of Garrity. Suffering from amebic dysentery. His treatment, Barr promised, with a droll little smile, would be a "real roll of the dice." I should have been on my guard but, as usual, I missed the irony in his voice.

Timothy "Big Tim" Garrity was a towering, fleshy figure with a voice like a howitzer and a personality to match. Back then, in the late fifties, he was hailed as one of the great professional gamblers of the day. Not even Jimmy "the Greek" Snyder could have held a candle to Big Tim in his prime. Garrity's fortunes rose or fell as much as a quarter of a million dollars after a night of stud poker, a presidential election, or a Cuban cock fight. Ownership in a string of hotels and casinos from Las Vegas and Reno to Vera Cruz and Havana financed his highrolling lifestyle and staked infamous gambling "vacations" to Monte Carlo, Cannes, and Rio, where he shared the faro table with the likes of King Farouk and Aristotle Onassis.

I had heard of Garrity, of course, and most of what I'd heard I hadn't liked. At the time, I was spending a few weeks in Cuba at the beginning of each summer helping Cornell medical students set up experimental studies, not bothering to report back to my hardworking colleagues at Cornell that the golf at the Havana Country Club was superb. Havana, in those pre-Castro days, tried hard to live up to its reputation as a wide-open, wicked city and mostly succeeded. It teemed with the variety of fast action and faster women favored by Garrity and his crew of hangers-on, all of whom Big Tim put up free of charge at his garish Casablanca Havana hotel and casino. Tales of this unlikely playboy's legendary excesses in bar, casino, and boudoir circulated freely in the large expatriate American community, where it shocked the wives and induced in the men a kind of dreamy, contemplative silence.

I could afford to take a dim view of Garrity because gambling, amazingly enough, was not among my vices. My Owenite parents had seen to that long ago. So thoroughly had I been indoctrinated, in fact, that now, at age forty-five, a five-dollar bet on a friendly round of golf struck me as a sinful extravagance— although I would think nothing of dropping many, many times that on a good meal and a bottle of wine. Still, it was amebic dysentery, one of my medical specialties, not gambling, that forced me to contemplate meeting Big Tim and, from a purely ethical point of view, I reasoned, I was duty-bound to treat him. Secretly, of course, I was burning with curiosity. Garrity, whatever else could be said of him, was a gold-plated American original. What possible harm could there be in having a look?

This was naive. In getting involved with Big Tim, I would, as it turned out, be putting my practice, my bank account, and my good name on the line.

"Bring him on," I told Dr. Barr, with all the confidence of the consummate sucker.

The next morning I was sitting in my office at 728 Park Avenue, reviewing some blood studies, when Cora Burke buzzed me on the intercom. Her voice was on edge.

"Oh, Dr. Kean, there's somebody here who says . . ."

At that instant the door flew back on its hinges to reveal the enormous, hulking figure of a man that filled the entire doorway and blotted out the light from the waiting room like an eclipse of the sun. He had a shock of bright orange hair, a blotchy, port-wine complexion, and a huge grinning mouth full of huge grinning teeth. He wore an expensive Western suit with three musical notes embroidered above the breast pocket, hand-tooled cowboy boots, and a lariat necktie with a lucky horseshoe clasp clustered with tiny diamonds.

Gazing at this alarming apparition, it suddenly occurred to me that I might be having a nightmare. But this was no bad dream. This was Big Tim Garrity.

"Call me Big Tim," he bellowed, sticking out a huge paw for me to shake, while his face turned such a violent shade of purple I thought his head would explode. When he could contain himself no longer he detonated the longest, loudest barrage of laughter I have ever heard.

"Dr. Barr's told you I've got the runs," he boomed, the windows rattling violently. "Had 'em for six months," he went on, pounding a meaty fist on my desktop. "Now goddamnit, Doc, cure me already, will ya?" His voice was nothing like I'd ever heard before. Part foghorn, part Gatling gun.

Too shell-shocked to speak, I simply pointed in the direction of the examination room and watched in awe as Big Tim squeezed himself through the door. Suddenly I began to worry if my examining table would be sturdy enough to support his weight, which I estimated at a minimum of 375 pounds. To properly assess whatever damage the amebas might have done to his intestinal tract, I would have to do a proctoscopic exam.

The thought of this gigantic specimen crashing to the floor in the middle of it was almost too terrifying to contemplate.

While I considered the odds, and decided to proceed anyway, the gambler removed his suit and shirt, revealing a layer of heavy woolen underwear of the old-fashioned, "trapdoor" variety. I asked him to strip to the waist so I could listen to his heart and lungs. "Nope," he said, setting his jaw and slowly shaking his huge head like a four-year-old child. Why not, I asked. He eyed me skeptically, as if wondering what kind of nincompoop doctor he had gotten himself tangled up with, and roared, "Get serious, Doc, I'm a fragile flower from the Havana sunshine. You'll give me pneumonia!"

Defeated, I inserted the stethoscope under his protective wool hide. It was then that I saw something strange. There, on the calf of his left leg, readily visible through his long underwear, was a large lump roughly the size of a pack of cigarettes but more ovoid in shape. I reached out and touched it. It was firm, and just slightly mobile.

"How long has that been there," I asked.

"About three hours," Big Tim said nonchalantly.

"That's impossible. A tumor that size couldn't have grown there in only a few hours."

"Oh yes it did," he insisted. Grinning fiendishly now, his eyes disappearing into a gorge of puckered flesh, he peeled back his woolies to show me the lump. Out fell a big wad of dollars tightly bound with several thick rubberbands. When I bent down for a closer look, it appeared to be a roll of thousand-dollar bills. Feigning complete surprise, Big Tim asked my startled nurse if she would be so kind as to deposit his "tumor" in his jacket pocket.

The examination proceeded uneventfully. Garrity did have a serious case of amebic dysentery, all right, one that would have put most men out of commission for weeks. I prescribed the appropriate medication and, true to form, Big Tim staged a spectacular recovery. "It would take a small A-bomb to kill Garrity," one of his associates told me later. At that point, fat, sassy, and in his prime, I believe it would have.

Everything would have gone smoothly, had Big Tim not tried to incorporate me into his bizarre lifestyle. His highly mobile profession brought him to New York often. Strong as an ox, he rarely needed medical attention, but he insisted on dropping by for an "office call" anyway. The real purpose of these visitations was usually to show off some terrified new girlfriend or introduce to me an emaciated, booze-riddled crony, who he'd then entrust to my care with orders that all bills be sent to him in care of the Casablanca Havana. He was forever inviting me to ball games at Yankee Stadium, which seemed innocent enough, or trying to coerce me into spending an open-ended vacation in Havana, which did not.

It was hard to keep turning him down, but I did. I was determined to maintain a healthy professional distance between me and this frightening, flamboyant character. Each time I resisted his "friendship," however, he redoubled his efforts to shock and pester me. One tactic was to send me a sudden rush of patients—collapsed gamblers, faded show girls, men of ambiguous professional standing—each one more sinister or outlandish than the last. His most startling blandishment came to my office one morning in a plain brown wrapper. Inside was an expensive, leather-bound photograph album displaying in *Playboy* centerfold fashion the nude anatomies of some fifty remarkably robust young women. Leafed inside was a note from Big Tim. "Cut the crap, Kean," it ordered. "Get your ass down here to Havana on the double. Your friends are lonely!"

Long afterwards, I concluded that, for all his freewheeling bonhomie, Big Tim was indeed a desperately lonely man. Back then, though, his advances plagued and puzzled me. I became convinced that he was committed to my destruction, for he seemed to derive no end of diabolical pleasure from contemplating the seduction of a man of science into his shadowy, turbulent world.

Big Tim Garrity, I vowed, would never be anything to me except a highly troublesome patient. But vows did no good. On his next visit to New York, Big Tim came armed with a scheme that ate away at my resistance like a hungry virus.

Because of his ever-expanding bulk, Garrity had a hard time squeezing his sumo wrestler's frame into any ordinary chair, so I'd purchased an oversize leather recliner for his use, a contraption that allowed the occupant to adjust the angle of incline by manipulating a series of levers and buttons. He liked his new armchair. Sitting there majestically, playing with the dials, raising and lowering the level of his feet, he introduced a subject new to our relationship.

"Tell me, Doc, do you ever bet on football?" he asked.

My early-warning antennae shot up immediately. My medical duties, I told him, left me little time for that sort of thing.

Big Tim was shocked. "You mean to tell me," he shouted, "you've never bet on a goddamn football game? Why, every red-blooded American male has wagered on football!"

I chose to ignore this double-barreled assault on my manhood and love of country. Garrity, meanwhile, had flipped another dial and was now inadvertently staring at the ceiling, his feet resting at considerably greater altitude than his head. He fished around in his coat pocket and produced a single sheet of paper, which he held aloft.

"Take this," he said, rattling the paper. "But you've got to swear you won't show it to anybody else."

Warily, I took the paper and looked at it. It appeared to be a roster of professional football games scheduled for the following Sunday. Opposite each matchup was a number—"Giants by seven," "Raiders by twelve," and so forth. Although the numerology made little sense to me, I wasn't completely naive. Anybody could see this was what professional gamblers called a "line," a ranking of teams favored to win or lose and by how many points.

Garrity, the chair having catapulted him bolt upright, was now looking me squarely in the face with his crafty gambler's eyes. "I bet a hundred thousand dollars on each of ten teams each week," he announced proudly. "My record last season was incredible. Give it a whirl, Kean. What've you got to lose?"

I thanked him primly, but repeated—a little less adamantly than the first time—that I didn't think I would have much time to follow the games, given the demands of medical practice and all. But I held on to the roster, anyhow.

As soon as Garrity had left the office, I telephoned Bill Harder. Harder, a tough, smart, street-wise little man who was then president of a big Wall Street investment firm, I knew to be a gambler of maniacal intensity, a man who would bet on any sport where a ball either moved or was likely to be in motion—football, baseball, sometimes even croquet.

"Bill," I said, "I'd like to bet on some pro football games this Sunday."

"Do you have a line?"

"Of course I have a line," I sniffed. "I want to bet ten dollars a game on ten games."

Harder laughed. No self-respecting bookie, he explained, would take a bet of less than fifty dollars a game. All right, so it had been a while since I placed a bet, I said huffily. If fifty was the going rate, fifty it would be. I read Harder the games and the point spreads from Garrity's list.

"Jesus Christ, Ben," said Harder, "I can't turn this line into my bookie. He'll laugh himself silly. Your numbers are way off. Are you sure you really want to do this?"

I said I was sure. Okay, to save us both the humiliation of going through a bookie, Harder said, he would cover the bets himself. It would teach me to stick to doctoring and leave gambling to the real gamblers, and he would get a good laugh out of seeing me humbled.

The following Sunday some now-forgotten medical crisis kept me at the hospital all afternoon and evening, so I missed the chance to keep tabs on how things were panning out for me on the gridiron. Around eleven o'clock I'd just returned home and was sitting down to a late dinner when the telephone rang. It was Bill Harder. He sounded flustered.

"This is the craziest thing I've ever heard! You've got eight wins, one tie, and one loss," he told me. He demanded to know where I'd got my line.

"Can't tell you, Bill."

"Goddamnit, Kean! I'm not going to pay you a cent until you tell me."

"Okay, keep the money. I still can't tell you. I'm sworn to secrecy."

Harder's check settling our wager arrived the following Thursday. Later that same day, Garrity called. He had followed a floating poker game to Tulsa. Had I bet on any games last Sunday? Yes, I told him, I certainly had. That was a marvelous line he had given me. I thanked him profusely.

Would I care to bet again? Of course, I said. Garrity then read me a new lineup of teams for the following Sunday. When he hung up, I again telephoned Bill Harder. Again he agreed to cover the bets himself. This time, I won all ten games. Harder now owed me five hundred dollars. I was beginning to develop a new appreciation for Big Tim Garrity.

My relationship with Harder, on the other hand, was taking a turn for the worse. I detected a distinct coolness in his voice when he called on Monday morning. He would no longer be covering my bets himself, he informed me. Instead, he gave me the telephone number of his bookie.

"Come on, Ben," he pleaded. "If you don't tell me where you're getting those spreads, I'll have a heart attack. You're my doctor. Save me!"

"Sorry, Bill," I said. "I'll give you the name of a good cardiologist, but I can't tell you where I'm getting my numbers. I promised."

Another Thursday rolled around. Another call from Garrity, this time from Miami. Another fresh line. More winnings. In the meantime, I telephoned Harder's bookie, who turned out to be located, of all places, in Tampa, Florida. A man with a deep, well-lubricated voice answered the phone. Yes, he'd be happy to accept a few bets each Friday. He promised to send a messenger to my office each Monday morning. If I came out ahead, the man would leave an envelope filled with cash. If not, I would leave enough money to settle the score. It was a very nearly perfect setup.

For the next two years the system ran like clockwork. Toward the end of each week, Garrity would call me from wherever Lady Luck happened to have led him and give me the point spreads. I would then call my man in Tampa. On Monday mornings, I made it a point to stay out of the office, which was on the ground floor, for that was when the bagman, "Moe," arrived. Moe would knock three times at the window closest to my receptionist's desk, whereupon she would open it and make the exchange.

Not all of Garrity's picks were winners, of course. But I won enough to keep my attention focused. Quite soon, I was betting a hundred dollars a game. Not long after that I had bumped it up to a cool thousand, for a total of ten thousand dollars a Sunday.

Occasionally, Big Tim would call and tell me to double my bet on a particular team. The advice varied according to intelligence he'd received from local scouts who kept an eye on each team and its players. Garrity liked to boast that he had at least one spy on his payroll inside every locker room in the country. Their job was to troll for scraps of gossip that could have a bearing on the outcome of a game. New York's star quarterback had another knee injury this week? Garrity would shave a few points from the Jet's advantage over Pittsburgh. A key linebacker was broken up because his wife had tossed him out for carousing with gridiron groupies? Garrity would bet more heavily on the opposing team. Big Tim insisted that no bribes ever changed hands.

In time, Garrity directed me to new opportunities for fun and profit to be had in wagering on college football. Two years after my first innocent bet, I was regularly plunking down money on an average of twenty games each weekend. Then, late one Saturday night, it all came to an abrupt end.

That was when I found myself working the telephone in a panic, calling one local television and radio station after another in a frantic attempt to learn the results of a college game between the University of West Virginia and Virginia Tech, and getting nowhere. I cursed my luck. Beads of cold sweat dotted my forehead. My skin felt clammy and my stomach churned. And with good reason. I had bet twenty-three thousand dollars on that one game, and hours after the players had left the field, I still couldn't find out whether my team had won or lost.

At last, I reached the sports editor of a small newspaper in Charleston, who told me that my team had won. I should've been overjoyed. Instead, I was terrified. As I hung up the receiver, my hands shook violently. I was in the grip of an insidious, destructive disease, and I knew it. The unflattering self-diagnosis was now obvious: I was a compulsive gambler, heavily and hopelessly addicted. From that moment on, I vowed, I would never again place another bet on football, horses, or even something as seemingly innocuous as Ping-Pong. Though I had promised to mend my ways, however—and did—the wheel of fortune was still spinning.

My number finally came up one day the following June when a friend telephoned to ask me if I'd seen an article that morning in one of the New York tabloids. Soon the headline screamed up at me from my own desktop: "Park Avenue Doc Nabbed in Gambling Raid." My heart plunged. So much for an otherwise promising career in medicine, I thought. Frozen with dread, I read on.

The details were appallingly straightforward. The Florida state police, the article said, had raided a bookie joint the day before and turned up a list of "celebrity patrons." Among those being subpoenaed to testify in the case were "prominent Wall Street investment banker William Harder" and "Park Avenue physician B. H. Kean."

There was that "Park Avenue" again! Over the years, I had noticed how the simple geographical epithet always seemed to act on the media like a spell, summoning up images of a world of unspeakable privilege and wealth, jewel-bedizened matrons and suave, shifty-eyed tycoons. Park Avenue doctors were well-known scoundrels, buttering up and bilking the ruling class for their cash. Finding one of them with his hands planted firmly in the cookie jar had an almost irresistible reverse snob appeal. In short, it made great headlines.

All of this now struck me as a little unfair. Nowhere was there any mention of Big Tim Garrity who, I had managed to discover, used the same bookie. He had gotten me involved in this scam in the first place. Surely he deserved some publicity, too. But no, it was the "Park Avenue" doctor that appeared to be stealing the show. My mind started to swim with imagined headlines: "Patients Dump Park Avenue Doc," "Park Avenue Doc Forced to Resign College Post," and so on.

While I was brooding over what fate had in store for me, the telephone rang. It was a reporter from the local newspaper in Tampa, calling to confirm the story. Still in shock, I babbled incoherently for a few seconds but, when the conversation ended, I couldn't for the life of me remember what I'd said. Again, however, Park Avenue was destined to make the headlines. The front page in Tampa the next morning read: " 'Oh, My God,' Says Park Avenue Physician." In any event, it was an accurate enough assessment of my mood.

That afternoon I was served a court summons at, appropriately enough, my Park Avenue office. I decided to telephone Big Tim Garrity for some guidance. Tracking him down wasn't easy but I finally got through to him. He was back at the Casablanca Havana—safely out of reach of the U.S. authorities. But guidance, I was about to discover, was not Big Tim's strong suit.

"You *are* in a mess," he bellowed.

"What do you mean, 'You're in a mess'!?" I gasped. "You got me into this. For godsakes, man, help get me out!"

Compassion wasn't one of Big Tim's fortes, either. "In a situation like this," he said, "it's every man for himself."

"How the hell did you keep your name off the list?" I demanded.

Garrity launched a cannonade of laughter so deafening I thought the receiver would split in half. "What kind of bum do you take me for, Doc? You don't think I'd be dumb enough to use my real name, do you? Only a Park Avenue genius like you would do that." He tried to shatter the telephone with another superdecibel guffaw and then rang off.

On a sweltering afternoon a month later I found myself sitting glumly in the Tampa District Court. Next to me in the witness box waiting to testify was an equally grim Bill Harder. We had flown in together and were represented by the same lawyer. Big Tim, of course, was nowhere to be seen. Not only had he never been subpoenaed, his name had never once been mentioned by police, prosecutors, or the press. But he was there in spirit. Early that morning the hotel bellhop had delivered a bouquet of three dozen lilies of the valley to my room. Tucked inside was a card which read simply, "Nice Knowing You, Doc." Some joke.

The courtroom was packed with law-abiding Floridians, there, I was convinced, for the sole purpose of stealing a glimpse at the gambling fiend from Manhattan, the dreaded "Park Avenue Doctor." Whispers, punctuated with clearly audible "Park Avenue"'s, circulated through the airless courtroom when the judge called me to the stand. The prosecutor, a short, pudgy, balding man with large glasses, rose to his feet and began his examination. He appeared not to like me very much.

"Yours is an incredible tale of vice and gambling," he began. The defense attorney complained loudly. Objection sustained.

The prosecutor then pointed to the defendants themselves, a group of a half-dozen beefy looking men, who had allegedly run the bookie operation. I took a good look at my partners in crime. They were dressed in loud plaid jackets with wide lapels, for the most part. Two of them wore black silk shirts unbuttoned far enough toward the navel to expose hirsute chests festooned with gold medallions. They answered to names like "Charlie" and "Al."

"Will you please tell the court where you first saw these men," the prosecutor said.

"I've never seen them before in my life."

The prosecutor cackled theatrically and gave me a sly wink. He did not believe me, and said so. So I explained how the system worked, how the bets were placed by telephone, and how Moe, the messenger, came to my office each Monday and stood outside the window. To wit, I had no way of identifying any of the defendants.

"So for two years you placed large bets with men you say you never saw—just spoke to on the telephone? How did you know they would pay you if you won?"

"Sir," I said, "everyone knows that professional gamblers are honest about paying debts, otherwise they would have very short careers."

My worldly logic failed to impress the prosecutor, who smirked in the direction of the jury.

"I'm sorry, sir," I said, "but I've told you exactly what transpired. I've never seen any of these men before today. With due respect, I really don't care whether you believe me or not. I'm telling you the truth."

Suddenly all six defendants jumped to their feet and clapped their hands enthusiastically. The judge barked at them to sit down, stop their racket immediately, or he'd have them all handcuffed. I was then quietly told that I could step down.

With the sound of applause still ringing in my ears, I fled the courtroom, and headed for the airport as quickly as my rubbery legs would carry me. Back in New York City I sat in my office on sinful Park Avenue waiting for some dark figure to step forward and shame me with the incident. Mercifully, no one ever did. I never found out whether my patients and colleagues were simply ignorant of the whole affair, or just chose to ignore it. Whatever the case, it took me months to stop feeling like a real fool. I think I did learn my lesson, though. Big time gambling, unless you are a Big Tim Garrity, is a strictly no-win proposition.

But even Big Tim's luck could not last forever.

After the Tampa incident, I didn't hear from Garrity for years. Then, in the fall of 1977, I was packing to leave a Los Angeles hotel room when the telephone rang. From the thunderous boom at the other end of the line, I knew it could only be Big Tim. He said he'd seen a writeup of a speech I'd given in one of the Los Angeles newspapers and used that to track me down. He was in Tijuana, he told me. He was only calling to say goodbye. Then, in such deeply lugubrious tones that I almost fell for it, he informed me that he was dying. Could I ever find it in my heart to forgive him for Tampa? Only then could he go to his grave in peace. This was followed by a burst of laughter so intense that the connection was momentarily swamped in a tidal wave of static. Pure Garrity hokum, I thought. He hasn't changed one bit.

But I was wrong. When his voice resurfaced, it was not the old Garrity talking. He sounded somehow subdued, somber, beaten. Maybe a little scared. Could I make a housecall, he wanted to know. His back had been killing him for weeks. Couldn't shake it. Couldn't sleep. Going out of his mind. Ordinarily, he said, his humor rekindling, "I would fly to your arms, pal, but pressing business matters demand my presence south of the border." Against my better judgment, I agreed to see him.

When I arrived at the address Big Tim had given me, a vermin-infested apartment block smack in the middle of Tijuana's notorious red-light district, I did indeed find a changed man. Big

Tim looked awful. Pale and unshaven, he had, if it was biologically possible, grown even more fantastically obese than before.
Sprawled on a greasy couch, rolling bloodshot eyes and complaining of constant pain, he looked like a battered whale heaved
up on some unfriendly beach. One look at this grim scene and
I knew what had to be done.

"Get a few things together," I said sternly. "You're going back
to LA but pronto for X rays and treatment. There's no telling
what's wrong with that back and we'll sure as hell never find
out in Tijuana."

"No soap, Doc," said Garrity, flashing his old lopsided grin.
"Got to stay right here on base. All leaves canceled till further
notice." Suddenly, everything made sense. True, I hadn't seen
Garrity since Tampa, but I'd heard plenty about him over the
years. I now remembered a particularly ominous rumor Bill
Harder had passed on just recently. Something about Garrity not
being able to cover massive gambling debts in Las Vegas. Trouble with the mob. No wonder he was suffering from insomnia,
bad back or no!

Although we'd had our sharp differences in the past, I suddenly
felt sorry for my colorful old nemesis. Trying to stay upbeat, I
told him I would hereby grant him complete absolution for
Tampa. After all, he'd done me a great favor. If he hadn't barged
into my life all those years ago, I might have remained forever
ignorant of my fatal weakness for gambling. This induced in Big
Tim a fit of laughter so powerful that it rocked the flimsy apartment like a small earthquake until a painful back spasm snapped
him out of it. Before I left, I loaded him up with painkillers and
sleeping pills. I promised to send him a back brace from New
York, which I did. I gave him my phone number and told him
to keep in touch, which he didn't. A few years later I heard from
Bill Harder that Tim, flat broke and deep into the bottle, had
died in Vera Cruz of a heart attack.

As I headed for the door, Big Tim held up a huge paw for me
to stop. There was something he wanted me to have—"In lieu
of the standard methods of payment, you understand." He then

dangled his lucky lariat necktie under my nose, the one with the diamond-studded horseshoe clasp. I refused to take it.

"Keep it," I told him. "You'll be back in action sooner than you think. You're going to need every ounce of luck you can muster." I'd meant that last part as a joke, but neither one of us laughed. It sounded too much like what it was: the cruel, unvarnished truth.

The Baptism of "Peter Smith"

Luckily, not all patients were as difficult to deal with as Big Tim Garrity, though their medical concerns could, on occasion, prove every bit as daunting. Take the frigid February morning in 1978 when I received a telephone call from Joseph V. Reed, who was then chief of staff to David Rockefeller at Chase Manhattan Bank.

"When can you leave for Sweden?" asked Reed, in his blunt, no-nonsense way.

"May I ask why I'm being exiled to the North Pole in the dead of winter? Something I said, perhaps?"

Normally, Reed would have responded to my feeble attempt at humor with his throaty, patrician laugh. Instead, he was silent for a moment, then said, "Marcus Wallenberg is very sick. They say he's dying."

I recognized the name immediately. Wallenberg was one of the most powerful businessmen in Europe, the central figure in a banking and industrial empire worth many billions of dollars. Reed handled the Wallenberg account at Chase.

"What do they think is wrong with him?" I asked.

"That's just it—nobody knows. He's in a hospital in Stockholm getting sicker by the day. His doctors haven't been able to come up with a diagnosis, and now they're worried about his survival."

"Has he got a parasite?"

"They don't know what it is." He explained that Wallenberg had just returned to Sweden after a brief stay in Hobe Sound, the Florida resort community where for the past thirty years I've taken my semitropical winter vacation, my escape from the hated northern cold. "They think he might have picked up a bug down there."

"There's nothing special about Florida," I said. "Hobe Sound has no unique diseases that I know of. I don't see how I can help."

"That's not important," said Reed, trying to be patient with me. "What matters is that they *think* you can help."

Clearly, Reed had been a patient of mine far too long—he was even beginning to think like me. Any doctor–patient relationship worth a damn has to be based on trust, a point I've tried to hammer home for years. If a patient trusts his doctor, the benefits, both psychological and somatic, can be enormous. If he doesn't, he should "fire" that physician immediately and find one he *can* believe in. But I confess that I didn't much like being on the receiving end of my own good advice. Besides, it was the middle of winter and, despite the tantalizing prospect of unexplained illness looming on the horizon, the thought of flying off to frozen Sweden did not excite me.

"Look, Ben, they have no other solution right now. Just do it, okay?"

"Okay," I said irritably, "when do I leave?"

"You'll hear from the Wallenbergs within the hour."

As I went home to pack, I began to warm to the idea of meeting the great Marcus Wallenberg. To many Americans who lived through the Second World War, the Wallenberg name is famous because of Raoul, the Swedish diplomat who risked his life spiriting Jews out of Nazi-occupied Hungary before disappearing at war's end into the Soviet gulag. Marcus and Raoul were cousins, Marcus also gaining something of a reputation during the war for his diplomatic efforts in representing neutral Sweden in its dealings with the Allies.

By the time he fell ill, Marcus, as head of Skandinaviska Enskilda Banken, his country's most influential bank, controlled about a third of Swedish industry and employed, directly or indirectly, a third of all Swedish workers. Through his bank, Wallenberg also commanded an empire of companies, including Saab, the automaker, Scandinavian Air Lines, and Ericsson, the telecommunications giant.

Formidable as his economic muscle was, however, Wallenberg was the rare business tycoon widely respected by his fellow countrymen. For all that, though, he seemed genuinely proud of only one accomplishment: in 1922, he had been the first Swede to play on center court at Wimbledon, where he was known for a particularly wicked slice.

No sooner had I unlocked the door to my apartment than the telephone rang. A man with a deep, mellow voice introduced himself as Erik Orinius. In the lilting accent of the Swedes, he said that he was Wallenberg's personal physician and was delighted that I would be joining them in Stockholm. Would it be convenient for me to leave that evening? A ticket would be waiting for me at the SAS desk at Kennedy Airport for the eight o'clock flight.

Two hours later, a black limousine picked me up at home and deposited me at the airport. Two airline officials took my bags and ushered me onto the plane. I had as yet seen no ticket, but, as I was already being treated in the manner of Viking royalty, I secretly hoped that I would be traveling first class. That, as it turned out, was not the case.

A name had not yet been invented for the class I was to travel. The plane, a standard 747, had the usual placement of first-class passengers in the forward compartment, far away from the cattle-car atmosphere of economy where I had normally traveled as a humble scientific researcher. I could see the flight was crowded and thought I would be lucky enough just to get on board. So I resigned myself to the prospect of skulking to the aft cabin and squeezing into a tourist seat.

But no, a mustachioed steward took me by the elbow—"Right this way, Professor Kean"—and guided me up the spiral staircase to the upper deck. There a bed with a goose-down comforter occupied the rear of the cabin, in front of which a single over-stuffed chair faced a fully stocked bar and a coffee table spread with canapes. A stewardess of sparkling blonde beauty materialized and plied me first with champagne and caviar, then, after takeoff, with smoked salmon, steak, and cheeses, each course accompanied by an appropriate bottle of vintage wine.

Hurtling through black space toward Stockholm, I enjoyed an after-dinner Cuban cigar of great quality (and stole one for later). This was no pleasure trip, however; I was on a serious medical mission. So I tried, with some considerable effort, to focus on what I might find waiting for me when I arrived.

Orinius had told me a little about Wallenberg's condition, but the details remained nearly as sketchy as Joseph Reed's initial report. On the flight back home from a Florida vacation, the patient had come down with a blistering fever that had persisted for two weeks now; despite all efforts at diagnosis and treatment (including one, then another, then a third and a fourth powerful antibiotic), the patient was getting progressively weaker.

After eight hours of food, wine, and sleep, I arrived in Stockholm rested and eager to meet my patient. I was met at the aircraft door by a husky man with thinning blond hair and ruddy cheeks, who introduced himself as Peter Wallenberg, Marcus's son. Peter instructed me to forget about my baggage and passport as he led the way to a glistening royal blue Saab parked on the tarmac. "We have no chauffeur," said Peter, adding apologetically, "I wanted to talk to you privately, so I will drive you into town myself."

THE BAPTISM OF "PETER SMITH"

Once behind the wheel, Peter proved himself a driver of grand prix virtuosity. It was winter and the roads were icy. Snow was banked high on both sides of the highway. We hurtled along like a bobsled in a chute, doing close to two hundred kilometers an hour most of the way into downtown Stockholm. Peter pointed out "our bank" as the huge Skandinaviska Enskilda Banken blurred by.

At the Grand Hotel, I was deposited in a suite with bulging bay windows that wrapped around the fourth floor. Cigars and smoked salmon on the plane had been one thing, but the continuous unfolding of ever-greater luxuries was beginning to make me feel uncomfortable. The four huge rooms were exquisitely furnished, antique tables offering up baskets of fruit and bottles of expensive liquor at every turn. Only the muffled thundering of multiple jackhammers from construction going on in the street below disturbed the atmosphere of serene elegance.

Peter waited for me downstairs while I shaved and changed clothes, all the while stealing glances of the intoxicating view of ferry boats crossing the indigo waters of Blasieholm Bay, the huge Parliament House standing on the opposite shore and, just beyond that, the battlements of the royal palace, with the royal ensign ahoist and rippling in the wind, signifying that the king was in residence.

When I mentioned the jackhammers to Peter, he chuckled and said apologetically, "It's one of our companies." My introduction to the Sweden of the Wallenbergs was now complete, I thought; I had flown from New York on SAS, which was "owned" (meaning they controlled the majority of its stock) by the Wallenbergs, driven in a car made by Saab, which was "owned" by the Wallenbergs, checked into a hotel "owned" by the Wallenbergs, and been disturbed by a construction company "owned" by the Wallenbergs. The next stop was a private hospital supported by the ubiquitous clan.

The hospital, a posh clinic on a quiet street about a half mile from the hotel, was one of the few medical institutions in "socialized" Sweden not under direct government control. Waiting at the entrance to greet us was Erik Orinius, who led the way to a small, tastefully furnished room on the second floor.

Sitting up in bed was an elderly man, who, though gray and gaunt with illness, wore the inquisitive expression of a man given to quick, shrewd appraisal. Marcus Wallenberg welcomed me graciously in his correct, elegant English—obviously, he had put me to great inconvenience, he said, but he hoped the flight had been tolerable. In addition to Orinius and Peter, we were accompanied by a man of skeletal thinness, with a dark suit and a cleanly shaven head, who was referred to as Dr. Munck. I would later learn that Munck, who looked like a Scandinavian version of Boris Karloff, functioned as aide-de-camp, financial confidant, and trustee to the elder Wallenberg.

I asked Wallenberg to remove his pajama top and proceeded to examine his lungs, heart, and abdomen as best I could, and found nothing unusual. I then retired to an adjoining room with Dr. Orinius to review the chart, laboratory tests, and X rays. I developed an instant liking for this tall, lean, handsome man. That he was an accomplished physician became quickly apparent; Erik Orinius was a respected cardiologist, and there is very little that would have escaped his meticulous clinical approach. Of his great devotion and love for old man Wallenberg there could be no doubt whatsoever. All the more reason why he was deeply distressed by his inability to fathom his patient's illness.

A stream of Swedish infectious disease and tumor specialists had already flowed through Wallenberg's hospital suite but had contributed little to the understanding of the illness. Their working diagnosis was of an "atypical pneumonia following influenza." Atypical, indeed! There wasn't the slightest evidence of inflammation in the lungs. The X rays looked bafflingly normal to me, although my Swedish colleagues insisted they could see faint traces of disease. I asked Erik to show me the hospital laboratory, where I inspected specimens cultured from the patient's sputum for further clues. Nothing.

After three hours of fruitless review, I was sure of only one thing—I had a dying patient on my hands and nobody, including me, had the slightest idea of what was killing him. It was time to come up with a medical hunch or quit the case and fly back home to New York in defeat.

I needed time to think. I asked Peter to drive me back to the hotel, where I wrapped up in three or four sweaters and an overcoat and went for a walk. It was late afternoon and the quay outside the hotel was dark and nearly deserted. A brutal wind whipped off the bay. Icicles formed on my nose as I trudged along. Then suddenly, just as I was about to give up, return to the hotel, and examine myself for frostbite, a parasite broke through the surface of my frozen brain and presented itself as a clear mental image.

That's it, I thought, that's the little bastard! Although every laboratory test done by the Swedes had turned out negative, they hadn't thought of the bug that had now wriggled its way into my consciousness and, hence, they wouldn't find what they weren't looking for. The brainstorm gave me little pleasure, however. The pathogen was so elusive that researchers still had a hard time identifying it. Worse yet, there was no easy remedy. If I was right, only a medical miracle of considerable magnitude could save the life of the great Marcus Wallenberg.

Back then, in the winter of 1978, the parasite, *Pneumocystis carinii*, which produces a form of pneumonia with a particularly vicious twist, was quietly working its way toward unanticipated notoriety in the gay bathhouses of New York and San Francisco, although its discovery as a leading cause of death in AIDS patients was three years away, and the opportunistic little killer was still virtually unknown outside the serried ranks of the world's parasitologists.

We've learned a fair amount about the parasite since 1981,

when Henry Masur and his colleagues at the National Institutes of Health in Bethesda, Maryland, first made the connection between pneumocystis and AIDS. We know, for instance, that it's a minute parasite, one of the tiniest, with a diameter about a third the size of a red blood cell. Like most terrorists, *P. carinii* travels in gangs; its preferred hangout is the lungs, where up to a dozen parasites band together behind a thin, translucent membrane. Heavy infection produces thousands of these cysts, which seriously impair the respiratory function. For all that, though, *P. carinii* remains a mysterious beast; some scientists argue that it isn't even an animal parasite at all, but a type of fungus. Without special staining techniques, *P. carinii* is invisible to the human eye, no matter how powerful the microscope. No wonder even the most scrupulous physicians are apt to overlook it.

The parasite was first described by the great Brazilian parasitologist Carlos Chagas in his original paper on Chagas' disease, the American form of African sleeping sickness, in 1909. Chagas "discovered" it in the lungs of guinea pigs infected with *Trypanosoma cruzi*, although he mistakenly concluded that it was part of the life cycle of the trypanosome, the cause of Chagas' disease. A year later, in 1910, fellow Brazilian Antonio Carini found the same bodies in the lung tissue of jungle rats. This time, Carini correctly identified them as "new" entities, and coined the name *Pneumocystis carinii*—*pneumocystis* for "lung cyst" and *carinii*, well, for the usual reasons. But it wasn't until 1942 that *P. carinii* was recognized as a distinctive "personality" in the parasite world and the causative agent of a rare type of interstitial pneumonia.

The question of why Carini's creatures are so destructive in the bodies of AIDS patients remains a riddle. The few of us who had previously studied the parasite, however, pegged it early on as one of the great invaders of the immunosuppressed. Originally, it was thought to be a disease primarily of underfed babies and the very old. Since then, it has been demonstrated that cancer patients of all ages frequently become infected when their immune systems break down under heavy chemotherapy.

Wallenberg snapped perfectly into my mental profile of the

kind of patient who died of pneumocystis infection: he was old—
seventy-eight—and exceedingly thin, as though malnourished,
or suffering from tuberculosis or cancer. More important, his
elaborate series of lab tests had failed to turn up any of the more
routine pathogenic suspects. That, and the sheer spookiness of
Wallenberg's condition, seemed to point toward pneumocystis.

P. carinii and I were old foes, and it had slipped away from
me before. In Panama during the forties, when I routinely autopsied young, malnourished children and elderly cancer victims
in my role as pathologist at Gorgas Hospital, when I began to
notice something odd about these two groups at opposite ends
of the age scale. Very often, the alveoli, or air pockets, in the
lungs of these individuals would be clogged with a foamy, lat-
ticelike exudate, the nature of which I couldn't identify.

Then one day it came to me in a flash. How had I been so
stupid! The mystery substance in the lungs could be only one
thing—milk. Intravenous feeding of patients was still considered
an innovation at the time and not much used. Instead, gravely
ill patients were normally kept alive on milk. Somehow, I concluded, my autopsy subjects had managed to inhale milk into
their lungs just prior to death. Buoyed by this brilliant piece of
deduction, I started work on a paper about my "discovery," with
the working title, "Inhaled Milk Pneumonia," and would have
published it had the U.S. Army not saved me from broadcasting
an embarrassing scientific error by transferring me to Berlin in
1945.

Still, I clung loyally to the milk theory. When I visited the
refugee camps in Germany, where the survivors of Auschwitz
and other Nazi death camps were housed, I couldn't help but
notice numerous cases of what appeared to be a strange new form
of drug-resistant pneumonia. Although the onset of the disease
was relatively mild, the patients frequently developed bouts of
rocketing fever and extreme respiratory distress, which almost
always ended in death. Talking to a group of German pathologists one day, I was intrigued to find that they had discovered
a mysterious milky material in the lungs of the deceased. Several

years later I made the critical connection—the peculiar honey-combed pattern of pneumonia "caused by milk" was in fact pathological evidence for pneumocystis infection; by then re-searchers, using special stains, had discovered that the "milk" simply represented massive concentrations of the tiny parasite.

The collapse of my milk theory had taught me to maintain a healthy suspicion of my own medical guesswork. So on that cold, dark afternoon in Stockholm, as I walked back to the hotel, trying to mentally construct a case for pneumocystis, I realized that what I'd managed to come up with was still only an inspired hunch. Guesswork improves with age and experience, but a hunch is still a hunch.

When a man's life is clearly at stake, though, it is sometimes proper to act on such impulses. A doctor who is too cautious runs the risk of watching his patient die as he stands by helplessly. In Wallenberg's case, however, there was another serious prob-lem. The only possible treatment for pneumocystis then available was pentamidine isethionate, a dangerous experimental drug. Given Wallenberg's weakened state, it was very possible that the drug could kill him before the disease got the chance.

Back at the hotel I telephoned Orinius and asked him to meet me at the hospital at 5:30. I also requested that Peter Wallenberg be present, in addition to the austere Dr. Munck and a Lutheran pastor (I had assumed that Wallenberg, like most Swedes, was a registered Lutheran). Erik seemed a little alarmed by the calling in of religious expertise but agreed to comply.

Having arrived promptly, I stood at the foot of Wallenberg's bed and addressed myself to the old man, turning from time to time to look at Peter or Dr. Munck, who stood at the door in funereal fashion. Only the pastor had failed to show. What trans-pired next strikes even me, in retrospect, as hard to believe, but the others who were there have repeatedly assured me that my memory is correct.

"Mr. Wallenberg, I have come to some conclusions about your

health," I said, taking a deep breath before plunging ahead. "There is a very good chance that you are going to die. I trust your affairs are in order?"

Wallenberg seemed not the least surprised by my bluntness. He simply stared at Munck, who said, first in Swedish, then in English when rebuked by the boss for not taking my linguistic limitations into account, "We have made the few corrections you requested this morning. Things are the way you want them."

"Good," I said. "Now that you have nothing else to worry about, we will make a major effort to cure you." I then proposed my course of treatment. "First, I want to transfer you to Bellevue Hospital."

"Bellevue Hospital?" said Wallenberg, looking a little startled. "That is in New York, is it not? That is where the poor people go."

"Precisely," I said.

Perplexed, Wallenberg asked, "Do you really think I am strong enough to fly to New York and enter Bellevue Hospital?"

"No," I replied. "To put you on a plane for a ten-hour flight would, at this point, kill you."

"Then how can I go to Bellevue Hospital?"

"There must be a 'Bellevue Hospital' right here in Stockholm. In fact, I have visited it myself. I want you to go to the public hospital at the Karolinska Institute."

"But why a public hospital, when I have a good private clinic here with the best doctors and nurses?"

"There are two ingredients essential to your recovery," I explained, "that can't be found here and that you cannot buy. These are things found only at a large public institution, where hundreds of patients are seen each day, many of whom suffer from pneumonia. First, you need a large house staff—bright, young people with new ideas and with daily experience in dealing with desperate situations. Second, you need a laboratory with specialized technicians available around the clock to monitor your breathing, to do special culture work for bacteria and parasites.

This is a lovely private hospital, but the kind of help you need isn't available here."

Wallenberg thought for a moment, his wise, old eyes taking a slow survey of the faces in the room. "All right, Professor Kean," he said at length, "we will do what you say. But tell me," he asked, still puzzled, "why on earth did you ask for a pastor to be present? We thought you were ready to announce the time had come for the last rites."

"Nothing of the kind," I said. "I simply wanted to change your name."

"What name do you wish me to have?"

"Peter Smith."

"Peter Smith? But I have been baptized Marcus Wallenberg."

"That is why I wanted your pastor. We need to get you re-baptized. If you go into 'Bellevue Hospital' under the name of Marcus Wallenberg, you will probably die. As 'Peter Smith' you'll have a much better chance."

While I let that reasoning sink in, I wondered how often in my years of dealing with economically privileged patients I had seen them receive some of the poorest quality medical care possible. Too often the rich or famous were victims of their own wealth or social status. People tend to think that money, power, and prestige will buy better medical care than the ordinary patient can expect to get. In fact, the reverse is often the case. Fearful of making the wrong decision when the life of some big shot may be at stake, doctors tend to opt for conservative decisions—even when drastic action may be called for. The wealthy become prisoners of their expensive private clinics, where they are cut off from the enlivening, if sometimes chaotic, intellectual and technical resources of great public medical institutions. Often-times, a "Peter Smith"—in other words, an ordinary patient—is much better off.

Why "Peter Smith"? Peter Smith, who Wallenberg was now about to become, was, in real life, a New York banker and a patient of mine. I had seen him just prior to leaving New York for Stockholm, and his medical problems were still in my

thoughts. And, of course, he was blessed with a suitably anonymous name.

"I see your point," said Wallenberg at length. "I agree to
'Bellevue Hospital' and I agree to 'Peter Smith.' "

"Good," I said. "Now, let's get an ambulance and get moving." I turned to Orinius and asked him to telephone the hospital
and let them know that "Peter Smith" was on his way.

Twenty minutes later an ambulance arrived, and, in keeping
with the Bellevue Hospital image, it was a battered wreck—
small, narrow, unheated, with a canvas cot and two metal stools
that screeched and skidded along the chipped enamel floor. We
put "Mr. Smith" into a wheelchair, wrapped him snugly in blankets, and hoisted him into the suspect vehicle for the short drive
to Roslagstulls, one of the many health facilities at the sprawling
Karolinska complex. I climbed in beside Orinius. Peter and the
glum Munck followed in the Saab.

We drove through determined snow flurries and up a long
access road as it wound through the vast, frozen tundra surrounding the hospital before stopping at a side entrance of the
main building. Up a dozen treacherous, ice-covered steps was
an anteroom for coats and boots, which, in turn, opened onto
a typical hospital room whose other door led to a long corridor
with the usual nurses' station at the end. It was a perfect arrangement; we could visit Marcus from outside without going
through the hospital proper, but via the other door he was part
of the routine of a great public hospital—a noisy, bustling, earthy
city hospital.

Orinius and I then met with the chief resident and outlined
our plans for "Mr. Smith." First, we stopped all medication.
Next we arranged for daily studies of the patient's blood, sputum, and pulmonary gases. Specimens from the lungs, blood,
urine, and stool were cultured to see if we could encourage the
elusive pathogen to colonize a petri dish. I still suspected pneumocystis but kept quiet for fear of needlessly depressing everyone.

For the next two days I slept in the hotel but lived at the hospital. I looked at every laboratory examination that was done. I examined Wallenberg himself three or four times each day. I spent hours at the microscope looking in vain for the presence of the pneumocystis parasite, hoping to find it and dreading I might. I watched in agony as the patient's fever spiked up and down the temperature chart in a troubling crescendo. On the morning of the third day, I could stand it no longer. I assembled Orinius, the chief resident, and several junior physicians in a small office next to the sickroom and said, "Now, we will treat the patient."

"Treat what, and with what?" was the astonished response. It was a good question. How do you treat a patient when you have no idea what is ailing him? For a time, I thought about treating him for malaria, but I had been unable to find any trace of the parasite in his blood, and it was hard to believe that his fever would remain so stubbornly persistent without the bug making an appearance.

Liver abscess was another possibility. Wallenberg had traveled widely. He could be harboring colonies of amebas inside his liver that wouldn't show up on his tests. He could also be treated for a kidney abscess, another occult disease; in that case, however, the drugs he'd already been given should have brought some improvement. Cancer was also a consideration, of course. Bone marrow studies had tested negative for tumor, but the differential diagnosis of "fever of unknown origin"—FUO—is enormous and includes cancers that may be buried deep within the internal organs.

Good doctors, like good billiard players, have to think at least three moves ahead. A consensus exists inside the medical community on which drugs should be given first and, if those fail, which should be given next. The problem with Wallenberg was that, after three weeks of illness, virtually all standard antibiotics had been used without success, and he was getting worse. His daily bouts with fever left him exhausted. Three days in the hospital without medication, without diagnosis, without improvement, and without the luxury of many more days to experiment, left the situation at a complete intellectual and medical impasse.

So I said to my Swedish colleagues, "First, we will treat him for tuberculosis." The resident, awed by the situation, made no objection. But a gutsy young intern, with a scraggly blond beard and dark circles under his eyes, stood up and protested, "There's absolutely no evidence for tuberculosis as an important factor." Orinius, normally polite beyond reason, was edgy—and told him to sit down.

"A man of Mr. Wallenberg's age," said the older doctor, "may, as Professor Kean suggests, have tuberculosis without our being able to find the focus. Besides, there is some suggestion he may have had the disease as a young man." This was true, but then what man of Wallenberg's age didn't have vestigial scars at the apex of his lungs to suggest an undiagnosed tuberculosis infection overcome early in life? The intern had been right to raise the question.

Why Orinius trusted me I will never know. Maybe he considered me his specialist of last resort, since so many Swedish experts had already failed his patient. Or possibly he was simply sick at heart for seeing his old friend Wallenberg wasting away before his eyes. He may have been as desperate as I was to take some reasonable action—and as ready to accept the risk of being wrong. Whatever the cause, he was clearly in my corner and I felt reassured by his support.

"We will use all three drugs available for the treatment of tuberculosis," I continued, "and use them at the same time. Unfortunately, it could take weeks to show definite progress. Meanwhile, he could die of something else while we're trying to treat him for a disease he may not have."

It was then that I dropped my bombshell. "Since time is running out," I said, feeling a sudden surge of nerves, "I want the patient to be treated with large intravenous doses of chloramphenicol simultaneously administered with hydrocortisone."

This last piece of news rattled even the even-keeled Orinius.

How could I blame him? Chloramphenicol was generally regarded as a highly dangerous drug. Developed in the early fifties, it was one of the first major antibiotics after penicillin. It was a real powerhouse, capable of knocking out a wide range of infections, especially those of the lungs. Anything that effective, of course, is bound to be abused—and it was. Soon doctors were using it to treat simple colds and flu. Unhappily, a few patients—one in every twenty thousand or so—acquired a brutal blood disease called aplastic anemia and died. As the horror stories spread, chloramphenicol rapidly fell into disuse.

The drug would have been banned outright had it not been for its special role in controlling typhoid fever—a tropical disease. And since I was a tropical medicine man of a certain age, I was probably one of only a handful of doctors worldwide who had administered vast quantities of chloramphenicol for the serious purpose it had been intended.

"Why do you want to use chloramphenicol?" asked Orinius. Secretly, I felt that it was at least possible that the drug, one of the few antibiotics that hadn't yet been tried, might just prove effective against an atypical pneumonia. Conceivably, it might even work on pneumocystis, although a connection between the drug and the disease had never been established. But how could I explain to my medical colleagues that my gut told me it was the right medicine to use? Try as I might, I couldn't think of a scientifically acceptable answer at the moment, so I made one up.

"His fever could be due to typhoid," I said. "The blood titers are not positive, but there are instances in which the test does not become strongly positive until some weeks have elapsed. He could have acquired typhoid in Florida. It *is* semitropical territory."

Orinius was reluctant. "Why the cortisone?" he asked.

I had a better explanation for that. After weeks of taking potent antibiotics, Wallenberg's blood was full of harmful toxins, both from the drugs and from the infection itself. Another superdrug might send him into shock, which had already happened once earlier in his illness. The cortisone would help prevent a recurrence and might actually amplify the efficacy of the antibiotic.

Orinius and the others still weren't happy, so I suggested that we take the case to the patient himself.

Once again, we assembled in Wallenberg's room. Present were Peter, Dr. Munck, Orinius, and, this time, the chief resident. The old man's entire demeanor had changed. All the forced good humor of the first two days had fled. No question about it—he was now fighting for his life. He listened to me with eyes half closed.

"We still don't know what's wrong with you," I said, embarrassed by our inability to crack the case. "Nevertheless, I feel we should treat you for tuberculosis, which I do not think you have, but the drugs won't hurt you and can be stopped at any time."

Wallenberg nodded weakly, so I continued. "The other drug I want to use," I said, "could kill you. It kills one individual in twenty thousand, though you are probably at somewhat greater risk given your condition and the high dosage you will require. At the moment, I think that's a chance we've got to take. You should also realize that this program has been designed by me, and I am responsible for anything that goes wrong. Dr. Orinius here is fearful that you might be damaged by the therapy. The choice is up to you."

Wallenberg clenched his teeth and tried to prop himself up on his elbows; he wanted to look me in the eye. He stared at me for a few moments, then at Orinius, his old friend. "How long will it take to know whether the drugs you suggest are working?" he asked me.

"Let's try it this way. I'll come back in one week. If you're not better then, we'll have to give up and try something else."

"All right," Wallenberg said. "I will take my chances." I shook hands with the dying man and left straight for the airport. I was feeling very sad. It was all too possible that my patient would be dead within forty-eight hours.

Three days later I received a telephone call from Orinius in Stockholm. "He's cured," he said.

"What?"

"Yes, Mr. Wallenberg's fever completely disappeared the day after the treatment was started. This morning he ate a big breakfast. You have saved a great Swede," Orinius went on, beginning to pull my leg a little, "which makes you a great hero, too."

I could barely wait to return to Stockholm to confirm the miraculous cure. What had happened?

There were a number of possibilities. The antituberculosis drugs couldn't have been responsible for the swift drop in fever—they didn't work that way. That left cortisone and chloramphenicol, either of which could have brought down the patient's temperature, although the evidence suggests that the chloramphenicol acted against the mystery infection, whatever it was. As for *Pneumocystis carinii*—well, it was a nice try on my part. You can hardly blame a parasitologist for wanting to get one of his favorite villains into the act. Recent studies provide powerful evidence, however, that chloramphenicol simply does not work against this deadly parasite. In any event, no one has ever been known to recover from pneumocystis in just one day. The plain truth is that to this day I don't have the faintest idea what Wallenberg had or why he was cured.

Would Wallenberg have recovered as Marcus Wallenberg, or did his "rebaptism" as Peter Smith, and his change of hospitals, help save his life? That, too, is impossible to say, although I cling to the perhaps somewhat romantic notion that at least one of my theories paid off.

PART III

THE SHAH'S DOCTOR

CHAPTER 11

Operation Eagle

Tuesday, September 27, 1979, was a gray, humid day in Washington, D.C. I was sitting in the headquarters of the Pan American Health Organization talking about two of life's perennial problems: diarrhea and money. Haiti had too much of the former and not nearly enough of the latter, and I was there in my role as professor of tropical medicine at the New York Hospital–Cornell Medical Center to persuade PAHO officials to part with enough funds to build a badly needed diarrhea control clinic on the outskirts of Port-au-Prince. Since I am the world's worst fundraiser, it was depressing duty.

The officials listened politely but impassively. It was going to be a hard sell. No sooner had I launched into my pitch, however, than I was called away to the telephone. Annoyed, I stalked to a secretary's desk in the outer office and, picking up the receiver, was surprised to hear the familiar voice of Joseph Reed.

" 'Peter Smith' rides again," Reed said.

Peter Smith? What the hell was he talking about? "Peter Smith" had been our code name for Marcus Wallenberg when the Swedish industrialist had staged his miraculous recovery. Had he fallen ill again? "I don't understand," I said. "I just spoke to 'Peter' last week and he's never felt better."

"Wrong 'Peter Smith,' " Reed said. "We've got a new one."

"Where?"

"South of the border. In Mexico. The local doctors say he's got malaria and jaundice. Will you fly down and examine him?"

Good Lord, I thought, he's talking about the Shah of Iran. It was hardly a brilliant deduction. The media had been full of speculation about the Shah's uneasy Mexican interlude. How long would the government of President José López Portillo let him stay? Would President Carter ever admit him to the United States? The prospect of treating someone at the epicenter of world events was electrifying. "Of course I'll go," I told Reed.

Although I was flattered that Reed had called me, I was not completely surprised. Having been a patient of mine for twenty years now, he knew of my passing acquaintance with the Shah and his people. I had met the Shah himself, though briefly, on three previous occasions—once when he was admitted to New York Hospital thirty years before and twice when my medical travels had taken me to Iran. I had treated both Princess Shams, the Shah's elder sister, in Teheran, and his former brother-in-law, Chafik, in New York. But I was first and foremost a malaria man, and if his Mexican doctors were correct, a malaria man was precisely what the Shah needed.

I flew to Mexico City the next afternoon. On the plane, my sense of excitement grew. The political drama unfolding around the Shah promised the intrigues of a good spy novel, and here I was, a graying parasitologist with an adolescent nose for adventure, about to dive into the middle of it all. As the plane dipped and rattled through a patch of rough weather somewhere over the Caribbean, I decided to review what little I knew of the patient's medical history. Were the Mexican doctors right? Could the Shah have malaria?

Geographically speaking, it was entirely possible. True, malaria was not a common ailment in Mexico, but it did occur, and travelers who were not adequately medicated were especially vulnerable. Something didn't quite fit, however. The Shah, I recalled Reed telling me, also suffered from jaundice, a yellowing of the skin and eyes that signals a dangerous buildup of toxins in the liver. From experience, I knew jaundice was only rarely a symptom of malaria. So where had he picked *that* up?

Then I remembered. The Shah's escape from Teheran had taken him briefly to Cairo and then on to Morocco and the Bahamas. Any student of epidemiology knew that hepatitis was endemic to North Africa and not rare in the Caribbean. And hepatitis—an inflammation of the liver usually caused by a viral infection—was a primary cause of jaundice. If the Shah did indeed suffer from malaria and infectious hepatitis, there was a good chance that I could have him on the mend very soon. Both diseases were serious, but with early detection and the right drugs they could be treated easily enough.

By the time we reached the coastline of Mexico, my excitement had faded and I felt truly miserable. For some reason I couldn't quite fathom—occupational skepticism, ESP, or indigestion from a very bad airline meal, perhaps—I was more and more uncomfortable with the Mexican diagnosis. My paltry supply of clues about the patient's condition and my forced inaction now tortured me. Settle down, Kean, I told myself. You don't have a parachute, so you'll just have to wait.

Two hours later I found myself in a battered black Cadillac hurtling through the low, peaceful hills surrounding Mexico City at astonishing speed. The sun was shining hotly. Accompanying me were Richard Armao, the younger brother of Robert, the Shah's American spokesman, whom Robert had deputed to guide me to my patient, and Mark Morse, Robert's assistant. At the wheel was a loquacious Mexican chauffeur with a stereotypical "bandido" mustache. Our destination, barring slaughter on the road, was the sleepy resort town of Cuernavaca sixty miles south of the capital, where we would come to a house-turned-fortress called the *Casa de las Rosas*. Holed up inside this Villa of

Roses we would find the man our driver referred to as *el máximo jefe*, the Shah of Iran.

Just before we reached the Cuernavaca city limits, the car lurched up a steep, twisting road and stopped abruptly at a dead-end. Before us a heavy iron gate rolled noisily back on its hinges and we drove into the courtyard of the Villa of Roses. The main house, a sprawling hacienda, sat at the edge of a river and was encircled by a high wall and terraced gardens dripping bougainvillea, frangipani, and other unfamiliar tropical flowers of startling reds, greens and yellows.

Given its name, I had expected the place to be exploding with roses. Oddly, though, I can't recall ever seeing a single one. My most vivid memory—appropriate enough for a parasitologist—is of the clouds of anopheline mosquitoes that hung like halos over the garden lamps in the sultry evening air. That part of my brain reserved for recording medical clues automatically noted this possible indicator of any one of three varieties of malaria. The Shah may or may not have malaria, I thought, but he is certainly in the right neighborhood for it.

We drove through the gate and were greeted by a pleasant-looking woman with coppery skin and big, sad eyes, who Richard Armao introduced as Dr. Liossa Pirnia, the pediatrician for the royal family, who had chosen to follow her monarch into exile. Together we walked up the cobblestoned drive and entered the big house through a cavernous garage. Inside were a dozen or so heavily armed Mexicans, some with submachine guns slung from their necks, others fingering carbines and revolvers. On the outer perimeter of the compound alone, I later learned, there were some thirty machine-gun emplacements all manned around the clock and synchronized with interlocking fields of fire. Assassins trying to stage a raid were likely to succeed only in stopping large amounts of hot lead. Bribing their way in would prove difficult, too. The local chief of police, Armao said, was a very happy man these days. Having been duly entered on the Shah's payroll, he was making many times his regular salary in "consulting fees."

We proceeded into the main house and up a deeply carpeted stairway. Entering a large, airy bedroom on the second floor, we were suddenly standing before His Imperial Majesty, the Shahanshah. The deposed monarch was lying on a canopied bed in his robe and slippers, but got up when we walked in and said, "Thank you for coming, Dr. Kean. I hope you can help me. As you can see, I am a very sick man."

He was indeed. I had last seen the Shah in 1967 when I'd visited Teheran to study an affliction called schistosomiasis, or "snail fever," which still causes several million serious cases of liver and bladder disease in humans in the Near East each year. I'd found him a gracious, friendly host. He had an incisive mind and a soft but compelling way of speaking, and I had enjoyed my conversation with a man who looked the picture of health and fitness.

But now, in Mexico, he was a man transformed by disease. The Shah had become a sad, shrunken figure who looked like the victim of some viciously accelerated aging process. The thought that someone could have changed so profoundly so fast depressed me.

Armao had already taken me aside and coached me on how to behave; I would always address the Shah as "Your Imperial Majesty"; I would speak only when spoken to; I would never sit in the royal presence, and so on and so forth. All the pomp and circumstance, I must confess, went against my grain. My populist parents had taught me to take a dim view of what they called "putting on airs," so it was small wonder that lofty titles like "You Imperial Majesty" did not roll lightly off my tongue. I tried—and fumbled. There was a trace of a smile on the Shah's face when he told me, "You may call me 'Sir,' if that is easier for you."

I started the examination. The afternoon light was fading fast, so I had the patient step to the window where I lifted his eyelids with my thumb. The whites of his eyes were a scaly yellow. Even in the gathering shadows I could see he was severely jaundiced. I next examined the Shah's urine specimen, a thick, mahogany-colored syrup in clinical harmony with his jaundice.

Then an important fact emerged. The Shah informed me that his stools were whitish, and a warning flare went off inside my head. The discoloration raised the possibility that something was blocking the bile duct and preventing the liver from discharging its normal secretions. If true, that would mean his jaundice was caused by neither malaria nor hepatitis, but by an obstruction of some kind. And that meant either gallstones or a tumor.

The Shah removed his pajama top, and I felt the back of his neck for enlarged lymph nodes. Cancer, especially of the pancreas, stomach, or liver, can cause pronounced yellowing of the skin. More often, however, it first manifests itself in enlarged lymph glands in the neck. Stomach cancer is a fairly common disease among Iranians; circumstantial if not scientific evidence points to the heavy concentration of salt and spices in their national diet.

The Shah's neck appeared to be normal, however. I then listened to his chest and took his pulse. His heart, lungs, and blood pressure all seemed to be in good order. But I was now convinced the Shah's condition was more complicated than I'd been led to believe. Arriving at an accurate diagnosis was not going to be easy.

When the examination was over, I told the Shah and Empress Farah, his wife, that I would return the following morning and said goodnight. But as I left the room, I was more troubled than ever. The facts had begun to speak for themselves. For weeks now, the Shah had complained intermittently of fever, chills, and abdominal pains. His Mexican doctors had given him chloroquine, a powerful antimalarial drug, but his symptoms had persisted. The diagnosis of hepatitis rang false, too. Tests done by the local doctors were puzzling; levels of the enzyme normally signaling infection were only slightly elevated. Jaundice as deep and persistent as the Shah's should have resulted in sky-high readings.

I asked the Mexican doctors to show me the slides that had

persuaded them the Shah had malaria and they set up a microscope in an anteroom just outside the Shah's bedchamber. Having prepared and examined thousands of malaria slides, the process was as familiar to me as brushing my teeth. I knew what to look for, and I did not see it in any of the specimens they now presented.

Granted, the malaria parasite is not easy to spot. It is a single-celled creature far too small for the naked eye to perceive. Usually transmitted by a mosquito bite, it is one of the true mass murderers of human history; it has killed more people than all the wars from Carthage to Vietnam combined and all the violent purges from the time of the Spanish Inquisition through Stalin. Before the Second World World malaria was a leading cause of human mortality worldwide and to this day routinely kills nearly a million and a half people each year.

Given its grisly past, the parasite's physical beauty comes as something of a surprise. To see the beast clearly, it must be viewed under a high-power microscope. To do that, you first smear a thin layer of red blood cells from the human host across a glass slide and then stain the cells so they turn a pinkish, crepuscular color. If the elusive parasite is present, it will stand out against the rainbowed backdrop of the microscopic field—a tiny, soft blue halo encircling a nucleus of ruby red. The staining is all-important; clumsily done, it can be worse than no testing at all, because it inevitably leads to a mistaken diagnosis when platelets, elements in the blood that help clotting, are confused with the pathogen. It can be a fatal error.

Sure enough, when I asked the Mexican doctors to point out the "parasites" that had confirmed their diagnosis, again and again they pointed not to malaria but to platelets, their microscopic imposters. When I explained their error, the senior Mexican physician greeted the news huffily. I felt my blood pressure rise a little, too. But there was no use in either of us getting angry; the mistake was as common in hospitals in Cleveland as it was in Cuernavaca. And no harsh words or hurt feelings would change the painful fact that the diagnosis was wrong. The patient did not have malaria.

As it turned out, the tests the Mexicans had done for hepatitis were equally dubious. So I was back to the question I had pondered on the flight from New York: If the Shah didn't have malaria or hepatitis, what *was* wrong with him?

I reconsidered my earlier hunch that the Shah had obstructive jaundice—something was blocking the bile ducts leading from the liver to the intestine. But was it gallstones or cancer? Either way, major surgery would almost certainly be required. Only reliable blood tests, followed by a battery of X rays, would pinpoint the real culprit. And there was no way we could find the answers we needed as long as the Shah stayed put. He would have to leave his Cuernavaca fortress for a major medical facility.

The next morning Dr. Pirnia and I went to see the Shah. A long sleep had done him good. He had lost his melancholy of the previous evening and spoke animatedly—and a little eerily, I thought—about how he hoped to return shortly to the glories of court life, his "beloved" people, and a Peacock Throne that no longer existed.

In the bright daylight, the depth of the patient's jaundice was startling. I continued hunting for gallstones or cancer, but solid clues were hard to come by. The Shah flinched slightly when I began working my fingertips along his abdomen, feeling for the spleen. I asked him to take a deep breath and, once or twice, I thought I felt the edge of the organ, but then decided I was imagining things. For the spleen to be palpable, it must be twice or three times its normal size. In a man of fifty-nine, with both severe jaundice and weight loss, a palpable spleen would almost certainly signal cancer. But, try as I might, I could feel nothing. How I ached for a battery of sophisticated laboratory tests. Somehow, I thought, I've got to get this man to a first-class hospital and pronto.

Before that, though, there was one last check I had to make.

Jaundice can also be caused by a toxic reaction to drugs. While I thought this unlikely in the Shah's case, I broke off the examination momentarily, mumbled an excuse, and went into the royal bathroom. Lined up in neat rows on the counter were more than two dozen bottles of pills and tubes of salve. Just what I had suspected. The Shah, like many international travelers, was a "hotel medicine" junkie, a collector of the chemical garbage that is peddled in every port around the globe to great fanfare and little curative effect. The Shah's cache was pretty harmless stuff—mostly what the French call *digestives*, or antacids. It contained nothing that would either explain the Shah's symptoms or relieve them.

When I returned to the bedroom, the Shah looked at me expectantly. "You do not have malaria," I said bluntly. "You probably never did." I told him hepatitis would also probably have to be ruled out. "You have obstructive jaundice," I said, "and we need to find out what's causing it."

I told him that I was not enthusiastic about the lab facilities in Cuernavaca, and the Shah nodded in agreement. On the other hand, I said, Mexico City did have excellent pathology labs. The Shah could not visit the city in person for fear of being killed by assassins, but we could certainly take a vial or two of his blood there without incident. I suggested sending samples to the two top hospitals in the city. Another test tube would return to New York Hospital with me as a fail-safe.

The Shah smiled softly, but shook his head. "I spoke with my French doctors on the telephone last night," he said. "They encouraged me to continue taking the cortisone they prescribed some weeks ago for my hepatitis. You will understand that I feel obliged to follow their advice."

I was flabbergasted. French doctors? No one had ever mentioned them before. Whoever they were, I didn't think they were behaving very responsibly. For one thing, the idea of treating somebody so seriously ill by long distance was absurd. More to the point, the diagnosis of hepatitis, though still a remote theoretical possibility, flew in the face of the mounting medical evidence. But the prescribing of cortisone was incredible. It was no longer the treatment of choice for hepatitis, and for a very good reason. Using it for the wrong ailment was not only dangerous— it could be fatal.

As diplomatically as I could, I told the Shah how I felt. "You require much more sophisticated care than you're now getting," I said. "If you are going to be treated by your French doctors, I urge you to have them come to Cuernavaca and be responsible for you. Either that or seek the best possible medical care in Mexico."

The Shah was polite, but adamant. He made it clear that he intended to call his own medical shots and trusted his French doctors. Above all—and this I found downright peculiar—he wanted absolutely no blood tests. Having firmly outlined his plans for treatment, which did not include me, he thanked me for coming. As I was leaving, Empress Farah presented me with a lovely silver box engraved with the royal peacock crest. It was the classiest brush-off I had ever experienced in forty years of making house calls, but there was no mistaking the message: my services would no longer be required.

Flying home to New York, I was both puzzled and angry. The patient, I was convinced, was hiding something from me. There was not a damn thing I could do about it now, however; I had just been fired.

Two weeks later, Joseph Reed was on the telephone again. "We've been lied to," he said. "The Shah's got cancer. He's had it for years. You've got to go back to Cuernavaca. He wants you to treat him now." The next day I was on a plane back to Mexico City. I suppose I should have been pleased at having been called back into the case, but I was too wrapped up in the serious business at hand to feel any satisfaction. Cancer and jaundice were a disastrous combination.

When the gates to the Shah's hacienda rolled back this time, I was met by Robert Armao himself. Slightly built, polished, and intense, Armao was then in his early thirties. He had met the Shah while working for Nelson Rockefeller when Rockefeller was Governor of New York and, later, Vice President of the United States. These days Armao ran his own public relations firm in Manhattan, and since the Shah's escape from Teheran in January he had been spending virtually all of his time trying to sort through the logistical twists and turns of his client's troubled hegira.

Something in Armao's manner told me the whole atmosphere had changed. Normally exuding the cheerful, unflappable demeanor of the consummate spokesperson, Armao now looked worried. "They didn't level with us," he said testily. The Shah's cancer had obviously come as a shock to him, too.

Standing next to Armao was a tall, youthful looking man with a head of light-brown hair, gold-rimmed glasses, and a jaunty European manner. Armao introduced him as Georges Flandrin, one of the Shah's two mysterious French physicians; the other one, I learned, was a man named Jean Bernard, head of the Institute for Research on Leukemia at the Hôpital Saint-Louis in Paris. So that was it, I thought. Bernard and Flandrin. Now I knew why the Shah had tried to keep the two doctors in the background. Both were prominent cancer specialists with international reputations. Mentioning Professor Bernard's name, in particular, was equivalent to shouting "lymphatic cancer" from the rooftops.

So the secret was finally out. The Shah had lymphatic cancer, and Flandrin was eager to brief me, as if he wanted to share an uncomfortable burden. Handing me a thirty-five-page report on the Shah's condition, he apologized for the haphazard care the patient had received but, as he summarized the dossier for me orally, it quickly became apparent that I had judged the Frenchmen too hastily.

The Shah, Flandrin explained, had had cancer for nearly seven years. During all that time, he had refused to let his doctors perform the tests necessary to establish a definitive diagnosis. The Frenchmen could hardly be faulted. The Shah's care had long since become hostage to the patient's overriding fear of publicity. Beginning in the early seventies, his political opponents inside Iran had been gaining strength underground. World opinion was starting to tip against him. News that he was suffering from a possibly terminal illness, he seemed to feel, could only compromise the achievement of his driving ambition: to survive long enough, both physically and politically, to see the Pahlavi Dynasty pass safely into the hands of his then teenage son Reza. So, in the spring of 1974, when Flandrin and Bernard found his spleen enlarged and begged him to undergo thorough testing and a biopsy, he had not only refused, but had threatened to fire them and find new doctors.

It was, medically speaking, a foolish decision for the Shah to make. The French physicians could only theorize that the Shah suffered from a cancer of the lymph nodes and spleen, probably lymphatic lymphoma. They had put the Shah on chlorambucil, a mild anticancer drug that seemed to have held the disease in check for nearly five years. Then, in January of 1979, when the Shah was forced to flee Teheran, it was almost as if the sudden shock of exile had started the cancer cells spreading again, this time with a special vengeance.

"By then," Flandrin explained, "the Shah had developed hard lymph nodes in his neck. But again, we were not permitted to do a biopsy." Flandrin started him on a five-month program of chemotherapy that included the puzzling cortisone the Shah had mentioned during my first visit to Cuernavaca. That explained why, by the time I first examined the Shah in September, both his neck nodes and his spleen had shrunk back to within normal limits and I could feel nothing unusual. The treatment, at least for the time being, had been a great success.

"When the patient became ill here in Mexico," Flandrin went on, "we all accepted the local physician's diagnosis that he had simply picked up malaria." But now the Shah's condition had taken a dramatic turn for the worse. The hard, walnut sized tumors in his neck had reappeared and begun to grow. Again, his spleen had become swollen and tender. Flandrin knew that the chemotherapy was no longer working. Visibly agitated, the Frenchman flung both hands in the air and said with frustration, "It has been absolutely *impossible* from the very beginning."

Freighted with bad news, I went upstairs to see the Shah. He looked ten times worse than the last time I had seen him two weeks before, and he had looked on death's doorstep then. Any first-year medical student could tell he needed to be hospitalized immediately.

He looked at me and smiled. "You must understand that for reasons of state I could not before tell you the nature of my illness," he said apologetically. "I must think of my country's survival and of passing on the mantle to my son."

"Your Imperial Majesty," I said, "we must get you to a hospital right away. You have multiple life-threatening illnesses. We've got to develop a comprehensive diagnosis, and that won't be easy. Your case is too complicated for any one doctor or pair of doctors. You will almost certainly require surgery. What you need is a medical team—a diagnostician, a surgeon, an oncologist, a hematologist, a radiologist, a nutritionist, an infectious disease specialist, and a supportive house staff."

"Where might such a team be assembled?" the Shah asked.

That was by no means an easy question to answer in his case. He was so plainly unwelcome almost everywhere in the world. What could you possibly say to reassure such a patient? That was when I invented the "Mali Option." We could, I told him, charter an airplane, gather the right people and gear, pitch a hospital tent, and get the job done anywhere—even in a place like Mali, one of the smallest, poorest, most underdeveloped countries on earth. The place was not important; the medical team and the machinery were the real keys.

Still, there were many more attractive alternatives to operating in Mali. I rattled off a list of countries where we would need take no such extreme measures—Britain, Switzerland, Brazil, Canada, Australia, Argentina, Japan. As each country was mentioned, the Shah shook his head. "I am not welcome," he said. Maybe he should go to France then, I suggested, since French doctors had been treating him all along and were familiar with his case. Again he said, "I am not welcome."

It was then that I told my story about how changing Marcus Wallenberg's name to the anonymous "Peter Smith" had helped save his life. "Maybe it's time we rebaptized you, too," I said.

The Shah grinned. "You forget," he said, "I am a Muslim and cannot be baptized." We both laughed at the gallows humor. Adopting a new, anonymous identity might be possible for a mere millionaire or movie star, I realized, but it was out of the question for the self-proclaimed Shah of Shahs. There was nowhere on earth the Shah could go and not be immediately recognized.

For the moment, then, the options boiled down to either Mexico or the United States. The Shah was not enthusiastic about Mexico. There he would be battling a language barrier; only the top Mexican doctors spoke English, and none of the Shah's advisors spoke Spanish. Security was another headache. The array of equipment needed to diagnose and treat the Shah—sophisticated CAT scanners and sonograms for imaging tumors, for instance—were spread out over three hospitals. The Shah would have to shuttle among them and, with the Ayatollah's "death squads" still rumored to be on the prowl, his bodyguards worried about his exposure.

From a medical standpoint, I strongly favored the United States. There were at least seven U.S. cities boasting world-class medical centers where an exceptional team of physicians, nurses, and technicians could be quickly assembled. I mentioned Houston, Los Angeles, Palo Alto, San Francisco, Chicago, Boston, and, of course, my own home turf, New York City.

The Shah bridled with anger at the mention of the United States. Under Jimmy Carter, he said, the United States, an ally of thirty-seven years, had betrayed him. Washington had given him conflicting advice about how to handle the Islamic revolution. Ultimately, he believed, American stupidity and duplicity had cost him his kingdom.

If that wasn't enough, the Shah went on, the Americans had tacitly promised to invite him to stay in the United States if and when he found it necessary to abandon Teheran. So he had left quietly only to have Carter renege on the deal. The Shah insisted he was too much of a realist to be shocked by such behavior. Nonetheless, he had made no secret of his bitterness toward the American president and had repeatedly vowed to his friends and retainers during his first months of exile that he would never go to the United States, even if formally invited.

But it was now the middle of October, the tenth month of his hegira, and the Shah's rapidly deteriorating physical condition was working a slow, grudging change of heart. He posed the question to me: "If one were to go to the States for treatment," he asked, "where would one go?" The language was guarded, but clearly, even in the Shah's own mind, the question was anything but hypothetical.

The diplomatic problems swirling around the Shah were every bit as complicated as his medical condition. His sudden departure from Iran had created a vacuum. The Ayatollah, though celebrated as the hero of the revolution, was still struggling to consolidate his hold on power. The government of Prime Minister Mehdi Bazargan, a moderate, was proving hopelessly ineffectual in accommodating the more radical aims of the country's fundamentalist Islamic clergy and its militant students.

The Shah's demise had also dropped a bombshell on Washington. Perhaps America's greatest friend in the Persian Gulf, the Shah had been the anchor of U.S. strategy in the oil-rich region and his collapse had shaken American confidence. To keep the turmoil in Iran from destabilizing the entire Middle East, Jimmy Carter had to search for ways to establish ties with Iran's new rulers. The Shah's appearance on American soil would effectively cancel out that option.

With presidential primaries only a few months away, Carter was clearly on the spot. As evidence mounted that the Shah was indeed gravely ill, it was growing increasingly difficult for him to ignore a former friend now so clearly in need of help. In New York and Washington, the Shah's staunchest American friends—David Rockefeller, Henry Kissinger, and establishment insiders like John McCloy—were not about to let Carter forget his responsibilities to an old ally. While the Shah languished at Cuernavaca, negotiations between his men and the State Department were suddenly thrown into high gear.

The whole business was deeply frustrating. Here I had a dying man on my hands, and I still had no idea where he would be treated. Time was running out, and the bureaucrats were, in effect, still bickering over the shape of the negotiating table.

Then, on October 19, 1979, Dr. Flandrin officially withdrew as the Shah's chief physician. Paris was too far from Cuernavaca, and he felt he was no longer in a position to provide the kind of intensive care the Shah now required. So out of the swirl of events, at least one thing had resolved itself: I was now the Shah's doctor, and there was much work to be done.

That night, back in New York, I telephoned Dr. Eben Dustin in Washington. Dustin was the State Department's chief medical officer, who, alerted to my involvement in the case, had called me before my last trip to Cuernavaca and asked me to brief him on the Shah's condition when I returned. "Should I assume that this report might be sent to the president?" I asked.

"That's a good assumption," said Dustin.

"All right," I declared—a little too preciously, I thought later—"I will make it with all the accuracy and earnestness that I would give if I were reporting directly to the president." I told Dr. Dustin that the Shah suffered from at least five distinct conditions, all demanding immediate treatment: obstructive jaundice due to cancer, type undetermined, or gallstones; lymphatic lymphoma of his cervical lymph nodes (on the neck); splenomegaly (swollen spleen), probably due to lymphoma; leukopenia (low white blood cell count); and anemia (low red blood cell count), both also probably linked to his lymphoma. He would need surgery to relieve the obstruction, chemotherapy or radiotherapy for his neck tumors, transfusions to rehabilitate his blood, and removal of his spleen when he was strong enough to tolerate the surgery.

Throughout the conversation, I consciously avoided mentioning the United States or New York City. I wanted no part in any political decision. I would tend to the medicine and let the government boys draw their own conclusions.

"How much time do we have?" Dustin asked.

"Days. Maybe weeks. We do not have months."

He paused, drew a clearly audible breath, and asked the sixty-four-million-dollar question: "Where do you feel is the best place to treat the Shah?"

"Frankly," I said, "I would prefer my team at New York Hospital, but any of the other major medical centers in the country are perfectly qualified."

"Can you treat him in Mexico?"

"Not as easily or as quickly, but it could be done."

We left it at that. Dustin, an experienced general practitioner of excellent reputation, grasped the need to move swiftly. He said he would confirm my diagnosis through his own channels, but there would be no need for further time-consuming examinations of the Shah himself. The Shah's condition, while complicated, was straight from the textbooks and there could be little debate about what had to be done. Or so I thought.

Science magazine, in a story purporting to analyze the basis on which the Shah was admitted to the United States, would later claim that I had lied to get the Shah into the United States. It accused me of telling Dustin that the Shah was at the point of death and could only be treated in the U.S. That may indeed have been the message, purposely garbled or not, that eventually worked its way up the bureaucratic ladder to the ear of the president. But it did not come from me nor, I am confident, from

235

Dr. Dustin. There were many layers of officialdom between Dustin and the president and many senior bureaucrats with their own vested and often opposing interests in the outcome of the Shah's odyssey.

In any event, the *Science* allegations were ridiculous. I was identified as a paid minion of David Rockefeller, despite the fact that I had never met the man (and the Shah, you can be sure, paid all of his own medical bills). What's more, I was accused of performing a flawed and superficial diagnosis. The magazine would eventually retract its judgments about me when my medical colleagues stepped forward to vouch for the thoroughness of my diagnosis and affidavits from key U.S. government officials showed I was telling the truth. Annoying as the incident was to me personally, however, it was a good barometer of the emotion and conflicting perceptions that the Shah's presence in the United States had stirred up.

That is not to say that the "Rockefeller interests" weren't busily at work. They were. David Rockefeller and the Shah were old friends. In 1953, the CIA had helped topple the nationalistic government headed by Mohammed Mossadegh and restored the Shah to power. Since then, Rockefeller's Chase Manhattan Bank had managed many of his important financial dealings. His powerful friends in Washington had frequently lobbied the White House and the State Department on the Shah's behalf.* But since I knew none of these titans personally, I remained a cog lost among the big wheels.

Nonetheless, it became perfectly clear that my visits to the Villa of Roses and my reports on the Shah's fitness were getting attention at the highest levels. After each of my trips to Mexico, I telephoned either Armao or Rockefeller's chief of staff, Joseph Reed, and told them about my findings. They, in turn, would report, as I learned later, to David D. Newsom, undersecretary of state for political affairs, who had been tapped by Secretary of State Cyrus Vance to handle the diplomatic back channel.

---

*See Pierre Salinger, *America Held Hostage: The Secret Negotiations* (New York: Doubleday, 1981), 20–21.

OPERATION EAGLE

During one of our conversations, Reed began referring to someone or something called the "Eagle." I was confused, until I realized he meant the Shah. I had to chuckle to myself. Obviously, the "Peter Smith" code name was now passé and had to be replaced by a handle more worthy of a bona fide international intrigue. Soon Reed was talking about "Operation Eagle," by which I understood him to mean the campaign by Rockefeller and others to get the Shah admitted to the U.S. Just how this "old boy network" functioned and how much it influenced President Carter's ultimate decision is impossible for me to say, although political observers far more astute than I have suggested that its pull was relatively inconsequential—and I suspect they are right. Whatever the circumstances, Carter decided on October 20, 1979, to admit the Shah "for humanitarian purposes."

I was at New York Hospital that afternoon when Armao called from Cuernavaca. "Get ready," he said, trying unsuccessfully to keep his glee in check, "the Shah's finally coming." There would be a brief delay, however. "The Pentagon," Armao explained, his tone growing suddenly somber, "wants to get more marines into several of our embassies around the world in case there's any trouble." His stress fell ominously on that final word.

The Mexican Bombshell

The "Eagle" landed at New York's La Guardia Airport on October 22, 1979. It was nearly midnight by the time the Shah's Gulfstream jet rolled to a stop on an isolated stretch of runway that had been cordoned off by the authorities. Police patrol cars, lights flashing and sirens screaming, escorted the Shah's bulletproof limousine through the late-night traffic toward Princess Ashraf's house at Beekman Place, so that the Shah could have a few minutes alone with his children, who were staying with their aunt. But when the entourage arrived in midtown Manhattan, word came over the car radio that a photographer was lurking outside Ashraf's townhouse. Fearful of publicity, the party immediately changed course and drove to the corner of York Avenue and Seventieth Street and the towering gray buildings of the New York Hospital–Cornell Medical Center.

I was waiting at the main entrance and watched as the Shah's wheelchair came into view. He looked so weak and fragile that my stomach churned. "Welcome to New York Hospital, Your Imperial Majesty," I said.

The Shah smiled thinly. "I can't say it's good to be back," he said, "but I am glad to finally be here."

Having escorted him to his seventeenth-floor room, I told the patient that I had taken the liberty of admitting him under the name of David D. Newsom, the State Department man, and I handed him his hospital identification bracelet. He laughed for the first time since his arrival.

Hibbard Williams, chief of medicine at the hospital and my old friend, was also in the room, as was Richard Cohen, the chief medical resident, who would deftly coordinate a thousand details during the Shah's stay. As they went to work examining the patient, I returned to my apartment across the street from the hospital for a shot of Jack Daniels, a cigar, and a good night's sleep. Thank heavens, I thought, as I slid under the covers, the Shah is finally where he belongs.

Events now seemed to speed up with a vengeance. In the two days since my return from Mexico, I'd assembled the medical team that, through Dr. Dustin at State, I had assured the president was needed to properly treat the patient. Williams and Cohen would be in charge of the Shah's immediate medical needs. Waiting in the wings were a surgeon specializing in gallbladder disease, an oncologist, a radiologist, and a hematologist—all seasoned pros, each with his own crucial role to play.

Within twenty-four hours, ultrasound tests confirmed that the Shah did indeed have gallstones which were surgically removed. Two days later, on his sixtieth birthday, the empress gathered a few doctors and retainers in his suite for a quiet celebration. The Shah was cheerful and, in keeping with the nonalcoholic rigors of Islamic custom, much orange juice was consumed.

Then came the first really bad news. A biopsy of one of the Shah's neck tumors showed that the patient, contrary to the educated guesswork of his French specialists, was no longer suffering from lymphatic lymphoma, if indeed he ever had been. He now had histiocytic lymphosarcoma, a much more lethal form of cancer.

This finally solved the Mexican puzzle; the Shah had been suffering from both gallstones *and* cancer. We decided that when he had sufficiently recovered from his gallbladder surgery we would take out his spleen as well.

But the crowning complication had nothing to do with medicine. On November 4, thirteen days after the Shah's arrival in New York, his former subjects seized the U.S. embassy in Teheran, taking sixty-five Americans hostage and, as a precondition for their release, demanding the immediate return to Teheran of "the greatest criminal history has seen." Both medically and politically, we had entered a whole new ball game.

The oncologists had by now determined that the Shah's cancer was metastasizing rapidly throughout his body. Even so, they held out uphill hopes for a cure. But it would require radical action. Radiation therapy would be used to attack the Shah's neck tumors, which by now had grown to the size of golf balls. His spleen would have to come out as soon as he was strong enough to withstand another round of major surgery. Finally, he would need at least eighteen months of intensive chemotherapy.

I didn't dispute the proposed course of action, but I was less sanguine than the oncologists about the long-term prognosis. To confirm my suspicions, I reviewed the slides of the Shah's tumor with the pathologists who had rendered the report, and then with two of my most trusted colleagues: John Ellis, Cornell's senior professor of pathology, and Philip Lieberman, chief of pathology at Memorial Sloan-Kettering. Both confirmed the distressing diagnosis.

As the dismal medical reports piled up, I found myself getting angry with my patient. If he had only let his French doctors do a proper biopsy when they first suspected cancer back in 1974, we might now be talking about his optimal survival in terms of years, not weeks or months.

Meanwhile, ripples from the Iranian revolution were already spilling over into Manhattan. The streets outside the hospital were inundated with placard-waving protesters, mostly Iranians, many of them chanting "Death to the Shah." Hospital switchboards were flooded with calls from people threatening to kill the Shah, blow up the building, kill themselves kamikaze-style, or engage in some other form of extreme violence unless the Shah was sent packing back to Iran to stand trial.

Police patrolled the grounds for intruders around the clock. Outside the Shah's suite on the seventeenth floor security guards carefully screened all visitors. At home, my telephone rang constantly. Anonymous Iranian groups from around the country kept calling me to suggest a variety of bizarre schemes to use the Shah as bait to spring our hostages.

Then one night a caller, hissing into the receiver, threatened not only to take me hostage unless the Shah was handed over, but to kidnap Carnoustie, my West Highland terrier, the friend and colleague who had accompanied me to medical school every day for a decade. Now they had gone too far; I stopped answering my telephone.

My medical colleagues had mixed reactions to the Shah's presence. Many were supportive. A few thought the Shah should never have been admitted to the hospital in the first place. Others felt that, for humanitarian reasons, he should be treated and then returned to Teheran and the tender mercies of the Ayatollah. (That logic, I always felt, bore an uncanny similarity to the insane proposition espoused by some of our government and military officials during the Vietnam War that American troops had to destroy a peasant village in order to save it from the enemy.)

Many of the dissenting doctors were simply upset by disruptions they blamed on the Shah. Tight security, unfortunately, made special treatment unavoidable. Radiation therapy, for instance, became a logistical nightmare. The machines were located at the Memorial Sloan-Kettering Cancer Center on the opposite side of York Avenue. To use them, we had to wait until three or four o'clock in the morning when the pedestrian tunnels running beneath the street were judged "secure." This went on for weeks, while orderlies and technicians were paid double and triple overtime for staying up all night. Angered by the intrusion and tired of seeing sleepy-eyed orderlies stumbling through the corridors, one prominent doctor at Sloan-Kettering tried to withhold the radiotherapy—despite the fact that the Shah had previously donated a million dollars to the institute in gratitude for treating his mother!

Most of my patients were sympathetic to my involvement with the Shah. But not all. On March 28, 1980, long after the Shah had left the United States, one long-time patient, a philanthropist widely known for his compassion and deep insight into the human condition, wrote to me, saying, "The spectacle of distinguished physicians . . . scampering on the trail of the rejected Shah is shameful . . . Why? Is there something besides money and influential friends that makes famous doctors willing to pant along in [his] wake?" He asked that I remove his medical records from my files immediately. This was not the first time a patient had fired me, nor would it be the last.

During his forty-one days at New York Hospital, I saw the Shah at least twice, sometimes three or four times each day, and got to know him well. Our morning meetings were largely devoted to medical matters—giving him his daily examination, checking his drug dosage, outlining his treatment schedule. The evenings were different. At six o'clock I would return to his suite to review the day with him, and we would fall to talking, often for several hours.

The Shah seemed to find my tales of tropical medicine diverting; at least he laughed a lot. In return, he provided me with a view inside a world of wealth and power someone born in Valparaiso, Indiana, was not likely ever to experience firsthand. He was proud of the billions of dollars of arms he'd bought to bolster his military muscle and liked to recount particularly complex deals involving the exchange of massive oil revenues for the latest high-tech weapons systems he hoped would make both the United States and the Soviet Union respect Iran's potential for keeping peace in the Persian Gulf.

The Shah had been an imperious ruler, one who relished flaunting his opulent lifestyle. Yet he was also a devoted leader with ambitious plans for his country. His dream, I learned in our talks, was of a modern, industrialized Islamic state. Indeed, he had been industrializing his nation with a vengeance, but, in so doing, had run afoul of the country's hidebound, xenophobic mullahs, who opposed not only his efforts to change the old ways, but criticized his lavish spending on military hardware and, most of all, his close ties with America, the Great Satan. The clash of wills had been shattering, and now the Shah's big plans lay in ruins.

Invariably, our discussions wound up addressing the progress—or the lack of it—in the hostage crisis. His sharpest words were always reserved for President Carter, who was then scrambling to find a diplomatic opening to Iran's new leaders in hopes of cutting a deal for the release of the Americans. During one of these sessions I was foolish enough to suggest that Carter's approach seemed to make sense to me.

"How naive of you to suggest a rapprochement with Iran might be possible," he snapped, his voice thick and raspy as sandpaper from the radiation treatments. "Don't you realize that is the last thing in the world Khomeini wants? He doesn't need a good relationship with the United States. Quite the opposite. He needs to hate the United States. Without the Great Satan to blame, he is nowhere. It will stay that way until Khomeini dies or is overthrown himself."

The Shah's outburst startled me. Eager to shift the subject, I asked him what he thought Carter should do.

"Easy," he said, his dark eyes narrowing stubbornly. "If I were in his shoes, I'd set a date for destroying the oil fields. I'd give the militants holding the hostages enough time to turn them over to the government so that they could, in turn, be safely handed over to the Swiss embassy. But whatever Carter does, he shouldn't bluff. He should assemble a thousand bombers and start printing maps of the oil fields, not just the storage terminals. If the militants don't meet the deadline, Carter should attack." The Shah paused and looked me squarely in the face, before adding, "I don't favor such action, mind you. After all, those oil fields belong to my country and we can't get along without them. But that's not Jimmy Carter's concern, nor should it be."

I could tell the Shah was still angered, but my curiosity got the best of me. At the risk of infuriating him further, I said, "Some people say that, from a purely tactical point of view, you should have killed Khomeini while he was in exile in Paris. I'm not suggesting for a minute you should have, but, frankly, that's what many people expected. Surely it could have been arranged. Why didn't you do it?"

The Shah smiled at my bluntness. "Yes, that option was open to me," he replied. "I could have killed Khomeini in France in much the same way Stalin had Trotsky killed in Mexico. But there's one thing all of those people upset by my presence in your country—those people outside this hospital protesting my so-called human rights violations—don't understand. I was never a Stalin," he said with heavy emphasis, adding that his secret police, the feared SAVAK, was no match for Stalin's NKVD.

I had heard the stories of SAVAK brutalizing Iranian citizens and they had sickened me. I had read of the mass public demonstrations against the Shah's bloated, grandiose administration and his high-handedness and felt saddened that things were going so badly in a country I had become fascinated with in my medical travels and some of whose doctors had been my students at Cornell. Since Mexico, however, I'd begun seeing the Shah through the eyes of a doctor caring for a sick patient and I grew to like him. The man I'd come to know—gracious, wise, sober, more like a quiet French scholar than an oriental despot—did not fit his widely publicized image of an oppressor of his people.

The Shah's voice then sank to a whisper. He could not, he said, bear the thought of continuing to spill the blood of his own subjects simply to stay in power. Yes, his people were childish; they had been misguided by that madman Khomeini; but he could stomach no more violence. So he had left his country. Now, ten months later, however, the bloodshed had only accelerated under Khomeini. "Every time I pick up a newspaper and see what that man is doing to my country," he said, clenching his fists into tight balls, "my heart bleeds."

What a strange, enigmatic man, I thought, as I watched the

Shah regain his composure and again become the urbane, un-flappable conversationalist.

With the crisis in Iran deepening, and no sign that the Iranians were about to release the hostages as long as the Shah remained in the United States, it became increasingly clear that Washington wanted him out of the country. In late November, Robert Armao alerted the domestic staff in Cuernavaca to lay in supplies. The Shah would be returning to the Villa of Roses.

Then the Mexicans dropped their bombshell (as the Shah himself later described it). On November 30, less than forty-eight hours before the Shah was scheduled to leave the hospital, the Mexicans informed Armao that his client was no longer welcome in Mexico. The next day Lloyd Cutler, chief White House counsel, met with the Shah behind closed doors. Cutler apologized; he told the Shah that the Carter administration had done everything in its power to get Mexican President José López Portillo to change his mind, but López Portillo would not budge.

The Mexican foreign minister issued a statement to the effect that allowing the Shah to return would open Mexican citizens and embassies abroad to possible terrorist reprisals. To a political greenhorn like me, that sounded perfectly plausible.

What I did not know, of course, was that the White House boys had struck a secret deal with López Portillo before the Shah ever set foot in the U.S. The Mexican president had promised to not only welcome the Shah back to Mexico after his medical interlude in the States, but to allow him to stay there indefinitely. So Carter was flabbergasted by the Mexican about-face. Hamilton Jordan, Carter's White House chief of staff, wrote later that the President shouted, "López Portillo is a liar!" adding icily, "They just double-crossed us."*

The Shah, as usual, saw things differently. Sitting at his bed-

*Hamilton Jordan, *Crisis: The Last Years of the Carter Presidency* (New York: G. P. Putnam's Sons, 1982), 72.

side, I told him how sorry I was that Mexico had fallen through, and apologized once again for my own government's inhospitable behavior. He looked at me blankly for a few seconds and then, his mouth flattening into an ironic smile, he said, "But it's all my fault. After all, I did not follow the advice of my good friend, the president of Mexico."

"What advice was that?" I asked.

"Oh, he told me it would be a good idea if I gave him fifteen million dollars in American currency, so that he could 'distribute' the money properly in my behalf."

Incredulous, I asked him if he was suggesting that the president of Mexico had asked him for a bribe.

"I'm not suggesting any such thing," the Shah said, smiling at my simplicity. "I'm telling you that's exactly what happened. People like to talk about corruption in monarchies such as mine. What they don't realize is that what goes on in the so-called democracies, particularly those in the developing world, is far worse." Well, I thought, if these allegations are true, that gives the Shah and Jimmy Carter at least one thing on which they can agree—the character defects of Señor López Portillo.

Whatever their real motives, the Mexicans had beaten a hasty retreat. But Lloyd Cutler, always the resourceful tactician, had a series of fallback plans. He brought with him to New York a short list of countries that he said might be persuaded to take the Shah. When these choices proved unrealistic, he extended an invitation from the United States for the Shah to go to Lackland Air Force Base in Texas. The Shah could convalesce there, Cutler said, away from the prying eyes and ears of the media.

Cutler touted Lackland's excellent medical facilities, but I knew the truth; the base hospital was good by any standards, but it was no match for the best public hospitals. Lackland's overwhelming appeal to the bureaucractic mind was that it boasted one clear advantage no nonmilitary venue could provide: the security of an air force base. (Although, Lackland, unlike other military facilities, had no surrounding security fence or closely monitored front gate.)

This offer of a temporary safe haven was a backhanded gesture at best. Washington had granted permission for the Shah to enter the United States, but it was equally clear that Carter intended to hustle his unwanted guest out of the country as quickly as possible, and that remote Lackland was to be the last stop on his brief American journey.

In any case, the Shah had no choice but to accept. Where else could he go? On December 2, 1979, after six weeks at New York Hospital, the Shah's hegira folded its tents and moved south.

Lackland Air Force Base was a gloomy scene. The Shah and Empress Farah occupied a three-room apartment in a drab, clap-board building formerly used by visiting Air Force officers. It was a depressing affair, with its threadbare carpets, sun-bleached curtains, and bargain-basement furniture. Not exactly what the doctor ordered to boost a patient's spirits.

While I sat there talking with my patient on the cold, blustery afternoon of December 14, an impressive assortment of two dozen men—top military brass, Air Force doctors, U.S. State Department officials, and lawyers for both the American government and the Shah—had gathered in the building next door, where they now waited for me to bring them word on the Shah's condition. Chief among them were Lloyd Cutler and Hamilton Jordan.

Like me, Cutler and Jordan were intensely concerned about the Shah's prognosis, but for very different reasons. With the controversy over the Shah's presence on American soil metastasizing into the American body politic at a frightening rate, they wanted to excise him as quickly and as neatly as possible. But, as any good surgeon could have told them, removing an irritant of that magnitude was bound to be a messy job.

What would happen, for instance, if the Shah, an American ally of thirty-seven years, died as the result of being ignominiously shunted off to another country? His powerful friends inside the American establishment could make things very rough on Carter should he bungle the maneuver. So the question loomed: Could the Shah travel without putting his life in danger?

That put me in a terrible spot. As a loyal American, I felt deeply for the hostages and their families. Yet protecting them was the president's responsibility. As a doctor, I was bound to devote my energies and emotions to keeping my patient alive, regardless of his political record or public image.

Medically speaking, the situation was clear enough. Removing the Shah's spleen would be a highly delicate operation. Without access to plentiful blood supplies he could easily hemorrhage to death. His blood elements were so disastrously low to begin with that standard transfusions would not suffice. Only the most advanced computerized blood-separating equipment available would do. Common sense, at least in a doctor's mind, dictated only one thing: the Shah, no matter what Washington said, would have to stay in the United States.

"You've got to listen to me," I said, as the Shah prowled restlessly around his cramped sick room, pausing only to close the door so that the empress, who was in the adjoining room, wouldn't overhear our conversation. "You need that operation. Your life depends on it."

The Shah stopped pacing and shot me a sardonic glance. "Carter wants me out of your country," he whispered hoarsely. "He is not a very sophisticated man. He thinks my going will help free the hostages. He's quite wrong, of course, but I won't stay where I'm not welcome."

It was painfully clear to me now that, in spite of his failing health and spirits, the Shah's monumental pride wouldn't allow him to save himself. His decision to leave the United States was tantamount to suicide and both of us knew it.

The situation was further complicated by the place Carter's men had arranged only hours before as the next stop on the Shah's hegira. Of all the countries in the world, only one, the Republic of Panama, a little country with a big reputation for political skulduggery and haphazard medical care, was now open to him, and Hamilton Jordan had jumped at the chance to clinch the deal.

"Your Imperial Majesty," I pleaded, "no matter how much you loathe Jimmy Carter, you should not let that get in the way of your proper treatment. Your spleen will kill you if we don't act soon. Here, not in Panama."

"You're the one who told me how the operation could be done anywhere in the world," he said, smiling slyly. "Why not Panama? You may think I'm being foolish," he continued, "but I am a superstitious man. I know I am going to die. It's just a question of when. So for now, I want you to put me back on chlorambucil (the mild anticancer drug his French doctors had prescribed for him years earlier). It worked before; it just might work again."

He was right: I did think he was being foolish and, as diplomatically as possible, I told him so. Relying on chlorambucil now, with the cancer cells about to overrun his major organs, I explained, would be like taking aspirin for appendicitis.

"This is no time for halfway measures," I said. "You've had cancer for seven years. Time is running out."

"If the drug doesn't work," the Shah insisted, "then you can take out my spleen—but in Panama, and only after the holidays."

The Shah had spoken. Going to Panama was a big mistake—I could feel that in my bones. How could I possibly care for my patient in a foreign country with limited hospital facilities?

Then it came to me: we could go to Gorgas Hospital! Gorgas, the venerable institution in the American Canal Zone that had once led the world in research on tropical diseases, the hospital where I'd interned forty years earlier. I had a few qualms about how well the facilities had been maintained over the years, but at the very least, they would be vastly superior to anything we were likely to find inside Panama itself.

Everything now depended on my ability to sell my plan to the emissaries of President Carter, and, at the age of sixty-six, after a life studded with occasionally stunning lapses in tact, I had learned one sobering truth: I was no diplomat.

Depressed and worried, I walked down the stairway from the Shah's second-floor suite and headed for the adjacent building where Cutler and Jordan waited. Standing on the tarmac beyond was the small jet with the blue and white presidential markings that had brought me from New York that morning, its fuselage now shuddering in the icy wind that howled across the treeless Texas flatlands.

This has been one of the worst days of my life, I thought. I felt completely exhausted. Two weeks earlier I had been operated on for the removal of a kidney stone and I was still in pain. That, in addition to the strain of caring for the Shah, overseeing the weeks of intense therapy in New York, the sleepless nights, the burden of trying to keep up my regular medical practice—all combined to make me wonder whether I was physically up to continuing. Nonetheless, the mere thought of how our government was now giving the Shah a diplomatic form of the bum's rush after all those years they'd counted him as ally and friend was enough to keep my adrenaline flowing. To hell with politics, I thought, as I opened the door to the temporary White House "situation room."

Lloyd Cutler looked up as I entered and motioned me to take a seat. Eyeing me expectantly, Jordan hushed the others.

"Every shred of medical evidence at our disposal," I began, "says we should remove the Shah's spleen right away." I paused and looked at Jordan, who suddenly seemed deflated. "But we're not going to take it out just now," I said, adding with finality, "the Shah wants to leave."

The change in Jordan was instantaneous. Delighted, he jumped from his chair and asked, "How soon can he go?"

"Within the half hour."

Jordan let out a short, whooping rebel yell and sprinted for the telephone.

"Not so fast," I said. "The operation has to be done at Gorgas Hospital in the Canal Zone—and only at Gorgas. You'll have to agree to that. You'll also have to agree to provide whatever backup is necessary. If I need a B-52 flown in with hospital supplies, surgeons, and staff, you'll send it. If the operation can't be done at Gorgas, for whatever reason, the Shah will be allowed to return to the United States for treatment. This must be a solid commitment," I said. "Only then will the Shah go to Panama."

Cutler seemed at a loss for words. He looked at Jordan, who hesitated, but then nodded in agreement. Cutler turned to me. "You've got it," he said. Jordan immediately picked up a direct line to the White House and reported the breakthrough in negotiations.

Jordan had good reason to be pleased. Panama was ruled by military strongman General Omar Torrijos Herrera. Two years earlier, in 1977, the resourceful Jordan, who called Torrijos "Papa General," had helped successfully negotiate a treaty for the eventual return of the Panama Canal to Panama. Now he had called in a chit from his friend, and the general had been eager to oblige, especially if it meant winning him credit for the release of the hostages. With any luck, the Americans might even be home for Christmas—or so the men in the White House thought.

The Shah had maintained all along that this was nonsense. He was convinced that his transfer to Panama would make absolutely no difference in the hostage situation. But when I had encouraged him to speak up, he refused. With everybody convinced that his only interest was in saving his own skin, who would have taken him seriously? In any event, he was right about the hostages. The American prisoners, who had so far been held for 40 days, would remain captive a total of 444—until long after the Shah was dead and buried and Jimmy Carter had died a political death of his own, losing to Ronald Reagan in the 1980 presidential elections.

But all that lay in the future and, for the moment, I was confident that the Shah would be reasonably well provided for medically. Conditions in Panama wouldn't be ideal, but I had been promised the full support of the United States government. I could put a modified version of the Mali Option into effect, flying south from the States whatever medical supplies or personnel might be lacking inside Panama. I had the president's word on it. What could possibly go wrong?

I left Cutler and Jordan to huddle with Robert Armao and Bill Jackson, the Shah's Manhattan lawyer, to hammer out the terms of what would come to be called the Lackland Agreement and went to cheer up my patient.

The Shah sat alone in his shuttered room. Normally relaxed and friendly with me, he was now remote and cool. When he finally spoke, his voice had a bitter edge to it.

"Well, your president just called me."

"What did he say?"

"He called to thank me for leaving your country," the Shah explained with a mirthless laugh. "That was our first conversation since I left Teheran. When I really needed his help during my stay in Mexico, during all my weeks at the hospital in New York, he never once called me. Now that he's rid of me, he calls to thank me for leaving the country. I must commend him," he said acidly, "on his excellent manners."

Awkwardly, I tried to administer some placebo talk about Panama. I sang the praises of Contadora, the resort island in Panama Bay where he and the empress would be living. I told him about its salubrious climate and great natural beauty, and how its beaches, tennis courts, and scuba diving would appeal to his children.

All the while, the Shah sat silently on the edge of his iron-frame cot in that disheveled bedroom of his and stared ahead into the darkness.

Showdown in Panama

It was Thursday evening, December 20, 1979, as my wife, Collette, and I were packing to fly down to our vacation place in Florida for the Christmas holidays, that Liossa Pirnia, the Pahlavi family doctor, telephoned me from Contadora Island. The Shah's cancer was spreading rapidly. Worse yet, local doctors, operating under orders from General Torrijos, were insisting they be allowed to handle the Shah's case on their own. The Shah was in Panama now, they argued, and it only stood to reason that he be treated by Panamanians. Kean and the other gringo doctors would no longer be needed.

I told Pirnia not to worry; I would fly down and straighten things out as soon as I could. Damn, I thought as I put down the receiver, the Shah's barely arrived in Panama and already things are coming unglued. I decided to put the Lackland Agreement to its first test.

The next morning I picked up the phone and called Colonel Paul Anderson, chief of medicine at Gorgas Hospital, to discuss the Shah's treatment. I suggested he get in touch with Lloyd Cutler at the White House to confirm my understanding of the Lackland Agreement and to get whatever authority he needed to prepare

Gorgas to receive its new patient. Anderson was friendly and helpful, and said he was eager to see me when I arrived in Panama.

As part of our Lackland deal, and in their apparent haste to get the Shah out of the country, both Cutler and Jordan had assured me that government transportation would be made available to me for shuttling to and from Gorgas. Since I knew that Roman Catholic Panama would be completely shut down for the holidays, I arranged to travel south the day after Christmas. But when I telephoned the State Department on Christmas Day to confirm the flight, I was told that the trip had been canceled. "Who the hell has done that?" I demanded. The duty officer did not know.

David Newsom at State knew. He told me that Robert Armao had called the whole thing off. I was astounded. Why would the Shah's own man interfere with the execution of the Lackland Agreement? Newsom said he thought it had something to do with the question of who would pay for the airplane charter. I prepared myself for the Catch-22 and, sure enough, here it came; at Lackland, Newsom explained, the United States government had agreed to *supply* the transportation—not to *pay* for it. When State had called Armao asking him to confirm that the Shah would be picking up the tab, Armao had refused.

"I don't give a good goddamn who foots the bill—the White House, the State Department, the Shah, or me," I told Newsom. Including myself in the list of possible sponsors was somewhat reckless, since I had no idea how much chartering an airplane actually cost.

I phoned Armao and proceeded to blow my stack. Armao, who had never known me to be other than the calm, reasonable physician, seemed shocked at my belligerence, so it didn't take long to persuade him to change his mind. Within a few hours, arrangements for my flight were resuscitated; I would leave for Panama the next day.

I felt a little foolish making such a big deal about getting the government to provide the damned plane. Taking a commercial flight would have been a thousand times easier. On the other hand, I wanted to remind the White House of its commitments to my patient. And now, more than ever, I thought I had good reason to be concerned: Cutler and Jordan already seemed to be developing conveniently short memories when it came to honoring the letter of their Lackland promises. (Armao later explained his refusal to pay for the plane, saying it was *his* ploy to jog White House memories.)

The day after Christmas I flew into Panama on a sturdy little Lear jet bearing the emblem of the United States of America. Hibbard Williams, my colleague from New York Hospital, accompanied me. At the local airport we transferred to a cramped, single-engine airplane for the fifteen-minute flight to Contadora Island, where the royal couple occupied an airy bungalow on a bluff overlooking the sparkling waters of the Pacific.

When we arrived, the Shah was seated on the veranda looking out to sea, but rose when he heard us come in. He wore a flowered *guayabera* shirt and sneakers and raised his hand in welcome. He looked relaxed and cheerful. His face and arms were tanned, and he had put on at least ten pounds since I'd seen him last. His robust appearance was a pleasant surprise. After Dr. Pirnia's dour report, I had expected to see a walking dead man.

As the three of us talked, the Shah's four children, home on school holiday, were outside on the large veranda punching tunes on an ancient jukebox, mimicking American rock-'n'-roll dancers and making a terrible racket. The Shah, swiveling in his seat to observe them, smiled at their antics. I felt encouraged by his mood. The lonely figure I had observed at Lackland had vanished, and in his place had emerged a more confident, buoyant individual. This was just what he had dreamed of during his confinement in Texas; however briefly, he had brought the family together and they were happy again.

"I made the right decision to come to Panama," the Shah said, turning to look me in the eye. The children, two boys and a girl, were ecstatic about Contadora, Empress Farah seemed content, and, he added with clinical seriousness, "the drugs even seem to be doing me some good."

Meeting General Torrijos had been a stroke of good luck, too, the Shah said. His host had turned out to be a real friend; he had personally found the Pahlavis an excellent cook and had taken the family for a cruise around Panama Bay in one of his gunboats. More important, the general had promised the Shah that he would deal harshly with anyone who tried to profit from his presence in Panama. After all, Torrijos had said, "Señor Shah," as he called him, was not some wealthy tourist, but the personal guest of the general himself. The Shah had yet to recognize his own serious misunderstanding of Torrijos.

The next morning at ten o'clock I went to Gorgas Hospital to arrange for the Shah's preoperative laboratory tests. Since I had so far made all arrangements by telephone from New York, I was eager to see how the place had changed since the good old days, but I was not prepared for the transformation that awaited me. The old buildings of the hospital pavilion were still there on the brow of Ancon Hill, overlooking the canal and occupying the prime real estate of the entire Zone. But the white stucco structures had recently been converted into condominium-style apartments. The hospital proper was now a half mile away at the base of the hill, a brand-new, high-rise, air-conditioned, nondescript modern building of glass and steel. Just about everything about Gorgas had changed except the name. The old romance had fled.

Hibbard Williams and I met in the conference room with Colonel Anderson and his colleague, Colonel Ardeth Huffacker, who headed the hospital laboratory. Huffacker introduced us to two Panamanian doctors—Adán Ríos Abrego, a hematologist–oncologist, who served as consultant to Gorgas, and Carlos García Aguilera, who was described as chief thoracic surgeon at Paitilla

Medical Center in Panama City and as General Torrijo's personal physician.

I briefed them on the Shah's illness, his current condition, and the plan to arrange for a splenectomy in the near future. I asked Ríos if he would agree to visit the Shah at regular intervals to monitor the state of his blood. He cordially accepted the assignment. The tests were to be done in the laboratory at Gorgas Hospital and the results telephoned to me in New York. It was a comfortable arrangement, especially since Huffacker was an old, trusted friend.

I was especially pleased with the appearance of the U.S.-trained Ríos, who would be my eyes and ears in Panama while I was back in New York. Moreover, he could do what I could not: he could bridge the gap between the Panamanians in Panama and the *norteamericanos* in the Canal Zone. The two worlds were still separated by a vast gulf of colonial antagonism, and Ríos, I hoped, would be able to ease any friction that might arise.

Dr. García, dark and silent, said little but welcomed us in the name of General Torrijos and promised "complete cooperation" from the Panamanian medical community. That evening Ríos and his wife, also a physician, hosted us at dinner in Panama City and we drank numerous toasts to the spirit of "complete co-operation."

The next morning Williams and I flew back to New York feeling completely satisfied with Panama. How silly I had been to worry. After all, we had now received the official blessings of General Torrijos himself; above all, in Ríos we had a competent local doctor, who seemed to be cooperating admirably with his American colleagues. Our patient, meanwhile, was gaining back his strength, and very soon we would be able to set a date for the removal of his spleen. The Shah's hegira was, at long last, beginning to run in a more promising direction. I should have guessed that I was pounding myself on the back a little too hard.

By mid-January, Operation Eagle, the Panama Phase, still seemed to be going smoothly enough. The Shah remained a very sick man, to be sure. But his condition had stabilized; he had put on twenty-four pounds since arriving in Contadora and, from the way his stamina was rebounding, it would be possible to take out his spleen any day now. Dr. Ríos had been calling me in New York each week to report on the Shah's blood tests, and the levels of his red and white cells and platelets were building nicely.

Then a series of relatively minor events rekindled my fears. First, I stopped hearing from Ríos; I telephoned him but he did not return my calls. Dr. Pirnia's reports, meanwhile, became increasingly anxiety-ridden. She told me that, instead of sending the Shah's blood to Gorgas for testing, as we had previously agreed, Ríos was taking it to the Paitilla Medical Center, in downtown Panama City, which was owned and operated by the cabal of doctors surrounding Torrijos. I was reassured only by the fact that Gaspar García de Paredes, head of the surgery department at Paitilla, had been a student of mine at Cornell many years earlier, and I knew him to be the most patient and reasonable of men.

Then, in the middle of February, the Shah came down with a respiratory infection which required hospitalization. The fear was that, being immunosuppressed, he might develop pneumonia. But instead of sending him to Gorgas, as had been previously agreed, he was admitted to Paitilla. When Dr. Pirnia had meekly protested the arrangement, Carlos García, known locally as "Charlie," was overheard saying that, if she made too much trouble, he would simply have her thrown in jail. I developed a new respect for Dr. Pirnia's intuition.

Telephone reports from Robert Armao expanded the scope of the problem. He told me the Shah had received a bill from one Panamanian doctor totaling $14,791.73 for three trips to Contadora and a few routine blood tests. It was accompanied by the demand that it be paid at once and in cash.

Disgusted, Armao complained that the Panamanians appeared

to have declared open season on the Shah's pocketbook. The authorities, suspicious of the Shah's American advisors, had installed a telephone bugging device in his bungalow so that they could record and translate his international calls. A few days later a bill arrived for $500 for the machine! Even the Shah's "friend," General Torrijos, eventually got into the act, asking his guest for a loan of $15 million for "economic development" and offering to arrange the sale of Contadora itself for $10 million.

The Shah had grown particularly suspicious shortly after a French lawyer and a shadowy Argentinian business consultant, both representing the new Iranian government, showed up in Panama City to press the case for the Shah's extradition to Teheran. New rumors began circulating that Torrijos and his cronies planned to "sell" the Shah to the highest bidder. Indeed, the machinations of which Torrijos was capable seemed endless. Eager to help his "amigos" Carter and Jordan free the hostages, desirous of playing an important role in the international arena, and disappointed at the Shah's reluctance to cough up the money the Shah said he'd asked for, he was prepared to place his guest, "Señor Shah," under house "detention" while the Panamanian courts listened to Khomeini's agents. Still, he swore that confining the Shah to quarters would be a mere legal formality designed to buy time to arrange the release of the hostages; he vowed he would never send him back to Iran.

But how could the Shah trust Torrijos? The general continued to drop heavy hints about his financial requirements. The Shah could see a bidding war approaching, and he was convinced that he would lose out to the Ayatollah. "Interesting, don't you think, Dr. Kean," he said some weeks later, "that both López Portillo and Torrijos suggested the same sum—fifteen million dollars. Did they speak to one another, I wonder, or is that simply my Latin American value?"

Oppressed by his surroundings, fearful of arrest, the Shah grew quiet and withdrawn. Meanwhile, as the weeks went by, his spleen again showed signs of enlarging. The operation could be delayed no longer. I flew down to Contadora.

No sooner had I arrived at my hotel than Charlie García presented me and Robert Armao with an astonishing ultimatum.

"I have received word from the general," he said perfunctorily, "that the Shah will be operated on at Paitilla Hospital, not at Gorgas. If he so much as enters the Canal Zone, he will not be permitted to return to Panama. He will be treated at Paitilla or he will not be treated in Panama at all. The choice is up to him."

I was stunned. I reminded García of the promise that the Shah be operated on at Gorgas—the U.S. government had given its word.

He looked at me without expression for a moment, and then smirked. "We don't care what you were promised," he said. "You're in Panama now, and this is an order from General Torrijos."

"I dare you to say this to the Shah's face," I said.

Jutting his chin, García replied truculently, "Take me to him."

We immediately headed for the royal bungalow, walking along the lawns, then over the airstrip, and up the winding road to the top of the bluff. We found the Shah sitting on the veranda with the empress. He looked up when we came in, quiet, calm, but clearly perplexed by our unexpected appearance. We adjourned to his bedroom and shut the door.

"Tell him," I said, staring daggers at García.

As much as I despised him at that moment, I had to give the man credit. He pulled no punches for the Shah. He told him where he would be operated on and under what conditions.

I was amazed. This must be a first, I thought—a medical minion giving the Shah of Shahs a direct order, as if he were a fifteen-year-old boy. But the Shah responded with perfect aplomb; he said he would defer a decision until he could give the matter further thought. He then said goodnight and ushered us to the door.

For all our differences, García and I could agree on one thing— the Shah needed to have his spleen removed as quickly as possible; we simply could not agree on where the operation was to be done or who was to do it. Ríos suggested that we invite Charles McBride, a surgeon from the M. D. Anderson Hospital in Houston, to fly down and operate at Paitilla. He had already engaged Jeane Hester, a hematologist from Anderson, to set up an IBM blood separator that would provide the leukocyte and platelet support needed for the procedure. To my dismay, the Shah had not objected to this plan. In fact, no one, not even Armao, seemed to understand my dogged insistence on Gorgas. The reason was so elementary: it all boiled down to control.

Simply put, the proper treatment of a patient cannot be decided by committee. Second, third, even ninth and tenth opinions can, and often should, be sought out. Sometimes, doctors can agree on the right course of action. Oftentimes, though, sharp differences emerge. This is particularly true when the case is complex and life-threatening. Ultimately, someone has to make the tough decisions. That duty falls to the physician whom the patient has hired to oversee his case. In the Shah's case, I was that physician. No matter what the Panamanians said, it was my duty to continue to coordinate his care unless or until the patient said otherwise.

At Gorgas, with its American staff, I could coordinate the medical team and make the necessary decisions. At Paitilla, I would be a mere bystander, a peripheral physician watching doctors call the shots on the treatment of a patient whom I knew so much better. I knew the Shah could never be treated properly by committee. What would happen when the doctors disagreed on life-or-death decisions?

Nonetheless the time for compromise had come. I had no choice but to agree that the operation be done at Paitilla; I had been outvoted. So I consoled myself with the knowledge that whatever equipment we needed could still be flown in from the States. But we still needed a world-class medical team, including a surgeon of surpassing quality. Moreover, we needed a surgeon with a reputation so big that no one would dare buck him.

Then I had a brainstorm: Michael DeBakey, the famous heart

surgeon from Houston! He was a man of vast international acclaim; along with Christiaan Barnard of South Africa, DeBakey was considered one of the two best cardiac surgeons in the world, but I vividly remembered his earlier reputation as one of America's great abdominal surgeons. He had also performed surgery in more than thirty world capitals. If I could get him to agree to operate, I thought, the Shah will get the best possible treatment and the Panamanians, out of deference and respect, could not possibly object.

I telephoned DeBakey at the Baylor Medical Center in Houston. Much to my delight and the Shah's good fortune, he told me he'd be happy to come to Panama—provided he could bring his own surgical team with him. I told him he had a deal.

The Panamanian doctors were, as I had hoped, elated by the news of the great surgeon's impending arrival in Panama. They said it would be a great honor for the country. Charlie García, wildly enthusiastic, began making plans to throw a big party at his house in DeBakey's honor. At Paitilla, Dr. García de Paredes was equally enthusiastic and agreed to help DeBakey in any way possible. Impressed with my flair for diplomacy, I decided to return to New York briefly to catch up on my regular patients.

On March 14, 1980, Hibbard Williams, Robert Armao, and I accompanied DeBakey to Panama along with his handpicked medical team, including Gerald Lawrie, his chief surgical assistant. DeBakey proved to be a marvelous traveling companion with a repertoire of medical stories he spun in his gracious, witty manner. We arrived in Panama in good spirits, thinking all would be well.

But the visit got off to a puzzling start. For one thing, no one was at the airport to meet us. This seemed odd, especially given the exuberance expressed earlier by the Panamanian doctors over DeBakey's involvement. A lone stateside television crew intercepted us as we deplaned and DeBakey issued a benign arrival statement; he said he was glad to be in Panama but could not comment on the patient's condition until he had had a chance to examine him.

At Paitilla Medical Center our entourage was blocked by three swarthy armed guards who refused us entry. "We have orders," one of them said in halting English. "No papers, no get in."

My blood began to boil. Here I was in the company of one of the world's most distinguished surgeons and a full team of medical experts, and we weren't going to be allowed to see our patient. What the hell was happening, anyhow?

Robert Armao excused himself to exercise some telephone diplomacy with Torrijos. Almost an hour later, Ríos magically appeared and apologized for the delay. We must understand the need for tight security, he said. Leftist students had been rioting in the streets protesting the presence of the Shah, whom they saw as a puppet of American imperialism. The hospital and its staff had to be protected, he said, as he led the way to the patient's room.

DeBakey examined the Shah for the first time and estimated that his spleen weighed at least two kilograms, which meant it was considerably larger than it had been even at Lackland three months before. Moreover, his white and red blood cells and his platelets had again dropped to dangerously low levels. DeBakey and I agreed that a splenectomy was now vital. Given the dilapidated condition of the Shah's blood, the longer we waited, the greater the risks would become.

When we broke for the evening, Ríos informed our team that a meeting with all the Panamanian doctors had been scheduled for nine o'clock the following morning. DeBakey, Williams, and I said goodnight, and then hung back, eager to give the hospital a quick inspection tour. As we prowled its corridors, we were appalled. True, the facilities themselves were better than we had expected—clean and up-to-date, if not exactly bursting with state-of-the-art technology. Still, the ambience was disturbing. The operating theater was empty. So was the anesthesia area. And the storeroom. Indeed, there didn't seem to be a soul in the entire wing. Hibbard Williams remarked on the absurdity of Panamanian claims of "tight security." "What's to prevent anybody from sneaking in here and dosing up the Shah's IV drip with poison?" he asked. No one wasted his breath on the obvious reply: nothing at all.

The real showdown came the next morning. Hordes of local reporters and journalists from the States waited outside the Paitilla entrance amid a pandemonium of strobe lights and television cameras. We quickly proceeded to the hospital library. Many of the Panamanian doctors had failed to show, but Gaspar García de Paredes, in his role as hospital superintendent started anyway. He wasted no time in getting to the point, and—to my astonishment—I was the target of his complaints.

Wagging his finger in my direction, my former student accused me of leaking stories to the Stateside press that had impugned the integrity of the Panamanian medical team and called their competence into question. Furthermore, I had endangered the security of patients and personnel at Paitilla with all my loose talk. Panamanians from all walks of life felt insulted and humiliated. Panamanian doctors refused to be displaced in their own country. As a result, the deal was off—DeBakey would not be allowed to operate on the Shah.

The intake of breath on our side of the table was audible. I was thunderstruck. Press reports? What the hell was he talking about? I had scrupulously avoided speaking to reporters about any aspect of the Shah's treatment, either in Panama or anywhere else. To be sure, the U.S. media had been full of speculation about the latest leg of the Shah's medical odyssey, but none of the information came directly from me, and I told García de Paredes as much.

Clearly, he did not believe me. Having worked himself up into an ecstasy of outrage, he now turned his ire on Michael DeBakey. He referred to him as an "itinerant surgeon," and, thumping the table for emphasis, continued to insist that the Shah's splenectomy could only be performed by Panamanian surgeons. He complained about the five-person team accompanying DeBakey. Surely a retinue of that size was meant to supplant the Panamanians in every phase of the operation.

The meeting ended on a highly acrimonious note. The Panamanian contingent withdrew. DeBakey, Williams, and I were too bewildered and angry to do anything but shake our heads. DeBakey, the man the Panamanians had said they would delightedly welcome as a "great teacher" only ten days before—the man the absent Charlie García had been struggling to honor with a party—was now described as an "itinerant surgeon"!

Almost immediately the Panamanians had second thoughts about offending DeBakey. In a separate meeting a few hours later, García de Paredes backed off somewhat, saying the Panamanians would now permit the surgeon to be present in the operating room, though he skirted over exactly what DeBakey's role would be. Nonetheless, he made it plain that the Panamanians would do all the serious cutting.

It was at this point that DeBakey's great skills as a diplomat came into play. Later that day, Mike told García de Paredes he would accept the Panamanian invitation on one condition—that the surgery be postponed until the Shah had fully recovered from his respiratory infection. This, he suggested, might also allow the atmosphere between the Panamanian and American doctors to settle down and assume a more professional tenor. The Panamanians agreed, and went about preparing a statement for the press. When we informed the Shah about the postponement, he seemed relieved.

Meanwhile, Armao, DeBakey, Williams, and I were having second thoughts of our own. Mike was worried about assuming responsibility for an operation over which, as an "observer," he would not have complete control. Hibbard was bothered by the ad hoc arrangements for laboratory tests and blood support at Paitilla. I had long since come to the conclusion that the atmosphere at Paitilla was so highly politicized and poisonous that it would simply not be safe to operate there under the circumstances. Mike and Hibbard agreed. The Shah would have to leave

Panama. By indicating he would go along with the Panamanian plan, DeBakey had bought us some precious time. Now we would have to try to get our patient out. But how? I decided to play my final card—the Houston card.

I asked the hospital switchboard to put a call through to Lloyd Cutler at the White House. I reminded Cutler as diplomatically as I could of our agreement at Lackland—that, if necessary, the Shah would be allowed to return to the United States for medical treatment. Medically speaking, I told Cutler, it was now imperative that the Shah go to Houston where DeBakey, relaxed and unfettered by political complications, could operate on the patient in peace.

Cutler listened patiently to what I had to say and then, in his mellow courthouse baritone said, "It cannot be done."

In hindsight, I can't really blame Cutler for backing away from the promise he'd made the day he'd looked me straight in the eye and said, "You've got it" to my Lackland demands. After all, he was merely following orders. President Carter had to weigh the worth of a pledge given to the doctor of a dying autocrat in exile against the lives of the American hostages, who had now been held captive in Teheran for a total of 133 days. At the moment, however, I was angry.

"Mr. Cutler," I said, my voice rising, "you don't seem to understand. This is no place for the Shah, or anybody, to be operated on. The patient needs to return to the United States." DeBakey waved his arms at me to stop shouting and Williams whispered, "Cool down, Ben." (Hibbard was nervous about being spied on by the Panamanians, and now his suspicions focused on the "cleaning man," who had just entered the room for the fifth time and was pretending to empty an already empty wastepaper basket. We were all feeling a bit paranoid by this time, but not without reason.)

Cutler then warned me to watch what I said about the Panamanians, since the telephones were surely tapped. "Good," I said. "I hope Torrijos personally hears every word." This was not a smart move on my part, since, as I learned later, the government had already placed me on an enemies list. Now I had undoubtedly been overheard calling Torrijos himself "that obtunded gorilla." But my rage did nothing to change Cutler's mind. Reluctantly, DeBakey, Williams, and I returned to the United States to consider our next move.

There was one last, faint glimmer of hope. One—and only one—escape route remained open to the Shah, and it was Empress Farah, not the Shah himself, who would take the initiative. She did this by placing a telephone call to Jihan Sadat, wife of Anwar Sadat, the president of Egypt. The Sadats were old friends. They had hosted the Pahlavis on the first leg of their exodus from Teheran the previous year and had invited the royal couple to settle in Egypt, an offer that was later renewed when it became clear the Shah's plans to move to the United States had crumbled. The Shah had always declined, out of deference to the wishes of Jimmy Carter and a genuine concern for his friend Sadat.

By setting foot in Egypt, the Shah was almost certain to worsen Sadat's already delicate ties with his Arab neighbors. Sadat was also having problems with antigovernment nationalists and Muslim fundamentalists inside Egypt itself. Carter, in particular, worried that the Shah's presence in Cairo would make it increasingly difficult for Sadat to keep the peace at home, and a stable Egypt was essential to his dreams of a durable peace in the Middle East. More important, the president was not eager to have the Shah leave Panama when he believed negotiations for the release of the hostages had reached a critical point.

Empress Farah, however, was fed up with diplomatic priorities. Her husband was sick and hunted, and she was determined to save him. She explained to Jihan Sadat that the Shah was now a virtual prisoner of the Panamanians. If extradition proceedings began, they would be completely immobilized. She expressed her fears that Torrijos (who had made several thinly veiled sexual passes at her) just might allow the Shah to be sent back to Teheran. Knowing the line was tapped, she spoke in French, hoping the Panamanians wouldn't bother to translate the conversation into Spanish.

It took only a few moments for the Sadats to make the arrangements; both of them wanted the Pahlavis to come to Cairo as soon as possible. It didn't take Farah long to persuade her husband that hospitable Egypt offered the best hopes of survival.

When Lloyd Cutler heard of the Shah's plans, he immediately flew down to Contadora and tried to talk him out of going. But it was too late. The United States had broken too many promises. Sadat had offered to send a plane. The royal couple's baggage was already crated and piled on the tarmac at Contadora, waiting to be loaded for shipment. And both the Shah and his empress were eager to redirect their hegira back toward the Middle East and home.

Always the swashbuckler, Torrijos offered, as a favor to his friend Hamilton Jordan, to force the Shah to stay in Panama and be operated on there. Jordan quickly—and wisely—dissuaded the general. After all, how would it look if the United States appeared to be encouraging one American ally to hold another friend and former ally captive? Instead, the White House persuaded the Shah not to wait for Sadat's jet to arrive, but arranged for a special charter flight.

So it was that the Shah left Panama quietly at two o'clock on the afternoon of March 23, 1980, on board a vintage DC-8 from Evergreen International Air Lines, a charter operation that had had longstanding ties to the CIA. (Again, the U.S. government had arranged the transportation, but the Shah received a bill for $255,120.) Thus ended his hundred days on Contadora. He did not leave, however, before executing one final diplomatic flourish; he wrote General Torrijos a personal letter thanking him for his "friendship," "hospitality," and "human understanding."* Somehow, the Shah had managed to retain his exquisite sense of irony.

Back in New York I watched the departure of the royal family

---

*Salinger, 216.

on television. I couldn't help but feel a little guilty, wondering whether I should have stayed in Panama and flown directly to Egypt with my patient.

But there really was far too much work to do. DeBakey needed help in assembling his surgical team and gathering the sophisticated gadgetry he would need to operate in Cairo. I had to arrange to turn my practice and laboratory duties over to colleagues. And finally, I had to work on Hibbard Williams. Probably the most sensible man among us, he needed to have his arm twisted often and hard before agreeing to embark with me on the eighth—and final—leg of the Shah's medical odyssey. "I will regret this," he said portentously. How soon I would share his sentiments.

Death on the Nile

By late March the Shah was at long last out of reach of both the grasping Panamanians and his Iranian pursuers, and safely settled in Cairo. Overnight, the atmosphere around him grew buoyant.

But Cairo soon presented challenges all its own. The first problem was a logistical one: how to get our flying medical circus, with its doctors, nurses, and panoply of delicate equipment, gathered together and transported to yet another farflung capital in a matter of a few days. DeBakey came up with the solution, arranging with a friend, a wealthy Texas oil man, to borrow his private Boeing 707. The passenger cabin was large and outfitted with full-size mattresses so that the surgeon and his people could stretch out and sleep. Once an IBM blood cell separator, frozen plasma and packed red cells, medications for anesthesia, and surgical instruments were securely tucked into the cargo bay, the "Cairo Airlift" left Houston on March 26. I set off from New York the same day on the Concorde. Georges Flandrin flew in from Paris at Empress Farah's request.

We were now in the hands of a real statesman. Anwar Sadat had seen to it that there would be absolutely no funny business where the Shah was concerned. The royal couple had arrived a few days before our medical team and the Sadats, on hand when they deplaned, had whisked them by helicopter to Maadi Hospital, stopping briefly en route to show them around Kubbeh Palace, the official guest house for heads of state, where the Pahlavis would stay following the operation. Sadat had told the Shah he wanted him to feel "at home" and, in sharp contrast to Omar Torrijos, he seemed determined to show him that he meant what he said.

The next morning the seven members of the "American team," along with Georges Flandrin, assembled outside the hotel coffee shop. Together we pushed our way through the lobby, where armies of photographers, television camera crews, and reporters waited in ambush. Happily, the media were almost exclusively infatuated with the famous Dr. DeBakey, which made it easier for the rest of us to bolt to our waiting cars for the short drive to the hospital.

From the outside, Maadi Hospital was an imposing sight. A squat, rectangular building of considerable age perched on the banks of the Nile, it belonged to the Egyptian army and sat in the middle of several acres of dusty, necrotic lawns ringed by layers of cyclone fencing. Scores of military police, plainclothesmen, and sharpshooters patrolled the building and grounds, giving the impression of great efficiency and professionalism.

Inside was an entirely different story, however. As we walked through the corridors, my eyes and especially my nose told me that the hospital was a hygienic disaster area. Dirt and crud caked the windowsills. Toilets overflowed with unflushed feces. Hallways smelled of urine. I suddenly realized, my heart sinking, that we had ended up not merely in a second-rate hospital, but in a fourth-rate one.

Our Egyptian colleagues greeted us affectionately and, for the moment, the warmth of the reception helped distract me from the hospital's shortcomings. They led us to the Shah, who looked grim and determined, but smiled when he saw our combined group of more than a dozen doctors troop in and fill up his cramped quarters. His face was drawn, creased by lines of illness and worry, but he seemed cheerful and well prepared for surgery. And a good thing, too. Hibbard Williams, who had arrived from New York that same morning, examined him and found that, in the almost two weeks since Panama, his spleen had started to balloon massively once again.

Tucked up under the rib cage, a normal spleen cannot be felt by an examining physician. The Shah's spleen now measured six fingerbreadths below the bottom rib—an enormous swelling. To complicate matters, the patient's blood counts had also dropped dramatically.

We retired to a small room off the Shah's suite to discuss the operation. The Egyptian team was led by Zakaria El Baz, chief of medicine at Maadi, L. El Baz Rihan, a well-trained consulting internist, and Amin Affifi, a hematologist and oncologist. In staggering contrast to Panama, all the Egyptian doctors agreed: the Shah needed immediate surgery and DeBakey and his team would take command.

Throughout our conference, Crown Prince Reza played the role of royal inquisitor. While we were trying to make major decisions about the operation, the prince not only refused to stay out of the room, but demanded to participate in the decisions. The empress tried to curb him, but he persisted in asking questions: What's the spleen? Where is it? Will the operation hurt? In contrast, his younger brother, Ali, was no problem at all—he simply stood on his head in a corner of the Shah's room practicing his yoga exercises and occasionally shouting for his father to look as he tried some new meditative maneuver.

When we left for the hospital at six that evening, the hotel entrance was barricaded by reporters, so our entire team ducked out through the exit normally reserved for the removal of garbage. When we arrived at Maadi, everybody went their separate ways—DeBakey and Gerald Lawrie to the operating room to prepare the equipment and scrub down, me to the pathology lab to arrange for the proper examination of the spleen after its removal.

An hour or so before the operation, President Sadat and his wife arrived to pay their respects. While the two leaders met behind closed doors, the American team learned that the president wanted to meet us and we were asked to line up in the corridor outside the Shah's room.

After a few minutes, the door opened and out stepped Sadat, tall and relaxed, his salt-and-pepper mustache poised over a friendly warm smile. He looked like everybody's favorite uncle. I stood the closest to him and, when he stuck out his hand, I shook it energetically. Sadat spoke first. He thanked me for coming all the way to Egypt to look after "my dear friend, Pahlavi."

I suddenly felt inspired to say something that would do justice to this historic occasion, so I told him how much I appreciated his cooperation and how much his hospitality and friendship had meant to our patient. Unfortunately, I did not stop there. "When the history of the twentieth century is written," I went on, my voice threatening to crack with emotion, "there will be two towering figures—Sadat and Churchill."

Sadat winced. He then eyed me questioningly for a moment. Recovering his composure, the president nodded coolly and moved off down the receiving line.

His response puzzled me. Naturally, I had intended my remarks as the highest compliment—I really did consider Sadat one of the world's greatest statesmen, especially after his courageous visit to address the Knesset in Jerusalem in 1977 in an effort to forge a peace treaty with Israel. But obviously my words had not had the desired effect.

Several days later, when the Shah had sufficiently recovered from surgery, I told him about the encounter. His eyes widened in disbelief, and he laughed so explosively that I worried he would pop his stitches. "Dr. Kean," he said dryly, once he had his amusement under control, "you are a far better doctor than an historian. Remember, Winston Churchill once put Sadat in jail for almost three years!"

At precisely eight o'clock the Shah was wheeled into the operating room and placed on the operating table. The anesthetist covered his nose and mouth with a rubber mask and started the endotracheal anesthesia.

Suddenly a small controversy erupted. One of the Shah's retainers happened to notice that the monarch's head was facing north. This would never do, he complained in bursts of wildly broken English punctuated with Farsi exclamations of horror. In Iranian custom, the king had always to lie with his head pointed toward Mecca or something terrible was bound to happen. So the operation was delayed while the direction of the Holy City was determined and the operating table was swung around, with much commotion and moving of equipment, so that the Shah's head would assume the more auspicious angle.

Finally, DeBakey was ready. Moving with verve and confidence, the surgeon made a sweeping cut from the breastbone to the pubis. He took more time than usual in opening the peritoneum, the transparent membrane covering the visceral organs, as it had been less than five months since the Shah had been operated on in the same vicinity for the removal of his gallstones.

Empress Farah, the children, Princess Ashraf, and assorted members of the imperial retinue viewed the operation on closed-circuit television in a small room next to the operating theater while I explained to them what they were seeing. Several Egyptian physicians were there, too, as were three armed guards. Farah was visibly nervous as she made game, but unsuccessful attempts to cheer the entourage and quiet the children, all the while staring intently at the screen.

The operation seemed to go beautifully. The spleen was easily lifted from the abdominal cavity, then placed in a large sterile box and carried out into the corridor where I was now waiting in the company of five Egyptian pathologists. Inside the operating room, DeBakey finished the operation by sewing shut the Shah's belly. The entire procedure took eighty minutes.

I repaired to the pathology laboratory with the boxed spleen, accompanied by the crown prince, who, fancying himself a camera buff, now insisted on playing official photographer of the royal organ.

I placed the spleen on a small table for examination. It was an ugly monster—twenty times normal size. It was a foot long and weighed 1,990 grams. The angry red surface of the organ was mottled with white and gray areas ranging in size from the barely visible to some as much as a half-inch in diameter—a depressing road map of tumor.

With its antique electric fans and dusty equipment, working in the pathology laboratory was like stepping back through a medical looking glass into the 1920s, and the scene there could hardly have been more confusing. A group of Egyptian physicians, who had not been allowed into the operating room, crowded in, using the lab as a focal point for gossip and review. The crown prince, meanwhile, hovered over the organ with his expensive cameras, changing lenses, standing on stools, kneeling on the dissecting table itself, and, in the process, clicking off hundreds of frames of film.

Later, I would ask for copies of the photographs to include in my report, only to have the prince sheepishly admit that none of the pictures had "come out." Not a single one! Apparently he had purchased his film at the street bazaar in Cairo, not knowing (as any experienced traveler would) that exposed film and fake medicines topped the list of bogus goods routinely flogged by flimflam artists inhabiting souks throughout the Middle East.

But the spleen was now of only secondary importance. During surgery, DeBakey had taken a small biopsy of the liver, and microscopic examination of that specimen would tell the real story. Everyone knew that the spleen was shot through with tumor, but involvement of the liver would represent a much more serious condition. Sure enough, the tests disclosed lymphosarcoma of the liver. The Shah's days were now clearly numbered.

DeBakey, Williams, and I returned to the hospital early the next morning. The Shah had had a good night and looked remarkably healthy. The color had returned to his face, and his test results showed the reason why—all his blood counts had returned to normal! It was by any standards a breathtaking rebound, and Farah, Ashraf, and the children, who were gathered around his bed, seemed very pleased at how well the operation had gone.

I alone was not sanguine. My concern was already focused on the dismal results of the liver biopsy and the questions they raised about the long-term prognosis. We now faced a serious new dilemma—we could put the Shah back on a regimen of heavy chemotherapy, which might help apply the brakes to a quickly accelerating cancer and buy him a few more months of life, or we could dial back on the drugs and allow him to live out his time in as peaceful and painless a way possible. Which course should we choose?

While agonizing over that question, I broke the news about the biopsy results to Farah, who became deeply distressed. She pleaded with me not to tell the Shah and to withhold the information from the press. Otherwise, she reasoned, her husband's morale would be destroyed. But when I presented her views to the rest of the American–Egyptian team, DeBakey objected strenuously. There would be no way of concealing the truth from the press, he argued; the proper course would be to report everything we knew accurately, but to portray it in a positive light.

As he spoke, I realized DeBakey was right, so at a press conference that afternoon, we made a full disclosure—but with an optimistic spin. We told the reporters of the liver involvement, but expressed the hope that chemotherapy, which had previously kept his condition under good control, would continue to be effective.

I had my doubts. When I had sectioned the small piece of liver, it appeared that at least half of the tissue had been replaced by tumor. Yet when the patient's gallstones had been removed at New York Hospital the previous October, the liver had been entirely normal. In less than six months the lymphoma had become a rampant, metastatic disease signaling the final stage of malignancy—a stage not to be reversed by treatment.

There was now no hope of a cure. Given the circumstances, the application of aggressive chemotherapy seemed unnecessarily gruesome and debilitating. Yes, the drugs would buy the Shah a little more time, but they would also make him desperately ill. After much thought, I had reached a conclusion: chemotherapy should be used, but sparingly, and only to enhance the quality of the patient's life—not to effect a cure that couldn't be won at any price.

Throughout my medical career I had been a strong believer in what I called "coming out even." In treating terminal illness, there is a point at which the disease, and not the doctor, clearly takes command and the time comes to start increasing the morphine and easing off on life-prolonging therapies in order to make the end as peaceful as possible. It's a difficult balance to strike, but I wanted the Shah to "come out even."

My colleagues did not share my views. The Egyptians were eager to start chemotherapy at once. So was Flandrin. I disagreed vehemently. Vigorous chemotherapy, I should hardly have needed to remind them, would again depress the patient's immune system. This would put him at risk of serious infection that might impede his postoperative progress and could prove fatal. I argued that a hiatus of between one and three months should be observed before beginning treatment. We finally agreed that the Shah would be allowed a period of a few weeks to relax and build his strength before going onto a modest therapeutic program.

We had managed to paper over our differences, but just barely.

So far, Egypt had been a period of blissful concurrence among all the Shah's doctors, despite the various nationalities and specialties involved. The contrast with the nightmare in Panama couldn't have been sharper. But the honeymoon was now over.

On Monday, March 31, it was time for me to say good-bye. I had spent six months attending the Shah virtually full time. Now that his spleen had been removed I would be able to return to my duties as professor and practitioner in New York. So it was agreed that the Shah's care would be entrusted to two Egyptian physicians, namely Drs. El Baz and Affifi, and that Georges Flandrin would continue to consult on a regular basis from Paris. This formal transfer of authority, which was consummated by a series of handshakes in the doctors' lounge at Maadi, was very important to me; it was the only way of ensuring that the Shah's treatment wouldn't lapse into chaos. How naive my quaint insistence on ritual would seem only a few weeks later!

Before leaving for the airport, I took Empress Farah and Princess Ashraf aside for a detailed discussion of the Shah's condition and prognosis. DeBakey and Williams were also present. I told them that the Shah might be lucky enough to enjoy another Christmas, a holiday his children favored despite their Islamic upbringing. He had had his cherished family holiday in Panama the previous year. He might well have another one. But I did not think he would live to see a third. Again, I strongly advised against extraordinary means to keep him alive. I said my farewells to Farah and Ashraf and went to say goodbye to the Shah.

Sitting down on the bed, I felt the Shah's pulse and listened to his heart. I glanced at the wound on his abdomen, all the while trying to think of what to say. Finally, I said, "Your Imperial Majesty, I am about to leave you in the hands of our Egyptian colleagues," adding emotionally, "I'm not worried about you now." The Shah looked at me with those penetrating eyes of his and seemed to toy with the idea of calling my bluff but, at length, chose to let me wriggle off the hook. "I understand," he said, a sad smile flickering at the edges of his mouth.

I continued with my placebo talk, as the truth fled hopelessly into the distance. It was easy to rattle off isolated facts about his improved blood count to camouflage my pessimistic prognosis, but my underlying gloominess did not escape his careful scrutiny. I told him that with the removal of the spleen, the rapid rise of the cells and platelets in his blood, and with no evidence of tumor in the bone marrow, the only attitude should be one of optimism. I chose not to discuss the results of the liver biopsy. "In about ten days you will leave the hospital," I told him. "You should eat well and rehabilitate yourself. I expect to see pictures of you on the tennis court."

"Thank you for all you've done," he said. "When will I see you again?"

"As a doctor, only when necessary." We shook hands and parted. I couldn't bring myself to admit that, after all the hours we had spent together, my service to the Shah would come to an end the moment I walked out that door. But deep in my gut I knew that I would never see him again.

The Shah left the hospital in mid-April and took up residence in Kubbeh Palace. Despite my warnings, the Egyptians had already started him on a heavy regimen of chemotherapy. For the next two weeks the Shah seemed to be doing nicely. Then, toward the end of the month, his condition suddenly deteriorated. He became feverish and sick to his stomach. His abdomen became hard and swollen. His blood counts headed for the cellar once again.

Farah and Ashraf, never on the closest of terms, now had a major falling out over how aggressively to treat the Shah. Ashraf was obsessed with her belief that the Shah could be cured if only the right doctor with the right "magic bullet" could be found. Her latest medical magician was Dr. Morton Coleman, who had been the original oncologist on the New York Hospital team.

Coleman endorsed one of the most aggressive courses of chemotherapy going; to the standard four strong drugs he added two others, both highly toxic. The program was viewed by some, including me, as unreasonably adventurous for a patient in the Shah's condition.

Coleman's unannounced appearance in Cairo that spring took Georges Flandrin, who was there to monitor the Shah's progress, by complete surprise. Their disputes over how to treat the patient grew heated.* The poor Egyptians, trying their best to treat a fading patient, were caught in the crossfire of opinion and grew frustrated, then angry.

In late June, after weeks of agonizing indecision, a French surgeon operated to drain the Shah's distended abdomen and syphoned off a quart of infected fluid, presumably from the pancreas. The French began spreading word that the great Michael DeBakey himself had caused the infection by inadvertently nicking the pancreas while removing the spleen, an allegation I knew to be completely unfounded.

Meanwhile, the patient grew progressively weaker. He now suffered not only from his abdominal infection, but from pneumonia and pleurisy as well. Cultures of the pleural fluid disclosed *Salmonella typhosa*, the cause of typhoid fever.

Empress Farah asked Flandrin to assemble a full French team to rescue the Shah. The Egyptians, who had been diplomatic, helpful, and generous to a fault, now bridled at being ignored and were openly hostile.

Allegations continued to fly thick and fast among the competing medical interests. Much of the dispute was leaked to the Egyptian and French press, and the publicity added fuel to the controversy. No one doctor was now willing—or able—to take ultimate responsibility for the patient's care. The Shah's loved ones could not agree on a concerted course of action. It was, quite simply, a tragic mess, and I blamed myself; I had thought

---

*William Shawcross, *The Shah's Last Ride: The Fate of an Ally* (New York: Simon & Schuster, 1988), 398.

I was doing the right thing when I turned over the Shah's care to others. Now it seemed like a big mistake.

On Monday, July 21, Robert Armao was on the telephone. "There's been a palace coup in Cairo," he said, explaining that, somehow, Princess Ashraf had managed to wrest command of the Shah's medical care from the empress. And now Ashraf wanted our American team to return immediately. Would I go? Having felt helplessly sidelined while the Shah suffered, I jumped at the chance.

Immediately DeBakey and I made plans to fly to Cairo. At noon the following day, as I was literally going out the door for the airport, Armao telephoned again. The news was not good. Farah had now regained the initiative in the internecine struggle for control of the Shah's bedchamber. The French doctors had informed her that, if we Americans returned, they would walk out, and she would have to accept the consequences. After all those years of dependence on Flandrin, her decision was not surprising—but the French tactics, bordering on medical blackmail, were questionable, to say the least. "You can unpack your stethoscope," Armao said. "The trip is off."

Somehow, this final exercise in futility seemed wholly appropriate. It was a maddening end to what had proven to be a thoroughly frustrating, ill-starred affair from the very beginning. When I contacted DeBakey later that afternoon, he sounded uncharacteristically bitter and disgusted. "To hell with them," he said. "They don't appreciate what we've been trying to do." He got no argument from me. I felt the same way about the bickering doctors and the indecisive royal family—but how sad it all was for my patient. So late in his illness, nothing would have saved his life. He might have ended it peacefully, however, and he did not.

The Shah died at 9:56 on the morning of July 27, 1980. In the spirit of Islam, Anwar Sadat gave him a state funeral with full military honors. Mercifully, the Shah's hegira, his long, tortuous odyssey, had finally come to an end.

As events roared by, his demise almost became lost in the blur of media coverage. Three months before his death, on April 24, President Carter's attempt to rescue the hostages had ended in ignominious failure, leaving eight American commandos dead on the sands of the Iranian desert alongside the smoldering wreckage of their helicopters. Then, on January 20, 1981, as Ronald Reagan took the oath of office in Washington as the fortieth president of the United States, Teheran announced that it was finally freeing its American prisoners after fourteen agonizing months of captivity (timing that guaranteed that Carter, who had done the real work, would get little of the credit). The following October, the Shah's one true friend among world leaders, Anwar Sadat, died in a hail of bullets, the victim of the Muslim militants he had angered by providing the Shah with a safe haven.

How will history judge the Shah? That, of course, is impossible for me to say. My job was to care for a sick man, not to judge him, and my views on the subject are necessarily fragmentary, biased, and sympathetic. Nonetheless, I do feel qualified to comment on the key medical question at the heart of his case: Could things have turned out differently?

The answer is yes, most definitely. Had the Shah been allowed to return to New York Hospital from Lackland Air Force Base, or even Panama, the story would certainly have been different. A quick removal of his spleen, uncomplicated by political entanglements, might even have saved his life; it would surely have lengthened it.

That leaves only the one enduring irony about the Shah's odyssey that for me, as a medical man, eclipses all others and haunts me to this day. Here was one of the world's wealthiest men, who for a time was also one of its most influential leaders, a man who should have had access to the best medical care on the planet.

And yet, quite literally for the life of him, he could not obtain the proper treatment. Why not?

When both Ronald Reagan and Pope John Paul II were shot by would-be assassins in the spring of 1981, they were taken to the emergency rooms of ordinary hospitals in their respective cities and treated as ordinary patients. They survived because they received the standard, competent care provided by a good municipal hospital, an institution designed for the democratic care of the average citizen—the Peter Smiths of this world.

This option was not open to the autocratic Shah. He had been forced, while still on the Peacock Throne, to hide his illness from friends and foes alike while he tried to quietly search out the "best" foreign doctors money could buy. Later, when his illness was advanced, time was short, and he was on the run, he had been forced to look for a country where transplanted physicians could perform eleventh-hour services on an ad hoc basis. What he had really needed all along was the comprehensive, long-term care and medical teamwork available at a first-rate public hospital. Early on, medical democracy could have saved the Shah. In the end, it was politics that killed him.

PART IV

MEDICAL SLEUTHING

CHAPTER 15

The Steak Tartare Defense

A s studies in human nature, my patients have never ceased to amaze and fascinate me. I've relished the education. Still, I must confess that the real magic in life has come from another, older source. Ever since my mentor, Francis O'Connor, infected me with a love of scientific sleuthing as a student, nothing has equaled the overpowering attraction of an honest-to-goodness medical mystery—the more involved the plot, the more elusive the culprit, the better. Luckily, the past fifty years have brought me into contact with many such puzzles.

September 1986 was a case in point. I had just put a match to my after-lunch cigar when my secretary asked me to pick up the phone. Gary Wadler, a former student of mine who practices internal medicine in Manhasset, Long Island, was on the line and he sounded worried.

"Ben, I'm in big trouble."

"What's wrong?"

"Do you remember Martina Navratilova?"

How could I forget? The long, angular Czech—now an American citizen—was arguably the greatest player in the history of women's tennis. At twenty-nine, she had won every major pro tournament, some of them more than once, and had earned over $10 million in prize money. More to the point, she had been the subject of repeated conversations between Wadler and myself in the fall of 1982 when the superstar was a very sick woman and Wadler had called to ask me for advice.

"Certainly I remember her," I told Wadler. "She's not sick again, is she?"

"No," Gary explained, "it's just that I've got to appear in court at ten o'clock tomorrow morning to testify on Martina's behalf. Maybe you read in the newspapers that she's being sued for two million dollars. I need you to confirm our original diagnosis. Toxoplasmosis is central to her defense."

"Toxo" and I went back a long way and I cringed at the mention of the name. I had been its sworn enemy ever since that day at the autopsy table in Panama in 1945 when I had first witnessed how the evil little bug had reduced a newborn baby's brain to nothing more than a pulpy mass of collapsed tissue. Since then, I'd spent years trying to publicize the dangers of the disease, and yet it had remained as little known as it was widespread. But this was the first time I'd ever heard of the parasite worming its way into a lawsuit! I asked Gary to review the details of the case.

On the afternoon of September 7, 1982, Wadler reminded me, Martina had stepped into the crisp sunshine on center court at Flushing Meadows to square off against Pam Shriver in the quarterfinals of the U.S. Open. Despite her string of tournament successes, an Open victory had eluded her, and now, determined to rectify all that, she raced to a 6–1 win in the first set. Then, early in the second set, Shriver lost her footing and collided with a courtside flowerbox. Martina's army of fans cheered loudly, sure she would now close in for the kill.

It was at precisely that point that the champ seemed to falter. Her returns began to whiffle and float. She had trouble running up on the shots Shriver was now shrewdly dropping just over the net on her visibly weary opponent. Navratilova boosters gasped, then fell silent. Shriver won the second set in a tiebreaker and gained an easy victory in the third set. Once again, Martina's dreams of an Open triumph had collapsed.*

---

*For an account of the athletic drama, see Martina Navratilova with George Vecsey, *Martina* (New York: Alfred A. Knopf, 1985).

Wadler, who was then serving as official Open physician, and had been watching the debacle from the stands, groaned inwardly. It was just as he had predicted: the longer she played, the weaker she would get. "I'd warned her not to risk it," Gary said. "Why hadn't she listened to me?"

Ten days earlier, Martina had visited Wadler at his Manhasset office, complaining of a variety of troubling, though somewhat confusing symptoms. Her arms and legs ached terribly, she said, and she had lost power in her swing. Knotting muscle spasms struck without warning day and night. Even walking became a chore and climbing stairs was special agony. After six weeks of this, Martina felt completely drained. Normally so unflappable, she told Gary she was having a hard time keeping the lid on her emotions. All she wanted to do was go to sleep.

Wadler pondered the possibilities. On the surface, the symptoms suggested nothing very serious. A little aggravated anemia, perhaps, or a viral infection. Both were common problems of women tennis champions wedded to life on the grueling pro circuit. As soon as Wadler began the routine physical examination, however, he quickly changed his mind. Behind her ears, on the back of her neck, and down the sides of her chest, Wadler found a network of swollen lymph glands—"in places," he said, "that were disconcerting."

Muscle weakness, irritability, a case of "the blahs"—these by themselves were ordinary enough complaints. Combined with enlarged, walnut-hard lymph nodes, however, they could mean real trouble, and the grim choices raised a number of red flags in Wadler's mind. Hodgkin's disease? A different variety of lymphatic cancer? Acute leukemia?

It was then that Wadler remembered the warning I had repeated time and again as he'd sat as a student in my classroom: "Before you send a patient under the knife for a cancer biopsy, send me a blood sample for toxo testing!" Martina's blood arrived by messenger, and sure enough, her tests revealed the presence of the disease. We felt reasonably sure that Martina had acute toxoplasmosis.

Weak, frustrated, and still shadowed by the possibility of cancer, Martina contemplated Wadler's advice to withdraw from the tournament—then gamely decided to go ahead and compete anyway. Her loss to Pam Shriver wasn't the last of Martina's problems, however, since her condition was about to be compounded by some messy legal complications.

As Martina left the court in defeat and headed for the showers, she was mobbed by the usual crowd of photographers. Shielding her face with a towel, she lowered her head and tried to push her way through the confusion. Suddenly, a scuffle broke out. In the next instant, Martina was holding a camera in one hand and ripping out the film with the other, while a bewildered freelance cameraman named Arthur Seitz picked himself up off the ground. Seitz had learned the hard way that you didn't tangle lightly with the powerful young Czech.

But he wasn't about to let the incident pass. Attorneys acting on Seitz's behalf filed suit in a Long Island court claiming $2 million in damages. Navratilova had not only damaged Seitz's camera equipment, they said, but had injured his shoulder and caused him mental anguish.

"Here's where it gets complicated," Wadler told me on the telephone. "The lawyers have picked up on a newspaper story which alleged that Martina routinely took anabolic steroids to build up her muscles and endurance. They may try to portray her as some kind of steroid-massive Amazon with the strength to beat up on males and inflict serious bodily harm.

"On the other hand," Wadler speculated, "her lawyers might argue that the toxo parasites had invaded her brain, causing abnormal cerebritis [inflammation of the front, or 'thinking' part of the brain] or possibly encephalitis [inflammation of the entire brain], and that was what made her lose control." Pausing briefly for me to consider the argument, Wadler then asked, "Does that make sense to you?"

"It's going to be hard to prove," I replied. Acute toxo of the brain *is* possible, of course. The disease has been known to cause bizarre behavior changes when it occurs as a potentially deadly complication in immunosuppressed patients, especially those terminally ill with cancer or AIDS. But that was unheard of in the normal course of the infection, and I told Gary as much.

Wadler had his own theory. "Martina was beaten by Pam Shriver because she was in an ailing, weakened condition," he said. "That much is obvious. Instead of being a steroid-hyped maniac, she was suffering from extreme fatigue and muscle spasms. After three sets of championship tennis, she couldn't have had the strength to hurt a fly."

Precisely! I agreed and encouraged Wadler to go with that line of argument. But I was now more intrigued than ever. How would a jury weigh such seemingly arcane medical evidence? The next few weeks would tell. Meanwhile, I relighted my cigar, took a deep puff, and paused to consider the long, tangled mystery of toxoplasmosis and how I came to be caught up in it.

Toxoplasmosis, readers may be surprised to learn, is a disease of truly panoramic proportions. It is caused by a rapacious little protozoan that infects an estimated one out of every three Americans—and probably a billion people worldwide! It remains one of the leading causes of birth defects in the United States and, since 1981, has emerged as a major opportunistic disease causing dementia and death among our growing population of AIDS victims.

For all that, though, toxo is hardly a household word. Why have so few people ever heard of it? Toxo, to put it simply, is a parasitic master of deception. It is a bug that frequently produces no significant illness at all or whose transient symptoms—fever, rash, headache, and enlarged lymph nodes—are frequently passed off by the victim as a "touch of the flu." It is, in the jargon of tropical medicine, a nearly "perfect" parasite, meaning it can, and most often does, live inside its human host for decades undetected and doing little serious harm.

In most cases, our body's natural immune system sees to it that toxo behaves itself. The disease police, cells called macrophages, patrol the parasite colonies, limiting their size and preventing a population explosion that would endanger the host. But the odds can shift suddenly and with a vengeance. When an individual becomes immunosuppressed, for whatever reason, previously quiescent toxo cysts suddenly explode, releasing hundreds of individual parasites. Greedily expanding their turf, they burrow deep into the vital organs—the heart, liver, brain, and eyes. At this stage, the damage is permanent and often fatal. When a pregnant woman becomes infected, toxo can ravage her unborn child with blindness, heart and liver damage, or severe brain deformities.

So how do humans acquire this menace? How can it be prevented? The answers to those questions lie at the heart of a riddle of sickness that has literally taken centuries to fathom. Toxo, with its most elusive of symptoms, has probably been bedeviling the human race since the very beginning. Evidence indicates that the parasite was flourishing along the arc of northern Africa when Hannibal first set out to sack Rome from his native Carthage in 218 B.C. It wasn't until 1908, however, that scientists stumbled across the first important clues as to toxo's true identity.

The adventure started one steamy morning in the Tunisian capital of Tunis. Two French scientists, Charles Nicolle and Louis Herbert Manceaux, were hard at work in their laboratory at the local branch of the Pasteur Institute. Before them on the dissecting table was the unimposing carcass of the gondi, a small, white African rodent that looks something like a cross between a guinea pig and a rat.

Peering into his microscope, Manceaux suddenly spied something so unusual that he called his partner over for a look. There, amid a smear of blood and tissue from the gondi, Nicolle observed several tiny, crescent-shaped objects he had never seen before. Indeed, further study persuaded both men that what they had witnessed was not only a parasite of great rarity, but one completely new to the annals of medical science. The jubilant

Frenchmen named their discovery *Toxoplasma gondii* (*toxo* from the Greek meaning "arc," and *plasma* because it was found in the cells or cytoplasm of the gondi).

Three days after Nicolle and Manceaux had published their findings in Europe, serendipity struck again, this time in South America. A Brazilian investigator named Alfonso Splendore, who was working independently in São Paulo, recorded yet another encounter under the microscope with the newly christened parasite, this time in one of his laboratory rabbits. So it was that, after millennia of anonymity, toxo had finally stepped from the shadows.

Still, the parasite's belated debut on the scientific scene failed to raise much of a fuss. Most parasitologists of the day simply passed off the curious little protozoan as an insignificant agent of infection in small, fur-bearing animals. Yet its appearance did raise a question that now plagued the inquiring few: Could *T. gondii* also be a parasite of man? It was to that very question that toxo would respond with its next dramatic appearance.

On March 5, 1922, Josef Jankü, a pediatrician and ophthalmologist in Prague, was faced with a grim chore. One of his patients, a sixteen-month-old boy named Victor, had died that very morning after a long, doomed struggle for life. Grotesquely deformed, Victor had been born with a large, swollen, pear-shaped head (hydrocephalus) and a drooping, malformed left eye (microphthalmus). Now the grieving parents, wanting to know exactly what had killed their son, had asked the trusted Jankü to perform an autopsy.

Jankü disliked postmortems and only rarely did them himself, but he felt obliged to honor the wishes of Victor's parents. Very soon, however, his scientific curiosity was piqued when the autopsy revealed the most peculiar phenomenon. Clustered in the decedent's brain tissue and in the retina of the left eye were thousands of microscopic parasites encased in scores of tiny podlike cysts. They looked to Jankü like seeds in a pomegranate. Each

pocket of infection was surrounded by a crimson corona of in-
flamed tissue, a pattern that Jankü later described as a curtain of
half-furled bat wings. Not well read in the literature of parasitology, however, he had no idea how to identify the arc-shaped
creatures under his microscope, nor did any of his colleagues in
Prague. What could they be?

Leave it to a tourist to come up with the answer. While vacationing in Prague in 1928, Claude Levaditi, the French microbiologist, overheard someone talking about Jankü's strange
findings and thought he'd have a look. He soon found himself
in Jankü's study, staring at a speck of tissue from Victor's eye,
as Jankü loomed over his shoulder. Voilà! Levaditi recognized
the phenomenon immediately. This was the very same parasite
first described by his countrymen, Nicolle and Manceaux, that
scorching day in Tunis twenty years before. Science, at long last,
had recorded its first clinical case of toxoplasmosis in humans.

The narrative now jumps another two decades ahead to the hot,
sticky evening of October 6, 1945, when I, now senior pathologist at Gorgas Hospital in Panama, was standing in the morgue,
smoking a cigar and mopping my brow with a handkerchief.
Suddenly the huge swinging doors flew open and in rushed Alleyne, my Jamaican assistant, wheeling a gurney in the middle
of which lay the tiny, lifeless body of a newborn baby boy.
Alleyne handed me the hospital report, and the story was a sad
one.

Earlier that afternoon the infant's father, one Pedro Torres,
had stumbled into the emergency room in a highly emotional
state. Clutched to his breast was the unnamed son, who had been
born ninety minutes earlier at the Torres home. The shrewd old
midwife handling the delivery had been alarmed by the child's
wizened, dwarfish features and his irregular breathing and had
insisted that he be taken to the hospital. On admission to Gorgas,
the Torres boy was examined, but, when no serious abnormalities were found, he was placed in an incubator for observation.

A few minutes later, he suddenly turned blue, began gasping for breath, and died.

While I pondered the report and tried to imagine what on earth might have killed the child, Alleyne readied the body for autopsy. Having participated in some 15,000 postmortems in his long career at the Gorgas morgue, the venerable old Alleyne had developed an eagle's eye for aberrations. So when the first dramatic illustrations of congenital toxo in the brain were published in 1942, I had been careful to show them to him and told him to keep his eyes peeled.

Alleyne knew better than I that a normal brain looks something like a large, gray sponge a deep-sea diver might pluck from the ocean floor. But that is not what he saw when he peered inside the infant's braincase. Instead of two firm hemispheres with their distinctive, anemonelike convolutions, Alleyne saw collapsed on the floor of the skull a gelatinous mass of watery brain tissue flecked with sickly yellow spots.

Nearly speechless with excitement, Alleyne turned to me and stuttered in his fruity island baritone, "Dok-tor, dok-tor . . . tok-zoo-plaz-moh-seez . . . at laazt!" He was quite right, of course. A thorough microscopic examination revealed that the parasite that had invaded the brain, as well as virtually every other organ in the child's body, was indeed *Toxoplasma gondii*.

It didn't take me long to figure out why the child had died so suddenly. It was perfectly obvious that his mother had unwittingly infected him. Yet the mother herself hadn't succumbed to the parasite. Why not? And how had she acquired the disease that had so ruthlessly destroyed her child?

I decided to visit the Torres home to search for further clues. The family lived about ten miles outside of Panama City in a particularly poor barrio where man and animals commingled in undifferentiated squalor. Cats, dogs, goats, chickens, pigeons, and rats roamed freely in the Torres barnyard. All of the villages in the area, Mr. Torres informed me, were tormented by large mosquito populations. Nearly all of the dogs were infested with a common canine tick. In other words, the number of possible vectors for the transmission of disease to the human population seemed almost infinite. I was now more confused than ever.

Back at the hospital, a study of the individual family members was equally unhelpful. Asked how she had fared during her term, the twenty-four-year-old Mrs. Torres allowed that it had been by far the easiest of her six pregnancies, and delivery had gone smoothly. Blood, urine, and stool tests revealed no noteworthy abnormalities. The thirty-year-old father did have a history of inadequately treated syphilis, but otherwise displayed no symptoms that might have harmed his unborn child. Baby Torres's four surviving brothers and sisters were all in good health.

So there it was. We had witnessed the twenty-seventh case of human toxoplasmosis so far recorded, and we still hadn't the faintest idea, none whatsoever, of how the disease might be stopped or even how it was transmitted.

That didn't prevent me from offering an opinion, of course. My autopsy report and an article I later published in the *Journal of the American Medical Association* concluded, "on extremely tenuous grounds," that the disease might have been transmitted by Mr. Torres's pigeons, the species of bird in question having previously been identified as a carrier of other deadly infections. Admittedly, it was a stab in the dark, and, as it turned out, spectacularly wrong. Nonetheless, I was convinced that the answer lurked somewhere beneath the feathers and fur in that woebegone barnyard. But where? Before I could investigate any further, my pursuit of toxo took an unexpected turn.

The war in Europe had been over for four months when I finally received my orders to report to General Stayer in Berlin in the fall of 1945. During a layover in New York, I decided to pay a call on the famous Abner Wolf, the toxo expert at Columbia-Presbyterian Hospital and my former teacher at Columbia P & S. (It was his illustrations of the disease that Alleyne had seen and remembered.) The great doctor was a taciturn man, with bushy eyebrows and cool gray eyes, and it was clear from the outset that he was in no mood to waste his valuable time on some young military hotshot like myself. I noticed him brighten perceptibly, however, when I told him that I was about to leave for Germany.

"Any chance you'll be getting over to Czechoslovakia?" he inquired, before adding with feigned disinterest, "If you do, of course, you could render medical science an invaluable service."

An invaluable service? Me? Dr. Wolf's words had a magical ring. The hint of some kind of secret mission in Soviet-occupied Eastern Europe was wildly seductive. What exactly did he want me to do?

The doctor was pleased by my enthusiasm, which he somehow seemed to anticipate. In Prague, he explained in a hushed, conspiratorial tone, I would find a man named Herman Sikl. Herr Professor Sikl was a celebrated pathologist at Charles University, and, as it happened, possessed certain bits of embalmed tissue that he would turn over to me to eventually carry home to Dr. Wolf. The times were still precarious in Europe, he wanted me to understand, and only a fool would entrust such valuable scientific artifacts to the mails. All I had to do was pick up the goods in Prague and deliver them to Wolf when my tour of duty in Europe had ended.

I knew Dr. Wolf was no fool, and Sikl, from Wolf's account, didn't sound like one, either. But why all the fuss over a few scraps of tissue, I wondered aloud.

Dr. Wolf seemed visibly staggered by my ignorance. "Because," he said evenly, as if explaining the rules of basic anatomy to an exceedingly dense first-year medical student, "Sikl inherited the autopsy remains of Jankü's baby boy."

Those "scraps," Wolf would have me know, just happened to be the very same remnants of brain, eye, and heart tissue taken from Jankü's autopsy on the famous Victor, his young toxo victim, way back in 1922. They had been preserved all these years, and Sikl, on a visit to the United States just before the war, had promised to pass on to Wolf the remaining samples. There was only one stipulation—the specimens had to be hand-carried.

I had been in Germany five months before I worked up the guts to ask General Stayer to let me go to Czechoslovakia. My position as chief health officer for the state of Hesse provided frequent excuses for seeing the old man, so I telephoned for an appointment, ostensibly to discuss bottlenecks in the delivery of medical supplies. On the appointed day I flew from Wiesbaden to Berlin on the military shuttle. When I walked into his office, I stood at attention and fired off a snappy, by-the-numbers salute. Since I had already earned a reputation for my occasional embarrassing lapses of military bearing, Stayer sensed something was up.

"What is it you want, Kean?" he growled, looking up from his desk.

"General," I said, "I want to go to Czechoslovakia."

"No you don't," he said, looking down again. "Four American officers went on a drunken rampage in Prague a couple of weeks ago and simply tore the place apart. Thanks to them, Prague is now off limits. The Russians don't want us there, the Czechs don't want us there, and I certainly don't want *you* there."

"But General," I pleaded, "I promised Dr. Wolf." I then explained how vital my mission was to the advancement of human knowledge.

Stayer cut me off. "Impossible," he said. "There is only one way of getting into Czechoslovakia now, and that's in the event of an outbreak of typhus on the border. So far as I know, though, there is at present no typhus *on* the border."

I should have been disappointed, but I was not. I thought I had detected a sly smile flickering at the corners of the old soldier's mouth when he assured me of the sheer impossibility of epidemic typhus. Okay, I thought, it's worth a gamble. If I read the general correctly, he had just given me my ticket to Prague. If I was mistaken, of course, I could wind up facing a court-martial.

I returned to Wiesbaden on the first available flight and loaded my jeep with a few cartons of C-rations and plenty of cigarettes. Leaving my bewildered army driver standing forlornly outside the officers' quarters, I roared off alone toward the Czech border.

It was late winter, cold, and the roads were slippery with ice and studded with detours. I circled Darmstadt on the shattered autobahn, drove past Nuremberg, and stopped for the night at a "liberated" castle at Amberg, a place catering solely to GI brass, with soft sheets, a bed warmed by a hot brick, and a brandy nightcap for "the important major." On the road again before dawn, I neared the village of Fürth im Wald. All I had to do now was find a hospital. As my jeep skittered around a sharp bend in the road, I saw a bomb-scarred, one-story wooden building with a battered tin roof. It would have looked like a pathetic dump to anyone else, but to me it was a glorious sight. A faded red cross unmistakably identified it as the local hospital.

I skidded to a stop in the gravel courtyard and announced to the duty nurse, in my farcical German, that I had come to see "Herr Doktor Commandant"—whoever he might happen to be. The head doctor soon appeared. He was balding and scrawny, with a long white laboratory coat that flapped around him in the chill breeze, making him look like a scarecrow that might have just wandered out of one of the neighboring fields.

He greeted me with heartbreaking formality. For a man in his position, a visit from an occupation health official usually meant trouble. He spoke little English, but we communicated easily enough by shouting universally understood medical words at one another. I gave him to understand that I wanted to tour his venereal disease ward on the double.

Joined now by two junior physicians, the head man obligingly ushered me into a long room with two rows of about twelve beds each. My eyes wandered over the sleeping patients, who were emitting throaty, muffled snores. Then I saw her—just the sort of woman I had been hoping to find. She was sitting up in bed at the far end of the room, thumbing listlessly through a dog-eared magazine. As we approached, I could see that she was really only a girl, no more than sixteen or seventeen. "*Prostitut*," my guide told me in a loud whisper. The girl pretended not to notice as I stepped in for a closer look. She was a study in scarlet, all right. Her narrow head of stringy red hair framed a hard, pallid face dotted with small crimson spots. An obvious case of secondary syphilis.

Turning to my German colleagues, I announced in a voice loud enough to wake the dead, "Ah, typhus fever!" and rushed out of the ward. Horrified, the Germans ran after me, wailing, "*Nicht* typhus! Syphilis! *Nicht* typhus!" When I reached my jeep, I looked over my shoulder one last time at my frantic pursuers and shouted, "*Nicht* syphilis! Typhus!" and sped away. At the border station a few miles down the road, I asked the MPs to relay an urgent message to General Stayer in Berlin. It read simply: "Outbreak of typhus at border near Pilsen. Undertaking investigation. Report soon. Kean."

I entered Prague about noon. In spite of the war, the city's classical features, its curved bridges, glittering domes, and stone turrets, had survived intact and now lay as snow-crusted ornaments under the low gray skies.

When I reached the doorstep of the Hotel Europa, a crumbling five-story building just off the central boulevard, I parked my jeep on the sidewalk, heaved the extra gasoline cans inside, and locked it ostentatiously. I wasn't taking any chances. Czechoslovakia was now under Russian occupation, and its elegant old capital was starving, shivering, and immobile. Anything that could be eaten, worn, or driven could disappear with breathtaking speed.

The interior of the hotel was a dismal sight. Only a few bare bulbs burned dimly in the gloom of the winter afternoon, casting the once opulent lobby, with its baroque wall carvings, heavy tapestries, and pathetically threadbare carpets, in sepia tones. Faking a typhus epidemic at the border had been an exhilarating experience, but now I was beginning to surrender myself to all this Central European angst. The Soviet presence only seemed to contribute to the leaden atmosphere.

My sense of mission revived, however, when I asked the desk clerk if he could direct me to Charles University and he said, in halting English, that the school was only a few blocks away. As if to make up for his linguistic shortcomings, he drew me an exquisitely detailed street map, and soon I was standing in the dank, barren corridors of the department of pathology.

Herr Professor Sikl was a man in his early fifties and a gentleman of the old school, erect, gaunt, and cordial. He bowed, snapping his neck forward in the European manner. Inviting me to sit down, he ordered an assistant to bring us coffee—an unspeakable luxury, considering the privations of that starving metropolis. Reaching into a desk drawer, Sikl produced a small silver box containing three wrinkled cigarettes, one American and two of unknown but somewhat dubious origin, probably Russian.

The professor looked a little crestfallen when I selected the American cigarette, but listened attentively when I told him of my assignment from Dr. Wolf. He quickly grasped the desire of a young pathologist to accede to the request of an honored mentor. Sikl then grew morose. For a moment I thought he was going to cry; maybe he did. In any event, I averted my eyes in embarrassment. For twenty years, he told me, he had painstakingly gathered the finest collection of pathology specimens to be found in Europe, perhaps the entire world. His department had housed a museum that was the mecca of every pathologist on the Continent.

As founder and curator of this hall of wonders, Sikl had become a famous man. Specimens in glass jars filled shelves that lined the labyrinthine corridors of laboratories, autopsy rooms, and classrooms. A ghoulish form of interior decorating, perhaps, but there was real genius in the layout; wherever they moved, Sikl's students were always within sight of the basic raw materials of their craft. The collection contained thousands of specimens, and had, in that precomputerized age, been catalogued and cross-indexed with withering efficiency to allow for rapid access and recovery of items.

When war came to Prague, life under the occupying Germans had presented many hardships. Sikl and his colleagues tried to remain philosophical; at least they were allowed to go about their business without much interference. The Nazis even accorded them a certain icy respect. Then, in the spring of 1945, the Russian army was suddenly on the outskirts of the city. May 18. Sikl remembered the date vividly, for that was the day the Germans paid a final call on him at the museum. The soldiers had marched up the stairway to the second floor and began methodically removing all of the jars from the hall cabinets, laying them gently on the floor. "What luck," the good professor remembered thinking. "They're worried the specimens will be damaged in the fighting and are removing them for safekeeping."

Just then, one of the German officers had blown a whistle. On command, the soldiers picked up the jars and started tossing them out the windows. Horrified, Sikl watched the courtyard below fill up with debris—islands of shattered glass joined by rivulets of formalin. The specimens themselves, now stripped of their scientific context and reduced to meaningless heaps of offal, were so scattered and crushed as to defy identification. As Sikl looked on, the Germans climbed into their canopied trucks and back and forth over the puddled courtyard, destroying the last vestiges of his fabulous collection. "They worked very hard," said Sikl, his bony fingers squeezing the bridge of his nose. "It was impossible to understand."

We said farewell sadly. After hearing Sikl's story, I didn't have the heart to ask him about the Jankü specimens. They, too, had obviously gone the way of the rampaging Nazis. As I was about to leave, however, Sikl held up a skeletal hand for me to wait and, reaching into his desk once again, he retrieved three small bottles neatly labeled in English, "heart," "brain," "eye." Inside floated wafers of tissue somewhat larger than aspirin tablets.

Sikl gave me a final, snappy nod, and said, "Give these to your Dr. Wolf. I went downstairs after the Nazis had finished and salvaged what I could. I'm afraid this is all that remains of Jankü's autopsy on little Victor."

I never saw Sikl again, but I protected those bottles as if my life depended on it.

When I returned to Berlin with my trophies, I fully expected to be arrested on sight and hauled off to jail to await court-martial. I made for General Stayer's office straightaway to face the music. But instead of ordering me bound and gagged, the old man greeted me warmly. Offering me a cigar, he began to talk animatedly about a forthcoming visit of prominent stateside newspaper editors. He never once mentioned my trip to the Czech–German border. No further investigation of the great ty-phus "epidemic" there was ever made.

One day in the early winter of 1947, when my tour of duty was finally over and I was back in New York, I paid a call on Dr. Wolf at his laboratory at 168th Street and Broadway. I pulled the three bottles Sikl had given me from my coat pocket and handed them over. The great doctor thanked me profusely and then turned his back on me and proceeded to examine Jankü's lost treasure greedily. But his enthusiasm was misplaced. Wolf would examine the material for the next two years, slicing section after section of wafer-thin sheets from the tiny blocks and look-ing at them under his microscope.

But he would never find a single trace of *Toxoplasma gondii*. The parasite had vanished. Had Sikl plucked the wrong stuff from the soup the Nazis made of his collection? Had the leftover tissue never been infected in the first place? Whatever the reason, with the disappearance of the physical evidence from Victor, Josef Jankü's enormous contribution to the understanding of toxo was played out.

My wartime fling with toxo quickly became a thing of the past as I spent the postwar years building up my Park Avenue prac-tice. Then, in the mid-sixties, I was eager to find an area of medical research that I could conduct close to home. That's when

I remembered my fascination with toxo. It was high time, I decided, to rekindle the relationship—and with good reason.

Medical science had now identified toxo as a true national tragedy. Improvement in testing procedures had helped us map out the scope of the disease for the first time, and we were genuinely shocked to find so many people affected. The postwar "baby boom" in this country alone had brought thousands of infants into the world with hideous deformities linked to toxo. Since the war, we had learned that the body's natural immune system rendered toxo relatively harmless to the majority of its adult victims. Not equipped with the same defenses, however, an unborn child was utterly helpless in fighting off the marauding parasites acquired from the mother. To complicate matters, toxo was so insidious that the average expectant mother never knew she was being infected. Typically, she would explain away the symptoms as a "touch of the flu," unaware that her baby was in mortal danger.

We found toxo sneaky in other ways, too. Children might develop normally throughout childhood and into their late teens, for instance, until toxoplasma cysts, long buried in the back of the eye, would burst without warning. Thousands upon thousands of parasites thus released would quickly set about destroying the cells of the retina (chorioretinitis). The result was badly impaired vision, if not total blindness.

Because only a few institutions in the country were set up to perform the complicated testing then required for the detection of toxo, New York Hospital became a leading diagnostic center. The humble tropical medicine unit I headed took on a sudden prominence as doctors from across the United States consulted us for guidance on this "hot new disease." It was at that point that serendipity landed on our doorstep and did not just knock politely, but tap danced, stood on its head, and whistled for attention.

THE STEAK TARTARE DEFENSE

The date of its arrival was March 5, 1968. That evening hundreds of Cornell students crowded into Uris Auditorium to hear the celebrated guest speaker, Dr. Christiaan Barnard, the Cape Town surgeon famous for his role in pioneering the techniques of the heart transplant operation. To ensure getting a seat for the talk, many of the students had gone across the street to grab a quick hamburger at the dormitory cafeteria.

The snack bar was run by a large, matronly woman named Betty, who fussed over the young medical students as if they were her own children, constantly admonishing them to clean their plates. For all her maternal concern, however, Betty was not a gifted cook. Her burgers were famous for invariably coming off the grill blood rare, regardless of how they had been ordered. With the sudden surge of business on the night of the big lecture, Betty's offerings gave the word *rare* new meaning.

Exactly one week later, on the morning of March 12, two students limped into Cornell's student health clinic complaining of fever, rash, headache, and enlarged lymph glands in the neck. That afternoon, three more showed up. Two of the five had experienced a loss of feeling in their feet and legs, and two others were suffering from nausea. All of them said that muscle cramps, painful and persistent, were by far the most unpleasant feature of their condition. Blood tests confirmed the impossible: all five had come down with acute toxoplasmosis!

In contrast with the plagues of old, the numbers involved were hardly staggering. Scientifically speaking, however, they were sufficient to establish the first epidemic of the disease ever recorded. Since our famed South African colleague was responsible at least indirectly for the outbreak, I felt obliged to credit him by naming it the "Christiaan Barnard Epidemic."

Why did my colleagues and I suspect the beef? The science is called epidemiology, but the process was simple common sense. What, we asked ourselves, is the one thing all five infected students swallowed, inhaled, or otherwise came into contact with—and more or less at the same time—to make them sick? Questioning of the victims pointed the finger straight back to that culinary evening at Betty's. The students vividly recalled their surprise at suddenly encountering the raw beef between their burger buns and then gamely, if queasily, wolfing it down.

Simple arithmetic also helped. Before toxo, or, for that matter, any other infectious disease, can claim its victim, it must undergo a set incubation period during which organisms multiply inside the body to the point that they begin to disturb normal bodily functions. By counting backward from the onset of symptoms as reported by the students, we were able to establish a rough time frame for the original infection. Then, by linking the five students directly to Betty's burgers, we accomplished something highly unusual in the annals of epidemiology; we established the exact hour of the natural infection—between 6:00 and 7:00 P.M., March 5, 1968. Like clockwork, the first symptoms had appeared seven days later, and all of them within a fortnight.

Other scientists, of course, had already done most of the really tough detective work for us. That toxo could be transmitted through undercooked lamb and pork had been well established back in the fifties by researchers at the U.S. National Institutes of Health in Bethesda, Maryland.

Dr. Georges Desmonts of the St. Vincent de Paul Hospital in Paris uncovered the next major piece of evidence when he studied a group of young tuberculosis patients and found that those children who had been living in a local sanitarium were five times more likely to come down with toxo than those who remained as outpatients. The findings stumped Desmonts until one day, like any good Frenchman, he found himself reviewing the hospital menu with an appraising Gallic eye. Each day, he noted, the TB patients were given generous helpings of blood-rare meat, a dietary regimen designed to help build their stamina. When, acting on a hunch, Desmonts ordered the staff to increase the size of the daily meat ration, the rate of infection doubled. Desmonts had confirmed his suspicion; the more raw meat the patients ate, the greater their exposure to the toxo parasite and, hence, the more likely they were to acquire the disease.

The Barnard epidemic really made me see the light. Thousands of babies were being born in the United States each year with birth defects deriving from toxo, and I now knew that the "raw," the "rare," and the "medium-rare" were the true villains. At New York Hospital alone, one child in a thousand was born damaged by the disease, a rate higher than defects from German measles, congenital syphilis, and all the viral diseases combined.

It all seemed so tragically simple. If there was a pregnant woman in the house, why not cook the family roast a few minutes longer or give the sirloin another turn on the grill? Expectant mothers had to be encouraged to police their diets more carefully. Doctors had to be advised to make testing for toxo a routine part of prenatal examinations. Once the word went out, I was confident the number of birth defects from toxo would drop dramatically in no time.

Before I knew it, I was embarked on a major effort to publicize the dietary dangers facing pregnant women, and I undertook the work with the fury of a convert. I started by giving interviews for a series of articles in minor patient-oriented magazines, the kind that gathers dust in every doctor's waiting room. Then, in November 1968, *Time* magazine weighed in with an article entitled "Dr. Barnard's Epidemic," and alerted millions of Americans to the dangers of toxo for the very first time. The story quoted me as saying: "If this epidemic had occurred in five pregnant women [instead of the five medical students], the potential danger to their unborn children—either fetal death or severe brain damage—would have been enormous." My vision of educating the American public about this hidden health menace was becoming a reality.

That started an uproar, of course. Many of my colleagues did not share my zeal, and the obstetricians at New York Hospital mounted a full-scale attack. The *causus belli* was simple. Evidence linking undercooked meat and toxo had been building for years. Obstetricians routinely warned their patients to stop smoking, abstain from martinis, and avoid certain drugs. Astonishingly, though, they ignored toxo as a possible complication of pregnancy. Women continued to eat rare beef as a means of counteracting the anemia common to expectant motherhood. And so the number of damaged babies and needless abortions continued unabated. Understandably, not a few obstetricians were sensitive to the implications that, in neglecting the issue, they had been responsible for the carnage.

Late one afternoon in the early winter of 1968, two hundred angry obstetricians and gynecologists affiliated with New York Hospital descended on one of the hospital's large amphitheaters for an emergency meeting. The purpose of the war party was ostensibly to "more accurately assess" the health threats posed by toxo. The real purpose, of course, was to flatten me. A handful of the aggrieved had already approached Cornell's dean to persuade him to get me to stop talking. The maneuver hadn't worked, and now a larger lever, in the form of a mass gathering, was seen as necessary to pressure me into silence.

The attention was flattering, but somewhat misplaced. After all, my primary contribution to shedding light on toxo had been a handful of papers written many years before while still a pathologist in Panama. I hadn't made any of the key discoveries linking the disease to the unborn. Because I was responsible for putting out the word to the general public, however, I was depicted as having set out on some kind of misguided, publicity-hungry campaign.

Indignant, one of my colleagues rose to his feet and said, "Your alarmist articles have gotten my patients so upset they're calling me night and day demanding to be tested for your disease." As others rose to speak, the charges against me all boiled down to one damning indictment—I had been trying to educate patients and their doctors.

Finally, it was my turn to speak, and I decided to counterattack. Rising slowly, I asked if any of the doctors in the audience had routinely warned prenatal patients in the past twenty years against eating red meat. Silence. I asked for hands. Not a single palm was raised. "Gentlemen," I said, angrily, "each of you is guilty of malpractice. Yes, malpractice! You knew about the rare meat problem for years and did nothing about it. I will gladly testify in court against any one of you if even one of the children you have delivered in the past ten years has had congenital toxo."

The very mention of the word *malpractice* had a magical effect. It is the only incantation powerful enough to browbeat large numbers of agitated medical practitioners into submission almost immediately. The meeting was quickly adjourned, and the case against Ben Kean, toxo evangelist, was dropped.

Had my critics only known enough about the disease, they could have shut me up in a minute, for while I was railing against the evils of raw beef, new evidence came to light that toxo occurred in people who had never eaten a single morsel of beef in their entire lives!

This perplexing news arrived by way of India. Studies there had shown that both the country's large Hindu and Moslem populations shared virtually identical rates of infection for toxoplasmosis. That made perfect sense where the Moslems were concerned; they had always eaten great quantities of beef and mutton. But the Hindus? They ate no meat whatsoever. They were the world's most scrupulous vegetarians. How the hell could they have become infected? Obviously, there had to be another way for the disease to enter the human body.

A Scottish researcher named W. M. Hutchinson thought he had the answer. Hutchinson knew that many parasitic diseases were transmitted by eggs deposited in the feces of the host. Why not toxoplasmosis, as well? To find out, he encouraged his lab cat to dine on mice infected with toxo parasites. Sure enough, the feline droppings, when transferred in minute quantities to other laboratory animals, did indeed spread the disease. And on that triumphant note, Dr. Hutchinson took a turn in the wrong direction by erroneously concluding that the tiny infectious agent

309

passed through cats was concealed inside the egg of another larger parasite, the roundworm.

In 1968, scientists at the University of Kansas Medical Center finally forged the missing link when they demonstrated that the intestinal tract of the cat was not only a way station for the toxo organism, but its home; the feline bowel was the natural incubator, the primary host, of *T. gondii*. So that was it! Exactly sixty years after Nicolle and Manceaux had discovered their crescent-shaped parasite in the modest gondi of Tunis, we finally had our answer—toxo, that most elusive of parasites, was not primarily a disease of humans at all, but of cats. Man, in toxo's cosmic scheme of things, was merely a second-rate host.

The Kansas team, led by Jack Frenkel, an old friend, didn't stop there. The single-celled parasites, they went on to show, are lusty little devils with complicated sex lives. For years researchers had surmised that they simply divided, ameba-style, before invading the tissue of the host. Not so. Jack found that each parasite produces male and female cells inside the feline gut which then unite to produce an egg. Each egg, or oocyst, only a little larger than a single red blood cell, acts as incubator in which eight new parasites form. Deposited by the cat in its feces, the oocyst is virtually indestructible; it can survive vast temperature extremes, from scorching desert heat to numbing subarctic cold, all the while remaining poised to adhere to the hands of whoever has the dubious chore of emptying the family catbox. The accidental ingestion of any oocysts clinging to the hands starts the infection in humans.

Obstetricians tend to have short memories, so the furor stirred up by the Barnard Epidemic, though intense and unpleasant, faded quickly.

The cat lovers were a different breed, however. I soon learned that they are as powerful, pervasive, and prickly an interest group as one is likely to find in American public life. They did not react at all well to the suggestion that their beloved housepets might be responsible for spreading a serious disease that maimed babies. Word spread quickly that some crank doctor at a fancy New York hospital was openly advocating the wholesale slaughter of cats. Obviously, he needed to be taught a lesson.

One especially irate guardian of feline sanctity was Cleveland Amory, a nationally known columnist who often wrote on animal affairs. After giving my crimes some thought, he came up with what he deemed a suitable punishment; he would ask a million cat lovers across the country to each send me one postcard a day for a full year. This "inundation technique," as he called it, would so disrupt the running of my practice that I would be forced to abandon my radical views on cats. Luckily, Amory turned out to be a paper tiger; he never did make good on his threat. Meanwhile, I managed to remove much of the rancor myself by loudly and repeatedly denying in public that I wanted pregnant women to kill their cats.

I wasn't entirely off the hook, though. I had now been targeted as a toxo "expert." My telephone rang endlessly. Public concern was so great that I could easily have stopped practicing any other kind of medicine and made a perfectly good living as a "one-disease" doctor. I wanted out. Yet how could I turn away people frantic with worry about a legitimate health menace? That was the terrible dilemma. Then, a single, baffling, heartbreaking case persuaded me to stop trying to save the world single-handedly.

In 1969, my colleagues at Cornell and I completed a study of nearly five thousand expectant mothers at New York Hospital's prenatal clinic, and we had some very good news. Our findings confirmed that once a person acquires toxo, he or she is infected for life. This meant that once the mother had established her immunity to the disease, she would pass on that protection to her unborn child. A mother could only transmit the disease to her child if she became infected for the first time while she was pregnant. If she was already infected, the baby would be protected. Or so we thought.

One day in the summer of 1973 Mrs. S visited me in my office at New York Hospital. She had been referred to me by her obstetrician after having experienced a stillbirth some months earlier. The baby had been horribly damaged by toxo. Mrs. S was utterly distraught. She was again pregnant and scared to death of transmitting the disease that had killed her first unborn child to her second.

"Are you sure, Doctor, that this baby won't get it, too?" she asked, fighting back the tears.

"Absolutely," I said, smiling confidently. "There isn't a single case on record in which a mother had a baby with toxoplasmosis in two different pregnancies. It's impossible. You've had the disease, you're now immune, and that will protect your next baby. Cheer up!"

A few months later, Mrs. S gave birth to a second hideously deformed, stillborn baby. I was devastated. So was Anne Kimball, the quiet, capable infectious disease expert, who had been assisting me in our studies. The two of us spent days poring over tissue samples from the child. We examined every identifiable body organ under the microscope for the presence of the parasite. We found nothing, not one speck of evidence to indicate that the child had ever had toxo. To our great relief, though with a lingering sense of responsibility, Anne and I had to conclude that the child's deformities had been caused by another factor—genetic, viral, a toxin, perhaps, but not by toxo.

Dr. Kimball explained our findings to Mrs. S. I could not muster the courage. Understandably, she refused to believe our story. She called us liars. Quacks. She threatened a malpractice suit. She fled the office in tears, her trust in doctors, I am quite sure, shattered forever.

Medical research can be a painfully fickle business. In the case of toxo, however, the intervening years, and the growing mass of evidence, have only confirmed our belief that a mother can infect only one unborn child. But the experience with Mrs. S was too traumatic. I decided to begin offering my services as an unpaid consultant to any physician who wanted advice or information, but I would see no more patients with toxo.

To this day there are still only two surefire ways of avoiding the trauma of giving birth to a baby damaged by toxo or of having to contemplate a preemptive abortion. Every pregnant woman susceptible to toxo should, at all costs, avoid eating raw or rare meat. And if there is a cat in the house, it should be sent away for a nine-month vacation. At the very least, good husbands everywhere should take over the responsibility for cleaning kitty's litter box until the baby is born.

Although my own involvement eventually wound down, medical science's biggest challenge from toxo was only just beginning. Doctors at Memorial Sloan-Kettering in New York reported the first death in a victim of AIDS directly linked to toxoplasmosis in December 1981. By 1988, several thousand such deaths had been recorded. In France, toxo had emerged with pneumocystis as a leading opportunistic killer of AIDS patients. The way AIDS destroyed the human immune system created ideal conditions for the parasite to flourish. Suddenly, people were hearing about this "rare" illness for the first time as it attacked friends, lovers, and relatives.

But I was as puzzled as ever. Why should toxo, out of all the other parasitic enemies of man, play such a prominent role in AIDS? Clearly, we still had a lot to learn. Eight decades after coming to light in Tunis, *Toxoplasma gondii* remained an enigma. It was reassuring to know, however, that, in the tradition of Nicolle, Manceaux, and the others, a new generation of researchers was hot on toxo's trail. The answers would come, and they would arrive by the same hard-fought, quirky, serendipitous route they had always traveled.

There was little doubt that Martina Navratilova had been stricken with a serious case of acute toxo on the eve of the 1982 U.S. Open. It had spoiled her chances of a tournament victory. Her forfeit of over a million dollars in potential winnings while she recuperated had inspired courtside reporters to dub toxo the "Million-Dollar Disease." Worse yet, it had embroiled her in a bitter, time-consuming lawsuit. And still the big question remained: How did a member of the glitterati of global athletics acquire such a decidedly unglamorous disease?

Gary Wadler's curiosity led him to a cat named Baby Jesus. The cat lived in San Francisco and belonged to Rita Mae Brown, Martina's friend and former lover. As Martina tells the story,* she had visited Rita Mae at her apartment in the summer of 1982, a week or two before she noticed her first symptoms and more than a month before going east for the tournament at Flushing Meadows. While she and her friend chatted, a pair of frisky housecats had gamboled around the house, stopping occasionally to stick a paw into one of the bowls of snacks Rita had laid out.

Wadler, nothing if not meticulous, requested that Baby Jesus and his alleged accomplice be hauled in for testing. The results were negative, however, and both feline suspects were cleared—they had never been infected with toxo.

Wadler also grilled Martina about her dietary habits, of course. He later recalled raising an eyebrow when she told him of her passion for undercooked beef. She ate her hamburgers rare. She also admitted frequently succumbing to a craving for steak tartare (ingredients: raw chopped beef, a raw egg, chopped onions, capers, and freshly ground black pepper).

Concrete evidence, obviously, would have been hard to come by in any event, since it had probably long since been eaten and digested. Still, the case against raw beef was strong, and Martina vowed to exclude it from her diet. Her muscle spasms and weakness persisted for several months, but by late October tests were beginning to show that the toxo antibodies in her blood were returning to normal levels, as time allowed the immune system to bring the numbers of parasitic intruders under control. Drugs were not used; biopsy was not needed. Ultimately, it took six months for her glands to return to normal size.

---

*Navratilova, 230.

THE STEAK TARTARE DEFENSE

Things started looking up for Martina. The following year, she finally won her coveted Open, beating Chris Evert in the finals. In September 1986, Gary Wadler, having reviewed the case with me, testified in a Long Island court that toxoplasmosis had been responsible for the unfortunate events culminating in her courtside scuffle with photographer Arthur Seitz four years earlier. On October 9, 1987, a jury threw out Seitz's claim for $2 million in damages and instead awarded him $50 dollars for the roll of film that had been exposed in the incident. For all practical purposes, the case against Martina had collapsed under the weight of the medical evidence. The steak tartare defense had triumphed.

Montezuma's Revenge

T here is nothing like a doctor falling prey to a disease himself to fuel the search for a cure. Little did I suspect I was about to enter that category, however, when I received orders one day in the fall of 1946 to leave Wiesbaden and report to General Stayer's office in Berlin on the double.

Word had come down the GHQ grapevine that the number of American military medical officers in occupied Germany was about to be reduced from 450 to 45 within nine months. With similar cutbacks in store for Italy, the responsibility of providing health care for huge numbers of civilians would have to be transferred back to our former enemies, and fast. This was the problem with which the general was wrestling when I walked into his office.

"Kean," he demanded, "what do you think of Aldo Castellani?"

I had learned not to mince words with Stayer, so I spoke bluntly. "He's a bum," I said, "a medical bum."

"Good," said the old man, cracking a flinty smile, "we finally agree on something. Now all you have to do is get the pope to concur. One of his cardinals is pushing Castellani for the job of Italy's civilian health chief. I want you to go down to Rome and impress on His Holiness that the man is not fit for the job."

"But General . . ." I stammered, nervous at the prospect of meeting the Vicar of Rome, then Pope Pius XII.

Stayer cut me off. " 'But General' nothing," he said. "Tell me what you know about Castellani."

"That's easy," I said. "As a young researcher, he somehow stumbled across the parasite causing African sleeping sickness. It was a major discovery, and he's been getting full mileage out of it ever since."

Stories of Castellani's medical mountebankery were well known—how over the years he'd routinely laid claim to scientific discoveries he hadn't made, how he'd shamelessly curried favor with Mussolini and, for his efforts, had become the medical darling of Italy's Fascist hierarchy.

Stayer smiled sagaciously—a sure sign that he knew something I did not. According to information he had obtained from our Counterintelligence Corps, he said, Mussolini had ordered Castellani to stamp out typhoid fever among his troops after they invaded Ethiopia in 1935. It was an enormous responsibility, but Castellani had attacked the problem with his reputed panache and brilliance. Somehow he managed to have every single soldier in Ethiopia vaccinated against the disease, a phenomenal rate for wartime. Not one soldier ever contracted the disease. Or so Castellani reported to Il Duce.

CIC investigators told a different story. "Not a single case of typhoid was ever reported in Africa," boomed Stayer, with obvious pleasure, "because not a single field study was ever done! No soldiers were ever vaccinated! Castellani fabricated the whole campaign on paper without ever leaving Rome. It was pure baloney!"

Before the war, Stayer went on to explain, Castellani's imaginative approach to medicine had made him the toast of European royalty. Castellani's own staff, however, hated the arrogant doctor, and so they'd tipped off investigators to the secret of his popularity, which lay chiefly in his capacity for giving an injection—*piqûre*, as it was called on the Continent—without leaving the slightest blemish on the body of the patient. No

mark, no blood, none of the unpleasant feeling of needle penetrating tissue. Because of its obvious cosmetic advantages, the
procedure was especially popular with the royal ladies. Castellani
gave most of his injections in the derrière, and the sole complaint
was that they were always accompanied by a slight pinching
sensation. It became known as "Castellani's pinch."

It was a simple trick, but an effective one. With an ostentatious
flip of the wrist, the distinguished Castellani would draw into
the syringe whatever substance was about to be inoculated (usually some kind of superfluous vitamin supplement). Next, having
shaken the instrument to eliminate the air bubbles, he would
swab the site with alcohol, wait for it to dry, and then gently
pinch the skin of the proffered buttock between thumb and fore-
finger. The contents of syringe, meanwhile, were injected not
into the patient's backside, but into a large silk handkerchief Castellani kept tucked in his left cuff.

After finishing his tale, Stayer snorted, "This man should not
be allowed to become dogcatcher. That's why you're going to
see the pope. Everything's arranged. Tell His Holiness that one
of his own men is backing Castellani. Tell him that the American
high command is eager to know if the cardinal's view represents
that of the Holy See. Would an American veto of Castellani be
looked upon favorably or unfavorably by the Vatican?"

I arrived in Rome late the next day, a glorious autumn afternoon,
and checked into the Excelsior Hotel. The U.S. Army was still
in control of the exquisite old building on the Via Vittorio Veneto
and my rank of major, in addition to an announcement of my
mission to the Vatican, obtained for me not just a room, but a
cavernous suite with a huge marbled bathroom. Buoyed by my
good fortune, and since I wasn't due at the Vatican until ten
o'clock the following morning, I spent the rest of the buttery
Roman daylight walking up and down the Via Veneto, stopping
for a cup of hot chocolate at a sidewalk cafe and fighting off an

endless parade of aggressive prostitutes from the bars across the street.

That evening it was my luck to fall in with a somewhat raucous group of three American officers and an appealing quartet of British army nurses I'd met on the train earlier in the day. Hell-bent on enjoying ourselves, we found a restaurant, a noisy, crowded bistro about a block from the hotel, where it looked as if this might be possible. After so many months of eating the mystery meat and lumpy mashed potatoes served at the officers' club in Wiesbaden, the Italian food was like a miracle: seafood pasta in a rich, creamy sauce, grilled paillard, and a variety of delicately textured pastries filled with fresh whipped cream. The wine was cheap and plentiful. We drank. We danced. We drank some more. At midnight, in a rare display of self-discipline, I shouted my apologies over the increasingly frenetic band and returned to the hotel. I was eager to get a good night's sleep so as to make a good impression at the Vatican the following morning.

At 3:00 A.M. I suddenly snapped to attention, sitting up sharply in bed. Something terrible was happening to me. My stomach boiled. My limbs shook. The sheets were drenched in sweat. My body was about to erupt like Mt. Vesuvius.

I jumped up and ran for the bathroom, but I did not make it. Halfway there, I stumbled and collapsed in a heap, as all orifices concerned with the emergency elimination of bodily wastes simultaneously opened and functioned unremittingly for the next three hours. At dawn, I managed to summon the strength to stagger into the bathroom and flop into the tub, where I stayed for an hour before hobbling back to bed.

The mess, it must be said, was spectacular. Mortified, I bribed three chambermaids to clean up, but only after agreeing to part with most of my cigarettes and a large wad of American one-dollar bills.

In the middle of Operation Cleanup, the manager, a pious Italian who had been much impressed with my impending audience with Il Papa, appeared briefly in the doorway clicking his tongue in disapproval while shrewdly making arrangements with the maids for his cut of the baksheesh. But he was a charitable man. At eight o'clock he sent up two sturdy young bellhops to help me get into my good uniform.

At nine o'clock a car arrived and took me to the Vatican. I was ushered into a small, ornate room and told to wait. I felt faint with weakness, my bowels making dangerous gurgling noises. After a minute or two, I was admitted to the audience chamber, a room of modest proportions, but richly decorated, with mahogany paneling on the walls and heavily embroidered draperies. The pope approached, extending his hand in blessing, and smiled wanly. He was an ascetic-looking man, with hollow cheeks and eyes that looked out on the world from sockets buried deep in his skull. His cool serenity made me nervous, which, given the delicate state of my intestinal tract, was not a hopeful sign.

His Holiness spoke to me gently, in English: "In which language would you like me to conduct this audience?" I had barely enough energy to ask, "What are my options?" a question I asked out of sheer idle curiosity, since I have only ever spoken the native tongue of Valparaiso, Indiana, with any confidence.

"There is English, French, Italian, German, and Spanish," said the pope, "but, if you prefer, we can always speak Latin." We spoke Valparaiso.

I explained my mission. What did His Holiness think of Dr. Castellani?

Having listened attentively, the pope spoke in a manner that could only be described as Delphic. If the military government was *not* prepared to appoint Dr. Castellani, there would be no complaint. However, if the military *was* planning to make the appointment, His Holiness would like to be so informed in advance, so that he could take appropriate measures. The message seemed clear enough: thumbs down on the Castellani nomination was okay by the pope; thumbs up, and he wanted time to raise his own objections. I repeated his remarks as clearly as I could to make sure I had understood him correctly. He nodded and said, "I think you understand me perfectly."

Aldo Castellani did not get the job.

The mission had been a great success. The next day I found myself back in Berlin, standing in front of General Stayer's desk and receiving his benediction on a job well done. At length, he noticed my dilapidated condition. "Good god, Kean," he said. "You look terrible. What on earth happened to you in Rome, anyway?"

What on earth, indeed? I am not a religious man (my socialist mother saw to that long ago). But as I lay panting on the floor of the Excelsior Hotel that horrifying night, I prayed for a miracle. I solemnly swore that, if I somehow recovered sufficiently to keep my appointment with His Holiness, someday I would first determine the nature of the disease that felled me and then do my damnedest to find a cure.

For years, I speculated as to what, from a purely medical standpoint, had hit me. As a tropical medicine man, I knew what I did not have. I did not, for instance, have salmonellosis or its malignant form, typhoid fever, diseases caused by well-known bacterial culprits that require a long incubation period and did considerably greater damage to their victims. Nor did I have shigellosis—also known as bacillary dysentery, or "the bloody flux," which has been endemic to many parts of the world throughout recorded history and is thought to have been the disease that felled Napoleon's soldiers on the march to Moscow. (How often do we pause to consider the humble microbe's role in shaping the course of human history?) I also knew I did not have amebic dysentery, the result of infection by Francis W. O'Connor's favorite parasite, *Entamoeba histolytica* (which he liked to call the "bread and butter of tropical medicine"), because the symptoms needed a fortnight to develop, were rarely so acute, and recovery was never so rapid.

No, those forms of diarrhea were real killers. And although I felt for a while as if I would die that night in Rome, I somehow sensed the diarrhea that had attacked me was the same disease that had set upon wayfarers since time immemorial. No less an authority than the Bible describes the clinical symptoms in a verse from the Twenty-second Psalm: "I am poured out like water, and all my bones are out of joint; my heart is like wax; it is melted in the midst of my bowels." (I only belatedly realized the danger of making this point too sharply when I spoke to a group of religiously inclined colleagues one evening and was promptly accused of blasphemy.)

Millions upon millions of modern travelers have grown uncomfortably familiar with the syndrome, which lasts anywhere from one to three days, has a low trough, but features a mercifully rapid recovery. It has been honored by many imaginative and graphically descriptive names: "Delhi Belly," "Casablanca Crud," "Aztec Two-Step," and, perhaps the name most popular when we did the research in Mexico that finally helped crack the code of the disease, "Montezuma's Revenge." For simplicity's sake, however, my colleagues and I chose to use the Spanish nickname, Turista.*

But how to zero in on the cause of this most cosmopolitan of all human afflictions? Back in the late forties, the explanations of its origins were many and confusing. They ranged from abrupt changes in climate, contaminated water, the consumption of too much olive oil or not enough calcium, to the proximity of pernicious brainwaves. Nearly everyone who went abroad fell victim, at one time or another, to this disease, but nobody—the best and brightest medical brains included—had the faintest idea of what caused it. For a man of science like myself, who was also a former victim, this was a most unsatisfactory situation.

---

*Purists will point out that the villain that attacked me in Rome was not Turista at all, but most likely a preformed toxin of staphylococcus in the cream employed either in the seafood pasta or dessert I had so mindlessly consumed in the company of those British nurses. It wasn't until the mid-fifties, however, that I was able to establish scientifically that Turista rarely develops so rapidly.

MONTEZUMA'S REVENGE

From the beginning, I was convinced that we were dealing with a single disease, with a single cause. Identifying the cause of Turista became my Holy Grail, and my brief audience with the Vicar of Rome marked the beginning of a scientific quest that would last for the next thirty years.*

In 1952, shortly after my teaching appointment at Cornell, I began pursuing Turista in earnest when I designed the protocol for our first major experiment. Simplicity in design is the key to all good scientific work, and this project was nothing if not simple. We would examine the stools of a group of college kids going to Europe for the very first time—once on their way out and again on their way back. We would then match the two sets of samples. The subjects would either develop diarrhea in Europe

---

*In lecturing on Turista over the years, I could never bring myself to tell the story of my audience with the pope, which I found too embarrassing, so I used an account belonging to Bill Schaffner, one of my Cornell students. In an article published in November 1963 in *Annals of Internal Medicine*, I quoted Bill as follows:

"At 4 A.M. the patient awakened with a start, desperately aware that he was about to move his bowels. He traversed the bed-to-bathroom distance in what must have been record time and relieved himself of a totally watery bowel movement which was accompanied by transverse colon cramps. The patient returned to bed in a stunned state, only to discover that no sooner had he arrived than he was constrained to leave again, with uncustomary alacrity. This staccato ballet continued at fifteen-minute intervals with the patient exhibiting progressive weakness, profound malaise, increasingly severe cramps, almost constant nausea, and several episodes of vomiting.

"He remained afebrile and had no chills. Examination by a colleague at 7 A.M., after he had had approximately ten bowel movements, confirmed the diagnosis of Turista. He was given paregoric, and the diarrhea was lessened, but the patient remained very weak and was unable to leave his bed. During the day he took fluids, usually tea or ginger ale, and ate some cooked rice with apple sauce. The next day he felt stronger and, despite five soft bowel movements, he was able to leave his room in the afternoon. On the third day he resumed his responsibilities but at a reduced tempo; on the fourth day after the onset he felt completely well."

or they would not. They would either pick up parasites there or they would not. If those who got sick also displayed the presence of a particular parasite that the healthy subjects did not, we'd have identified our culprit. If no clear villain emerged, we could eliminate parasites and move on to the other possible pathogenic causes—bacteria or viruses.

The Second World War and its aftermath had done much to bring the rest of the world to the attention of the American public. By the early fifties, a new generation of American college students was bent on seeing more of that world than their parents had, and Europe was becoming an increasingly popular destination for summer travel, particularly among those attending schools on the East Coast. As happened in airline travel a few years later, several hundred students would charter space on the same cruise ship, scatter to spend several months traveling around Europe, and then reassemble for the trip home.

That made execution of the protocol a simple matter of placing a pair of medical students on board one of these vessels and having them obtain the necessary specimens. Laboratory facilities weren't necessary, because the stool samples could be easily preserved with a special iodine solution for later examination under the microscope. The next step was to ask for volunteers from among the hundred second-year medical students in my course on tropical medicine.

So I raised the question: Who wants to spend eight weeks in Europe, all expenses paid? One hundred hands shot up.

What really started the uproar, however, was when I announced to the overwhelmingly male class that the travelers selected for our experiment belonged to a group of 743 young women from Vassar, Bryn Mawr, Barnard, and Sarah Lawrence. The notion of coeducational travel was still poorly developed in America then, and the prospect of traveling as the only males among a group of nubile coeds from the Seven Sisters was almost too much for the struggling young physicians to bear. Shoving matches broke out in the back of the classroom. Normally docile students began shouting mild obscenities at one another. Order was restored long enough for two candidates to be selected—Charles Hoffman and William Van Stone.

So it was that the two lucky young scientists, seen of by none of their envious classmates, sailed from Quebec one day in late June on the Canadian liner *Skaubryn*, with all 743 potential subjects on board. Since I had already grown nervous about the prospect of being left behind, Hoffman and Van Stone agreed to send me a brief cable from shipboard each day, indicating their progress. Our goal was to get specimens from 300 of the outbound travelers and match them with samples from the same women on the return voyage in late August. That meant getting the cooperation of less than half of the questing coeds, a ratio that didn't strike me as overly optimistic, given the captive nature of the subject pool. After all, what intelligent, healthy young female wouldn't want to help out a couple of handsome male students who were embarked on an important scientific mission? Clearly, I did not know my coeds:

> DAY ONE: "Having a wonderful time. Thanks for the opportunity."
> DAY TWO: "Meeting subjects per protocol."
> DAY THREE: "Proceeding on schedule."
> DAY FOUR: "Experiencing difficulty."
> DAY FIVE: "Disappointment. Unable to get necessary specimens."
> DAY SIX: "Trouble continues."
> DAY SEVEN: "Defeat. Plan to return immediately after docking in Le Havre."
> DAY EIGHT: "Success is ours!"
> DAY NINE: "We are heroes. See you in fall. *Au revoir.*"

At that point all communications abruptly stopped. Those two little bastards, I thought uncharitably. Here they've disappeared into Europe for two long months, leaving me to contemplate nothing but a few cryptic trans-Atlantic cables. I began to harbor dark thoughts about Hoffman and Van Stone. Visions of homicide flickered through my head. But first I wanted those stool specimens! I tried reaching the vanished scientists through American Express offices in virtually every European capital. But it was no use. They had disappeared into thin air. It was the worst summer of my life.

Then one day in early September, Hoffman and Van Stone turned up at my Cornell office with a very large suitcase containing 804 vials. "Your dirty work," Hoffman said, smiling broadly. The pair had managed to capture 200 matching specimens (samples from the same individual both going and returning), along with 404 single, unpaired samples. We had not met our goal, but we had plenty of material for statistical analysis. I decided to forgive Hoffman and Van Stone and turned the suitcase over to Pat Daniels, the same laboratory wizard who would, a few years later, tangle with C. P. Tetchner's monster tapeworm.

The results were readily apparent—and disappointing. Parasites were not responsible for the diarrhea of travelers in Europe. But there was one positive development: twice as many students who spent the summer in the Mediterranean developed diarrhea compared with those who went to Northern Europe and Scandinavia. Some other agent, then, was responsible for the disease, and, like most discerning travelers, the bug appeared to prefer the beaches of St. Tropez to the fjords of Norway. With the parasites eliminated, the next obvious step would be to single out a bacterium as the potential villain.

Before that, though, I had a score to settle with Hoffman and Van Stone. What had all those cables meant, first suggesting success, then failure, then triumph? What the hell had happened aboard ship, anyway?

Hoffman explained. Everything had gotten off to a glorious start. The first evening of the cruise, the two medical students successfully infiltrated a get-acquainted party attended by all 743 American coeds. As the only males under forty within earshot of the dance band, Hoffman and Van Stone found themselves in great demand. They spent the evening being passed from one set of soft, welcoming arms to another. In the process, they managed to arrange a number of "dates" for the following day. The women went off to their beds, a few at least presumably contemplating the possibilities of shipboard romance with a handsome young doctor-to-be. Hoffman and Van Stone retired to their cabin to discuss paired stool specimens.

Unhappily, charm and good looks will take you only so far in life, as Hoffman and Van Stone were about to discover. The next day the two men punctually appeared for each of their many dates. After some desultory small talk, they would open a briefcase and produce a small glass bottle and a sheet of paper explaining the nature of the experiment. They would then instruct the young woman to return her specimen to the ship's infirmary as quickly as possible after it had been produced. The young ladies responded variously. Some blushed and dissolved into giggles. Some walked off in a huff. A few tried to strike Hoffman and Van Stone with angry female fists. The majority of them, however, seemed puzzled, as if they couldn't quite figure out what the two men were after. They did not—or would not—understand, for instance, what was meant by the term "stool." Hoffman and Van Stone found themselves suddenly tongue-tied, since it would still be a decade or so before the four-letter word, so crude but so graphically descriptive of its substance, could be used comfortably in mixed company.

The young scholars grew depressed—and with good reason. A minimum of two hundred paired samples was necessary for statistical review. Five days into the voyage, however, they still had found only seven coeds willing to comply. On the sixth day, Hoffman crafted a cable, which the ship's radio officer refused to send. It read: "Have made major scientific discovery and plan to publish immediately on return. Finding is as follows: young, white females from Vassar and similar colleges do not defecate."

"Then how on earth did you turn it around?" I demanded. "How did you get all these specimens?"

Here I was about to learn an important lesson: second-year medical students are indispensable to all successful experimentation. Freshmen are too nervous to be intelligent. Third- and fourth-year students have convinced themselves that they've apotheosized into real doctors, and are, therefore, too godlike to be useful. The time to catch them is between the second and third years, when they are pretty sure they are going to make the grade academically, but are still curious and excited enough to be resourceful. Hoffman and Van Stone proved the point admirably.

By the sixth day, Hoffman observed, "The girls were getting pretty tired of dancing with each other." Their boredom was compounded by the absence of radio or television on shipboard. Hoffman and Van Stone approached the captain and explained their problem. They asked him if, in the ship's stores, there might not be a motion picture of such romantic allure as to attract the interest of 743 lonely college women. The captain was sympathetic. He had such a film, he said. It was *Red Dust*, starring Clark Gable and Jean Harlow. The captain would arrange for it to be shown in the ship's ballroom on the last night of the cruise. Hoffman and Van Stone set the price of admission: one stool sample, bottled and fixed with iodine solution.

It was a cheap trick, but, like Aldo Castellani's "pinch," it worked, and to much more legitimate scientific ends. Standing at the door, Hoffman and Van Stone collected 400 "tickets." On the return trip the movie was not necessary. After two months in Europe, the coeds had become sophisticated women of the world who recognized the importance of scientific endeavor. They graciously provided the crucial matching specimens without protest.

Hoffman went on to become an expert in infectious disease. Van Stone, for reasons presumably unrelated to the European cruise, became a psychiatrist. In 1954, our findings were published in the *New England Journal of Medicine*, and I embarked on the next phase of diarrhea research.

It was about this time that I first met Somerset Waters. Waters was a specialist in the economics of tourism who had developed an absolute fascination with diarrhea thanks to President Eisenhower. As a presidential advisor, Waters was involved in plans to encourage more Americans to go to Europe and spend money, and thus speed the recovery of the Continental economy from the war. Tall, suave, and irrepressible, Somer was convinced that many people who would otherwise travel abroad refrained from doing so because of their fear of getting sick, and so he dreamed about one day eradicating the ancient scourge of travelers. That made us natural allies, so we decided to team up in a research effort that would last for the next twenty years.

The first thing we did was to create the Travelers Health Institute, with Waters as president and me as medical consultant. Like most "nonprofit" organizations, the institute was designed to raise money—money we would need to fund experiments in various places around the world. Waters shrewdly recognized that big names always help in such endeavors, so we proceeded to pack the board of directors with people like his own father-in-law, Walter Fuller, then publisher of the *Saturday Evening Post*. General Stayer, retired and living in Pennsylvania, also agreed to join us. Our legal advisor was a young attorney from the New York firm of Milbank, Tweed, Hope and Hadley named Bill Jackson, the same man who would, years later, come to represent the Shah and accompany me that dismal day at Lackland Air Force Base in Texas, in 1979, when the Shah was elbowed out of the United States.

Our first official act at the Travelers Health Institute was to order stationery. Waters felt that a letterhead with a proper logo was essential. After all, he reasoned, we were establishing a new field of medicine, one devoted to the study of the diseases of travelers, and if there could be fields for children (pediatrics) and old people (geriatrics), why not travelers? The obvious name for this new specialty, Waters argued, was *emporiatrics*, since *emporos*, he reminded me, was the Greek word for "traveler." I objected strenuously. I was old enough to remember in the Midwest of my youth the ubiquitous "emporium"—an entrepreneurial euphemism for the musty corner dry goods store. The image hardly seemed appropriate for an international organization of style and sophistication.

But Waters was a stubborn man. He went around the corner to the New York Public Library and consulted the resident linguistics expert. Naturally, the expert agreed; the only proper word for our specialty was *emporiatrics*. So, the logo on our new letterhead would read, "Devoted to the Science of Emporiatrics." I was convinced the phrase was a real dud, but not being above a little honest self-promotion, I used it in a few speeches and papers and then let it drop.

Years later, while I was thumbing through *Dorland's Medical Dictionary*, my eyes stumbled on the term *emporiatrics*. How it got there I still have no idea. A short time later, though, I found myself reading about "Emporiatric enteritis" in the *Journal of the American Medical Association*. Soon I would discover a London publication, *Travel Magazine*, billing itself as "The Journal of Emporiatrics." So much for a parasitologist's flair for language. Emporiatrics has become the widely used name for a whole subspecialty of medicine that started with a trip to the public library. Waters was the genius, but I usually get the credit.

Our first experiment was so simple it seemed almost ridiculous. Waters flew out to the Los Angeles International Airport, where, between July 4 and August 3, 1957, he parked himself in the baggage claim area and interviewed 1,265 American tourists returning home from Mexico. A third of those who had spent a week or more in Mexico experienced one or more attacks of diarrhea. Of that number, two-thirds fell ill during the first week. Youngsters, we found, were much more likely to develop the disease than parents or grandparents. Most attacks lasted anywhere from one to three days.

While haunting the baggage claim area, Waters also questioned 210 tourists returning from Hawaii. Very few in this control group reported having had diarrhea of any kind, and virtually nobody had experienced intestinal upsets of the Mexican magnitude. Thus we could scientifically eliminate all those folkloric notions about the excitement of flying, change in climate and daily routine, and the various other psychic factors some people believed prompted the illness. Turista was a real disease with a real cause, and now we would have to find it.

Our focus shifted to Mexico. Beginning in 1957, I went to Mexico City for six weeks every summer in the role of teacher–researcher, leading a group of eager second-year medical students from Cornell and determined to finally get the drop on the elusive Turista bug. Thanks to the efforts of Hoffman and Van Stone in Europe, we had already eliminated parasites as the cause, so we could concentrate next on bacteria and viruses as potential villains.

Our experiments required large numbers of captive subjects, and, early on, I discovered a supply in many ways superior to even the shipboard coeds of Hoffman and Van Stone. Several thousand North Americans went south each summer to study at Mexican universities. Fearful of getting sick and seduced by the prospect of obtaining free medical care from a team of Cornell "physicians" (as we self-servingly referred to our second-year medical students), most of the young scholars were eager to cooperate.

Bribery helped, too. We set up a system of "door prizes"— transistor radios, meal tickets for the school cafeteria, tickets to the bullfights—to encourage collaboration. If all else failed, we simply bought our stool specimens outright. We would "hire" students at ten pesos a day for periods of two or three weeks, paying a special bounty to subjects who had the misfortune of contracting a particularly virulent strain of the Mexican Two-Step.

The ingenuity of my students knew no bounds. In 1963, having eliminated bacteria as a potential cause, we embarked on a sophisticated search for viral agents at the University of Mexico and what was then Mexico City College (now the University of the Americas), which demanded that we obtain specimens from patients as soon as possible after their diarrhea had commenced.

We then froze the specimens and sent them to the United States for complicated tests that took more than six months. But if a virus was the culprit, it was bound to be a highly delicate organism and would therefore have to be induced into suspended animation by flash freezing or it would become inactive within a matter of minutes.

If a student received the "call" while in school, there were few problems. He simply hobbled down to our laboratory, where we placed a portion of his specimen into a glass container, and then immersed it in a below-zero container of nitrous oxide for the trip to the States. But how could we get hold of the specimen promptly, if the diarrhea hit—as it most often did—during the middle of the night?

Two of my students, Elizabeth Barrett and Caroline Keegan, came up with a brilliant solution. They established a system involving four Mexican motorcycle policemen of their acquaintance and a central telephone number. In the event of a kamikaze attack of Turista, the student guinea pigs were warned not to flush their toilets, but to pick up the phone instead and call either Libby or Caroline. Whichever woman received the red alert would then ring up one of four night-duty cops, who would arrive at their apartment within three minutes. Our colleague, armed with a portable lab kit, would hop on the back of the motorcycle, clutch the policeman around the waist, and roar off into the steamy Mexican night in the pursuit of science, hair flying, red lights flashing, siren screaming. Scores of such midnight raids resulted in enough specimens to keep our virus laboratory at Cornell in New York busy more or less nonstop for an entire year.

It was our very successes in Mexico that eventually stymied us. After endless hours in the field and at the microscope, we had put dozens of theories about Turista to the test, demolishing many of them. We had created a clear profile for the disease and knew its symptoms and its course. We had confidently knocked not only parasites from the list of possibilities, but bacteria and viruses as well. Yet we still had not discovered the cause of the disease. We had worked ourselves into intellectual limbo and would remain there for ten long years while the pieces of the puzzle sorted themselves out.

But we were not idle. During that slow decade word of our efforts spread quickly. Following the publication of our report, "The Diarrhea of Travelers to Mexico: Summary of a Five-Year Study," in 1963, I was invited to speak at various medical schools around the country. It was during this period that my esteemed colleagues began referring to me as "Dr. Diarrhea." Unfortunately, the nickname stuck and was picked up by the medical press, where it became a time-honored epithet. Having never learned to exercise due caution in dealing with reporters, I became known as the doctor who said such things as, "The only way to sterilize lettuce is with a blowtorch."

Then, as not infrequently happens in medical science, human tragedy brought new scientific insight when the world experienced one of its worst cholera epidemics on record. Starting in the Celebes in Indonesia, a virulent new strain of the ancient disease roared through Southeast Asia in the late sixties, claiming hundreds of thousands of victims, before settling in Bangladesh in 1971.

I was all too familiar with classic cholera, having visited Calcutta a number of times in the fifties to witness the seasonal epidemics that started like clockwork in early May as the filthy Hooghly River flooded its banks with the combined feces of millions of Indians. Within forty-eight hours, the hospitals would be inundated with thousands of victims placed two or sometimes three to a bed. Miles of rubber tubing connected the patients to large steel pipes that ran the length of the cacophonous wards and carried saline solution designed to replenish the spectacular loss of bodily fluids associated with the disease.

Even so, cholera victims died with alarming speed. It was not uncommon for them to lose as much as a third of their body weight overnight as the disease drained virtually all vital fluids with ruthless efficiency (it is, of course, extreme dehydration and loss of bodily minerals, such as salt, that kills the patient). And therein lay the mystery: autopsies would routinely show the victims' intestinal tracts to be completely normal! How could this be?

As researchers painstakingly pieced together their profile of the epidemic, the anatomical irony of the disease became apparent. In cholera, the studies showed, the intestinal tract becomes a relentless producer of liquid, propelling quart upon quart of watery effluent through the anus and causing quick dehydration and death. Instead of destroying the delicate epithelial cells that form the lining of the intestines, as happened in other diarrheal diseases, however, the cholera bug produced chemicals that actually stimulated the tissue of the gut and encouraged it to produce its overabundance of waste fluids. Rapid dehydration, in fact, *depended* on the intestinal tissue remaining intact; had it been seriously damaged in any way, it could never have produced the amount of fluid it did. Therefore, if doctors could only win the battle to replace these lost fluids in time, the patient would recover quickly, since the toxins themselves were washed out of the body in the process of violent diarrhea.

While I was poring over the latest reports from the Cholera Research Center in Dacca one day, everything suddenly fell into place. Turista, I now realized, was nothing more than a mini-cholera. It was caused not by a bacterium itself, but by toxin *produced* by a bacterium. That's why patients recovered so rapidly and completely—no real damage was ever done to the intestinal tract. That realization made identifying the organism responsible for producing the evil toxin a relative snap. The culprit turned out to be none other than *Escherichia coli*, the bacterium that accounts for a full third of the material bulk of the human stool. It had been, quite literally, right under our noses all the time!

The pathogenic portrait of Montezuma's Revenge was now clear: the traveler swallows *E. coli* bacteria present in contaminated water, food, sauces, and even on "clean" spoons and forks. In the gut, these bacteria multiply and, reaching a critical level, release toxins that stimulate the lining of the intestinal tract to release fluids—water and salt—literally by the bucketful. The rapid loss of liquid is what produces the diarrhea.

There were hundreds of varieties of *E. coli* to choose from, of course, most of them benign. So we went to work trying to isolate those responsible.* Finally, on May 1, 1975, the hunt was officially declared over. That was the date the *New England Journal of Medicine* carried a report of our findings that traced the age-old bane of the tourist back to several of the rarer, toxigenic strains of *E. coli*, one of the colorful bacterial characters that Francis W. O'Connor had introduced me to more than forty years before.

But the riddle of Turista was far from solved. New studies would soon uncover new complexities. *E. coli* would remain the prime villain in the drama, but it has since been shown to be responsible for only about half of all cases of travelers' diarrhea. A dozen other agents of disease, including viruses and parasites, account for the rest. And, since there is no single cause, as I had long hoped there would be, there can be no single cure. Prevention must be general, not specific. Diagnosis remains difficult, treatment troubled.

As far as I was concerned, though, the investigation, which had started on the floor of my hotel room in Rome that uncomfortable night in 1946, had come to an end. Others would continue efforts to isolate the toxins, devise vaccines, search for new therapies. It was high time for me to bow out. Thirty years of the Mexican Two-Step, even if he is Dr. Diarrhea, is enough for any man.

---

*Our team consisted of Sherwood L. "Sherry" Gorbach, a former student and colleague, who had done important cholera research in Dacca and who was then head of the infectious disease department at UCLA; Dolores and Doyle Evans, superb husband–wife bacteriologists from Sherry's laboratory; the indispensable Somerset Waters, who arranged for final field testing in Mexico; and last, but not least, six second-year medical students from Cornell University Medical College.

CHAPTER 17

Mining An Abandoned Vein

The line between inventiveness and insanity, as everyone knows, can run exceedingly fine. In 1963, I came up with an idea that even I found a little nutty. Some of my more skeptical colleagues thought I was flattering myself; they said it was downright ridiculous.

To explain the controversy, let me first introduce the villain, a disease called schistosomiasis, which rivals malaria as the greatest threat to human health in the tropics, where it infects more than 200 million people and puts nearly a half billion more at risk. The cause of "schisto" is a parasitic blood fluke whose larvae inhabit various species of snails found along the banks of irrigation ditches, streams, ponds, and in swamplands throughout the Third World. Only in the veins of the human liver, however, can the larvae reach full adulthood, find a mate, and thus complete their reproductive cycle.

Humans acquire the disease when, swimming or wading in any suitable body of fresh water, they come into contact with schisto larvae, which have developed from eggs deposited there in the urine or feces of other humans. Entering the body through the skin, the young worms make a beeline for the liver, where they mature and mate. Each newly consummated schistosome couple then busily sets about transforming itself into an egg-

laying factory of truly terrifying productivity. A single female
(which spends her entire life lounging seductively in a lengthwise
groove in the body of the male, an arrangement looking a little
like a hotdog in a bun) can, depending on the species, produce
anywhere from a few hundred to many thousands of eggs a day,
often for many years.

It is this prodigious outpouring of eggs, swept into the major
organs by the circulating blood, that causes all the trouble. Each
egg comes outfitted with a sharp spine, something like a microscopic rose thorn, which irritates and scars the surrounding tissue
with spectacularly unpleasant results. Untreated, "snail fever,"
as schisto is widely known, can slowly destroy the liver, the
lungs, and the spinal cord; it can cause the spleen to swell to the
size of a football and the male testicles to shrivel to the size of a
pair of dried prunes; it can create varicose veins in the esophagus
that either slowly strangle the victim or, rupturing, cause sudden
death from internal bleeding.

To put a stop to this grim business, you have to find some
way of putting those prolific egg-layers, the female schistosomes,
out of commission. But how? Today a few doses of praziquantel,
a miracle drug developed in the late seventies, will do the trick
nicely. At the time of my disputed brainstorm in the early sixties,
however, there were no easy answers. None of the drugs then
available worked very effectively and nonmedical approaches,
such as trying to kill off the snails, were impractical, given the
range and biological diversity of the tough little mollusks.

My solution was simple. Why not just filter the offending
flukes from the blood? I have to confess that, on the face of it,
it did seem pretty ludicrous. After all, infections are, for the most
part, caused by microbial agents—bacteria and viruses, in particular—that can reproduce themselves at split-second intervals,
much too fast to be foiled by filtration. Take a patient with hepatitis, for instance. Say you somehow succeeded in developing a
filter with a mesh fine enough to capture a virus as microscop-
ically tiny as the hepatitis bug. Say you then somehow successfully filtered from the patient's blood 99.9 percent of the virus

particles. Within twenty-four hours the 0.1 percent you left behind would have produced a thousand new generations, bringing
the virus population right back to where it was when you started.
X So I did not blame my colleagues for their skepticism. It was
an eccentric idea and, for almost any disease you could think of,
it would be utterly useless. Not for schistosomiasis, however.

Schisto is different because it, like a number of other parasitic
infections, is a strictly mathematical disease. The infection starts
when a person's body is invaded by a finite number of agents,
which, when they mature, develop into male and female but
cannot reproduce themselves inside the human host. As adults,
all schistosomes can do is produce those damaging eggs. Eliminate the eggs and you eliminate the disease. That, in a nutshell,
was the basis for the concept of fluke filtration.

I foresaw no major difficulties in putting my theory into practice. In the first place, the adult schistosomes are big as pathogens
go—about half an inch in length—and easy to spot with the
unaided eye. They are also cowards with a highly predictable
pattern of cowardly behavior. After courtship and mating, the
adult worms leave the safety of their host's liver and set up house-
keeping in the biological suburbs of the intestines. At the first
sign of trouble, however, some nostalgic impulse stirs and they
scurry home toward their mother organ for protection.

This state of schistosome panic could be induced, I had learned
from earlier studies, by injecting the patient with a single dose
of a powerful medication called tartar emetic. All you had to do
then was block the escape route of the stampeding worms by
positioning some kind of filter in the portal vein, the large vein
channeling blood from the intestines to the liver. The blood could
go on its way uninterrupted, but the parasites would be stopped
cold. The best part of my plan was that in schisto, because it is
a mathematical disease, you didn't need to obtain a total cure. If
you could reduce the number of egg-producing adults by 90
percent, the patient, having 90 percent fewer eggs to irritate his
insides, would be 90 percent cured.

Today, the idea of trolling the blood for pathogens no longer seems so farfetched. Big international biotechnology firms routinely spend millions of dollars trying to develop ultra-sophisticated methods of screening cancer cells from the body. Back in the early sixties, though, I was starting from scratch and dealing with the most basic questions imaginable. Was it mechanically possible to put a filter into the portal vein? How big an operation would it require? Could a patient tolerate such a procedure? All that was required to find the answers was a little scientific teamwork.

But my colleagues were unhelpful. I mentioned the idea to almost everyone I knew—parasitologists, internists, and surgeons. No one was interested.

It was then I thought of Ed Goldsmith. Ed was a brilliant vascular surgeon and, since I was proposing to introduce a filter into the portal vein, he was just the man for the job. As everyone else had turned me down, Ed was my last hope. So I approached him gingerly, explaining how I planned to experiment first on monkeys to see if we could develop a technique that would eventually work in humans. "We'll share the glory," I promised.

Ed was in his middle thirties then, a tall, heavy, scholarly type, who was always fighting his weight and fretting about his family. He studied me suspiciously for a moment. "Let me think about it," he said, and walked away.

Schistosomes come in three varieties—*Schistosoma mansoni, Schistosoma haematobium,* and *Schistosoma japonicum*—and, despite relatively minor physiological traits, the differences among them are chiefly residential. The mature *S. mansoni* (named for Francis W. O'Connor's mentor, Sir Patrick Manson) lives and lays its eggs in the bulbous veins of the human colon, while *S. haematobium* favors the more alkaline neighborhood of the urinary tract, especially the bladder, and *S. japonicum* remains a devoted resident of the small intestine.

In the wider world, the worms' territorial imperatives are chiefly a function of their obsessive fondness for differing types of intermediate hosts, the species of snail in which the worm passes from its first larval stage to its brief career as the tiny, tadpolelike creature that eventually penetrates the human skin. S. *mansoni*, for example, is simply wild about the various members of *Biomphalaria*, a family of snails found in Africa, though the parasite has probably claimed more victims in Brazil, Venezuela, and the Caribbean islands, since it was carried to the New World inside the bodies of African slaves and managed to locate a sufficiently attractive snail cousin there. S. *haematobium* only has eyes (figuratively speaking, of course) for the burly, marble-size *Bulinus*, and so is found in the snail's main haunts—parts of the Middle East and much of Africa. S. *japonicum*, true to its name, has been faithful to Japan because of the presence there of *Oncomelania*, a twirled snail looking something like a flattened pea, although both worm and host are now far more prevalent in the less-developed areas of China and the Philippines.

The intricate life cycle of the schistosome begins when the infected human deposits schisto eggs in his local pond or stream. Concealed within each egg is a live ciliated larva called a miracidium, which, swimming at a velocity of 700 centimeters per hour, seeks out and invades its snail of choice. Thus begins the second phase of the schistosome's evolution. After a month or so of furious reproduction inside the minute liver of the intermediate snail host, thousands upon thousands of the larval changelings, now multiplied vastly in number and having entered their tadpole stage, leave the snail in regular daily blizzards.

The larvae, now known as cercariae, begin their final rite of passage when they make contact with the human skin, jettison their tiny forked tails, and tunnel into the body. After mating inside the veins of the liver, the newlywed schistosome couples migrate to the intestines where they settle down to a life more or less exclusively devoted to sexual intercourse and the resulting production of eggs. It is probably just as well that the victim remains oblivious to the swarm of aggressive creatures burrowing through his skin (they are too small to see with the naked eye), although soon thereafter he usually experiences the allergic reaction—a painful, itching rash—warning of their presence. It takes at least six weeks for the human subject to experience the first serious symptoms of the disease: high fever, swollen glands, aching joints, diarrhea, accelerated skin allergies, enlarged spleen, and eosinophilia. A particularly alarming symptom in *S. haematobium* infections is bloody urination.

On a good day, an *S. mansoni* female can exude three hundred eggs, the more prolific *S. japonicum* three thousand, which explains why, mathematically speaking, *Schistosomiasis japonica* is by far the most destructive form of the disease.

The schistosomes have been perfecting their curious calculus for a very long time. Petrified eggs have been discovered inside Egyptian mummies entombed two thousand years before the birth of Christ. This is hardly surprising, since pharaonic wall paintings dating from the period clearly depict field slaves standing knee-deep in water, operating one of the world's first irrigation systems and, no doubt, acquiring schistosomiasis in the process. (The more detailed murals suggest that the ingenious Egyptians not only grasped the connection between water and sickness but were thinking about prophylaxis, as well; male slaves are shown outfitted with a woven sheath, a sort of primitive condom, covering their penises, presumably in an effort to prevent the evil disease from entering their bodies and causing them to pee blood.)

In China, the Chou Dynasty (480–222 B.C.) tombs outside Changsha have yielded their own supply of mummified schisto eggs. In the fifties, Mao Zedong claimed to have eliminated the ancient scourge by instructing ten million Chinese workers with ten million Chinese hoes to turn over ten inches of Chinese top soil, crushing whatever snails they found in the process. Ignorant of Mao's ideological dictates, however, the snails survived; in the early seventies the World Health Organization estimated that as many as one in ten Chinese, something on the order of a hundred million people, were victims of snail fever, although the number is considerably lower now.

While it ravages the Third World, however, schisto is by no means exclusively a poor man's disease, as a group of American college students found out one scorching afternoon in March 1984, when they went for a swim in a slow-moving stream in the Machakos district of Kenya. Within hours, several of the swimmers, who belonged to an expedition sponsored by the Experiment in International Living, had developed the telltale red blotches on their skin. Within six weeks, fifteen of the eighteen students were experiencing fever, diarrhea, and rapid weight loss. One young man became permanently paralyzed from the waist down—the result of eggs concentrating in and destroying the cervical portion of the spinal cord.

I first encountered schisto at the autopsy table at Gorgas Hospital in Panama in the early forties. This was remarkable if only because schistosomiasis does not occur in Panama, at least naturally; the snails required to perpetuate the life cycle refuse to live there. The disease arrived in the bowels of Puerto Rican GIs brought in for jungle warfare training during the Second World War, a number of whom had the bad luck of succumbing to the local forms of violence—auto accidents and bar fights, chiefly—before getting the chance to face the Japanese in the South Pacific. Many of the deceased, when autopsied, had the disease. Puerto Rico had the right snails.

I remembered this when I took a part-time job as consulting parasitologist at Halloran Veterans Hospital on Staten Island after my return from Germany in 1947. We saw large numbers of demobilized Puerto Rican soldiers there, and I was determined not to miss a single case of schistosomiasis. The result was that all returning vets, no matter what their ethnic background, were required to submit to a rectal biopsy as part of the mandatory exit physical. A mountainous orderly would shove a tongue blade down the unsuspecting patient's throat and, while the patient was busy saying "Ah," would unceremoniously flip him over on his stomach. I would then appear on the scene with a short proctoscope to obtain a sample of tissue.

My investigations soon showed that as many as one-fifth of all the Puerto Rican veterans were infected, a figure later mirrored in samplings of the hundred thousand or so Puerto Rican emigrés then living in the New York area. Over the years, schisto would lose its status as one of the city's leading endemic diseases, however, as a highly effective campaign against worm and snail took hold in Puerto Rico itself. But in the late forties, the "tropics" of Manhattan faced an invasion of the exotic parasite, and we did our best to cope.

Conditions were not ideal. The only drug treatment then available consisted of multiple intravenous injections of tartar emetic, which the patients didn't like any more than the schistosome, and for a very good reason. The medication was toxic, hard to administer, and an overdose was not infrequently fatal. So we gave it sparingly and only to those patients whose heavy infections might otherwise kill them. Fuadin, a substance originally prepared in Egypt and named in honor of King Fuad, was the substitute, but few patients completed the treatment because the intramuscular injections were so excruciatingly painful. Even those who managed to tolerate the full three-month course had only a slightly better than fifty-fifty chance of a cure. Safe, efficient drug therapy still lay two decades in the future, and, meanwhile, I agonized over the suffering my patients had to endure.

In our determination to find a more reliable treatment, my colleagues at Cornell and I tried everything. For a time, I was convinced that, if one couldn't efficiently kill the adult worms, we could at least sterilize them, rendering the males impotent and the females incapable of producing eggs. So we raised thousands upon thousands of schistosomes in our laboratory. We bombarded them with X rays. We fed them hormones designed to confuse their sexual identities. Ultimately, though, nothing we tried had any effect whatsoever on those powerful little libidos. It was then, at length and out of sheer desperation, I came up with my crackpot blood filtration scheme.

I had given up on Ed Goldsmith, but he had not given up on me. Several weeks had passed without a word, when one day he suddenly appeared in my laboratory and said, "Count me in."

Ed had only one condition. Instead of monkeys, we should use baboons, which, he insisted, were superior in several respects. First, the baboon was bigger; its larger vessels would be easier to handle surgically. Moreover, Ed's meticulous search of the literature on schisto had indicated that the big simian was more susceptible to the disease. Most important of all, though, Ed had been toying with the idea of creating a primate research center at Cornell and just happened to have a couple dozen baboons on hand in his laboratory. I was now convinced I had made no mistake—Ed Goldsmith was the right man for the job.

"Of course," he observed nonchalantly, "placing the filter directly into the portal vein, as you propose, is asking for trouble." Instead Ed suggested running a tube into the portal vein and then using an electric pump to propel the blood out of the body and through a filtering device before returning it, strained of worms, back into normal channels. I could tell Ed was excited. "What should we call this thing?" I asked.

"We should call it," said Ed, a faraway look in his eyes, "extracorporeal hemofiltration."

Extracorporeal hemofiltration. It had a nice ring to it.

While Ed and I were working the kinks out of our antischistosome machinery, our lab technicians had painstakingly harvested large numbers of cercariae from *Biomphalaria* snails we had imported from cooperative molluscicidologists in Brazil and Puerto Rico. When our pumps and filters were finally in proper working order, we called in the baboons and introduced them to the schistosomes. A few weeks later we were finally ready for our first operation.

Having administered the proper anesthesia, Ed opened the abdomen of the first baboon and inserted a tube in its portal vein, so that all of its blood would be diverted out of the body, filtered, and then pumped back into a vessel in the leg. My role was to inject an appropriate dose of tartar emetic into a vein in the baboon's arm and wait to see if the parasites would release their grip in the intestines, flee in the direction of the liver, and become snared in our contraption.

The atmosphere was tense. Then, precisely six minutes after I'd squirted the chemical into the heavily infected baboon, the first worm came sluicing out of the tube and slammed into the filter. Then another and another. Soon we had captured nearly a hundred adult schistosomes. Ed Goldsmith tipped back his head and let out a triumphant war whoop. We had scored our first victory in the battle against schistosomiasis, and victory was sweet.

The results in all six baboons were so precise, so mathematical, and so predictable that we felt further experimental trials were unnecessary. It was high time, we thought, to try out our system on a human subject. And it was then that we encountered the most important, difficult problem facing all researchers who work in medicine: medical ethics.

How does one go about translating an animal experiment into a standard operation on a human patient? Neither Ed nor I had ever faced this situation before. According to long-established rules, the patient, whoever he might be, had to give his informed consent. This meant he had to understand the nature of his illness, as well as the hazards of the operation and its limited potential for a cure. But Ed and I were dealing with a disease affecting the poor, uneducated rural populations of the world's tropical zone. How does one get informed consent from an African tribesman, an Arab child, or a Chinese peasant?

To complicate matters, many of our potential patients inhabited cultures where the widespread phenomenon of teenage boys urinating blood was not considered a sign of disease, but a mark of manhood, a sort of male menarche. Moreover, the Helsinki Declaration, designed with the "scientific" excesses of Hitler's medical men in mind, was quite explicit on this point: every experimental procedure conducted on a human being must be designed to help *that individual*, not to benefit science or humanity in general.

Ed and I were in a quandary when the answer to our problems walked into our laboratory in the form of Dr. Aluizio Prata. Prata, then a visiting scholar at Cornell, was a gifted parasitologist from Brazil where *S. mansoni* was a raging national crisis, with no fewer than ten million confirmed cases on the books and another thirty to fifty million Brazilians at risk of acquiring the infection. So when Prata found out about our filtration scheme, he implored us to come to Brazil.

The profile of the disease in Brazil was a depressing one, to be sure. Many victims were young men and women in their teens and twenties whom the schistosome had marked for life. Swollen veins in the esophagus would burst and bleed, causing severe anemia, malnutrition, and weight loss. Patients might be unable to hold down a job simply because their spleens, swollen many times normal size, required too much energy to carry around. Livers stopped processing male hormones and men became eunuchoid, going through life with shrunken testicles and falsetto voices, unable to find wives or sire families. In Brazil, Prata informed us, the standard method of dealing with the disease was to cut out the spleen.

As I listened to Prata talk, I suddenly recognized a unique opportunity. Ed had been worried about cutting into the portal vein in order to introduce the tube that would carry the blood into our out-of-body filter. In removing the tube and sewing up the vein, he feared, a clot might occur that would block the passageway—and that, very likely, meant death for the patient. But Prata had a brilliant solution. "Why open the portal vein at all?" he said. "You could use the splenic vein, which is connected to the portal vein anyway. As the surgeon removes the spleen, he'll simply 'hand over' the splenic vein to you." Using that route, we could insert our tube and reach the portal vein very nicely; there would be no need to damage any vessels other than those cut in the course of routine splenectomy.

Thanks to Prata's brainstorm, our experimental blueprint gained the approval of the human rights committee at Cornell. The panel judged that, since we would merely be piggy-backing on an ordinary splenectomy, our momentary rerouting of the blood would, by itself, present little danger to the patient. It was then agreed that Dr. Prata should return to Brazil as soon as possible to select a surgeon who was doing splenectomies for the treatment of schisto, and to assemble a pool of patients who would stand to benefit from our procedure and who would be capable of appending an "X" to an informed consent document.

At long last, it was time for Ed Goldsmith and me to take our tubes, pumps, and filters on the road. We flew to Bahia, a lovely seaport on the northeast coast of Brazil famous for its beautiful beaches, its sultry women, and its "layer cake" effect—two lush urban tiers carved out of the green mountainside and connected one to the other by a huge open elevator.

There Prata introduced us to the chief surgeon at the Hospital Edgard Santos at the University of Bahia, and we spent the next several days rehearsing our procedure with our Brazilian colleagues and selecting our first three patients.

When the big day arrived, the observation balcony of the operating theater was filled with curious physicians, many of them with binoculars trained on the abdomen of the first patient, a twenty-nine-year-old farmer. The surgeon proceeded to the removal of the spleen, isolated the splenic vein, and moved to the opposite side of the table to make room for Ed. Ed carefully threaded a tube through the splenic vein and up into the portal vein to the point where it entered the liver. Once the tube was in place, I gave the signal to start the pump. Having worked in Brazil before, I had insisted that the pump be turned by hand; a sudden electrical failure and we could have a dead patient on our hands.

With the system up and running, the pumpman having caught his stride, I moved to center stage. From a bottle marked "tartar emetic" I suctioned off the standard dosage with a syringe, which I then squirted into the rubber tubing that would carry the fluid intravenously into the patient's arm.

For the next five minutes all eyes in the house were focused on the glass-enclosed filter resting on the patient's chest. All except mine, that is; I was too nervous to look. Then a cheer went up from the viewing area. Our observant colleagues had managed to witness the dramatic entrapment of the first few parasites through their field glasses even before I had a chance to utter a confirmatory, "Thank God."

Over the space of an hour we managed to bag 146 worms. The second patient, a fourteen-year-old male student, took the record the next day with 799 worms. From the third, a twelve-year-old boy, we extracted 157 schistosomes. All three patients had been ravaged by the disease, all three had large spleens and small, poorly developed testicles. Every single observation we had made on the baboons was confirmed in these first human trials. We were walking on air.

Ed and I left all of our equipment in the hands of our local colleagues and together with them established a protocol for subsequent operations. News of the results dribbled in over the next few months, and it was excellent: over 90 percent of the worms in each of the first twenty-three patients were removed. For all practical purposes, we had achieved a near-perfect cure. I was convinced we had made a significant contribution to schistosomiasis therapy. The *Journal of the American Medical Association* agreed by publishing as its lead article "Surgical Removal of Schistosomes from the Portal Blood: Treatment of the Parasitization in Man" in January of 1967.

Our procedure had one major flaw that could no longer be overlooked, however. It was too damned complicated. First of all, it required the use of relatively expensive medical paraphernalia that had to be administered by a full surgical team, so it could only be used in a select number of individuals under special circumstances. How many of the world's 200 million victims could afford that? We had succeeded, I realized somewhat belatedly, in developing a rich man's cure for a poor man's disease. I tried to be philosophical, though. If we couldn't operate on the suffering millions, at least the filtration system would allow us to advance our understanding of the biology of the disease and eventually open the way for a better form of therapy.

Our next target, *Schistosoma haematobium*, the urinary variety of schisto common throughout Africa and the Middle East, would force us to modify our methods. While the concept of flushing and filtering the parasite from the blood would remain unchanged, the fact that *S. haematobium* resides in a different part of the anatomy than *S. mansoni* (congregating around the bladder instead of inside the intestines) demanded different tactics. And that meant more baboon trials.

It was then that I first appreciated how environmentally fussy our blasted flukes could be. We had left over from our first baboon studies a plentiful supply of *Biomphalaria*, the home favored by *S. mansoni* larvae. *S. haematobium*, however, required *Bulinus* snails, which had to be shipped to us at great cost from suppliers in Iran, Egypt, and Africa. Unhappily, these new arrivals did not thrive in the demanding Manhattan environment. At length, we were forced to rely on a snail broker in Rhodesia (now Zimbabwe), who promised to ship us snails already infected with schisto larvae, again at staggering cost. Our efforts to coax the cercariae needed to infect our baboons from the Rhodesian snails proved just as fruitless, however, so I decided once again to bring in a medical student to save our hides.

The upshot was that we sent Mark Rosenberg, a second-year student at Cornell, to Rhodesia. His orders were to capture six baboons, infect them with schisto, and then escort the animals back to New York. He performed admirably in the tradition of diarrhea-busters Hoffman and Van Stone, but it was no easy task.

Naturally, I told him nothing of the details of his mission in advance. When he was safely in Africa, I informed him:

Dear Mark:

In the past three years, we have received at least eight batches of infected snails from Africa, Egypt, and Iran, yet we have been unable to get cercariae from them in a laboratory. Each one of our colleagues assured us that we would have no trouble with the snails, but the snails were not told about this. Therefore, you will please infect six baboons, with 5,000 cercariae each, and bring them back to New York as soon as possible.

Two weeks later, Rosenberg replied:

Dear Boss:

I have received your letter regarding the infection of baboons. I had to trek to a game park today to capture two more to round out the six animals. I'll try to infect all of them with 4,000 or 5,000 cercariae.

It has been quite an experience. I spent three days last week armed with a capture gun, stalking the kopje [rocky hills] for signs of the baboon. I now understand why they are so difficult to catch. The farmers have long shot baboons as pests, so that you can't get within five hundred yards of them if you're a white man, especially one with a rifle. Baboons will not enter traps unless they are permanent fixtures of their environment. Some quick talking, and promises of all sorts of recognition and money, was necessary, but we got the beasts.

Getting passage for the animals out of Salisbury was a trial. The only connection I could make is with Lufthansa. They're leaving Salisbury to Jo'burg to Frankfurt but should get to New York on schedule. The baboons will be arriving, some of them two to a cage. The others are not compatible.

By and large, South Africa is an extremely dull place. They have all the amenities of civilization that Bismarck, N.D., has, except more than one TV station. Perhaps I should have spent more of my time teaching the baboons how to talk.

The animals eventually arrived in New York in good shape. Unfortunately, for reasons I still do not clearly understand, extracorporeal hemofiltration in baboons infected with *S. haematobium* did not work.

Ultimately, Ed Goldsmith devised a theoretically brilliant operation for filtering *S. haematobium* from the blood, this time without opening the abdomen at all. The procedure featured a balloon, which would be inserted through the femoral artery in the leg to block blood returning from the leg, pelvis, and bladder to the heart via the major vein known as the vena cava. We could then artificially channel the flow through a tube to the femoral artery in the opposite leg for return to the heart. While passing through the tube, of course, the blood was strained through a filter that removed any worms present.

It promised to be technically much easier than the procedure we had used against *S. mansoni* in Brazil, and, because of the decidedly less invasive nature of the operation, it presented much less risk to the patient. As a result, we had no trouble getting clearance from the human rights committee at Cornell for trying it on humans. But where to operate?

I first thought of Africa. Several countries were possible, but the situation was complicated by the fact that, throughout large parts of the continent, areas infected with *S. haematobium* overlapped with those affected by *S. mansoni*, making experimentation a hopelessly murky affair. Egypt was another candidate; I had been there many times and knew the local brand of snail fever to be almost exclusively *S. haematobium*. But this was 1967, and escalating tensions with Israel that would soon culminate in the Six-Day War had left the Egyptians touchy about foreigners.

Iran, then, was the logical choice. Still firmly under the control of the Shah, the country was a bastion of stability in those pre-revolutionary days, although it wouldn't remain so for very long. I had met the Shah, but did not know him well. I had other Iranian connections, though, that could be helpful to our effort. Foremost among these was financier David Lilienthal.

Lilienthal, who had headed the Tennessee Valley Authority under Roosevelt and the Atomic Energy Commission under Truman, had long since been in private business. His company, the Development and Resources Corporation of Iran, had been largely responsible for building the massive Dez Dam in Khuzistan in the early sixties. Because of his experience at TVA, where he had learned how essential it was to raise and lower water levels regularly in order to destroy mosquitoes responsible for spreading malaria, Lilienthal was sensitive to the irony linking economic development to the dissemination of disease.

The Dez Dam was a perfect case in point. Designed to bring water and electric power to a half million impoverished people in Khuzistan, it would also inevitably bring disease. The same irrigation project that would make the desert flower would create a vast grid of freshwater sluiceways hospitable to *Bulinus* snails. So Lilienthal, fearful of the consequences, had asked Carl Taylor, an expert on tropical epidemiology from Johns Hopkins University, and Lawrence Ritchie, an expert on snails from Puerto Rico, to design a program to keep schisto from spreading after the completion of the dam. They could not. Later, as medical consultant to D & R and Lilienthal's personal physician, I was asked to find a solution.

One trip to the villages of Khuzistan was all it took to convince me that the project should go ahead regardless of the threat of schistosomiasis. The primary health problems there—malnutrition, infant mortality, blindness due to trachoma, and rampant venereal disease—were staggering, even for the Third World. Without the benefits of increased crop yields and electric power the dam would bring, there would be little hope of introducing even the rudiments of modern sanitation and medical care. Those issues took priority; schisto would have to come next. In my final recommendation, I had glumly but realistically noted, "Bring the water and see what happens. I know of no way to prevent schistosomiasis from spreading."

So it was that Ed and I turned up in Iran in May of 1967 to do battle with *S. haematobium*. In Teheran, we paid a brief courtesy call on the Shah, who gave our project his blessing in the presence of the foreign minister, Ademar Zahedi.

Ed and I had selected Ahwaz, a sleepy little oasis town in southwestern Iran, for our first series of operations. An unhappy place, it was one of the world's major foci of schistosomiasis. (The town was to become unhappier still when it was largely destroyed by Iraqi bombers during the Iran–Iraq War in the early eighties.) We checked into a dusty hotel off the main square and headed for the Pars Hospital. It was a simple institution, small and cramped, with two hundred patients on iron-frame cots sweltering in the 110-degree heat. There was no air-conditioning, even in the operating room, which, with its open windows, slowly revolving ceiling fans, and large population of stinging insects, reminded me of my intern days at Gorgas Hospital in Panama.

Our first patient was a twelve-year-old boy, who complained of painful, bloody urination. Ed went to work. It was my duty to stand guard at the unscreened windows and try to keep out as many flies as possible. As the operation proceeded, I made sure that the proper amount of tartar emetic was drawn into a syringe and then spent the rest of my time observing the parched town square. I was enchanted by the thought that the few people milling around out there, robed and exotic, represented a daily routine that stretched back to time beyond memory. It wasn't long, however, before I noticed that a sizable crowd had gathered. There must have been several hundred people, many of whom—a little oddly, I thought—were pointing admonishing fingers in the direction of the hospital. Some of the men carried rifles.

Gesturing toward the assemblage, I casually remarked to an Iranian colleague that today must be some kind of festival day to attract so many people. What holiday was it?

"The only thing that makes this day special from all others," he said with a grimace, "is that Dr. Goldsmith is operating on the first-born son of the local sheik." What did that have to do with all those people out in the square, I asked, suddenly anticipating the answer and feeling a little queasy.

"Well, if the operation is a success, they will cheer you as heroes and go back to their village," he said, pausing to add gloomily, "If not, well, all of us may just possibly disappear."

The operation, as luck would have it, was a complete failure. Not a single worm appeared in the filter. Thankfully, though, the boy was wheeled back to his bed in good condition, so we at least had some room to maneuver with the sensibilities of the expectant villagers. Given the circumstances, we decided that lying would be in the best interests of medical science; it would at least help ensure that Ed and I lived long enough to continue our experiments elsewhere.

Through an interpreter, we announced to the sheik's grizzled retainers that the injection took time to be effective (and, in truth, the single large dose of tartar emetic would produce a remission in symptoms, though not a cure). The sheik's men, who had apparently anticipated an instant and complete cure, looked ferociously displeased, but went away.

The next day we operated on a less politically risky child, the ten-year-old son of a farmer, and, the day after that, on a twenty-two-year-old religious student. All three operations were uniformly unsuccessful; not one parasite appeared in any of the filters. To this day our failure remains a mystery to me. Having so successfully challenged *S. mansoni* in Brazil, why should *S. haematobium* present such problems? Maybe the tough Iranian worms were unfazed by the influx of tartar emetic. Possibly, the extreme convolutions of blood vessels around the bladder prevented the schistosomes from moving freely toward the filter. Whatever the reason, it was a deeply disappointing experience.

Later that same year, the depression over our Iranian failures having lifted, I resolved to test the Goldsmith–Kean system against *S. japonicum*, the last and most severe of the three varieties of snail fever.

Having originally identified the disease at the turn of the century, the Japanese made short work of it after the Second World War when they launched an antischistosome campaign of withering intensity. Using a new generation of potent molluscicides, they bombarded the country's rivers and paddy fields, its ponds and irrigation ditches. Geography also helped, since the disease, bottled up as it was on the Japanese archipelago, occurred in a few relatively isolated areas and could be eradicated in comprehensive fashion.

This was not the case in China, where during the late sixties some seventy-five million cases of human infection were thought to exist in the sprawling Yangtze Valley alone. At the time, however, the Red Guards had plunged China into the Great Proletarian Cultural Revolution, and snails ranked low on the list of ideological targets. With *S. japonicum* so efficiently handled in the land of its discovery, and China politically embargoed, we turned our attention to the Philippines, the third major arena of the disease.

Arming myself with a letter of introduction from a Wall Street banker friend with business connections there, I flew to Manila to meet President Ferdinand Marcos. Little did I realize that approval of our project would depend on something so unpredictable as my skill—or, rather, lack of it—on the golf course.

I was met at the airport by three smiling officials, who escorted me to a waiting limousine. Motorcycle policemen leading the way, we drove at high speeds toward Malacanang Palace, where I was ushered into the president's office. While waiting for Marcos, I had time to size up the surroundings and noticed that, on the far side of the large, floor-to-ceiling French windows was a small plot of neatly trimmed grass bordered by a few tropical bushes, beyond which scowled a squad of lethal-looking armed guards. "How interesting," I remember thinking. "If this was not the office of a head of state, I'd swear that was a golf tee out there."

Then came the unusual request from one of the president's smiling men: "What shoe size do you wear, please?" He seemed inexplicably elated by the news that I wore a size ten. It was at that point that my jacket and shirt were forcibly removed and I was handed a silk sportshirt and a cashmere sweater, which I was instructed to put on. Another smiling attendant appeared pushing something resembling a grocery cart on which were displayed a remarkable assortment of golf shoes—all size ten. I selected a pair of shoes and accepted a pair of white golf socks that were handed to me.

Twenty-four hours in transit had left me badly jet-lagged, so it took a while to register that I was being groomed to shoot a round of golf with the chief executive. One of the officials, still smiling, informed me that the grassy area I had observed outside the office was indeed the first tee of the presidential golf course. It fronted an inlet about a hundred yards wide where a small gunboat rode at anchor. Lush, manicured links did not strike me as the most appropriate venue for discussing the problems of schistosomiasis among the rural poor, but since this was apparently how they did business in the Philippines, I decided to play along.

Ferdinand Marcos arrived. He was dressed informally and wore a floppy, narrow-brimmed cloth hat similar to the one he would be wearing on the day nineteen years later when television cameras showed him arriving, sick and feeble, at a military airport in Guam after he had been forced to flee his own country. But back in the late sixties, he was still in his mid-forties, a small, cheerful, vigorous man, with a wry sense of humor and a dark, lumpy complexion. The doctor in me entertained the idea that he might be suffering from a mild case of leprosy. Later I would learn that what he actually had was lupus, a tuberculosislike disease which can affect the skin of the face.

"You are our guest," said Marcos, gesturing toward me with upturned palms. "Your honor. Tee off."

Still mentally groggy, and not being a very good golfer to begin with, I got off to a poor start. The gunboat made me nervous. Marcos made me nervous. I dumped the first ball into the water about fifty yards from the tee, whereupon a young Filipino, clad in what appeared to be a loincloth, dove from the deck of the gunboat to retrieve it. A second ball, hit hard but sliced, entered the water at a wild angle, though at a somewhat greater distance. My third shot skimmed the surface of the canal and barely succeeded in reaching the far shore. Marcos, meanwhile, had no trouble laying a low, wicked drive up the center of the fairway.

The gunboat ferried us across the inlet where a half-dozen golf carts awaited—two for our foursome, one carrying an incredibly well-stocked bar, and the remaining three creaking under the weight of some very muscular-looking "caddies," who watched over a set of specially designed golf bags that nearly succeeded in concealing their collection of Uzi submachine guns, rifles, and shotguns. As we played on and the afternoon shadows deepened, a system of floodlights flashed on, illuminating the darkening fairways.

I am not a good golfer, I repeat—but I am a pretty good competitor and the president's bald desire to win at any cost got me involved in the game. I was also encouraged by the fact that I had been teamed up with Dindo Gonzalez, a former captain of the Philippine national golf team and a constant companion of the president. Marcos's partner was his friend and confidant, Manuel Nieto, nicknamed "Neling." His style of golf was memorable in that it was nearly as bad as mine. As we were pretty evenly matched, the play soon grew intense.

By the time we reached the eighteenth tee, the match was all tied up. Everything depended on the outcome of this one last hole, a par four with the green backing onto the same inlet we had traversed in the gunboat. All four of us hit pretty fair drives. Our second shots to the green demanded a nine iron for Marcos, the cabinet minister, and me, and a wedge for the powerful Dindo. The president hit first and landed his shot on the green, but at some distance from the cup. His partner also reached the green in two strokes. Nervous about performing well, I moved my head just enough so that my ball corkscrewed into the ubiquitous canal. Luckily, we were playing "best ball," meaning the player scoring the lowest number of strokes on the hole would win the match for his side. The final play belonged to none other than Dindo Gonzalez, champion golfer of the Philippines.

Dindo was close, about ninety yards from the pin, and, given his reputation, I would have bet my life on winning. So it came as a great shock when Dindo, so cool and self-assured, the model of athletic poise, hauled off and inexplicably shanked his ball to within a few feet of where mine had plopped into the waterway. "Oh, my god!" he groaned, good-naturedly. "When I saw your shot, Dr. Kean, I guess I caught the disease."

Inside the locker room, I approached Dindo and asked, "How could you possibly hit a ball like that when we were so close to winning?" He smiled at my innocence. "How do you think I get to play golf with the president so often?" he said, adding a little mysteriously, "Besides, now you will have no trouble getting full cooperation from the Government of the Philippines for your research project."

He was right, of course. The government proved so helpful, in fact, that I would later ask Dindo what kind of present he thought I should send Marcos as a token of appreciation. He thought a while and said, "Why not do what everyone else does? Send him the newest, most expensive set of golf clubs you can find." At the time a thousand dollars was a lot to me, but, in the name of scientific advancement, I dispatched through the Philippine ambassador in Washington the fanciest woods and irons then available. When the Marcos government fell, the media zeroed in on Imelda's closet, the one crammed with three thousand pairs of shoes, as a symbol of the excesses of the old regime. I waited—but in vain—for some enterprising reporter to discover the vault where Marcos kept his golf clubs!

A few months after my trial by golf, Ed Goldsmith and I found ourselves flying toward the island of Leyte, the epicenter of *S. japonicum* in the Philippines. We were accompanied by Lawrence Ritchie, the snail specialist from Puerto Rico and an old friend. During a brief stopover in Manila, Marcos had personally assured the three of us that he was making the complete eradication of schisto a top government priority—a promise I would remember with bitterness years later when it became obvious he had done next to nothing.

Marcos told us he would be sending along "someone special" to keep an eye on us. That someone turned out to be none other than First Lady Imelda, who "invited" us—if that is the polite term for "ordered"—to stay at the First Family's summer house on Leyte. Imelda's side of the family, the Romueldez clan, was bursting with rich landowners, who dominated virtually every facet of life in Leyte, where her brother, General Benjamin Romueldez, was then serving as provincial governor. In those days, Imelda, still in her mid-thirties, was a voluptuous Philippine beauty—gracious, capable, and ebullient—so unlike the overbearing, overstuffed prima donna of the last years of Marcos rule.

The "summer palace" was a large hacienda that occupied a low cliff overlooking the ocean. It was ringed with tropical gardens that were, in their turn, bounded by the cyclone fencing of a military compound. The entrance to the estate was from a private road, and heavily guarded. The male bathers who walked up and down the beach in front of the house, all rippling muscles and watchful eyes, bore a striking resemblance to the caddies I had encountered during my golf game with the president.

Imelda soon arrived with her entourage, which consisted of thirty ladies of the Philippine Red Cross. That evening, there was a luau on the spacious patio, and the First Lady entertained us by singing songs in her throaty mezzo-soprano voice. Her favorite seemed to be "Deep in the Heart of Texas," which she sang twice. In the background, her smiling duennas hummed the accompaniment. Ed Goldsmith, having had perhaps one more bottle of San Miguel beer than good sense required, joined Imelda at the microphone. He didn't have a bad voice, and soon the First Lady and the vascular surgeon from New York Hospital were performing inspired duets. These were dutifully tape-recorded and played back to us several days later. Ed tried to make off with the master tape but was thwarted by the watchful eyes of the Red Cross ladies. Somewhere in my possession there is still a copy of the Marcos–Goldsmith recording.

The following morning we drove to Tacloban, the capital of Leyte. With the First Lady and her brother the general escorting us, cooperation at the local hospital was enthusiastic. The medical picture there was even gloomier than Brazil, not surprising since Asian schisto was an even more brutal foe. Unhappily, we found many of the patients with hepatosplenic schistosomiasis too dilapidated to tolerate major surgery. There were a few, however, who, despite their enormous livers and spleens, were still young enough and healthy enough to benefit from the operation.

Gowned and masked, the First Lady stood in the operating room while we went to work on a thirty-three-year-old farmer. For all the fanfare, though, our efforts were disappointing. We failed to turn up a single worm. In contrast to the festivities of the previous evening, things were glum back at the hacienda that night. The next day, however, we redeemed ourselves with an operation on a sixteen-year-old girl. As the pump whirred away, 285 worms were trapped in the filter, 143 females and 142 males. This was more like it.

Imelda was ecstatic. She declared a local holiday for the following day and insisted on flying in an orchestra for a special concert in our honor. As the band played on late into the evening, and special presidential wines were uncorked, the Red Cross ladies danced innocently in one another's embrace. It was a lovely time. The worms were on the run and all was right with the world.

The following morning we had another successful operation, although only a paltry twenty-three worms were recovered. We learned what had been reported in the literature for a long time: *S. japonica* was much more serious than either of the other two forms, because, although individual infections normally involved fewer worms, each mated couple produced ten times more eggs. It was absolutely imperative, we concluded, to operate at a much earlier stage of the disease to be assured of any reasonable success.

On the flight back to Manila, I sat next to Mrs. Marcos. As we flew over a spectacular group of islands, emerald ameba shapes floating in a sea of startling blue, I remarked how surprised I was to find so many uninhabited islands in a country every inch of which, for some reason, I had imagined to be swarming with humanity. But Imelda wasn't listening to me.

"I have decided to honor you," she said, arching an eyebrow and gesturing toward the window. "Look down." I looked down. I could see three small islands framed in the cabin window.

"That," said Imelda, pausing dramatically, "is an archipelago. I have decided to name it after you. On the next map of the Philippines," the First Lady went on, "you will find your name over this spot."

For once in my life, I was able to think quickly. Instead of naming the islands the Kean Archipelago, I suggested, a better name would be Kegori, a vowel-softened word—*Ke* for Kean, *Go* for Goldsmith, *Ri* for Ritchie—that sounded somehow less foreign, less suggestive of colonial influence, more Oriental. She agreed. Kegori it would be. But either she forgot, or I was never able to locate a map showing enough detail, because I never found my name, either wholly or in part, hovering over any appendage of the Philippines.

Back in Manila, Marcos went on national television to proclaim—and wildly exaggerate—our accomplishments; he predicted, prematurely and falsely, the total elimination of *S. japonica* from Leyte. Goldsmith, Ritchie, and I were decorated with the Presidential Order of the Golden Heart in full view of the cameras as the cabinet applauded our achievements. We left town, our medals clanking in our suitcases.

Over the years, I watched from afar and with sadness as events overtook the Marcoses—the change in their mood and manner, their entanglement in the tragic killing of Benigno Aquino, and the slow political and economic disintegration of the country under their imperious rule. I regretted the perhaps inevitable transformation of two considerate, charming, though strangely immature people whose eagerness to see themselves as regal figures guaranteed a fall from grace that, though not quite as catastrophic as the Shah's (and, on the whole, a positive development for their country), would be every bit as humiliating. As for the schistosomiasis eradication program, reports from colleagues in the Philippines indicated that precious few funds were ever actually made available to combat the disease.

After our experiences in the Philippines, Ed and I were more aware than ever of the impossibility of using our operation on a big scale because of the need for highly skilled surgeons, for special equipment, and, above all, because of the dangers inherent in removing the spleen, especially in a Third World setting.

Then Ed, in his ingenious fashion, devised a major simplification of the procedure for *S. japonicum* and *S. mansoni*. The tube that we had once placed into the hepatic vein would now be passed through the forgotten umbilical vein. In babies, a large blood vessel extends from the liver to the placenta through the umbilicus. After the tying off and cutting of the umbilical cord at birth, this vein closes down and remains dormant for the rest of one's life. It was not widely known, but the vein could be reopened by gentle cannulization, allowing the probing surgeon to reach the main vein of the liver. No abdominal surgery would be needed.

When Ed conceived of adopting the vein for our purposes, he took full advantage of my friendship with Milton Helpern, New

York City's medical examiner, and made frequent visits to the city morgue, where he tried out the opening of the umbilical vein on a series of helpful and uncomplaining cadavers. On March 2, 1970, an editorial heralding Ed's work appeared in *JAMA* under the title, "Mining an Abandoned Vein." We successfully performed several of these procedures at New York Hospital and, later, colleagues in the United States, Brazil, and elsewhere did the same.

Ultimately, though, the age of extracorporeal hemofiltration proved to be a brief one. Soon clever pharmacologists sent all of our cumbersome tubes, pumps, and filters the way of the Edsel, platform shoes, and the four-track car stereo by developing drug therapies so effective as to render surgery for schistosomiasis utterly unnecessary.

I have no right to complain, however. During its brief heyday, our treatment did succeed in focusing attention on the absence of proper therapy for a major disease. Tartar emetic and Fuadin were gradually replaced by less toxic preparations, some of which were purchased by governments around the world for the treatment of millions of the infected. And finally, a few years ago, praziquantel appeared. Much of the pioneering work on the clinical use of this extraordinarily effective drug has been done by the schistosomiasis unit of the World Health Organization, whose chief is Dr. Ken Mott, a former student of mine. Under those circumstances, it doesn't bother me in the slightest to have labored in an abandoned vein.

CHAPTER 18

A Night on Bear Mountain

E arly one morning in the spring of 1964 William Watts woke up like a shot. Sitting bolt upright in bed at his home in Westchester County, New York, the fifty-nine-year-old executive with the New York Telephone Company wondered what on earth had hit him. His head throbbed painfully. His stomach churned with violent cramps. Other symptoms—vomiting and diarrhea—soon propelled the beleaguered executive into the small bathroom just off the master bedroom. Staggering back to bed a few minutes later, Watts reflected unsteadily on his activities of the previous evening.

All that rich food, Watts moaned to himself, as he remembered how he had entertained a group of coworkers at the Bear Mountain Inn, a famous dining spot not far from West Point. Then, of course, there had been the martinis before dinner. The wine with the meal. How many times had he told himself that he was getting too old to overdo in the food and beverage department? Satisfied that he had identified the source of his problems, and feeling a bit sheepish about his gustatory excesses, he shrugged off his symptoms and rushed to catch the commuter train for Manhattan.

Two weeks later, Watts was again awakened by a set of queer sensations even more unpleasant and baffling than the first. This time, his eyes were practically swollen shut. His chest was speckled with irritating red splotches. His muscles ached, his hands and lower legs were stiff and sore, and he sizzled with fever. This time, though, he didn't have a clue as to why he should feel so terrible. The night before this second attack he had been a model of moderation, having had a light meal at home with his wife before retiring around ten o'clock. Mrs. Watts took one look at her husband struggling to get out of bed and telephoned the family doctor.

Examining Watts in his office later that morning, the alert physician recognized the nature of the problem almost immediately, although it is a diagnosis that is missed far too frequently by doctors who should know better. The real clincher in the Watts case, his physician believed, was a test of the patient's blood that showed dramatically elevated levels of eosinophiles, specialized white cells whose overabundance can mean only one of two things—a severe allergic disorder such as asthma or an advanced parasitic infection.

To the doctor, Mr. Watts's eosinophilia, in addition to his telltale assortment of clinical complaints—and the absence of asthmatic wheezing—suggested that his patient was suffering from a worm invasion of some kind. The clinician guessed that Watts was probably a victim of *Trichinella spiralis*, the parasite causing the potentially fatal condition called trichinosis. To confirm his hunch, however, he would need to talk to a parasitologist right away. He telephoned me.

What happened next has to rank fairly high in the category of amazing coincidences. No sooner had I finished talking to Watts's doctor than my colleague, Don Hoskins, who then shared with me the practice at 728 Park Avenue and was at the moment sitting in his private office less than twenty feet from mine, received another call from Westchester County from another physician describing the case of yet another middle-aged man suffering from a suspiciously similar set of symptoms. This man, too, as it turned out, worked for New York Telephone.

Don and I could barely contain ourselves for the remainder of the afternoon. As soon as the last patient had left, we hopped into my car, now a blue Jaguar convertible, and roared off at unhealthy speeds toward Westchester and the home of the first victim.

Watts, feeble but friendly, greeted us at the door in his pajamas. Sitting in his living room, Don and I quizzed the patient on his symptoms before administering the routine physical examination, which quickly confirmed the clinical diagnosis of trichinosis. The story was much the same at the second executive's house, although this man was too sick to get out of bed, so we conducted our business in the bedroom. Don then borrowed the man's telephone to call an ambulance and arranged for him to be admitted to New York Hospital immediately. A second ambulance was sent to pick up Mr. Watts. I then phoned the hospital's pathology lab and arranged for both men to undergo the further blood tests that would provide more definitive evidence of trichinosis. Later, biopsies of the muscle would be taken to determine the severity of the infection.

In the meantime, our questioning had revealed some intriguing details. Had Watts known the other victim? Of course, he said. They both worked in the same department at the telephone company and saw each other every day. Had the two of them ever gone out for lunch? Sure, Watts said, they did that pretty regularly. Had they, I asked, happened to have lunch together a day or two prior to March 4, the morning on which Bill Watts had awakened with his initial set of symptoms?

The odds suggested that they had been infected from the same source. Invariably, that source was undercooked meat, specifically pork. The gastrointestinal symptoms of the disease normally appeared within two days of the infection. Tracing the infection to a specific meal the two men had shared wouldn't only single out the culprit but would tell us if anyone else might be in danger. Hence Don and I were disappointed with Watts's reply.

"No, we didn't have lunch that week," he said with finality. After a thoughtful pause, however, he added, "No, we didn't have lunch that week, but we did have a dinner together. We both attended a company dinner I hosted at the Bear Mountain Inn."

Hoskins and I turned to each other and smiled. The game was afoot. For the next three weeks, our practice, our laboratory, our friends, and families all suffered neglect as we became completely wrapped up in sketching in the anatomy of an epidemic.

The clues began to tumble together like the combination on a well-oiled lock. On March 3, 1964, eleven top executives of the New York Telephone Company had dined at the Bear Mountain Inn, just as Watts had said. The menu had been elaborate and included cocktails and hot hors d'oeuvres—namely, Vienna sausages, barbecued pork spareribs, and Swedish meatballs—followed by an entree of beef, vegetables, salad, coffee, and dessert.

Within two weeks of the dinner, six of the eleven men had become seriously ill with a disease later identified as trichinosis. Both cooks, a head chef and his young assistant, who acknowledged their habit of sampling their handiwork, had also acquired heavy infections. In the course of our investigations, Don and I were able to identify cases of asymptomatic trichinosis in two other executives. Two subjects were "clean," and the thirteenth man was on an extended trip out of town and couldn't be examined. But the discovery of the eleven "positives," including the two cooks, left little doubt that the banquet that night on Bear Mountain had been to blame for a serious outbreak of trichinosis, one of humankind's most persistent parasitic foes.

Trichinella spiralis is small enough to coil up inside the muscle tissue of a select group of warm-blooded carnivores, including pigs, bears, rats, and humans, yet big enough to be seen by the human eye. (Adult female worms measure about an eighth of an inch in length, their pint-sized male counterparts about one six-teenth.) These trichinae, as we call them, are acquired, for the most part, by eating undercooked pork contaminated with live worm larvae, which are found in podlike cysts in the musculature of the infected animal. A substantial bite of infected meat may include hundreds of baby worms.

Infection can be easily avoided by cooking pork to the tem-perature of a hot cup of coffee or freezing the meat at subzero temperatures for at least forty-eight hours. But there is, in truth, no accounting for tastes. Despite the fact that the dangers of trichinosis have been widely recognized in our society for decades now, the self-destructive urge to consume raw and undercooked morsels of meat not only persists but has become increasingly fashionable in a new culinary age in which the consumption of raw beef in dishes like steak tartare and carpaccio, not to mention the raw fish in sushi and sashimi—or even a stylishly rare but potentially lethal pork chop—has become the standard for many Americans.

Fortunately, the cycle of infection in humans is reasonably pre-cise, which helps the investigating parasitologist form an accurate diagnosis. After the offending bit of flesh has been swallowed, the trichinae spend the next few hours unfurling from their cysts as the walls of their incubating homes are digested by the acids in the stomach. Thus liberated, the worms burrow into the lining of the duodenum for protection. It is at this stage that their pres-ence, if not necessarily their identity, is often heralded by the onset of diarrhea, muscle cramps, or vomiting—symptoms which, as William Watts discovered to his relief, soon subside.

Over the next week or so the worms, still cozily ensconced in the lining of the small intestine, develop rapidly from infancy to full maturity and, as they do, they naturally enough become obsessed with sex. Seeking out their diminutive male partners in the darkness of the duodenum, the larger, more aggressive females instigate multiple unions which result in the production of astonishing numbers of viviparous larvae, all of which proceed to penetrate the intestinal walls and circulate freely throughout all organs of the body. That's why it takes between seven and fourteen days after ingestion before the patient feels the full force of the disease—the high fever, the swelling of the eyelids, and the severe pains in the muscles and joints. If the infection is very heavy, the patient can develop an inflammation of the brain (encephalitis) or inflammation of the heart muscle (carditis), either of which may prove fatal. A million worms in the body is normally considered a fairly tolerable infection from which the patient will usually fully recover; ten million is a virtual death sentence.

Given the parasite's wide-ranging talents for destruction, doctors have frequently mistaken trichinosis for a variety of diseases, including food poisoning, alcohol poisoning, arthritis, gastritis, colitis, malaria, venereal disease, cholera, and, of course, the ubiquitous "flu." It is hardly surprising then that many of the several million infections of trichinosis thought to occur each year in the United States go undetected and untreated. Flu, with its fever and muscle aches, is the usual misdiagnosis of the milder cases. Still, any physician so inclined can make the diagnosis fairly easily by reading the clinical symptoms carefully, noting the presence of eosinophilia, and by performing a biopsy of the muscle in which live larvae can be clearly seen under the microscope.

Trichinosis is not a tropical disease. It has, however, been an important affliction in the annals of parasitology. In 1835, Sir James Paget, still a medical student at the time but destined to become one of the leading figures of British medicine, first identified the trichinal cyst while watching an autopsy being performed on an Italian male of forty, who had died of pulmonary tuberculosis. The classic descriptions of the pathology of trichinosis were made in the 1860s by the German pathologists Rudolf Virchow and Friedrich von Zenker. A generation later, in 1886, Thomas Richardson Brown, a second-year medical student at Johns Hopkins in Baltimore, first established the connection between trichinosis and eosinophilia, opening the way for a more accurate diagnosis of the disease.

Trichinosis occurs mainly in countries where people are either affluent enough to afford high-protein, meat-oriented diets, or where they are free from the age-old religious taboos that still ban the consumption of pork in large portions of the globe. At the turn of the century, the major focus of the disease was in Central Europe. Horrible epidemics regularly swept Germany, particularly following big feast days, when whole villages would consume infected sausages. Hundreds would be stricken, many would die. "Pork poisoning" prompted the German government to adopt a rigorous system of meat inspection; in 1905, for instance, there are said to have been more meat inspectors in Prussia than soldiers in the U.S. Army.

European emigration and our rapidly growing population eventually shifted the focus of disease to the United States. For the forty years between 1920 and 1960, statistics suggest that at least one in ten adult Americans had acquired the disease. The "official" rate of infection has now dropped to less than five percent, although most cases still go unreported and small, serious epidemics, reported or not, are distressingly common.

It is unfair to saddle the hog with all the blame for spreading this terrible disease, however. The medical literature has recorded instances of trichinosis in hunters and trappers in the Rocky Mountains, who regularly dined on bear meat, and epidemics among Eskimo communities where walrus was on the menu. France has documented an epidemic associated with horsemeat, although it's unclear how the herbivorous horse could have become infected. In 1931, students at the University of California at Berkeley were stricken when they slaughtered an ancient grizzly bear as a practical joke and ate the charred, but under-cooked meat at a pep rally prior to the big game against the Stanford Indians. Some joke. The home team got clobbered, and, two weeks later, a dozen indiscriminately carnivorous football fans turned up in the infirmary with the classic symptoms of trichinosis. (A Berkeley undergraduate at the time, I attended the game but, fortunately, not the atavistic pep rally.)

For years, the epicenter of trichinosis in New York was York-ville, an ethnic German neighborhood centered on Eighty-fifth

Street and Second Avenue in Manhattan, where huge delicatessens would sell hams and sausages seductively hung in the shop windows. The sausages, by reputation, were delicious; the meat was normally heavily infected. Much of it came from New Jersey, where pig farmers fed garbage to their hogs. In contrast to the healthier, grain-fed hogs from the big, and more closely inspected farms of the Midwest, New Jersey swine, like those from small farms pretty much everywhere, were often fattened on slop containing uncooked meat boiling with trichinae.

Despite improvements in health and sanitation standards over the years, the dangers of trichinosis still lurk around many a corner in our fast-food society. Estimates suggest that at least ten percent of all hamburgers consumed in the United States are adulterated with pork in the belief that the admixture produces a more succulent meal. So if you are one of those intrepid souls who eats his hamburger rare, you also run the risk of contracting trichinosis. In the case of the ailing executives from New York Telephone, it was not immediately clear exactly what they had eaten to make them so deathly ill, but I was determined to find out.

Whatever it was, it had to be pork. The executives dined on Bear Mountain but, unlike my Berkeley classmates, they had not eaten any bear meat. No matter how rare the beef they had consumed as a main course, it couldn't have been the offending agent; cows simply do not eat meat, hence they do not become infected with trichinae, hence they cannot transmit the disease. But which items on the menu contained pork?

When Don Hoskins and I appeared at the Bear Mountain Inn one afternoon in late March of 1964 the head chef was eager to help us out. Haunted by the possibility of having caused an epidemic, he had given the problem considerable thought. As far as he was concerned, there could be only two prime suspects: the spareribs and the Vienna sausages. Both had been served as appetizers, and both were pork products of the first order. The

Swedish meatballs, of course, contained small amounts of pork, but the cook dismissed their importance out of hand, since they had been been thoroughly cooked. Or so he thought.

I was suspicious of the chef's easy exoneration of his meatballs, and I had my reasons. Interviewed by telephone, one victim had already told me that he remembered eating neither the spareribs nor the Vienna sausages. Furthermore, all of the diners who had sampled the spareribs swore that the meat had been extremely well done, peeling readily off the bone. The sausages were precooked, which, by itself, wouldn't automatically put them in the clear (precooking can be as haphazard as any other form of cooking), but several of the victims had testified that they hadn't consumed a single cocktail sausage. On the other hand, all of the men who developed the disease, including the cooks, remembered having consumed at least one Swedish meatball.

But surely the chef had cooked the meatballs before serving them? Oh yes, he assured me, he was always careful to cook them even longer than necessary, first braising them for twenty minutes, then allowing them to simmer on the stove for up to an hour.

It was then that the chef suddenly slammed a meaty fist against his forehead. He was remembering the night of the banquet and how, at the very last minute, one of his kitchen helpers had called in sick. That had left only the chef and a lone assistant to perform the chores normally done by three men. Pressed for time, the head cook had taken what he thought at the time was a permissible shortcut; he braised the meatballs as usual, but then skipped a step, transferring them straight to a large copper serving dish where they would continue to simmer over a low flame as they were put out for the guests.

Sure enough, when Don Hoskins and I canvassed the other victims, several of them recalled noticing how the gas flame under the chafing dish had gone out; the meatballs, they said, had been only lukewarm by the time they were devoured. So there was our answer. In an effort to save time, a harried chef had unwittingly infected eleven men, including himself, with a potentially fatal disease. Our case against the Swedish meatballs was now airtight. But what could we do to rout the enemy worms in the victims?

Until 1964 there had been no specific treatment for trichinosis. Patients were usually placed on bed rest and given plenty of fluids and enough pain killer, sometimes morphine, to make life reasonably tolerable. Then a new drug called thiabendazole had suddenly appeared, and just in the nick of time for our Bear Mountain men. The incident allowed Don Hoskins and me to publish one of the first reports on the use of the drug in a clinical setting, which appeared in the *Journal of the American Medical Association* under the title "Treatment of Trichinosis with Thiabendazole" in November of 1964. Thiabendazole remains the drug of choice for treating trichinosis.

So it was that the Bear Mountain story came to a happy ending, at least as far as Don Hoskins and I were concerned. All nine ailing telephone company executives staged full recoveries and went back to work—just in time, several of my curmudgeonly colleagues at New York Hospital observed, to put the finishing touches on the destruction of New York City's telephone system.

The legal aspects of trichinosis began to plague me sometime in the early fifties when I was struggling to keep my Park Avenue practice solvent. One day a lawyer representing Swift & Co., the large meat-packing concern, called to asked if I would help them review a case. It involved a woman who claimed to have developed trichinosis from eating infected breakfast sausage, which had been labeled "precooked." She alleged that she'd been unable to work for over a year as a result and was suing Swift for several million dollars for physical and emotional injuries.

I needed the money, so I took the case. Unhappily for the plaintiff, her claim was easy to disprove. She readily admitted that the suspect product had been in her deep freezer for months—far longer than the forty-eight hours scientifically proven to kill any and all worms present. Flushed with victory, and still financially fragile, I took on a number of similar cases during this period and was surprised to find that the stories were all remarkably similar.

Someone would develop trichinosis. The diagnosis would be confirmed. The victim would identify the alleged villain and contact a lawyer. Soon he would find himself recounting for a jury the precise moment of infection with startling clarity and frequently with a highly developed flair for courtroom drama—"It was a cold and windy morning, your honor. I was all ready for work when I sat down to my sausages and eggs. I usually enjoyed my sausages, you know, but this particular morning they tasted kind of funny . . ." The plaintiff would then name names, singling out the brand. Invariably, the product had been marketed by a rich meat packer, sometimes in its raw state, sometimes precooked, as in hams and hot dogs.

My role was to assess the story and decide, from a medical viewpoint, whether the claimant could be telling the truth. This was usually easy, because in most cases the plaintiff was either lying or fooling himself. Usually, it was his feeble grasp of the first principle of epidemiology, incubation, that tripped him up.

As I have said before, parasitic disease is often coldly mathematical: how sick the patient gets depends on how many parasites he harbors inside his body. Moreover, the worm requires a fixed amount of time to complete its life cycle. The victim of trichinosis may well develop minor gastrointestinal symptoms within forty-eight hours of ingesting poorly cooked pork; the vomiting, cramps, and diarrhea at this stage reflect the unraveling of the larvae in the stomach as they prepare to make their way into the duodenum. But a newborn baby cannot walk; it takes a year (unless it's your own, in which case only eight months are needed). Similarly, freshly ingested trichinae cannot produce larvae; it takes them at least seven days to produce the offspring whose dissemination throughout the body causes the major symptoms of trichinosis.

It is in the nature of legal claimants to try to be as persuasive as possible. As a result, they would often go to great lengths to specify not only what particular food they had ingested, but which symptoms followed and when. It was this zeal for precision that brought their downfall.

I could feel the displeasure of my mother's ghost witnessing her son defend the interests of the big meat packers. She had been a great fan of Upton Sinclair's bestseller of 1906, *The Jungle*, the famous muckraker's indictment of the meat-packing industry, and brought it up every time my father and I returned home from a baseball game and confessed to having consumed a hot dog or two. Nevertheless, when a plaintiff testified that he'd eaten a precooked pork patty on a Sunday night—being "extra careful to cook it all the way through, just in case . . ."—and that, by Tuesday, his eyes were swollen, his muscles ached, and, two years later, he was still unable to work, I felt fairly comfortable in stating that he was dead wrong.

Because of my long experience testifying as a coroner's physician in Panama, and my special knowledge of the parasite and its cycle, I was a good witness. This did not dissuade juries from instinctively favoring the "victims," although the meat packer was rarely guilty of anything except putting pork products on the market. Still, attorneys for the abattoirs found me useful, and very soon I was in great demand. What I had undertaken as a good side job to help pay the rent now threatened to earn me the unwanted reputation of corporate spokesman. I grew fearful of becoming too closely identified by the legal community as a "testifying doctor."

So I started to turn down all requests to serve as an expert witness. But lawyers are a persistent bunch, and turning off their largesse wasn't easy. This obliged me to put market forces to work in my defense by instituting a ploy I used successfully as late as 1986 when I received my last invitation to testify in a case involving trichinosis. The call was from a senior member of a distinguished Chicago law firm.

"Yes, I'll testify," I said cheerily. "My fee is $10,000 to review the case with you, and $10,000 for every scheduled court appearance, whether the case is postponed on a particular day or not."

The lawyer sounded a little stunned. "We know you're very good in this sort of situation," he said, "but don't you think your rates are a bit steep?"

"They're not steep," I protested. "They're outlandish, and I hope they will encourage you to call someone else who will be willing to testify for a fraction."

"I see your point. But tell me, how did you settle on the $10,000 figure?"

"After years of fighting off the legal profession," I told him, "I've found this particular sum most efficient in stopping all further discussion." And so it did. The demand for payment for each courtroom delay was particularly effective, I've been told.

It is not unusual for a medical mystery to yield some unexpected insight, and so it was with the Bear Mountain epidemic. During a presentation to the New York Society of Tropical Medicine some years later, I pointed out that one of the executives who had eaten the Swedish meatballs had not acquired the disease. I offered the somewhat facetious explanation that, since he was the heaviest drinker of the lot, it was entirely possible that the cocktails he consumed had poisoned the trichina larvae in the stomach before they had the opportunity to infect him. I calculated that he'd polished off the equivalent of twelve one-ounce shots of eighty-proof liquor during the course of the evening. As supplementary evidence, I produced a chart establishing an inverse proportion between the seriousness of the infection and the amount of alcohol consumed—the heaviest drinkers had the lightest symptoms, while those who drank sparingly were hardest hit. Though based on fact, it was meant as a joke and, I must say, it went over pretty well.

But not everybody was laughing. Dr. William C. Campbell was too busy taking notes. A crazy idea is rarely overlooked by an inquiring scientist. Campbell, a senior researcher at the Merck

Institute for Therapeutic Research, and a very fine parasitologist, embarked on an elaborate experiment, which he eventually reported in the *Proceedings of the Helminthological Society of Washington* in July 1977, under the title, "Can Alcoholic Beverages Provide Protection Against Trichinosis?"

Campbell explained how he'd infected large numbers of rats and pigs with trichina larvae. He also dosed the animals with varying concentrations of alcohol either before, during, or after they had ingested the worms. The experiment was a smashing success. Campbell was able to conclude that alcohol will indeed protect against trichinosis. However, the volume of liquor required as prophylaxis has so far prevented the treatment from becoming widely used. Campbell estimated it would take the equivalent of two quarts of Jack Daniels (my antihelminthic drug of choice) to provide total protection in the human patient. He dedicated his paper to me.

CHAPTER 19

The Last Autopsy

In the winter of 1983 I performed my last autopsy. It had then been forty-five years since the day Dr. Lewis Beals Bates guided me through my first fumbling encounter with a corpse at the Gorgas Hospital morgue in Panama. In the interim, I had performed hundreds of postmortems. But this last autopsy was utterly unique in my experience—because I did it without ever having seen the patient or the body.

It all started one morning when an attorney named Robert Hammond telephoned me from his office in Grand Rapids, Michigan. His firm, Hammond explained, was representing a group of doctors and their hospitals, the defendants in a $50 million malpractice suit. The case was being brought by the parents of a three-year-old girl who had died of a brain abscess after a bizarre set of medical circumstances. The suit charged—unfairly Hammond thought—that the doctors had repeatedly misdiagnosed, misunderstood, and mistreated the little girl's illness, and, in the process, caused a delay in proper treatment that was ultimately responsible for her death. A former student of mine, Jonathan Hopkins, a neurosurgeon who was familiar with the case, thought I might be able to help. Would I fly out to Michigan and review the facts?

I told Hammond I was sorry, but I would have to decline. I

felt obliged to stay put in New York while I worked on a new book. Besides, I was no specialist in abscess of the brain. Why had Dr. Hopkins thought to call me in the first place, I wondered out loud. It was then that Hammond pulled a nasty trick.

"Well, you see, there's a parasite involved," he said nonchalantly. I swallowed hard and thought I could feel the hook being gently inserted into my throat.

"Yes," the lawyer continued, "Dr. Hopkins told me to tell you that, during the early stages of her hospitalization, the child passed roundworms in her stool. He thought this might have a bearing on the case, and that you might tell us how."

I *was* hooked! Boxes containing medical records, pretrial testimony, and the written opinions of various experts soon arrived at my Cornell office. My secretary, who had been putting up with nonsense like this from me for twenty years, stacked the documents on my desk, quietly shut the door, and, without asking, canceled all appointments for the next three days while I burrowed into the medical record.

The first thing that caught my eye was the testimony of two leading experts on infectious diseases of the brain; each man, Robert S. Chabon, director of the Department of Pediatrics, Penn Health Group, Pittsburgh, and Stanford T. Shulman, chairman of the Department of Pediatrics, Northwestern University Medical School, argued persuasively and with the force of specialized knowledge that early, accurate diagnosis and swift, efficient treatment would have saved the child's life. I knew both men personally and respected their learning and honesty. Chabon's deposition ran to 182 pages, with footnotes, and Shulman's to 149. Only a fool would try to contradict their conclusions.

Since it appeared that I was dealing with a classic open-and-shut case, I was angry at Hammond for trying to involve me in a hopeless legal battle. However, my anger slowly turned first to fascination, then to indignation of a different sort, because, as I read on, it became increasingly clear that everybody had overlooked the key medical clues, and, as a result, several young doctors were about to have their careers needlessly ruined and three hospitals would be plunged into financial hot water.

It was a tragic case, to be sure. On the morning of August 9, 1981, a Sunday, Brenda Hansen, holding her daughter Roberta in her arms, had rushed into the emergency services section of Lee Memorial Hospital in Dowagiac, Michigan, a small farming community forty miles southwest of Kalamazoo.

Distraught, Mrs. Hansen told her story to the emergency room physician, a young resident. For the past week or so Roberta had become progressively ill. Her fever, slight at the beginning, had crept steadily higher, and she now seemed lethargic and irritable most of the time. She had been vomiting periodically.

To the doctor, the symptoms, while troubling, didn't seem out of the ordinary. He thought Roberta was probably suffering from any one of a number of routine childhood diseases—a viral infection, an earache, a mild case of pneumonia, or a communicable disease like chickenpox in which the rash had been overlooked. He did what most doctors would do under the circumstances; after carefully examining Roberta, he recommended that she be hospitalized and kept under observation while the symptoms sorted themselves into a clearer pattern.

Ten days passed, however, and the doctors at Lee Memorial were still no closer to a definitive diagnosis. They seemed to be doing something right, though; they had treated Roberta for an infection of undetermined origin with ampicillin, and her condition had improved. Her fever disappeared. She began eating regular meals again. As far as the doctors were concerned, the patient was on the mend. On the morning of August 18, they sent Roberta home with her mother.

Three days later, on August 21, Roberta Hansen and her mother were back in the emergency room, this time at a larger hospital, the Borgess Medical Center in Kalamazoo. Roberta's symptoms had returned in force. In addition, she now complained of muscle aches and soreness in her joints. The examining physician, another young resident, noticed that her heartbeat was rapid and slightly irregular.

Then a new fact emerged. While in the bathroom at the hospital, Roberta passed a roundworm about the size of a lead pencil—a beast not uncommon to the bowels of children in the South, though a little rarer up north in Michigan.

Like his colleagues at Lee Memorial, the ER doctor had been somewhat perplexed by the wide range of symptoms Roberta presented. He now reached the not unreasonable conclusion that she suffered from a common worm infection of the intestinal tract. Brenda Hansen was handed a prescription for the standard antihelminthic drug and told to bring Roberta into the pediatric clinic in a few days for a followup examination.

Five days later, on August 26, Brenda Hansen entered the Bronson Methodist Hospital, also in Kalamazoo, in a state of panic. Again Roberta was cradled in her arms, but now the little girl was drifting fitfully between consciousness and coma as she gasped for air. Every few minutes, her body shuddered through a minor convulsion. A CAT scan of the child's head revealed a huge brain abscess.

Roberta was operated on immediately. By this time, however, the abscess had grown to lethal proportions, so large, in fact, that when the neurosurgeon made his drainage incision a large, pressurized stream of pus shot over his shoulder. Complications required a second operation and then a third. The patient, now deep in coma, was kept alive on a respirator for the next ten months. Finally, on August 3, 1982, Roberta died, a full, agonizing year after the onset of her symptoms. At autopsy, no brain as such was found; disease had reduced the organ to a gelatinous mass on the floor of the skull.

To all appearances, it was a case of coldhearted incompetence by six doctors at three separate hospitals, each of whom had ignored a blatantly lethal condition and mistreated the patient. Incredible! That was the story emphasized again and again in the formidable testimony of Drs. Chabon and Shulman. The press, meanwhile, dramatized the image of a young mother shuttling

from one hospital to another, unheeded and intimidated, in the fruitless attempt to save her child's life. Powerful stuff. No wonder the parents, their neighbors—and their high-powered attorneys from Grand Rapids—had absolutely no doubts about who had killed little Roberta.

Emotionally, the response was perfectly understandable. But factually speaking, was it justified? Were the doctors really to blame for Roberta's death? Could they indeed have saved her?

Pushing myself away from my paper-strewn desk, I leaned back in my chair and reached for a cigar while I tried to piece things together. What I needed was a common denominator, a starting point. That was relatively easy. The handle was obviously the brain abscess. How did Roberta get it? How long had she had it? Was it the cause of all her symptoms? Should the doctors have recognized it earlier than they did?

The most common cause of brain abscess in children is the spread from the middle ear of a bacterial infection called otitis media. But Roberta's medical history was puzzling on this point. The doctors at both Lee Memorial and Borgess had examined her ears and found no evidence of the disease. Nonetheless, she had responded favorably to ampicillin, a standard remedy for otitis media. Why?

The first surgeon had removed large amounts of infected fluid from Roberta's brain. This he turned over to a bacteriologist, who, he hoped, could identify the offending organism and recommend the most effective antibiotic to use against it. Two of the organisms thus cultured could indeed be linked to an infection of the ear or upper respiratory tract. This bit of evidence supported the standard scenario: the doctors had missed Roberta's ear infection, and the oversight had allowed the pathogens to multiply and travel the short distance from ear to brain.

That didn't explain the presence of the other five types of bacteria that emerged from the culture dish, however; these were all essentially "good" organisms, ones that help digest food in the intestinal tract. In the brain, however, they were a long, long way from home—and highly toxic. How in the hell, I thought, did they get all the way up there?

Then I recalled something Jonathan Hopkins, my former student, had noted in his surgical report. It was Hopkins who performed the second and third operations on Roberta. Coming late to the case, he wasn't named in the suit, but he was familiar enough with it to provide an important clue. While recounting how he had drained pus from the abscess, he remembered experiencing the faint but unmistakable odor of fecal matter—not exactly typical of the normally odorless environment of the brain.

Voilà! I was now sure that I had all the major clues I needed to solve the "murder" of Roberta Hansen. I spent another week impatiently gathering corroborating evidence, then telephoned Hammond.

"I've solved the case," I said somewhat immodestly—and unwisely, since one never knew how the jury in a personal injury suit might decide, no matter how powerful the arguments for the defense. "But I still can't travel to Michigan."

"That's okay," said Hammond. "Michigan will come to you."

On the morning of Tuesday, January 18, 1983, eight lawyers appeared at the door of my second-floor office at Cornell. Hammond had made arrangements with the judge in Kalamazoo so that my testimony could be taken in New York. Present, in addition to Hammond and his associate, were four lawyers representing, variously, other doctors and hospitals named in the suit, as well as two attorneys for the Hansens. A device combining a video camera and a tape recorder was switched on to capture not only my words but, presumably, any facial tics or mannerisms that might be helpful later in judging whether I was telling the truth.

The Hansens' attorneys were full of forced joviality. They appeared comfortable in the knowledge that the high-megaton yield of their own expert testimony would easily flatten whatever feeble arguments I was about to muster. After all, as they took pains to point out, what could a professor of tropical medicine know about a case from Michigan? They had obviously been forced to fly all the way to New York on some kind of wild fishing expedition concocted by a desperate defense. Still, they were prepared to be good sports. So they sat back smugly while Hammond, camera rolling, questioned me about my background and qualifications.

No claim was made that I was an expert on the brain or its malfunctions. It was agreed, however, that, as a pathologist, I was no stranger to the cranial abscess. Neither did the Hansen men dispute my expertise in the field of parasitic infection, unimportant though that seemed at the moment.

Had I ever given medical testimony in court before, Hammond asked. Yes, I had. As a young pathologist in Panama, I explained, I had appeared in court many times. I told them how, in the days before television, the coroner's inquest, with its tantalizing mysteries of mortality, was considered big-time entertainment, and entire families would pack the courthouse gallery for the hearings. The Hansen men chuckled in a relaxed fashion. I could see that I was being perceived as a harmless old spinner of yarns, even less of a threat than they had anticipated.

"What is your attitude toward malpractice suits?" Hammond asked.

"Pretty neutral," I said. "I've never been sued."

"Would the fact that several of the defendants are physicians prejudice you in their favor?"

"No," I said. "I propose simply to give testimony based on the facts of the case." The Hansen men guffawed as though they'd heard this response before and weren't inclined to believe it now.

"How many times have you testified in malpractice suits?"
"Never."

"Never?" Even Hammond had a hard time believing this one. Many doctors, especially those who have survived fifty years in medicine, have either been sued for malpractice at least once or have been involved as a trial witness.

"Yes, this is my first malpractice suit," I said, displaying a halo of innocence and honesty. For the first time, the Hansen men shifted uneasily in their seats.

Hammond proceeded to ask me whether I'd had the opportunity to review all relevant records in the Hansen case. I told him I'd looked at every page of the voluminous material and read much of it sentence by sentence.

"And have you reached a conclusion about the cause of death, Dr. Kean?" he asked, a note of confident anticipation rising in his voice.

"I have," I said.

"And is your conclusion in harmony with the opinions of the medical experts who have previously testified on behalf of the plaintiffs?"

"No, it is not." The Hansen men hardly seemed surprised. They exchanged knowing smiles.

"Would you please explain?" asked Hammond.

"Well, in my opinion," I began, "the nature of the disease that killed Roberta has not been understood by anyone who saw the patient, including the physicians in the three emergency clinics, those who took care of her in the hospital, or the experts who reviewed the case."

"What then, in your opinion, Dr. Kean, caused Roberta's death?"

"Involuntary manslaughter," I declared. I had hoped to get everyone's undivided attention—and I succeeded. The attorneys for the plaintiffs rose involuntarily as if standing to attention, and then, recovering momentarily, sat back down. Hammond, who hadn't been expecting me to pronounce a verdict in the case, but only to render a medical opinion, swallowed hard, and asked, in a curiously fluty voice, "Involuntary manslaughter by whom?"

I paused briefly before saying, "Roberta's three-year-old cousin—although 'manslaughter' may not be entirely appropriate in this case." The roomful of lawyers sat in stunned silence. The division between opposing sides had dissolved temporarily, since everybody was now equally confused. Even Hammond sounded a little defensive. "Please explain yourself," he said.

"Gentlemen," I said, "it will take me forty-five minutes to explain to you exactly what transpired. I will go through a chronology of events at the end of which the identity of the murderer will be clear to everyone. Please bear with me."

After a brief recess, during which I assembled slides and diagrams to help illustrate my case, I began to explain the strange anatomy of Roberta Hansen's disease.

"Roberta Hansen," I began, "was killed by a biological bullet to the brain. I will explain the nature of that bullet, and then I will tell you who, in all probability, caused it to be fired."

I pointed to the first important clue—the bacteriological study of the brain abscess. I reminded them of the seven organisms discovered there, and explained why at least five of them, the normal inhabitants of the intestinal tract, had no business being inside the skull in the first place. Most intracranial abscesses are caused by one organism, sometimes two. Seven was almost unheard of—and five of the seven belonged in the gut! Bacteria coming all the way from the remote, unsanitary bowel had been responsible for Roberta's roaring infection. The fecal matter smelled by Dr. Hopkins was further proof of their presence in the brain. So how did they get there?

"The biological bullet," I said, "was a parasite, gentlemen— a parasite called *Ascaris lumbricoides*, the common roundworm." I looked around the small, impromptu courtroom and counted eight pairs of knitted brows.

I explained that *A. lumbricoides* had been vastly underestimated by the medical experts in this case. This was despite the fact that the record clearly showed the parasite in proximity to the scene of the crime. Roberta had passed roundworms several times— at home, in the outpatient clinic, and in the hospital. Indeed, an antihelminthic drug was prescribed. For the most part, however, the phenomenon was considered unrelated to Roberta's more baffling, more serious symptoms. The worm got lost in the shuffle. A lot of kids have worms—no big deal.

This reaction was not at all unreasonable. In the vast majority of cases involving humans, the roundworm is a fairly benign character. The patient becomes infected by swallowing eggs that have been deposited via another person's feces, usually in the soil (and raw vegetables, especially lettuce, are not rare vehicles for transmitting the infection). Once inside the stomach gastric juices obligingly burn away the eggs' tough protective coating and then gently shunt the little bundles along to the duodenum, where the larvae hatch and begin their bizarre trek to adulthood. Burrowing into the blood vessels lining the gut they hitch a short, turbulent ride to the liver where they stop long enough to gorge themselves on blood before tunneling on into the air sacs of the lungs.

Three weeks after entering the host, the worms, now in exuberant adolescence, are really ready to show their stuff. Shinnying up the major lung tubes, the bronchi, they slither past the larynx, reach the tip of the epiglottis, and then, using it as a kind of high-dive platform, plunge back into the digestive tract. Six weeks after arrival, the worms, now young adults, are back where they started and ready to get down to the serious business of reproduction. The average mature female is astonishingly prolific, producing nearly two hundred thousand eggs daily for five to seven years—or approximately a *half billion* potential parasites! Just what inspires the worms, which will eventually grow to lengths up to ten inches, to undertake their existential journey in the first place only to return to biological square one in the gut remains a mystery. Happily enough, most human victims remain oblivious to the parasites' comings and goings and, aside from a mild, flulike pneumonia caused by the larvae passing through the lungs, the worms do little actual harm.

"There is one important exception," I said, as I looked around the room once again to find the lawyers reacting queasily to the mental images produced by my rather graphic explanation. "Sometimes the questing larvae make a wrong turn," I said. "Instead of completing the circuit via the lungs and arriving back where they started—in the gut—they lose their way and wind up in exile in some remote organ, even the brain, *carrying many harmful bacteria from the bowel with them* as they go. The host organ reacts by forming first an abscess and then a cyst around the invaders.

"The specific symptoms these lost patrols of parasites produce, which can be very serious in nature, depend on where they get trapped. The boil formed around them is usually in a silent area of the body where it gets walled off and absorbed. Occasionally, however, the immune system fails to fight off the infection and the boil, instead of shrinking, gets bigger and bigger. The brain is a particularly poor resister.

"In the case of the child in question," I continued, "one or more of these maverick larvae entered her brain, carrying piggyback a collection of lethally infective organisms from the intestinal tract. So you see, gentlemen, Roberta did not succumb to complications arising from an ear infection that was overlooked by her doctors. The source of the abscess is clear. Roberta died of a tropical disease in northern Michigan."

One of the Hansens' lawyers stood up. Forgetting the video camera and the fact that, technically, the floor still belonged to Hammond, he blurted out, "But what about the cousin? You said the cousin was guilty of manslaughter."

I must confess to having used that statement mainly as a ploy to get everyone's attention. Okay, it was a shallow ruse—but it *had* worked. Furthermore, it pointed to a possible explanation for what was perhaps the most baffling question of all: How had Roberta Hansen acquired a tropical disease in chilly northern Michigan?

I explained: "Roundworms do exist in Michigan, even in northern Michigan, although the disease is much more common in the South. Many, many schoolchildren in Mississippi and Georgia become infected. The incidence of the disease in Michigan, on the other hand, is very low. So it is quite likely that, in this particular case, the source of infection was of a long-distance nature. Had Roberta ever traveled outside Michigan? No. Then the disease must have come to her. But how?

"We know that Roberta must have become infected sometime in May of 1981, since it would have taken that long for the roundworm wriggler to hatch, work its way to the brain, and produce the symptoms of severe infection the patient exhibited when she appeared at the emergency room of Lee Memorial in early August. The rest of my answer is to be found in the pretrial testimony of Brenda Hansen, Roberta's mother.

"Mrs. Hansen reported," I went on, "that, in the fall of 1980, her sister arrived on a visit from her home in North Carolina. She was accompanied by her three-year-old son, Roberta's cousin, who had a history of roundworm infection. For a period of several days, the children played in a sandbox in the Hansen backyard before the visitors returned to the warmer—semitropical—Southern climate.

I paused for a moment before presenting my final theme. The Hansen men had lost their earlier shine and sat there looking a little crestfallen.

"We can never be entirely sure," I said, "but my guess is that Roberta's cousin, in the informal toilet habits young children often display, deposited the eggs in the backyard during one of the play sessions. The child went back to North Carolina with his mother, but the eggs stayed behind.

"The eggs are tough little bastards, if you'll pardon the expression. They have a hard coating that allows them to withstand vast swings in temperature—even a Michigan winter. So there the eggs remained, buried in the sand, buried under several feet of snow. Come spring, Roberta was allowed out into the yard to play in the sandbox. The eggs were lying in wait. They stuck to her hands, the hands went into her mouth, and she managed to infect herself. Her cousin was the accomplice . . .''

"Are you saying, Dr. Kean," Hammond interrupted, "that, no matter what might have been done for the child, she would have died?"

"That's precisely it," I replied. "Up against that agglomeration of organisms, no antibiotic regimen could have been successful. The child was biologically doomed before she set foot in the first emergency room or was examined by a single doctor. Unfortunately, the result would have been the same in any institution in the world, New York, Nairobi, or Kalamazoo. She was killed by a roundworm—not by a doctor."

The Hansens' attorneys were beaten men. When Hammond offered them a chance to go at me, they simply said, "No questions." They seemed eager to return to Grand Rapids. The following day, Hammond wrote later, the Hansens agreed to drop their suit. Their lawyers, who had turned down repeated offers to settle out of court, were now willing to talk. A deal was eventually struck under which the hospitals helped defray the Hansens' medical bills. In return, the doctors were cleared of all charges.

I was happy at the outcome but couldn't help feeling a twinge of sadness, too. As autopsies go, I knew that the Hansen case would be a very hard act to follow. It had taken a lifetime of experience as a clinician, pathologist, and parasitologist to produce a satisfactory answer to a unique problem. I'd also been very lucky in stumbling across the right clues. So I vowed to myself to make this the last "autopsy" of my fifty years in medicine. That is the good thing about your average clinical patho-parasitologist—he usually knows enough to quit when he is ahead.

Déjà Vu All Over Again

The afternoon of Thursday, April 27, 1982, was an occasion of high excitement in my office on Park Avenue. While I was holed up in the safety of my laboratory, two dozen angry young men stormed up and down the waiting room, shouting bitter words at Mary Wilson, my secretary, and demanding attention. They had been provoked—and understandably so—by Ms. Wilson's announcement that the office could no longer accept their stools for examination.

The reason was unfortunate but simple. New York City's gay community was experiencing its worst outbreak of amebic dysentery in years. Stool examinations were needed to establish the diagnosis, but the disease had spread so rapidly, and the surge of patients had been so dramatic, that my already overflowing toilets and overworked lab technicians were threatened with complete breakdown. Reluctantly, I had had to call it quits.

"Gentlemen"—I could hear the courageous Ms. Wilson's muffled words through the wall—"you really must stop this racket and leave."

As I listened to the hubbub from my sanctuary (I wasn't a complete coward—I had spoken to the men earlier, but succeeded only in getting angry myself and had been banished to the lab by the even-tempered Ms. Wilson), I couldn't help but think how this episode contained a perfect example of the way my old mentor, the great Francis W. O'Connor, had marked me for life. When I had first witnessed the rapidfire spread of amebiasis in Greenwich Village in the fifties, I immediately thought of how O'Connor had triumphantly riddled the mystery disease of the Chicago's World Fair by tracing *amebas* to contaminated drinking water. This inspired me to write a series of increasingly heated letters to New York City's Commissioner of Health, insisting that the water supply in the Village had somehow become fecally tainted.

Looking back, it stuns me that I could have been so incredibly naive. It was a full decade later, however, during the sexual revolution of the sixties, when gays began emerging from the closet in significant numbers, before I realized what I'd been dealing with all along was a disease transmitted primarily by anal and oral intercourse.

Meanwhile, back in the waiting room, Ms. Wilson proceeded to supply the still-grumbling men with the name of a larger laboratory that could handle their tests, and eventually they went away. All but one, that is. Left behind on the couch was the solitary figure of Philip Williams, a prominent man on the New York literary scene, who had been my patient for nearly ten years. Slightly built, stoop-shouldered, and soft-spoken, Williams, like the others, was suffering from an obstinate case of diarrhea. But there the similarity ended. Williams had had bouts of *"ameba"* before. This time, though, the symptoms—nausea, cramps, watery bowel movements—were more pronounced. The old remedies, he complained, hadn't laid a glove on them.

"I'm telling you, Ben," he said, as he settled uneasily into the chair facing my desk, "this is something right out of deepest, darkest Africa," a sour joke (though, as I would have cause to reflect later, an eerily prescient one) suggesting the more pernicious forms of diarrhea normally associated with the remote tropics. Indeed, the intensity of his symptoms *did* suggest malignant cholera, a disease I had never before seen within eight thousand miles of Manhattan.

I told him not to worry. "Let's take some tests," I said reassuringly. "We'll get to the bottom of this but quick."

When the results came back from the lab a few days later, however, it was my turn to panic. The patient's stools were devoid of all known causes of diarrhea; his blood studies were perfectly normal. Meanwhile, Williams had been on the phone saying that his condition had worsened and he was becoming weaker by the day. I was completely stumped. Every treatment had been tried, nothing had worked. What did I do now? I sat back in my chair and tried to remember whether I had ever seen a case so ominously peculiar. It was then that I thought of Haiti.

Working on my hunch, I yanked the phone from its cradle and called Phil Williams. "Phil," I said apologetically, "this question may seem a little crazy, but how often do you go to Haiti?"

"All the time, Ben," Williams replied, sounding surprised. "It's my favorite winter getaway. Why do you ask?"

Bingo! Haiti is the answer, I thought, as I slammed my hand down on the desktop. I was remembering a particularly educational evening I'd spent at the bar of the Oloffson Hotel in Port-au-Prince not six months before.

Before it underwent some badly needed renovation in 1986, the Oloffson Hotel was an experience not to be missed. A quaint, creaky gingerbread palace (the architectural clone of a nineteenth-century New Orleans bordello), the Oloffson was an oasis of dog-eared civility in a country of brutal poverty, malnutrition, and rampant disease, conditions criminally unrelieved by Papa Doc Duvalier, Baby Doc, his son and successor, or any of the other dictators who had held sway there since I first laid eyes on the island on my voyage to Panama in the summer of 1937.

For all its many disadvantages, though, Haiti, with its sunny climate and rich supply of tropical maladies, its gracious people, and its haunting voodoo melodies, had lured me back many times over the years, and always to the Oloffson. Where else could you sleep in a bed affixed with a brass nameplate commemorating

Barry Goldwater's slumber there? How many hotels boasted a Rex Reed Suite? Then there were the wonderfully ambivalent culinary charms—breakfasts featuring exquisite French toast, thick and golden brown, and bacon the consistency of rawhide strips that had obviously been cooked ahead of time for the entire week.

But it was the bar of the Oloffson, with its high ceilings, slowly revolving fans, and large population of biting insects that made me feel right at home. Most important of all, the bar represented the fruitful end of the Haitian grapevine. All local gossip—true or false, critical or trifling—eventually filtered through this small, dimly lighted enclave. So it was there, one evening in late 1981, as I tucked into my third rum punch and fought off sorties of flying roaches with the bartender's pearl-handled flyswatter, that I first heard of a new, mysterious strain of diarrhea that had appeared on the island. The news came from Dr. Jean Pape, a former student of mine from Cornell, who now presided over the diarrhea control center that I had helped set up in Haiti in 1979. A normally reserved teetotaler, but a man hopelessly intoxicated by all aspects of his research, Pape was on this night uncharacteristically outspoken.

"Ben," he said in his musically accented English, "this stuff is not to be believed. Patients have anywhere from ten to thirty-five stools a day, sometimes for weeks. They routinely lose between thirty and fifty pounds and then they die. I've done every examination I can think of but can't turn up a thing. Nothing. It doesn't fit any pattern we know. It doesn't respond to any form of treatment. We think it might be a form of intestinal tuberculosis," he said, furrowing his brow. "What do you think? You've seen a lot of TB."

Indeed I had. TB had been widespread in Panama in the forties and, as pathologist at Gorgas Hospital, I had reported autopsy results on no fewer than 1,713 victims of the disease.

"Jean," I said, "patients with TB may have many intestinal symptoms, but not the diarrhea you describe. It has to be something else."

Unhappily, I was right. The mystery disease that Pape had encountered in Haiti and that had wandered into my office on Park Avenue inside the intestines of Phil Williams was caused, as it turned out, by the parasite *Cryptosporidium*. "Crypto," as the name implies, had remained an elusive creature ever since it was discovered in mice by a researcher at Harvard in 1907, but we knew enough to have a sketchy profile of the parasite: it carried on its complicated lifestyle in the cells lining the intestinal tract and was probably spread by contaminated water. Until 1976, however, it had been recognized as a parasite primarily of chickens, calves, and sheep. Then, all of a sudden, a half-dozen cases were spotted in humans, where the bug was shown to cause diarrhea in people who are immunosuppressed. In late 1982, a breakthrough in lab techniques finally allowed us to identify crypto as the very same beast that was responsible for the on-going epidemic in Haiti.

So now the question loomed: Why was this previously rare, mostly benign disease causing so much havoc in the bowels of Phil Williams and his scores of fellow victims in the Caribbean? We didn't have a clue.

To make matters worse, Phil Williams died in early 1983. I felt terrible. The immediate cause of death had been unstoppable cryptosporidiosis. Knowledge of the nature of the disease, how-ever, had not provided a cure, and I had to stand helplessly by and watch my patient fade. But as reports flowed in, it was clear that Williams was not alone; hundreds of additional cases of the disease in its killing form had been reported in New York and San Francisco.

It had become painfully obvious that something was interfer-ing with the proper functioning of the natural immune system, making it possible for this parasitic invader to run wild inside its victims. That something, of course, had by then come into sharper focus, as well; it was none other than the disease scientists were calling the Acquired Immune Deficiency Syndrome. The appearance of crypto, Jean Pape and I now realized, occupied only a small corner of something much larger—the vast, chilling panorama of AIDS.

After fifty years in medicine, I was no longer surprised by the irony underlying much of our medical efforts, the cruel twist of fate that too often decreed the diseases we had so painstakingly suppressed would come raging back to life a decade or two later in new, more virulent forms. But AIDS, so enigmatic and deadly, was something completely new in my experience. Although I would be little more than an armchair medical detective in the attempt to unravel its conundrums (the important research would be done by much younger men, many of them my former students), I couldn't resist being drawn into one last scientific manhunt.

There were two basic riddles to be solved: What caused AIDS, and where had it come from?

The first answer came relatively quickly. As the disease worked its way through the American population, claiming ever more victims among homosexuals and intravenous drug users, and making inroads among heterosexuals, scientists in the United States and France quickly eliminated bacteria (relatively easy to identify) and parasites (even easier, because of their relatively larger size) as possible causes. Whatever caused AIDS, it was so elusive it almost had to be a virus. Sure enough, in 1983, Robert Gallo, then virologist at the National Institutes of Health in Maryland, and Luc Montanier and his associates at the Pasteur Institute in Paris simultaneously identified the culprit—a strange retrovirus which became known as HIV.

That left the question of the origin of the disease, and thanks to my peripatetic wanderings as a tropical medicine man I had something to contribute. The first major clue, ignored by those less familiar with obscure illnesses, hit me like a ton of bricks. This was the sudden appearance among AIDS sufferers of a brutal cancer known as Kaposi's sarcoma. Named for the Hungarian pathologist who first described the condition back in 1872, it was a rare tumor in Europe and America, for more than a hundred years affecting almost exclusively white, middle-aged males. By 1982, however, hundreds of AIDS patients in New York and San Francisco had developed Kaposi's sarcoma. So had their counterparts in Haiti. Why?

I knew from experiences in Africa in the fifties and sixties that the only places Professor Kaposi's disease had occurred in great numbers were Kenya, Uganda, and Zaire, where I had personally seen the toll it regularly took among young male villagers. No wonder no one knew much about it. Kaposi's sarcoma was primarily a disease of Africa, and with the exception of all but a handful of dedicated people we had been neglecting the massive health problems of that continent for years. When Kaposi's surfaced as a prime component of AIDS, I tried to persuade some of the major researchers in the field to direct their gaze toward Africa, though, perhaps understandably, they were too busy searching for more clues as to the identity of the AIDS virus to be bothered with its African genesis.

For me, however, AIDS had become a geographic puzzle. What on earth was an African disease doing in New York and Port-au-Prince? What, if any, was the connection between the two cities?

By late 1983, scientists generally acknowledged the African connection, but the route of infection remained hazy. The "smart" money was betting that it had come into the United States from a point as yet undetermined and then traveled on to isolated Haiti. I had my own theory. My patient, Phil Williams, had contracted crypto in Haiti. Wasn't it possible, therefore, that he had also been infected with AIDS there, too? I decided to return to Haiti to see what I could find out.

As usual, the critical piece of information came to me not during the long hard days in the laboratory, but while I was seated at the bar of the Oloffson. It was there one evening that I discovered Phil Williams wasn't the only gay who had enjoyed vacationing in Haiti. When I questioned Sue Seitz, the attractive young widow of the long-time owner of the Oloffson, Al Seitz, she revealed that, since the fifties, Haiti had been the favored destination of group sex tours that originated in New York. The trips were overwhelmingly popular with gay men, who would check into special hotels, where it was customary for Haitian boys, wearing very little or nothing at all, to parade up and down the corridors. While a particularly attractive youth might make as much as fifty dollars by accepting an "invitation" to a "sponsor's" room, the going rate was usually five dollars. When I confirmed these stories with gay friends in New York, they offered the disconcerting information that ten "dates" per weekend was pretty average, though perhaps a little on the low side.*

Thus was the Haitian–American connection established. Next we needed to confirm where AIDS had originated. This we could accomplish by using Kaposi's sarcoma as a marker. (With the exception of blood tests, there is no better index of AIDS than the presence of this disfiguring tumor that most often affects the skin and the lining of the intestines.) So in 1982, I asked Jean Pape to make a thorough check of pathology records at all major hospitals, clinics, and morgues in Haiti. The results were crystal clear. Not a single case of Kaposi's sarcoma had been recorded on the island until 1979. Kaposi's sarcoma, an old disease in Africa, was new to Haiti. So then was AIDS. Now the $64 million question: How did they get there in the first place?

---

* The earnest epidemiologists trying to piece together a profile of the disease at the Centers for Disease Control in Atlanta were not privy to this inside information. Somehow the rumor had gotten around in the scientific community here that homosexuality was not tolerated in Papa Doc's oppressive country and, therefore, it did not exist. The result was that, when an alarming number of AIDS cases was diagnosed among Haitian boat people arriving in Miami beginning in 1981, Haitians were promptly targeted as a major risk group for AIDS right along with gays and IV drug users. The prevalence of homosexuality in Haiti is probably no different than it is anyplace else—an estimated 10 percent of males are gay. By April 1985, this fact had finally dawned on the CDC, which belatedly removed Haitians from the high-risk category.

I struggled for weeks with the question of how to tackle this problem. Then on my next trip to Haiti the answer appeared, once again in the bar at the Oloffson. It arrived in the form of Madeleine Boncy, a pleasant, smiling woman in her early fifties, a Haitian and a microbiologist of long experience.

"Oh, Ben," she teased, when I brought up the question of how Kaposi's sarcoma could have come to Haiti, "you're so naive. I'll tell you a secret. It came from Africa."

"I know it came from Africa," I said irritably, "but how can you prove that scientifically?"

For a period of some twenty years, beginning in the early sixties, she explained, thousands of eager young Haitians had left Haiti for Africa, recruited by various national governments there to help improve local medical, social, and educational programs.*

I gasped at the thought of Africa looking to impoverished Haiti as a bastion of Western know-how. Zaire, in particular, represented a land of opportunity for young Haitians eager to escape the poverty and political oppression of their own country. The majority had stayed on there, living the expatriate life. Then in the mid-seventies, the Zairean government grew tired of its Haitian expats and pressured them to leave. Many returned home to the Caribbean. Not a few brought Kaposi's sarcoma with them. Boncy had seen the pathological evidence with her own eyes.

To my mind, the epidemiological route of AIDS was now clear. It ran from Africa to the United States, and cut straight through the heart of Haiti. The disease had been transmitted to Haiti by the local equivalent of returning Peace Corps volunteers,

---

* Novelist Graham Greene knew about the Haitian exodus to Africa, too, it seems. In *The Comedians* (which features the Oloffson thinly disguised as the Trianon), Dr. Maigot, the "non-Marxist communist" who becomes Mr. Brown's (read Greene's, despite his disclaimer) father figure says: "In the last ten years three-quarters of the doctors who have graduated have preferred to go elsewhere as soon as they could buy an exit permit. Here one buys an exit permit, not a practice. If you want to consult a Haitian doctor, better go to Ghana."

and from there to New York. Like all good scientific reasoning, it was perfectly simple.

Maybe a little too simple, as it turned out. As data accumulated, some AIDS experts became convinced that a more likely route of entry into the United States was from Zaire to Europe and then to New York via emigrating Zaireans. A few assigned the start of the epidemic to a single homosexual male, a French-Canadian airline steward, known as Patient Zero, whose globe-hopping sexual activities ranged from Africa and Europe to New York and San Francisco with stops along the way. But an epidemic of this magnitude is not by one victim made. There is little doubt in my mind that Haiti, if not *the* route for AIDS into the United States, has certainly been an important portal of entry—in spite of the scientific community's general unwillingness to openly acknowledge the connection.

Whatever the route or routes, it became apparent, as the epidemic progressed, that what started as a disease of the tropics had evolved into a health crisis of truly global proportions. If anyone ever needed a reason for regarding the human health problems of our planet as an indivisible phenomenon (as I had been preaching with only limited success for many years), this was it. Epidemiologically speaking, the tropics had risen and penetrated the gates of Western civilization in a most disastrous fashion.

Granted, I found the AIDS puzzle utterly fascinating on the scientific level. Personally, though, it quickly became too emotionally wrenching, as one longtime patient and friend after another succumbed to the disease. In 1985, for that and other reasons, I decided to cut back my practice to the bare minimum of patients. At times, I wanted to retire altogether. But I couldn't bring myself to withdraw from the battlefield entirely. For fifty years, I had proven constitutionally incapable of ignoring a direct challenge from a parasitic foe. Now AIDS was bringing my arch-enemies back in force in the most bizarre and unexpected way.

Take *Pneumocystis carinii*, the cause of pneumocystis pneumonia, for instance. Having first encountered this strange beast on the autopsy table in Panama in 1943, I had followed it through the liberation of Hitler's POW camps after the war, where it infected thousands of former prisoners, and right up to the bedside (or so I thought) of financier Marcus Wallenberg in Stockholm in 1978. But I wasn't prepared for the news that, by 1983, *P. carinii* was routinely killing half of all AIDS patients in this country!

Then, as crypto, the little fiend that I had observed Jean Pape battling in Haiti, continued to take its share of AIDS victims, another old enemy, *Toxoplasmosa gondii*, the disease that had led me on a wild chase from the Gorgas morgue, through the war-ravaged Czechoslovakia of Herr Professor Sikl, and up to courtside in Martina Navratilova's bid for the U.S. Open in 1982, emerged as the cause of death in as many as one out of ten AIDS-related fatalities.

I reflected on the return of my parasitic foes with glum irony. It was, in the immortal words of the philosopher Yogi Berra, just like déjà vu all over again.

"Your Dr. O'Connor didn't anticipate anything like this, did he?" asked Jean Pape, as my former student and I sat at the counter of the Oloffson bar, reviewing the grim statistics of AIDS in Haiti. Pape had suffered through many a lecture at Cornell in which I had invoked the demanding ghost of my long-gone medical hero and mentor. "Did you ever think," he continued, "that we'd be sitting around talking about how parasites were dominating a brand new epidemic like AIDS?"

I shook my head and stared blankly ahead into the gloom. After a lifetime filled with encounters with strange parasites, to say nothing of even stranger encounters with some of my patients, even I found this final irony a little hard to swallow.

"Well," said Pape, breaking into his wide, warm grin, "I guess this means you'll just have to train a whole new generation of parasitologists to cope with the problem—the way O'Connor trained you and you trained me."

It was an appalling thought for a man entering his eighth decade. Fat chance, Jean, I thought smugly to myself. Then suddenly, I grew uneasy. I somehow felt as if the specter of Francis
W. O'Connor were glowering at me from the shadows of this
tropical barroom in much the same way he had glowered that
sunny afternoon in June of 1937, when he kicked me out of his
laboratory and down the decades. Typically, he seemed to be
waiting for me to stop my waffling and get on with the work
at hand.

"Enough!" I shouted in the abrupt, irascible manner of my
old teacher. "Bartender, bring me another rum punch, and step
on it!" Out of the corner of my eye I could see Jean Pape smiling
even more broadly now; he had me, and he knew it. I ignored
him. After all, I needed time to think about just how I was going
to tackle this new assignment.

B.H. KEAN, M.D. is Clinical Professor Emeritus of Tropical Medicine and Public Health at Cornell University Medical College, where he lectures regularly, and continues his research. He has published widely in medical journals, but this is his first general interest book. He is currently working on volumes III and IV of *Tropical Medicine and Parasitology: Classic Investigations*. He divides his time between Manhattan and Florida.

TRACY DAHLBY, a former managing editor of *Newsweek International*, is a writer living in New York City. An award-winning foreign correspondent, he spent thirteen years in Asia, covering events in Japan, Korea and China, and served as Tokyo bureau chief for both *The Washington Post* and *Newsweek*. Dahlby is currently working on a book based on his experiences as a journalist in Japan.